FROM PARNASSUS

A  BOOK

JACQUES BARZUN, 1950

Detail from a painting by Cleve Gray

FROM PARNASSUS

ESSAYS IN HONOR OF

JACQUES BARZUN

Edited by Dora B. Weiner and William R. Keylor

HARPER & ROW, PUBLISHERS

 NEW YORK, HAGERSTOWN, SAN FRANCISCO

LONDON

1817

Fragments from *From the Memoirs of Pontius Pilate* copyright © 1976 by Eric
Bentley. The complete play will be published in 1977 by New Republic Books.

Nell Eurich, the author of "Learning in America," is grateful to the Mark Van
Doren Estate for permission to quote from *Liberal Education*, by Mark Van Doren,
© 1943.

The essay "For Beckmesser" by Peter Gay is based on research supported by grant
RO 7779-73-224 from the National Endowment for the Humanities, whose help is
here acknowledged with thanks.

Research for "Three Champions of the Handicapped in Revolutionary France" by
Dora B. Weiner was supported by a grant under the "Distinguished Scholar"
program, National Library of Medicine, National Institutes of Health, whose help
is here gratefully acknowledged.

In "Translation or Adaptation?" by John Simon, permission to quote from Moliere's
The Misanthrope, translated by Richard Wilbur, copyright © 1954, 1955, by Rich-
ard Wilbur, is given by Harcourt Brace Jovanovich, Inc. And excerpts from *The
Misanthrope: A Modern English Adaptation*, by Tony Harrison, copyright © 1975
by Tony Harrison, are reprinted by permission of The Third Press—Joseph Okpaku
Publishing Company, Inc.

FIRST EDITION

Designed by Sidney Feinberg

Library of Congress Cataloging in Publication Data

From Parnassus: essays in honor of Jacques Barzun.
    Bibliography: p.
✓ 1. Barzun, Jacques, 1907-   2. Barzun,
Jacques, 1907-   —Bibliography. I. Barzun,
Jacques, 1907-   II. Weiner, Dora B. III. Key-
lor, William R., 1944-
AC5.F79 1976   081   76-9203
ISBN 0-06-014549-8

76 77 78 79 80 10 9 8 7 6 5 4 3 2 1

Contents

Essays

Polyhymnia ತಿ   CRITICISM AND LANGUAGE

Clio ತಿ   CULTURAL HISTORY

Melpomene ತಿ   DRAMA IN LITERATURE

Thalia ತಿ   THE HUMAN COMEDY

Foreword

The essential contributor to this book is Jacques Barzun himself. The editors chose theme and format and then approached an appropriate group of his friends, colleagues, students and associates. The book took shape virtually unaided: the very fact that a tribute was being planned elicited eager participation.

The choice of a theme was difficult. The editors knew that this must not be an "ordinary" *Festschrift*. The wide spectrum of Jacques Barzun's interests demanded diversity; the unifying bond must be the pursuit of excellence. Therefore we allude to Mount Parnassus and its hospitality to the Muses who inspire literature, music, teaching, criticism, history, tragedy, comedy, esthetics and science—the province of each Muse being delimited with much poetic license so as to suggest a link between the creative activities over which each Muse presided in Hellenic culture and cognate activities that the same Muse might inspire in our times.

We see Parnassus as a convivial and collegial place—much like Barzun's *House of Intellect*—where scholars serve the arts and sciences with interdisciplinary tolerance and willingly acknowledge the complexity of past and present. Less elevated than Olympus and set in a more southerly and gentler clime, Parnassus also symbolizes elegance and good taste and the distinction of our collaborators.

Their ranks could have been widened at will and our roster may seem invidiously sparse. May Barzun's many friends, in varied disciplines, consider the scholars and artists here gathered as their worthy representatives!

The essays in this book needed little editing. Each author seemed implicitly guided by Barzun's admonition that every word must say exactly what it means, that good prose is simple and direct. The Bibliography of Barzun's writings, spanning half a century, reflects the wealth and variety of his scholarship. The brief biographies of the contributors indicate the quality of their friendship and the diversity of their indebtedness. We are pleased to be able to include two portraits—one on canvas, one in bronze—by artists also his friends, and are gratified that Barzun's longtime editor at Harper & Row should so readily have agreed to publish this volume. Sadly we note that our undertaking has lost its herald: the "Personal Memoir" that gives this book the stamp of the lifelong friend and colleague *par excellence* lay on Lionel Trilling's desk, unfinished, at his death.

To all contributors our thanks for their ready response and cheerful compliance with our manifold admonitions and requests. To Virginia Xanthos Faggi, Barzun's assistant for many years at Columbia, and to Corona Machemer, our collaborator at Harper & Row, our special gratitude for expert advice and timely help in our attempt to meet the requisite standard of excellence. May this book provide entertainment, and convey the affection and admiration that prompt this gift.

DORA B. WEINER
Manhattanville College

WILLIAM R. KEYLOR
Boston University

Publisher's Note

To be Jacques Barzun's publisher is a rare privilege and a pleasure. Technically speaking, I have also been his editor, but that term suggests the making of changes in an author's manuscript, an exercise which I would no more consider with the work of Barzun than with that of Aldous Huxley, E. B. White, or Thornton Wilder.

Like Huxley's, Jacques Barzun's interests and tastes are wide-ranging—belles lettres, science, music, history, and the theater. And, in addition, he's an authority on the detective story, a hobby that has entertained Jacques in off hours when not pursuing his chosen profession of teaching. As a friend he is a delight; his perfection of style makes him a most civilized and agreeable companion. The world of literature and of learning is fortunate in having so distinguished an exponent.

CASS CANFIELD

LIONEL TRILLING

A Personal Memoir

[When Lionel Trilling died on November 5, 1975, he had barely got launched on his introduction to this volume. Throughout the early days of September, before he became aware that he was indeed seriously ill, he was full of fretful impatience because he was coming increasingly to feel that he lacked the strength to get on with a piece he was so eager to write: a recollection of his long years of association with a much-loved friend. With great effort of will he set himself to the undertaking and got as much done as appears here. With two of Jacques Barzun's books, *The Energies of Art* and *Teacher in America,* these pages were on his desk at his death.

My husband usually wrote slowly, making many starts and ceaselessly paring or elaborating even what he had supposed was finished. But these pages of reminiscence were obviously written in a different manner—I have been able to find among his papers only one other, very slightly modified version of the first three pages, from which I have taken a few corrections and changes, and an even less altered version of the last three pages, after which there follow some scribbled notes of reminder. The impression I have of this manuscript, as compared with his accustomed way of working, is of his having made what would, for him, have been the fastest possible, almost desperate running start in order to try to reach a goal—any decently accurate report of his complex, cherished association with Jacques Barzun— before it would be too late for him to make the attempt at all.

Apart from the trivial alterations I have mentioned, the text published here exactly reproduces the pages which remained on his desk, including words in brackets and even including a bit of the scrawl at the end. *Diana Trilling*]

To write about Jacques Barzun in the way that is called for by the present occasion, to speak of the temper and achievement of his mind, is an enterprise that naturally delights me. And my pleasure is the greater because, as will be generally understood, it would scarcely be possible to go about my task without touching on the close relationship in which for many years Jacques and I dealt with books and ideas.

It was in the autumn of 1934 that we began to sit side by side at the head of a long table for some two hours once each week during the academic year and tried to lead the members of a small class toward the better comprehension of certain books and some degree of adeptness in talking about them. In addition, we confabulated about what books to read, which students to admit to the class, what grades they ought to be given, and all the innumerable small chores that any course entails. We pursued no ideological program, in the sense of seeking to attach our students to some particular set of ideas, or at least we were not conscious of such a purpose; although generally our class sessions went in a lively controversial way, I don't recall that we generated any dialectical drama or had it in mind to do so. As between ourselves, there were sizable differences in taste, but no doctrinal issues that we thought it necessary to resolve.

Jacques and I did not begin our teaching collaboration as friends —our friendship grew out of our fellowship in work, though at the same time the two remained in some sense distinct from each other. For me the work-relationship figured as a salient element of the environment in which I had my intellectual existence. In saying this, I do not mean to suggest that Jacques was an "influence" upon me— he was that indubitably, but chiefly in other connections than the one to which I now refer. The metaphor, such as it is, by which I propose the importance to me of the work-relationship invokes the environment in which we have our physical existence, such elements of it as the terrain and the atmosphere: sitting side by side with Jacques at the head of a long table week after week made the intellectual ground on which I walked and the intellectual air I breathed. Jacques's mental character had been pretty decisively shaped, as mine had not been, before our relationship ever began, and I must suppose that the relationship figured for him in a quite different way than it did for me, though I don't doubt that for him as for me it was of sizable importance.

I have never thought of the closeness which developed between us as having needed any special effort to achieve, yet certainly it is the case that Jacques and I came together over a considerable distance. That we were both graduates of Columbia College, Jacques's class being '27, mine '25, cannot be thought to have done anything to lessen the intervening space, but, on the contrary, only served to increase it. Such awareness as we first had of each other was across a barrier which had about it something of the barricade. During my freshman and sophomore years I had made a series of rather half-hearted attempts to take part in college life and had "gone out for" *Spectator*, the college daily newspaper, and *Varsity*, the college literary magazine, neither of which held my interest for long, and had offered myself as a candidate for membership in Philolexian, the college literary society, and been rejected; I won a part in the Sophomore Show (censorious middle-aged secretary), and after the first performance I knew that "student activities" were not for me. I took my stand with a group of young men who held themselves apart in skepticism and irony; they could not properly have been called Bohemians and the category of "intellectuals" hadn't yet come to be freely used, but "intelligentsia" was available and on the whole appropriate, for they had, it seemed to me, a strong tincture of the young men in Dostoievski and Chekhov; they suited my taste until I graduated. Jacques's relationship to the undergraduate establishment was the exact opposite of mine. Where I began in passivity and deference and ended in contempt, he took the measure of every organization which might bear upon his interests and estimated what pleasure it might give him through making demands upon his energies and abilities. By the time he graduated, he was the dramatic critic of *Spectator*, editor of *Varsity*, president of Philolexian, and author of the 1927 Varsity Show. So far, then, as we were aware of each other, we had no reason to exchange approval, standing as we did on either side of the undergraduate cultural divide. When we came together at the head of our first long table, we each had a pretty clear awareness of what our different college pasts might imply of our present differences in temperament. Actually, however, the differences made no difference, or none that stood in the way of our being at ease with each other.

It was Jacques who judged that the distance between him and me might be overcome and who initiated our association. Jacques's academic career as an undergraduate had been of the very highest distinction, and, having given up earlier intentions of going into the law or diplomacy in favor of the study of history, with an emphasis upon the history of culture, which at the time was still unorthodox, he had been given, immediately upon graduation, a junior appointment in the History Department. By 1932, when I became an instructor in English, he was already a significant influence in the affairs of the college, and it was to be chiefly through his efforts that the course for which he found the name Colloquium—Colloquium on Important Books —would be instituted. Actually the course in its principle and substance was not new to the college, for in virtually every respect it followed the pattern of John Erskine's General Honors course, which had

played an important part in the life of the college during Jacques's
and my undergraduate time. It had been Erskine's view that an educated man, such as a college graduate was supposed to be, must know
the great works of the art and thought of his cultural tradition, and
that he had best begin his acquaintance with them as if they had
been created to be the object not of his solemn study but of his lively
interest. The course had always met with the resistance and hostility
of a considerable part of the faculty and when Erskine was no longer
on the spot to defend it, its enemies did away with it, in the name
chiefly of true scholarship: how could one possibly know Dante if one
did not read him in his own language; if, indeed, one took him at so
low a level as to think that one might read the *Inferno* in a week and
"cover" it in a discussion of two hours? Now, however, Jacques and
his confederates were able to move forward on the new impulse toward humanistic general education which was beginning to manifest
itself in the universities. One of the features of the old course as Erskine had designed it was that each of its small classes or sections was
led by two instructors, of different intellectual disciplines. When the
Colloquium was approved by the faculty, Jacques invited me to join
him in giving a section of the second year of the course and I was delighted to accept what I took to be a sizable compliment.

Like General Honors, which Jacques and I held in pious memory,
the Colloquium met, all sections of it, in the evening, at a time which
came to be regarded as canonical: Wednesdays from 7:30 to 9:30.
The curriculum of the first year began with the *Iliad* and did twenty-
eight great books up through the *Novum Organum*. The second year of
the course, which traditionally ended with Freud, began with Voltaire
and went on to Rousseau and Diderot.

The occurrence of these French names might make the appropriate place to touch upon a second circumstance which set between
Jacques and me a distance that had to be traversed, Jacques's national
origin. This might have constituted a quite considerable hindrance to
our being at ease with each other; that it did not is to be accounted
for chiefly by the nature and extent of Jacques's acculturation though
[also by his tact]. In regard to the acculturation, it is to the point that
Jacques had entered Columbia College after two years of American
high school, preceded by another year of tutoring with an American
schoolteacher. There was in his speech no trace of an "accent." In his
bearing, in what one American sociologist calls "the presentation of
self," there doubtless was something that was not American in that
it was touched with consciousness and with what might be called the
intention of precision; or put it that Jacques did not have in his demeanor the characteristic American air of intending to have no con-

sciousness of himself and no precision. It was plain that this young man knew who he was and I think this knowledge, which is much more accessible to Europeans than to Americans, was taken to be a sort of *hauteur*. But any antagonism that this may have aroused was very quickly dissolved by the sense which Jacques almost unfailingly communicated, of his commitment to American life. It was not merely that, out of politeness or tact, he made a point of not referring to French views or ways of doing things but that he naturally spoke wholly in the American context.

I may have contributed something to the ease between us by my somewhat stolid attitude to Jacques's native culture—I had never directed to France the admiring interest which it frequently receives from Americans of literary inclination. I had perceived, or decided, that I would never speak the language well, would never come into the happy possessive intimacy with French life which Americans sometimes long to achieve, and it may be that this relative indifference to French culture on my part made it possible for me to take Jacques for granted. Such positive relations with French literature and thought as I had established were of a kind to be reassuring to Jacques. I have no doubt, for instance, that my devotion to Stendhal, probably as strong as his own, did much to give us a common ground whose firmness we tested annually when we had to defend *The Red and the Black* from the assaults of our students, almost all of whom over the decades expressed an animus against the book and a disdain of its hero, whom Jacques and I adored.

Jacques spoke but little of his French boyhood, yet I did come to know that his father, Henri Martin-Barzun, was a writer and that early in the century, in 1907, which was the year of Jacques's birth, he had played a decisive part in initiating the short-lived community of writers and artists known as l'Abbaye, after the old house in Créteil, near Paris, in which the members of the group attempted to live together and to support their creative efforts by means of a printing press. It may be that Jacques volunteered information about l'Abbaye in response to my having spoken of my interest, a fleeting one, in Jules Romains, who had been a member of the group, as had also Georges Duhamel and Albert Gleizes. Only very slowly did I gain any fuller awareness of the cultural circumstances of Jacques's early life which manifestly played a decisive part in his intellectual development. Actually, indeed, I did not have an awareness of anything like the full state of the case until 1956; in that year, in the introduction to *The Energies of Art*, Jacques undertook to base an explanation of his complex views of Modernist art on an account of his early relation to it. "To be born," he says, "near the beginning of the decade before the

First World War and at the center of the then most advanced artistic activity in Paris is an accident bound to have irreversible consequences on the mind." He goes on:

> The first picture seen: Cubist; the first music heard: Stravinsky's *Sacre;* the first poetry and drama: Futurist, Simultanist, "experimental" like the first new building visited, which was Auguste Perret's "modernistic" skyscraper apartment, Rue Franklin—all this, thanks to childhood's uncritical acceptance of the given as normal, could not help forming the most natural introduction to art as it is made. Anything but strange, the sights and sounds and ideas that would later make the bourgeois howl were seen as the usual domestic occupations of family and friends; it was Apollinaire interspersing his critical arguments for the grownups with stories for the child; it was Marie Laurencin amid her pictures telling the boy to sit still while she sketched him; it was going to the studio of Duchamp and Villon in Puteaux, of Gleizes and Metzinger in Courbevoie, and while playing there seeing *The Harbor, The Nude Descending the Staircase,* the wonderful dynamic *Horse* in red clay and then in bronze, and other casts and canvases by the dozen.

And still the riches of the juvenile experience are not yet told:

> At home the scene was scarcely different. Every Saturday and sometimes oftener, the stage was full: Marinetti acting and shouting, Archipenko making Léger roar with laughter, Delaunay and Ozenfant debating, Paul Fort declaiming his ballads, Varèse or Florent Schmitt surrounded at the piano. Particularly vivid was the figure of old Georges Izambard, who had been Rimbaud's philosophy teacher and protector, and who was an admirable raconteur. On view at close range were also: Ezra Pound, Cocteau, Severini, Bérard, Kandinsky, Copeau, Bosschère, Polti, Milosz, Poiret, Brancusi, La Fresnaye, and many others fleeting or unremembered. Unquestionably, art and the discussion of art were the sole concern of all who counted in that particular universe.

There follows a grim little account of how the war gave the quietus to all this bright ebullience. It concludes: "Toward the end of the four years, pointlessness was the controlling emotion, and when the war was over, suddenly, it broke upon one"—at the age of eleven!—"that the self had been permanently loosened from the love of life."

I think it would be a correct though simplified paraphrase of Jacques's view of the history of contemporary high culture to say that the regenerative creativity of the Modernist movement having been brought to an end within less than a decade after its beginning, the moral prestige which had been given to its affirmativeness was transferred to the sense of the separation of the self from the love of life, to the nihilistic disgust which became pervasive after the war had destroyed the hope of Modernism. What came to be conceived of as the entity of twentieth-century art was not a coherent style developing according to the laws of its being, but, rather, a union of at least two styles which were not compatible with each other—Symbolism, the dominant advanced style of the end of the nineteenth century, and an impoverished version of Modernism contrived from such of its elements as had survived the war. In Jacques's view, what sustained this infelicitous union was the extent to which the two styles were marked by "anger or despondency," their expression of "disgust at the pointlessness of existence." Such disaffection from modern art as Jacques felt had nothing to do with its avowed ideal of innovation and experiment but was a response to its accessibility to one or another form of nihilistic disgust.

I myself was by no means in a simple relation to the high artistic culture of the modern age, to what I once called, in a phrase that seems to have come in handy, the adversary culture. Before most of it I stood puzzled, abashed, and a little queasy; I was at least as much alienated from it as I was from the culture to which it opposed itself. Yet to a certain few of its practitioners I gave my strong allegiance, Eliot and Joyce being pre-eminent among them. I took the view, pious and dull enough, that the advanced art of one's own age cannot possibly be irrelevant to one's own experience and that one is under the virtually moral obligation to keep one's consciousness open to it. This line, if it can really be called a line, is, I suppose, the Philistinism— and the Pharisaism as well?—of the avant-garde position and Jacques's experience of the avant-garde was too complex and personal to make it likely that he would give it credence. He did eventually, I seem to recall, give way to some extent on Joyce but nothing I might say induced him to regard Eliot with any degree of admiration. Such sympathy as he may have found it possible to give Joyce was probably in some part a response to Joyce's paronomasia, for nothing so bound Jacques and me as our love of punning and our confirmed belief that any notable practitioner of the art was bound to be of large and generous mind (e.g., Shakespeare, Swift).[1]

If, as Jacques's view suggests, it is of the essence of modern

---

1. One of the punning episodes of our Colloquium section seems to have established itself in legend and Jacques and I are sometimes asked whether, in the course of discussion of *An Essay on the Principle of Population*, I said of some opinion of the work that had been advanced, "Honi soit qui Malthus pense," and that to this Jacques replied, "Honi soit qui mal thus puns." Although I do not recollect the incident, internal evidence seems to indicate that it took place as recorded.

artistic culture that it confirms and expresses the idea of the pointlessness of existence, it might be said of the Colloquium that it was of its
nature inhospitable to modern artistic culture. The books we read were
massed against it—they were nothing if not affirmative. To begin at,
say, 1750 with *Tom Jones* and to read some twenty-eight "great" books
of the next two hundred years was to encounter a great many works
that committed themselves to hope, to the joy of discovery and reno-
vation [give examples]. To be sure, there was in the offing always the
possibility of pointlessness and the disgust it aroused, but almost always, as in Hobbes and Swift, in Schopenhauer, Balzac, Stendhal,
Dickens, Nietzsche, it was to be named forthrightly, identified as the
enemy and confronted with a heroic energy of resistance.

Whoever was involved in the Colloquium enterprise was committed to the heroic principle. The course seemed to be designed as if
its chief purpose was to give life such significance as derives from
achievement against odds. It consisted of a series of [dramatic struc-
tures], each of which came to its climax on Wednesday evening.
Thursday might conceivably accommodate gestures toward relaxation
and well-deserved rest, but by Friday one had to be getting forward
with next week's book, possibly with the illusion which might be maintained for the first day of the weekend, that one could get the work
done at a reasonable, deliberate pace. But this was never possible—
unfailingly one had to read faster and give more hours to reading as
each day passed. Wednesday afternoon was given to desperate efforts
to come to the end of the work, then to a call to reasonableness and
the jotting down of salient ideas. A shower before dinner was fortifying.

I speak of how I conducted myself in relation to the work of the
Colloquium. It never occurred to me that Jacques behaved in a similar way.

> Jacques and me/his ability/music/science
> J & me: my slovenliness—lack of system
> J & me: rigor, degrees of
> We were in our twenties when we began the Colloquium—not
> much older than our students—
> We could outwit them at every turn—
> Change to graduate seminar—

Calliope

THE ART OF WRITING

HENRY F. GRAFF

Presidents as Penmen

> "The Lincoln who speaks to me through the written word is a
> figure no longer to be described wholly or mainly by the old
> adjectives, shrewd, humorous or saintly, but rather as one com-
> bining the traits that biography reports in certain artists among
> the greatest—passionate, gloomy, seeming-cold, and conscious
> of superiority."
>
> JACQUES BARZUN, "Lincoln the Literary Genius,"
> *The Saturday Evening Post*, February 14, 1959.

Almost twenty years ago Jacques Barzun volunteered to criticize the
galley proofs of a new book of mine. He was soon at work with his
customary energy and wit. Along with wise and sometimes tart observations on my choice of words and my handling of ideas, he entered
next to what I was representing as a quotation from Lincoln the
dauntless comment: "This isn't Lincoln's music!" I have not forgotten,
nor do I expect to, how startled I was by the conception he had offered—or the endless hours I shortly spent trying to locate the original
words which I had managed to misreport. But most of all I wondered
about the sources of Lincoln's "music," Jacques's ear for it, and the
quality of the "music" to be heard in the writings of the Presidents
generally. Regarding this last aspect of the subject I have been able
to establish only that nothing significant has been written on it, possibly because nobody but Jacques has ever listened for it.

   From 1789 on, the Presidential voice has been that of a voice
from the Throne.[1] The Annual Address—the fundamental Presidential
writing—has been an Address from the Throne. The Constitution states

---

   1. The most convenient compilation is Fred L. Israel, ed., *The State of the
Union Messages of the Presidents, 1790–1966* (3 vols., New York: Robert Hector
Publishers, 1966).

simply that the President shall provide to Congress "from time to time . . . information on the state of the Union." But if there was an unnatural casualness in the words, "from time to time," Presidents were not misled, and from George Washington to the present day the State of the Union Message—as it has been called since the Second World War—has been a major event on the political calendar. And while the Message was originally considered an intragovernmental document, it quickly was disseminated widely and commented upon in the newspapers, and in recent years has been carried to the people through radio and television coverage.

Part of the luxuriant lore of the presidency which every school-child acquires is that Jefferson, out of deference to republican principles (or was it simply because he was a poor public speaker?), ceased the practice of delivering a speech "from the Throne" and instead sent his words to Congress by messenger. For more than a hundred years Jefferson's way was the *modus operandi*. Then, Woodrow Wilson, operating under other compulsions, including an inordinate affection for things English, once more appeared in person before Congress to demonstrate that he was, as he said, "a human being trying to cooperate with other human beings in a common service." With some exceptions the President has ever since appeared before Congress—and the cameras—and has, in effect, turned the Message into an oral presentation. The Message is now written to be spoken, not read.

The form today is thus different from what it once was, and therefore less useful for judging Presidential writing. But what do the old written Addresses reveal? They reveal that at least in those documents Presidents have not displayed much literary imagination. Lincoln's are the notable exceptions. They are full of evidence that the Emancipator *chose* his words and undoubtedly crossed out a few in the process of choosing—and that the cadences in his phrases were natural and necessary elements in their meaning and persuasiveness. A short sample—familiar and matchless:

> Fellow-citizens, we can not escape history. We of this Congress and this Administration will be remembered in spite of ourselves. No personal significance or insignificance can spare one or another of us. The fiery trial through which we pass will light us down in honor or dishonor to the latest generation. . . .[2]

Grover Cleveland's Messages stand in sharpest contrast. His words were flat and motionless, and if they conveyed any feeling at

2. *Ibid.*, Vol. 2, p. 1,084.

all it was surely one of ennui, if not of insincerity. A just example: "As public servants we shall do our duty well if we constantly guard the rectitude of our intentions, maintain unsullied our love of country, and with unselfish purpose strive for the public good."[3] Benjamin Harrison—known to some contemporaries as "Old Icewater"—also held his audience at arm's length, as if in imitation of Cleveland. He once presented these words: "Our form of government, with its incident of universal suffrage, makes it imperative that we shall save our working people from the agitations and distresses which scant work and wages that have no margin for comfort always beget."[4]

A further observation: as if by design each President invoked God's name with a different circumlocution, which may have been the focal point for Presidential literary inventiveness. So we encounter "the Supreme Ruler of Nations" (Washington), "Heaven" (Jefferson), "the Just and All-Powerful Being who holds in His Hand the chain of events and the destiny of nations" (Madison), "the Divine Author of All Good" (Monroe), "He who searches the hearts of the children of men" (John Quincy Adams), "that Power which superintends all government" (Jackson), "He who holds in His hands the destiny of men and nations" (Pierce), and so on.

Despite only modest indications while in office, some of the Presidents when they became ex-Presidents redeemed themselves in their personal memoirs and autobiographical reflections. Perhaps in their post-presidency they felt less constrained, less need to be formal, and less bound by the temptation to be mannered. Alas, the most recent Presidential autobiographies—those of Truman, Eisenhower and Johnson—bear the marks of ghost-writers, who always contrive to hide rather than reveal their subjects, as well as merely muddy our understanding of what constitutes Presidential writing. So we must turn to the pre-1930 Presidents, whose "ghosts"—if they existed at all—have fled forever.

The best autobiographical writing by a President was done by Ulysses S. Grant.[5] Too long has Grant lived in American minds only as a heavy drinker and cigar addict whose seeming callousness toward

---

3. *Ibid.*, Vol. 2, p. 1,624.

4. *Ibid.*, Vol. 2, p. 1,669.

5. Of the many pieces of such Presidential composition I have reviewed in arriving at my judgments in this essay I have excluded from consideration Theodore Roosevelt's *Autobiography* (New York, Charles Scribner's Sons, 1913), a book of impressive artistic merit. Roosevelt was so widely published by the time he was President that he must be regarded as a professional writer, whose work requires and deserves a different kind of analysis than that accorded here to the literary efforts of Presidents who were amateur authors.

human life, including especially the lives of his own troops, once converted the road to Richmond into a charnel house. But Grant was a man of sensitivity and cultivation, whose high aim as a West Point cadet was to return to the Military Academy as an Assistant Professor of Mathematics. A master horseman, his predilection for the outdoors kept him from literary pursuits when he was growing up. His early military career gave him ample time to write, but he took little advantage of it. Later, when the heavy responsibility of a command in the field came to him, his writing was confined to military orders. They were for the most part crisply and cleanly drawn up, but without distinction. The language of his Presidential deliverances was also unexceptional—if not, like his administration itself, disappointing.

Although we know only the superficial facts of Grant's emergence as a man of letters, it constituted the high drama of the last months of his life. The chain of events began some years earlier. Grant had allowed an unscrupulous young man named Ferdinand Ward to inveigle him into joining an investment scheme that eventually cost the Grant family most of their capital and savings. Grant's chagrin was complete when he had to seek and accept gifts and loans of money from friends and other well-wishers.

Grant's dream of living comfortably in his retirement from public life went aglimmering and he was forced to scramble in order to help support his family. An opportunity arose when *The Century Magazine* began to plan what became its famous series on the battles and leaders of the Civil War. Grant's account of the fighting was expected to be the centerpiece of the series as well as the *sine qua non* of its success. Reluctant to participate—the age of memoir-writing by the nation's giants was then only getting under way—Grant finally agreed to do four articles at $500 apiece. Eventually he prepared three articles, and the publisher provided a bonus of $1,500. The bonus was an inducement for Grant to compose a book of memoirs.

The articles were only ordinary, lacking the verve and narrative strength that the magazine's readers looked for, because what had been a brutal fraternal struggle was now, on the eve of the twenty-fifth anniversary of Fort Sumter, a glorified and exalting memory for millions of Americans. Grant might have left the world only this dull set of recollections but for the remarkable intercession of Mark Twain.

Mark Twain knew that Grant was fatally ill of cancer of the throat. Grant too was aware that his days were numbered, and he was tormented by the fact that he would leave his family in desperate financial straits. As an admirer and friend, Mark Twain was eager to help—especially when he learned how little Grant had been paid by the *Century.* He was convinced that Grant's memoirs would find a powerful reception among the reading public. Quickly he persuaded Grant to start writing, and then proceeded to make arrangements for two volumes of memoirs to be brought out by the Charles L. Webster Company, a subscription publishing firm which he had recently established.

Although sick unto death and often in excruciating pain, Grant doggedly set down his recollections. Sometimes he was so ill that he could not work at all. Despite such interruptions, in a little less than a year he finished the autobiography—a week before he died. Published in 1885–86 in two volumes under the simple title *Personal Memoirs of U. S. Grant,* the work is so full of good writing that a student of Grant's life must conclude that like all accomplished literary craftsmen Grant acquired his skill, hitherto unrevealed, through the force of model and example.

Readers discover quickly that Grant uses unornamented language as if he knows well that it will heighten the power of the awful tale he has to tell of brother fighting brother. His sentences are short, startlingly short for that day, and their variety shows the deftness of a wordsmith. Consider his description of his first attempt at contact with the Confederate enemy—a unit under Colonel Thomas Harris at the town of Florida, Missouri:

> As we approached the brow of the hill from which it was expected we could see Harris' camp and possibly find his men ready formed to meet us, my heart kept getting higher and higher until it felt to me as though it was in my throat. I would have given anything then to have been back in Illinois, but I had not the moral courage to halt and consider what to do; I kept right on. When we reached a point from which the valley below was in full view I halted. The place where Harris had been encamped a few days before was still there and the marks of a recent encampment were plainly visible, but the troops were gone. My heart resumed its place. It occurred to me at once that Harris had been as much afraid of me as I had been of him. This was a view of the question I had never taken before; but it was one I never forgot afterwards.[6]

Where did Grant acquire his training in expository prose? On this matter the *Memoirs* themselves are instructive. Grant tells us that he did not attack his studies at West Point with enthusiasm ("avidity" is his word, perhaps a better one); "in fact I rarely ever read over a

---

6. *Personal Memoirs of U.S. Grant* (2 vols., New York: Charles L. Webster & Co., 1885–86), Vol. i, pp. 249–250.

author: no one can confidently imagine that he would actually have hired someone to do this work, although it eventually netted him a small fortune. He seems to have begun writing it while still President. The book, originally published serially in *Cosmopolitan* beginning in the spring of 1929, does not bubble with views and information; but the words are good-spirited and didactic, and they are often uncommonly inspired. Of his forebears, for instance, Coolidge declares: "Most of them are gone now and their old homesteads are reverting to the wilderness. They went forth to conquer where the trees were thicker, the fields larger, and the problems more difficult."[14] And he philosophizes gently and tersely about the kind of world out of which he came:

> Country life does not always have breadth, but it has depth. It is neither artificial nor superficial, but is kept close to the realities.
>
> While I can think of many pleasures we did not have, and many niceties of culture with which we were unfamiliar, yet if I had the power to order my life anew I could not dare to change that period of it. If it did not afford me the best that there was, it abundantly provided the best that there was for me.[15]

On the subject of the presidency itself, Coolidge provides a number of select aphorisms embedded in brief, clipped paragraphs. A sample reveals a self-assured way with words as well as thoughtful consistency of mind: "It is a great advantage to a President, and a major source of safety to the country, for him to know that he is not a great man."[16]

Coolidge's mind may have been a limited one in the sense that it did not generate compelling new governmental programs, or deal with old ones in imaginative ways. Moreover, the man was not given to using abstract language to help him generalize about concrete matters. Yet, is there anywhere in Presidential literature a more profound or more elegant commentary on the nature of the Chief Executive's work than this one?

> I appreciate how impossible it is to convey an adequate realization of the office of President. A few short paragraphs in the Constitution of the United States describe all his fundamental duties. Various laws passed over a period of nearly a century and a half have supplemented his authority. All his actions can be analyzed. All of his comings and goings can be recited. The details of his daily life can be

---

14. *The Autobiography of Calvin Coolidge*, p. 6.
15. *Ibid.*, pp. 33–34.
16. *Ibid.*, p. 173.

made known. The effects of his policies on his own country and on the world at large can be estimated. His methods of work, his associates, his place of abode can all be described. But the relationship created by all these and more, which constitutes the magnitude of the office, does not yield to definition. Like the glory of a morning sunrise, it can only be experienced—it cannot be told.[17]

This statement, quite apart from being intellectually surefooted, is also perfectly composed. The first sentence, short and assertive, is ornamented by the word "realization" used with perfect aptness. The sentences that follow are varied in tense and in mood, and move easily from idea to idea. The conclusion that the "magnitude of the office" does not "yield to definition" has a majestic certainty worthy of the subject that cannot be conveyed by any variant phrase.

Coolidge is no less cogent in writing of what had come to be his legendary repugnance at wastefulness of any kind. His words even today seem eloquent, not trite:

> Wealth comes from industry and from the hard experience of human toil. To dissipate it in waste and extravagance is disloyalty to humanity. This is by no means a doctrine of parsimony. Both men and nations should live in accordance with their means and devote their substance not only to productive industry, but to the creation of the various forms of beauty and the pursuit of culture which gives adornments to the art of life.[18]

If these sensible ideas seemed old-fashioned to a generation that was hearkening to the teachings of John Maynard Keynes, so did Coolidge's ideas about a personal God. He expressed them touchingly as he wrote of the death of his young son, who had contracted blood poisoning from a blister raised while playing tennis: "When he went the power and the glory of the Presidency went with him. . . . I do not know why such a price was exacted for occupying the White House."[19]

In the half century since Coolidge served, we have become aware that some part of his taciturnity, which once seemed to be the prime stuff of vaudeville entertainment, concealed an able and comprehending mind. Reread a half century after they were written, the following paragraphs do not seem "too short":

> It is difficult for men in high office to avoid the malady of self-delusion. They are always surrounded by worshipers. They are constantly, and for the most part sincerely, assured of their greatness.

17. *Ibid.*, p. 195.
18. *Ibid*, p. 182.
19. *Ibid.*, p. 190.

They live in an artificial atmosphere of adulation and exaltation which sooner or later impairs their judgment. They are in grave danger of becoming careless and arrogant.

The chances of having wise and faithful public service are increased by a change in the Presidential office after a moderate length of time.[20]

Not every President has been so self-effacing—or so perceptive. The juxtaposing of the adjectives "careless" and "arrogant" appears ordinary today in the light of recent Presidential history. But carelessness and arrogance were unusual attributes of Chief Executives not very long ago; that Coolidge understood them to be latent in every man in "high office" is an indication of his perspicacity. The reader, incidentally, notices quickly that Coolidge did not use the word "leader" to describe the Chiefs he had in mind. As in all of the judgments he committed to the pages of his book, he was attentive to nuances that others might have missed.

In deciding to leave the White House after having served an elective term of his own, Coolidge explained that he was not simply seeking the delights of private life:

While I had a desire to be relieved of the pretensions and delusions of public life, it was not because of any attraction of pleasure or idleness.

We draw our Presidents from the people. It is a wholesome thing for them to return to the people. I came from them. I wish to be one of them again.[21]

Agreeably, there is no self-aggrandizement in that final sentence. Coolidge simply states a wish that every reader and every fellow citizen can understand. What he wrote conformed with his practice of trying to say what he meant in the best possible way. He was "mystified," he maintained, that some people did not understand his intention when he announced simply in 1927: "I do not choose to run." That sentence, he said, seemed perfectly clear to him, for "[i]n making my public statement I was careful in the use of words."[22] So he was in the writing of his autobiography, too; and those who study his times ought to feel grateful to him.

A vastly different kind of writer was William Howard Taft, who has given us the most extensive examination of the presidency we have yet had from the pen of a President. Taft had presented the

---

20. *Ibid.*, p. 241.
21. *Ibid.*, p. 243.
22. *Ibid.*

substance of his thinking on the subject in a series of lectures he delivered on the campus of the University of Virginia in 1915. Later in the same year he delivered virtually the same lectures at Columbia University, although embellished with more anecdotal material. The Columbia version was issued by the Columbia University Press in 1916 as *Our Chief Magistrate and His Powers.*

Nicholas Murray Butler, the president of Columbia University, himself already bitten by the Presidential "bug," wrote the Introduction to the book with understatement and self-possession. He offered the thought that the work was "more objective and more philosophical than any correspondence could possibly be." For that reason, he said, "it is more suitable to the purposes of the general reader . . . who would get a clear and exact comprehension of the functions and duties of him whom we proudly call our Chief Magistrate."[23]

Butler's own sense of how precisely the work of the President of the United States could be specified informs us well about the simplistic conception of the office in Butler's time. Unheralded to Columbia's president, however, a metamorphosis was in the making. The public interest in the presidency that the success of Taft's lectures seemed to register as well as reflect followed upon the dramatic administration of Theodore Roosevelt. To a fuller extent than ever in the past the President and his family had become semi-royal figures whose lives—personal as well as public—were now everybody's business and concern.

In the nineteenth century scarcely an article, let alone a book, had appeared on the subject of the presidency as an institution. This lack is to be explained not only by the fact that there had been too few Presidents (only twenty-four by 1900), but also by the fact that the bureaucratization of American life, including the White House, had only just begun. Woodrow Wilson had examined the legislative process in his magisterial work, *Congressional Government* (1885), but the Presidential office still awaited comparable analysis. Unhappily, Taft was not equal to the task.

Leaving aside a substantive consideration of Taft's words on the Presidential office, we find his writing style remarkably torpid and flinty. Thus: "The Cabinet is a mere creation of the President's will. It is an extra-statutory and extra-constitutional body. It exists only by custom. If the President desired to dispense with it, he could do so."[24] Nowhere in the ensuing discussion does Taft deal with *his* feelings

---

23. William Howard Taft, *Our Chief Magistrate and His Powers* (New York: Columbia Univ. Press, 1916), p. [v]–vi.

24. *Ibid.*, p. 30.

toward his cabinet officers or with *his* experience in submitting questions upon which he sought the cabinet's advice.

As if by stubborn choice, Taft concentrates upon the small rather than the large. And he does so in language that is variously strait-laced and banal. He recounts, for instance, how as Secretary of War he had dealt with a mother who importuned him to approve her son's appointment to the Military Academy at West Point. The obstacle was the youth's chest measurement, which was below standard:

> I said to the mother therefore that as I had no difficulty in filling out my chest measurement [Taft himself weighed 300 pounds], I thought it would be possible for her son, with his intellectual capacity, to follow a regimen to give his lungs the proper room, and that I was inclined to waive the objections. . . . [T]here spread over her comely face a wry smile, and she hesitated a moment to think what she could say to express her gratitude and her satisfaction with me, and then she said, "Mr. Secretary, you are not nearly as fat as they say you are."

He added tamely, "A recollection of that remark has enabled me to get through a good many scenes that were much more annoying and had a much less satisfactory issue."[25]

Taft's tone in writing about the presidency is that of a man who feels at one with all of his predecessors—almost as if they were his contemporaries. Jefferson's refusal to respond to a subpoena *duces tecum*, Grant's standing up to criticism for being so frequently at his summer place in Long Branch, Garfield's readiness to ignore the recommendations of a New York senator on an appointment in New York—all are treated with a pleasantness suggesting that Taft and those who came before him in the line of the Presidents are veritably interchangeable. The language Taft uses is that of a man who is so comfortable with his achievements and his place in history that he does not have to make a case for himself. He is not given to exhorting or preaching or inspiriting.

It is safe to assert that Taft's listless prose is a match for the mere modicum of ideas in his book. A sample of his writing on a major subject:

> I was much interested during my term of office in devising a system for the permanent promotion of efficiency and economy in the government service. I induced Congress to give me $100,000 a year for two years, to pay the expenses of an expert Commission, to examine the governmental business and make reports upon the changes needed by

---

25. *Ibid.*, pp. 74–75.

the introduction of modern business methods and economy, to enable the people to get more for their money.

Congress, Taft continued, thought little of the resulting reports, so it cut off the appropriation. But the work of the Commission was rewarding, he concluded, "and while the dust is accumulating on their reports at present . . . some day they will be made the basis for further investigation and for definite measures of reform."[26]

Taft's book on the presidency has also gathered dust. At my suggestion some years ago the Columbia University Press reprinted it, bringing it out in a paperback edition under the title *The President and His Powers*. It has served to help teach my seminar students about Presidential writing as well as about writings on the presidency.

Americans may be certain that their Presidents will continue to write about their labors not only in order to pay their post-Presidential living expenses but also to help them climb Mount Rushmore. Some of them, it is earnestly hoped, will write as attractively as Grant and Coolidge, and with more animation and insight than Taft. For Presidential writing may be the most distinctive personal legacy a Chief Executive bequeaths to posterity, invaluable to his fellow Americans in rendering judgment when the fires of his public life have finally burned down. And when one considers that on the usual scale for grading the Presidents, Grant and Coolidge are near the bottom, and Taft only a few cubits above them, their literary remains are highly important. They inform us that a revised estimate of Grant and Coolidge may be called for, and that Taft's traditional reputation is substantially confirmed. A shiny new tool could well be in hand for the close student of the presidency. Jacques Barzun's casual comment about my abuse of Lincoln's words may be worthy of elevation into a principle: "By their music shall ye know the Chiefs."

---

26. *Ibid.*, p. 64.

C. P. SNOW

The Classical Detective Story

"In all of Barzun's works there is a demand, and a frequent prescription, for order."

C. P. SNOW

❧

For the sake of argument, which is of course always simpler than the truth, there are two species of detective story. In the first, the detective solves his problem by reason—deductive reason based on observation —rather like recent models (hypothetico-deductive) of the scientific process. The progenitors of this category of story were Edgar Allen Poe and Conan Doyle, though ingenious persons have suggested earlier examples.

This category was at the height of its popularity and esteem just before and after the First World War. It attracted both as working practitioners and readers a good many professional academics, and among its readers there was a high proportion of trained professional minds. There were attempts to set down rigid rules of how such stories should be written, including prohibitions of "illegitimate" devices.

Since the thirties, this kind of story has been under continuous critical attack by such authorities on the whole detective genre as Julian Symons. However, within the last few years it has attracted some admirable new writers, such as P. D. James in England, who can be compared favourably with the writers of the twenties. She belongs to the family of what we now call the classical detective story.

The other family is slightly harder to define, but it has recognisable features. It is indifferent to the puzzle element, which is essential in the classical stories; it usually includes violence, and is most comfortable with one solitary person plunging into the murk of mysterious crime. It is happiest with a derelict private eye at its centre, as in the work of its first major exponent, Dashiell Hammett. Its vogue increased with the vogue of free expression in literature, and in literary terms it is obviously and passionately romantic.

It doesn't need saying, or it ought not to, that no serious investigation of crime has ever followed either of these two paper patterns. Both are conventions, and the romantic one, though somewhat better disguised, is as much a convention as the other. No crime has been solved by the intellectual operations of Sherlock Holmes, or his more sophisticated successors. Nor by private investigators wandering about, preferably in an impenetrable haze on the fringes of society, gun under the armpit and on the hip.

Real police work has not yet been satisfactorily conveyed in fiction, though John Creasey had a stab at it. All expert policemen are emphatic in their dissatisfaction, and the literary evidence is completely on their side. It would require both insight and knowledge of a very high order, such as Balzac used to explore the performance of early nineteenth-century French finance. There aren't enough Balzacs to go round, and a modern one is unlikely to devote himself to detective stories (Simenon is the nearest approach, but a long way off). Further, however well equipped the talent was, the result might be distinctly tedious. So we have to make the best of what we have, and not expect too much in the way of factual truth. Here is a minor art. As with many minor arts, each of its branches, sensation stories (to use the nineteenth-century name for the romantic ones) and classical detective stories, has often given more pleasure than works in a major art.

In the midst of his main avocations, so many more than most men's, Jacques Barzun has been an addict of detective stories for most of his life. Together with his friend Wendell H. Taylor, he has organised in *A Catalogue of Crime* by far the most scholarly treatment of the whole subject. But it will not surprise anyone that, between the two main branches of detective fiction as defined above, Barzun gives most of his interest, and all his affection, to the classical form. It isn't hard to divine at least one reason. There is an echo of Baudelaire's great poem. At the end of the voyage, there in the desirable country, one is invited to find *beauté, luxe, calme, volupté*. But not only those allurements. Also *ordre*. Most of all, and as a condition of the rest, order. In all of Barzun's work, there is a demand, and frequently a prescription, for order. In this minor formalised art, he has discovered at least a comforting hint of it.

Isn't that, in fact, true of a good many of us? People don't really read classical detective stories for excitement. It is doubtful whether they read them, as much as they think, for the puzzle: although it is nice to pick out the answer, even the most ingenious and conscientious puzzle solvers, such as the great mathematician G. H. Hardy, don't feel disagreeably frustrated if they fail. There is a satisfaction deeper than getting the answer right. The final blessing of the classical detective story is another of Baudelaire's invitations: it is *calme*. And it is the calm—moral calm, if one can use a pretentious phrase—which comes from order, and will come from nothing else.

Think of the Holmes stories. The plots are pretty unsophisticated by the standards of those that follow. Like other great originators, Doyle was in technical respects nothing like as good as the writers who wouldn't have existed without him. Holmes's detective processes seem often mildly absurd, set against the classical examples of the 1920s and 1930s. The atmosphere is marvellous, but the dialogue is frequently careless and inept. Nevertheless, there is magic. Doyle had a reassuring touch of genius, which supremely popular writers sometimes possess, and aesthetic writers don't. Who has finished a Holmes story without feeling sheltered in a secure world, where decency, honour, and courage in the long run triumph, and where with will and effort righteousness and order can be made to prevail? At the conclusion of a Holmes case, Baker Street, with supper sent in from Fortnum's and a couple of good bottles of wine, is a delectable representation of the end of Baudelaire's voyage.

That same promise of order is the emotional basis of the classical detective stories which succeeded Holmes. It isn't often so powerful, because the writers, though more ingenious and disciplined, hadn't Doyle's primary gift. But it is there.

The form developed and to an extent divided. Some of the practitioners carried ingenuity to the extreme, which is nearly always a mistake in an artificial form. A good many concentrated on the validity and honesty of the puzzle. Monsignor Ronald Knox laid down statutes, which respect-worthy detective writers were ordered to obey. These had an effect similar to Boileau's instructions about verse.

Classical art, even in its minor expressions, is a delicate growth, and tends to wither or, alternatively, to break out in non-classical offshoots, if it has too much regulation. Knox's own stories were not much good. He was one of those singular products of inbred English upper-class education who have enormous charisma at school and university and a lifelong impact on their contemporaries which is not easy for later generations to understand. Another of these phenomena was Max Beerbohm, and there are two or three recent examples.

However, minds addicted to classical purity paid attention to the Knox doctrine. My own taste in art is on the impure side of the classical. Barzun, a purer character, isn't as comfortable with departures from the strict form. But he has a comprehensive knowledge of all classical detective story writers, and his favourites carry their own message.

Let us have a look, in chronological order, from before the First World War into the thirties, at a few of the English examples: R. Austen Freeman, H. C. Bailey, Freeman Wills Croft, Anthony Berkeley, Dorothy Sayers—and in a sub-category of her own covering a much longer span of time, Agatha Christie. Freeman was himself a man of scientific education (there were several others, including an eminent professor of chemistry, who during the same period wrote detective stories—usually correct but not enlivening—in their off-moments) and invented a peculiarly austere medical detective, Dr. Thorndyke. The detection in these stories, granted the artificialities of the genre, is impeccable. Sometimes the presentation is as near systematic as a detective story can be: clues, presented with faithful scrupulousness and no tricks, and then afterwards the chance for deduction. There are no literary concessions, though now and then the massive integrity of the enterprise does produce, outside the domain of the puzzle, a suspension of disbelief. At the height of the classical vogue, people were known to work away at the clues and emerge with the right answer.

It seems unlikely that, in spite of the present renaissance of classical stories, which I have already hinted at and will return to, Freeman's will be much published again. One gets the impression that they are a bit too unalluring even for Barzun's upright mind. That, however, is not true of H. C. Bailey. Unlike most of Barzun's admirations, this, which other cognoscenti approve of, is one I can't share. Like Freeman, Bailey had some scientific knowledge, and his detective Reggie Fortune was a forensic specialist. The detection is as honest as Freeman's, and the plotting more ingenious and subtle. But the mannerisms, the general atmosphere of giggling and what the English now call jokeyness, for me take away from any kind of narrative conviction. Once again, I would bet heavily against a revival of Bailey.

Freeman Wills Croft is too much for Barzun and everyone else. His was the classical detective story carried to the limit of bathos. Crofts was by origin a railway engineer, and the stories depend on an exact and scholarly interpretation of the English railway system—in the twenties, a good deal more elaborate and widespread than it is now. The unfortunate Inspector French had to make more railway journeys and study more timetables than any detective in the literature. Railway addicts, of whom there were always a fair number in England, may have enjoyed the stories, but no one else did.

By the time of Anthony Berkeley, well into the twenties, detective story writers were beginning to show the first signs of restlessness at the classical confines. Just as Bailey gets on my nerves by his over-sprightliness, Berkeley seems to have the same effect on Barzun. But he was an interesting man. He was well-to-do, and wrote and reviewed detective stories for many years as a wealthy man's hobby. The result was a certain preciosity and over-elaboration. *The Poisoned Chocolates Murder,* bizarrely cunning, is a concealed parodic exercise on the over-elaboration into which others were developing the classical detective story. Berkeley had a good deal of wit and light-weight literary talent. In the thirties he wrote, under the name of Francis Iles (his real name was Cox), several suspense novels of crime, not detective stories, which were effective in a manner at the same time idiosyncratic and sur-reptitiously perverse.

Some of his books bear re-reading very well. I can forgive him a lot for certain of his jokes. In one story, he has an irascible colonel who finds it difficult to distinguish between poets and unfortunate coloured denizens of the former British Colonial Empire. In the course of the mystery, he is compelled to have social relations with some poets. "Kick them," he says heartily, "kick them. The only language they understand."

With Dorothy Sayers, there are other signs of the classical form becoming oppressive to a fine practitioner. It wasn't that she cheated on the detective story rules. She obeyed them as faithfully as any of the duller masters, and, being a scholar *manqué* as well as a kind of George Sand *manqué,* she wrote an admirable history and analysis of the genre. By purist standards, her only fault was that some of her methods of homicide were remarkably over-clever, and had the additional disadvantage, at least for an enthusiastic murderer, that they probably wouldn't have worked. (Incidentally, a great experimental physicist once proposed the most complex and sophisticated method of murder so far invented. In a detective story, the trouble would have been that the only possible culprit was bound to be the great experimental physicist himself.)

In all technical respects, Dorothy Sayers—more potent than other gifted women, including Ngaio Marsh and Margery Allingham—loomed in the thirties as the last larger-than-life figure in the classical detective story. She was only unsatisfactory in that role because she got tired of it and gave it up. She devoted herself to religious writing and Dante scholarship, and lived robustly the fag-end of an unhappy life. At the time, this seemed to symbolise the obsolescence of the classical story; but the prognosticators had read the symptoms wrong.

They ought to have paid more attention to the work of Agatha

Christie, whose books were becoming, through the forties, fifties, sixties, more popular than ever all over the world. (If any magazine in
the Soviet Union is getting into trouble with its circulation, there is
one simple prescription—publish a story by "Agta.") Agatha Christie
had begun writing detective stories during, if not before, the First
World War. The dates of her publications cover sixty years; there are
going to be some difficult problems for bibliographers and textual critics. In many ways, not only in her abnormal productivity, she wasn't
an orthodox detective story writer. She broke the rules of legitimacy
when she felt like it, often glaringly, as in *Roger Ackroyd* and in *Cur-
tain* (Poirot's last case). Her secret, and one which makes her in a
singular fashion supreme, is a trick—partly technical but much more
emerging from natural, intuitive cunning—of something like psychological sleight-of-hand, or a literary version of the three-card trick. In
the whole history of the detective story, she is perhaps the greatest
oddity; not the greatest writer, but quite alone, with no one remotely
like her.

Nevertheless, the theoreticians ignored her as they followed the
rise, and expected the complete domination, of the sensation novel.
In its twentieth-century manifestation, it began, as the classical detective story had begun, with a writer of major literary talent. Dashiell
Hammett, in a strict literary sense, was a better writer than any of his
classical contemporaries. That appealed to cultivated taste, and was a
factor, for a time a decisive one, in celebrating the death of the classical form and the take-over by the new one.

Right up to the present day, good writers have been attracted to it.
An excellent example in America is Stanley Ellin, who could have
written almost anything well. In England, Julian Symons, a good poet
and distinguished critic, was so impressed, on the literary evidence, by
the superiority of the suspense mode that he became its chief theoreti-
cian. Just to prove his point, he abandoned his own accomplished
classical detective stories, and proceeded to write even more accomplished suspense stories. He is properly respected in England, and,
through both theory and practice, his views carried much weight.

And yet, Barzun isn't alone in disapproving of this romantic wave.
Hammett was, of course, as romantic as Hemingway, and so have been
his successors. In the language of literary textbooks, this is a romantic
age, with all the consequences—good and bad, anti-rational, personal-
ised—which that means. Romantic art, though, has a tendency, at
least to sceptical and critical minds, to emphasize the virtues of its
opposite. One can't dispense with order for ever, either in society or
in the literature which emerges from it.

Minor arts often show an underground hunger some time before major ones. Certainly there have recently been sharp signs of a return to classical detective stories, both among readers and writers. In fact, the form never lost its readership as much as critical opinion suggested. (It is important to remember that this readership hasn't at any time, except for singular phenomena like Doyle and Agatha Christie, been an enormous one. Most well-known practitioners sold in hardback a few thousand copies, no more.) Agatha Christie, the sempiternal, has continued down the decades to attract a large audience. Her survival has taught, or ought to have taught, a simple lesson. People might predict that the classical detective story, or anything like it, was dead. A considerable public took not the slightest notice and went on reading it.

Further, while writers as good as Ellin were giving new sophistication to the suspense novel, others of comparable gifts were applying themselves to the classical. In England most of these have been women—Gwen Butler, Ruth Rendall, Elizabeth Ferrars, Celia Fremlin. Quite recently there has appeared another (mentioned at the beginning of this article) as gifted as any of the founding fathers and mothers—P. D. James. She is not only as gifted as the forerunners, but has added skills that they didn't possess. She is as scholarly as Dorothy Sayers, but much more cool-headed and critical. She would have made an admirable straight novelist. When anyone as good as this is bringing new excellences to a nice minor art, it is a fair presumption that others will follow. She is the best living testimony to the durability of the Barzun taste.

Euterpe

MUSIC IN HISTORY

DAVID CAIRNS

Spontini's Influence on Berlioz

"If we except the works of Beethoven and a few others we have only a very imperfect notion of what Berlioz's musical experiences were."

JACQUES BARZUN, *Berlioz and the Romantic Century*

⟿

The legend of Berlioz—the sport of musical evolution, a phenomenon *sui generis*—which was for long the received idea of him, was in part a rationalisation; it helped to explain why his musical style was so difficult to grasp. Yet it could hardly have implanted itself so deeply if the music of Berlioz's immediate predecessors in France had still been known and heard. To take one example, the huge forces and grandiose style of the *Requiem*, the *Te Deum* and the *Symphonie funèbre et triomphale* would not have come to be thought of as peculiar to Berlioz, and freakish, if the equally massive ceremonial works of Méhul, Gossec and Lesueur had not already been forgotten.

In some ways Berlioz is a composer who looks forward to the twentieth century; but he was also the heir and final representative of the French classical tradition. The eclipse of that tradition was as important a factor in his music's "difficulty" as the apparent eccentricities of his style; or rather, the two factors were part of the same thing.

This is not to suggest that there was nothing disconcertingly new about Berlioz's music. That would be absurd. His music would have created a problem no matter what period he had lived in. Like Biblical man, he was born to trouble as the sparks fly upwards. But the problem was exacerbated by history—that is, by the replacement of the musical tradition which had formed him by one quite different in its methods, if not in its ideals. It was above all the change in the context in which his music was listened to that made it seem eccentric and prevented it from acclimatising itself. If in such things as its emphasis

on rhythm and its linear, non-pianistic treatment of the orchestra it
was actually ahead of its time, in the era of Wagner and Wagnerism
it seemed already out of date. Conversely, the modern discovery and
gradual acceptance of Berlioz's music is due as much to the fact that
the historical causes which militated against it have run their course
as to the fact that the advent of the long-playing record has simply
made it more familiar than it ever was before. Our comprehensive
awareness of the past, our revival of more and more forgotten operas,
oratorios and symphonies, and at the same time the upheavals in
musical composition, have between them virtually obliterated the old
concept of a "norm," against which music such as Berlioz's used to be
measured and found bizarre. And, in the case of Berlioz, the more we
get to know the music that he heard, the less isolated and unique we
realise him to be, and the clearer his roots become.

In stating that we had "only a very imperfect notion of what Berlioz's musical experiences were," Jacques Barzun was not confining
himself to any one period of his career but speaking generally. Like
any other composer Berlioz went on learning and profiting from what
he heard. (Composers get their musical ideas as much from each
other as from, in Elgar's phrase, the air around them.) But the statement is particularly applicable to the decade from 1821 to 1830, the
period of his musical education, when the provincial youth who had
come to Paris with the instincts of a dramatic composer but without
the means to realise them was learning his art and steeping himself
in one vital musical experience after another.

The influences to which Berlioz was successively and voluntarily
subjected during this crucial formative period may be summed up
under the following headings: the operas of Gluck and Spontini; then
Weber (*Der Freischütz*, followed by *Euryanthe* and *Oberon*); and finally, from 1828, Beethoven. To them should be added the masses and
oratorios of Lesueur and Cherubini, the Mozart of *The Magic Flute*
and the Rossini of *Moïse* and *William Tell*, and various post-Gluckist
operas such as Kreutzer's *La mort d'Abel*, Piccinni's *Didon*, Salieri's *Les
Danaïdes*, Berton's *Virginie*, and Sacchini's *Oedipe à Colone*. But from
all the composers with whom Berlioz set himself to go to school at the
opera and in the concert hall, four—as he himself makes clear—stand
out in importance: Gluck, Spontini, Weber and Beethoven.

Beethoven was the turning point. The revelation of the expressive
potentialities of symphonic music, of what music can be made to do,
and at the same time how it can be made to cohere—its scope and its
structural principles—made the discovery of his music as it were the
destined culmination of Berlioz's apprenticeship. Beethoven com-

pleted and greatly expanded Berlioz's musical aesthetic. He was the catalyst that precipitated the *Symphonie fantastique.*

Weber first introduced Berlioz to Romanticism in music. After an exclusive diet of *tragédie lyrique,* the effect of music of such vivacity, charm and variety of colour, coming upon him unawares, must have been intense, even in the garbled form of *Robin des bois,* that characteristic Parisianisation of *Der Freischütz.* With *Freischütz* a new note had entered music: the breath of the natural world. Berlioz's feeling for nature, both as sensation and as idea, found in Weber the exemplar it was instinctively looking for. For proof of the affinity, only listen to the way the tone-colour of flutes in their lower register is used to evoke the stillness of a summer night, in Agathe's *scena* and in the garden scene in *Roméo et Juliette.*

Gluck's profound influence also needs no emphasising. For Berlioz he was the creator of dramatic music, and his own spiritual father. It was a belief that was to last all his life, surviving the discovery of music of far greater emotional range, richness of texture and external impact, and it showed itself in a consistent fidelity to the loftiest Gluckian ideals of correct expressive accent as well as in a Gluckian concern with pure melody.

Yet, when all these and other influences and affinities have been accounted for, it is arguable that the major force in shaping Berlioz's musical style was not Beethoven or Weber or even Gluck but Gluck's successor and inheritor at the Paris Opéra, Spontini. I use the phrase "musical style" advisedly. As a general artistic influence, Spontini is not to be compared with Gluck or Beethoven (let alone with Shakespeare). But if we examine *La Vestale* and *Fernand Cortez,* the two Spontini works that Berlioz heard and re-heard and copied and pored over during his years as a student until he knew them inside out, we find a remarkable number of stylistic features that tend to be thought of as specifically Berliozian. A study of these two scores with Berlioz's music in mind shows just how enthusiastically and thoughtfully he responded to them; we see his eager imagination—as indeed we would expect—fastening on point after point in Spontini's music in order to absorb them into his own still experimental, not yet fully formed style.[1]

1. *La Vestale* and *Fernand Cortez* were composed, respectively, in 1807 and 1809. I have largely excluded *Olympie* (1819) from this discussion, principally because I do not know it, but also because it was performed only five times at the Opéra in 1822–30 (whereas in the same period *La Vestale* and *Cortez* between them totalled nearly two hundred performances), and because Berlioz himself treats it much more cursorily in his writings. However, it is only fair to say that there are those who consider it as important an influence on Berlioz as its two predecessors.

He says as much in his *Mémoirs*, when recounting those formative years. But the influence is not confined to the period when on his
own admission he was "exclusively taken up with the study of . . .
tragédie lyrique,"[2] and when a prentice work like *La révolution
grecque* could "show on every page the powerful influence of Spontini's style"[3]—the years before the advent of Beethoven and the composition of the first thoroughly characteristic scores, the *Huit scènes
de Faust* and the *Symphonie fantastique*. It is writ large in *Les Troyens*, the work in which thirty years later Berlioz summed up all that
his art had stood for.

None of this should surprise us. His analyses of Spontini's music
read at times almost like a description of his own. He never concealed
his admiration and his indebtedness. "I loved him, by dint of having
admired him," he wrote, in February 1851,[4] just after the embittered
old man had died, an alien survivor in a world which had forgotten
him. Even when most repelled by Spontini's egoism and paranoiac suspiciousness, he never forgot what his music had meant and still meant
to him: "The temple may be unworthy of the god that inhabits it, but
the god is a god."[5] This remained his attitude; it was unshaken by the
almost total neglect into which Spontini's music fell in the middle of
the nineteenth century, and which his own advocacy of it in print and
on the concert platform was powerless to prevent. With characteristic
tenacity but also with deep, clear-sighted conviction he stuck to his belief that Spontini was a master, and that his greatness transcended
the superficial fluctuations of fashion and the temporary disappear-
ance of the great singing actresses whom music such as his presup-
posed.

Berlioz's published writings and his letters regularly ring with
praise of him. *La Vestale* is one of the five operas for which the musicians in *Les soirées de l'orchestre* suspend their chat in order to devote
themselves with fervour and punctiliousness to the performance (the
other four are *Der Freischütz*, *The Barber of Seville*, *Don Giovanni* and
Iphigénie en Tauride). *La Vestale* was particularly close to Berlioz's
heart; it was one of the works that he made his fellow students in
Rome sing with him on summer evenings round the little fountain in
the courtyard of the Villa Medici, to console himself for his exile from

———————
    2. *Mémoires d'Hector Berlioz* (Paris: Michel Lévy, 1870), chap. 17.
    3. *Ibid.*, chap. 11.
    4. *Hector Berlioz: Le musicien errant, 1842–1852*, Julien Tiersot, ed. (Paris:
Calmann-Lévy, 1919), p. 311.
    5. *Hector Berlioz: Correspondance générale*, Vol. II, *1832–1842*, Frédéric
Robert, ed. (Paris: Flammarion, 1975), p. 700.

Paris. Ernest Legouvé in his autobiography describes a memorable ad hoc rendering of the second act, with guitar accompaniment, which helped to relieve the tension of a crisis in Berlioz's courtship of Harriet Smithson. But he loved *Fernand Cortez* little, if any, less than *La Vestale;* the two works are placed on the same exalted level of merit in the long discussion of Spontini's career and achievement which occupies the thirteenth evening of *Les soirées de l'orchestre.* With *Olympie*, they make up a "great temple of Expressive Music," through which, he says, he never tires of wandering, losing himself "in its twists and turns, in the endless details of its rich architecture, in the dazzling profusion of its ornaments."

One could go on citing testimony to his regard for Spontini's music and his sense of its peculiar importance to him. Spontini is "the genius of the century"[6] (this of course was before Berlioz had encountered the music of Beethoven). While relating a conversation in which Berton chided him for his "great admiration for a composer who does not enjoy a very high reputation among connoisseurs," he comments: "Yes, and never was admiration greater or more justified."[7] A year or two later, in 1830, he pictures Beethoven, Spontini and Weber as his three guardian angels, and in the same letter he brackets Spontini's "passionate sensibility" with Beethoven's genius, Weber's poetic imagination and Shakespeare's prodigious power.[8] Spontini is a commanding figure in the mythology of Berlioz and his young fellow enthusiasts of the Opéra pit. To a friend suffering from severe toothache he sends, "as a New Year present, a sublime aria from *La Vestale* which you don't know because it's been cut for more than ten years. You seem to me sad, you have need of tears, so I'm giving it to you as a specific."[9] The idea that Rossini's *William Tell*, with all its distinction, could be put higher than Spontini's masterpieces moves him to indignation, and he is happy to report that M. de Jouy (Spontini's librettist), whom he met during a performance of *Cortez*, agrees with him: "Though the author of the poem of *William Tell*, he spoke of Spontini as we do, with adoration."[10]

Not that it was ever a blind worship, any more than it was with Berlioz's other fervent admirations. He felt perfectly free to criticise Spontini's music. Thus the rich but restrained orchestration of *La*

---

6. *Hector Berlioz: Correspondance générale*, Vol. I, *1803–1832*, Pierre Citron, ed. (Paris: Flammarion, 1972), p. 129.

7. *Ibid.*, p. 161.

8. *Ibid.*, pp. 314, 315.

9. *Ibid.*, p. 221.

10. *Ibid.*, p. 271.

Vestale, which in *Cortez* became more complex, grew in his view over-elaborate in *Olympie* and even, in places, turgid and confused. He adds that though Spontini knew how to juxtapose wind instruments effectively with strings, his handling of them was not in itself technically very skilled. Berlioz is candid about the great man's limitations. "Spontini had a certain number of melodic ideas for expressing nobility of one kind and another. Once the cycle of feelings for which these melodies were designed had been gone through, the source became less abundant. That is why there is less originality in the melodic style of the works . . . which followed *La Vestale* and *Cortez.*"[11]

Yet such limitations were unimportant beside the splendour and beauty, the "passionate sensibility" of *Cortez* and *La Vestale,* their grandeur and pathos, above all their depth and truthfulness of expression. The impact of those early experiences at the Opéra remained fresh and vivid. When he came to compose *Les Troyens*—an opera concerned with what he called "epic passion," and whose genre, an epic of the clash of peoples, had first been broached in *Fernand Cortez* —the example of his mentor was clearly very much in his mind. His anxiety lest the music of the entry of the wooden horse should be too long sends him straight to the score of *Olympie,* where he is reassured to find that the triumphal march in the same tempo is longer than his own by a hundred bars.[12] Spontini is the touchstone of dramatic *justesse* and effectiveness.[13]

Spontini was first and last a man of the theatre, and his music, Berlioz insisted, lost a great deal when transplanted to the concert hall; so many rich and telling dramatic effects went for nothing.[14] Even so, and despite a stiffness of musico-dramatic movement as compared with the post-Spontinian works which form the bulk of our operatic

---

11. Hector Berlioz, *Les soirées de l'orchestre,* 13th evening, *passim* (Paris: Michel Lévy, 1852). Berlioz also takes Spontini to task for presuming to rewrite and augment Gluck's wind parts in *Iphigénie en Tauride.* (See *Mémoires,* Voyage en Allemagne, I, 8th letter, and *A travers chants* [Paris: Michel Lévy, 1862], p. 224.)

12. *Correspondance inédite d'Hector Berlioz, 1819–1868,* Daniel Bernard, ed. (Paris: Calmann-Lévy, 1879), p. 240.

13. See *Correspondance générale,* Vol. I, p. 125, where Berlioz, writing to a librettist, cites the final scene of *La Vestale* as authority for a particular procedure. It is also worth noting that his first idea for the sentries' duet in Act 5 of *Les Troyens* was of a march in triple time, an idea which harks back to the ¾ march in *Cortez,* cited in the *Soirées* as "the first and only one that has been written in triple time."

14. "What the concert listener can grasp is the expressive truth that is apparent from the very first bars of each role, the intensity of passion that makes the music burn with a concentrated flame (*sunt lacrymae rerum*), and the purely musical validity of the chord progressions. But there are also ideas that can be perceived only in the theatre" (*Soirées,* 13th evening).

repertory (and as compared with the pre-Spontinian *Idomeneo*), a well-prepared concert performance of *Cortez* or *La Vestale* can be a startling experience to a listener who had supposed them to be dead beyond recall. To Berlioz, who came fresh to it all, the dramatic force of these works, and the size, the sheer sound of their choral and orchestral sonorities, must have been shattering. Once the first shock had passed, he studied them with clinical thoroughness. Between 1822 and 1830 *La Vestale* was performed 61 times at the Paris Opéra and *Fernand Cortez* 130. The *Mémoirs* speak of his going to hear everything that was given at the Opéra, score in hand, and of his "analysing the methods of those three modern masters [of the orchestra], Beethoven, Weber and Spontini."[15] If he didn't go to every Spontini performance, it is clear from his letters that he went to a great many. They were a systematic and essential part of his education.

How to write for the orchestra, how to "dramatise" it, was certainly one important skill that Spontini helped to teach him. "By continually comparing the effect obtained with the means used to obtain it I came to appreciate the subtle connexion between musical expression and the technique of instrumentation."[16] Until Weber and then Beethoven opened up new horizons for him, this meant above all Gluck and Spontini.

The first music by the latter that Berlioz heard seems to have been the ballet music that Spontini added to Salieri's *Les Danaïdes*. In his treatise on instrumentation, written twenty years later, Berlioz cited the bacchanal, for the striking orchestral effect produced by the combination of piccolo and cymbals: "The strange sympathy that is set up in such a case between these two quite different instruments had not been thought of before Spontini."[17] He remembered the passage when he composed the three biting chords to which Mephistopheles makes his appearance in *La damnation de Faust*: on the third chord the brass and bassoons are joined by a dazzling flourish for piccolo, flutes and cymbals.

Spontinian reminiscences crop up all over Berlioz's music. As we have just seen, even a work as far from Spontini in style and ethos as the *Damnation* contains them. The abrupt pause on a diminished seventh chord, followed by silence, at the beginning of the scene in Auerbach's cellar, recalls a passage from the barbaric Mexican rites in the first act of *Cortez*:

15. Chap. 13.
16. *Ibid.*
17. *Grand Traité d'instrumentation et d'orchestration modernes* (2nd ed., Paris: Schonenberger, [1855]), p. 164.

Fernand Cortez, Act 1

La damnation de Faust, Part 2

The use of flat sub-mediant modulations is a persistent dramatic device in *Cortez* and *La Vestale*—and in *Les Troyens*. In one case the connexion is specific: when we hear Cortez, in the finale of Act 2, rallying his men with a reckless call to glory, it is impossible not to think of Aeneas at a similar moment of crisis in the finale of Act 3 of *Les Troyens:*

Fernand Cortez, Act 2

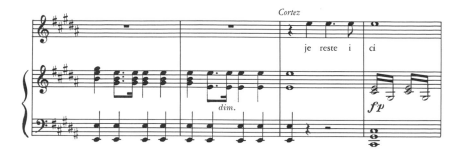

Perhaps it is fanciful to see the descending chromatic bass (B flat to B flat, with ten of the twelve notes included) which underpins Morales's narration in Act 3 of *Cortez* as a direct influence on Hector's recitative in Act 2 of *Les Troyens;* but in the following example the likeness is unmistakable:

Fernand Cortez, Act 1

Les Troyens, Act 5

Yet the kinship between the two composers goes deeper than mere reminiscence. It is a matter both of artistic climate—of tragic suffering, noble grief and indignation, heroic endeavour—and of actual musical style. As I have said, the traits that Berlioz singles out in his analyses of Spontini are very often those that are characteristic of his own music: the long massive crescendos, the undulating bass lines, the frequent accentuation of weak beats, the simultaneous use of different rhythms, the sharp juxtaposition of string and wind sonorities, the dissonances which resolve in a different part of the orchestra, the sudden, unexpected modulations. He made them his own, and indeed developed them into something more systematic, sophisticated and far-ranging. But the impetus came from Spontini's example.

Berlioz undoubtedly set out to emulate the rhythmic vitality and drive that he heard in Spontini's music, and to that end analysed it to discover the secret of his dynamic treatment of rhythm. In doing so, as I say, he carried it much further; but, to take one small example, his use of fanfare motifs to intensify the dramatic excitement, which we find not only (though especially) in *Les Troyens* but in *Benvenuto Cellini* and *Roméo et Juliette*, stems from *Cortez* and *La Vestale*.

Again, if Spontini did not go nearly as far as Berlioz in making the contrast and syncopation of different timbres an element in the energy and rhythmic propulsion of his music, he pointed the way:

In the second of these examples (rudimentary though it may be), the fortissimo string chord entering on the weak beat after two bars of woodwind and horns prefigures dozens of instances of dynamic tonal contrast in Berlioz's music (e.g., in the *Marche au supplice* or the goldsmiths' song in *Benvenuto Cellini*). And the first example, from *Cortez,* looks forward to the ravings of Herod and his soothsayers in *L'enfance du Christ,* and beyond that to the finale of Act 3 of *Les Troyens,* where the music's already considerable rhythmic tension is further increased by the superimposition of string and percussion chords in 3/2 time on the alla breve of the chorus, woodwind and brass.

Berlioz and Spontini also have certain harmonic procedures in common. The criticism of bizarre and awkward harmonisation which Berlioz incurred, just as Spontini had, must have strengthened the sense of identification; it was what innovators had to expect. One of the things the schoolmen could not forgive Spontini (another was his success) was that he broke the rules, especially the rules of harmony: he introduced dissonances without preparation, and harsh and unmotivated modulations, modulations "foreign to the principal key." "His crime was to write chords and modulations that had not yet become common practice, and before the pundits had decided whether they were permissible."[18]

Berlioz ranged himself firmly on Spontini's side: "I am of the faith of Beethoven, Weber, Gluck and Spontini, who believed and preached, and proved by their works, that the only test of whether something is right is what it sounds like."[19] (The classic answer to such criticism was the one given by Beethoven, when it was pointed out to him that a certain harmony was wrong, having been forbidden by Fux, Albrechtsberger and a dozen other theorists: "Very well—but I allow it.")[20] The creative imagination had to be free, or rather, bound only by its own constantly re-fashioned rules, and the criterion must always lie in the effect. By that criterion, he felt, Spontini's harmonic audacities sometimes failed; but far more often they were magnificently successful. Some of the most unconventional were flashes of genius, profound illuminations of the drama, like the change from D flat to C in the High Priest's recitative in Act 2 of *La Vestale* ("Vont-ils dans le chaos replonger l'univers?"), or the brusque movement from E flat to D flat in the chorus of mutinous soldiers in *Cortez* at the words: "Quittons ces bords, l'Espagne nous rappelle," where the listener is carried in an instant as though over an immense distance.[21]

Although Berlioz's own harmonic practice (once frowned on, but now at last beginning to be taken seriously) is far richer and more varied than Spontini's, once again Spontini's example left its mark. This is not the place to examine it in detail; but again and again some procedure in *La Vestale* or *Cortez* (for example, the fondness for mediant and sub-mediant relationships) points forward to Berlioz. (Even the occasional genuine maladroitness—a disconcerting return to the tonic after too brief an excursion into an unexpected key, or the addition of non-functional chromatic notes to a simple tonic-dominant pattern, which serves only to underline its banality—is faithfully reflected in the music of Berlioz's apprenticeship.)

The harmonic freedom and force of Spontini's recitatives was to remain an inspiration and an ideal. The recitative "Dieux immortels! il part," in the fifth act of *Les Troyens,* where to depict the fury and bewilderment of the abandoned Dido Berlioz stretches harmony almost to breaking point, is only the most audacious application of what he had learnt from Spontini. Spontini had shown him what a dramatic

18. *Soirées,* 13th evening.
19. *Mémoires,* Postscript.
20. *A travers chants,* essay on *Alceste.*
21. *Soirées,* 13th evening.

composer could and should do when the situation demanded it—for example, when Julia, the vestal, confesses to the horrified priest that she loves:

Yet perhaps Spontini's greatest influence on the formation of Berlioz's musical style was melodic. The influence may be most neatly illustrated by the mistake that Berlioz makes, in a letter to Spontini himself, when he quotes a phrase from *La Vestale*—the great sweep of melody, shared by clarinet and oboe, in the orchestral continuation of Julia's aria "Impitoyables dieux." By altering the descending quaver scale to triplets (at the point where the tonality has just shifted from C minor to B flat), he unconsciously identifies the music with his own, assimilating it more closely to the *idée fixe* of the *Symphonie fantastique,* which he had recently completed.[22]

He was, symbolically, right to do so. A characteristic interest in extended melody, which reaches its culmination in *Les Troyens* but which is a constant feature of his style, links Berlioz, as it links Bellini, with the composer of *Fernand Cortez* and *La Vestale.* Those huge but delicate melodic spans, with their subtly varied points of stress and repose and their ability to branch off in any direction, look back to Spontini's simpler but hardly less grand constructions. Here again Spontini did not so much implant an ideal as, by his example, provide a means of realising and formulating it, enable an innate faculty to emerge and take shape. In this he continued the work begun in Berlioz's consciousness by Gluck. But in Spontini the austerity of Gluck's melodic line is enriched by a new flexibility and a warmth of sensuous expression and a capacity to extend its length that suggest Berliozian melody itself, at its most soaring:

La Vestale, Act 1

22. *Correspondance générale*, Vol. I, p. 386. The autographs of this letter and of another (*Correspondance générale*, Vol. II, p. 178) in which Berlioz similarly misquotes the phrase have disappeared; their texts were transcribed and first published by Tiersot.

ton coeur _ s'é ga - re, ton coeur s'é - ga re et je _

trem - ble pour _ Ju - li - a, et je trem-ble _ pour Ju-li-

a, ma fil-le, ton coeur s'é - ga - re et _ je trem - ble pour Ju li - a

Fernand Cortez, Act 1

Allegro agitato assai

Amazily

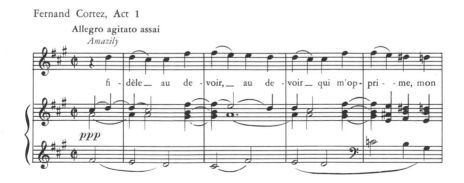

fi -dèle _ au de -voir, _ au de -voir _ qui m'op- pri - me, mon

The second of these two quotations suggests Berlioz, too, in the way the introduction of a new and vital rhythm in the accompaniment adds further to the growing exaltation of the vocal line. It could almost come from *Les Troyens*.

Enough has perhaps been said to indicate how greatly Berlioz was indebted to Spontini's influence—an influence of which he was thoroughly conscious and whose importance he tacitly acknowledged. It goes without saying that his pursuit of the ideal of a hyper-sensitive musical language able to reflect the subtlest movements of the human spirit led him into regions undreamed of by his master. But those profound and vibrant first impressions of Spontini's music—what he called "the grandeur and richness of its musical imagery," its heroic temper and noble pathos, the tragic world it inhabited, its magnificently vehement yet sober orchestration, its dramatic treatment of harmony, the stride of its rhythms and the great arch of its melodies— remained with him, only deepened by repeated study and fresh hearing.

Spontini has been for more than a hundred years a largely neglected figure. Yet, as recent concert performances have shown, these qualities can come alive again. In the theatre, with singers with a sense of the grand style, a serious revival of his operas might well be rewarding. It would certainly seem only logical and right to the disciple who learnt so much from him, and whose ancestry and achievements we are still discovering.

PETER GAY

For Beckmesser

"Hanslick was a far from stupid critic. . . ."
                    JACQUES BARZUN, *Darwin, Marx, Wagner* (2nd ed., 1958)

Critics, especially critics who write for the periodical press, are men who kill people for money. As professional assassins, theirs is a dangerous profession, for they invite counterattack, and the duels between creators and critics occupy a prominent, if rarely edifying, place in the history of high culture. Often, the critic survives the encounter he has provoked mainly as a warning to others: it is less his generosity or his prescience that is likely to preserve his name for posterity than his lapses. This is the way that Eduard Hanslick has survived, and not even under his own name. He is known, if he is known at all, not as Hanslick but as Beckmesser.

It was, of course, Richard Wagner who gave Hanslick this unwelcome sort of immortality by fixing his image as the egregious "Merker" who stumbles through the *Meistersinger*, the embodiment of the critic as conceited and incorrigible fool. Beckmesser, the pedantic and assertive guardian of high standards and judge of talents, proves himself to have neither; and opera-goers, exhilarated by the spectacle of a victim who deserves to be victimized, by a legitimate target for their free-floating aggressions, laugh, approve, and ask no questions.

Hanslick was admittedly vulnerable, but his vulnerability was less a quality of his person than of his position. By the 1860s, when Wagner completed the *Meistersinger*, Hanslick was an influential music critic writing for authoritative newspapers, in a city, Vienna, that was widely recognized as the musical capital of Europe. Vienna was a goal to which musicians aspired, a test that musicians feared. When Wagner chose to make Hanslick into his public victim, he knew what he was about; he was acting as the recognized leader of a musical party seeking to strike down a recognized leader of the opposition. His invention of Beckmesser, private as it may have been in its inception, had more than private implications.

By 1868, when the *Meistersinger* had its première in Munich, Hanslick and Wagner had been mortal enemies for several years, but their professional lives had been entangled for much longer than that. As early as 1846, the year that the young Hanslick moved to Vienna from his native Prague, he wrote an extensive appreciative essay on Wagner's *Tannhäuser* for the *Wiener allgemeine Musik-Zeitung*[1] and reviewed the career of Wagner, his casual acquaintance, at some length. Wagner, who had already drafted a *Meistersinger* poem containing the part of a self-important musical "censor," had no cause to be dissatisfied with Hanslick, and no reason to aim his satire at him. Even in 1854, when Hanslick explicitly and publicly rejected Wagner's call for a music-drama, the two men did not feel—certainly nowhere voiced—any mutual antipathy. All this was to change: in November 1862, Wagner came to Vienna and gave several readings of his *Meistersinger* libretto, in the version which permitted no doubt that Beckmesser was a scarcely disguised caricature of Eduard Hanslick—"the dangerous reviewer."[2] Hanslick was more than a dangerous reviewer by then; the feared music critic of the *Presse* was also a learned lecturer on music at the university, and the sociable acquaintance of everyone who was anyone in music. To affront him was to affront a person of consequence.

The hosts for one of Wagner's private readings—on this at least the autobiographies of Wagner and Hanslick agree—tactlessly invited Hanslick to attend. Wagner later recalled that Beckmesser "grew paler and more depressed in the course of the recitation," and could not be induced to stay. "My friends," Wagner innocently comments, "were agreed that Hanslick looked upon the whole libretto as a lampoon directed against himself," and he adds that from then on Hanslick's attitude toward him grew markedly more hostile.[3] Hanslick, for his side, reports no pallor and no depression, stresses his discriminating judgment of the *Meistersinger*, and gives cogent reasons for his detestation

---

1. "Richard Wagner, und seine neueste Oper 'Tannhäuser.' Eine Beurtheilung," reproduced in full in Helmut Kirchmeyer, ed., *Situationsgeschichte der Musikkritik und des musikalischen Pressewesens in Deutschland . . .* , Part IV, *Das zeitgenössische Wagner-Bild*, Vol. III, *Dokumente 1846–1850* (Regensburg: Bosse, 1968), cols. 147–184.

2. Richard Wagner, *Mein Leben* (3 vols. in one, Munich: Bruckmann, 1915), Vol. III, p. 341.

3. *Ibid.*, Vol. III, pp. 341–342.

of Wagner's character and dislike of Wagner's music.[4] One thing is plain: unlike Wagner, Hanslick found it possible to say some kind words about his enemy; like Wagner, Hanslick responded to a more than personal affront. He was, like Wagner, a representative figure, and he found it not merely insulting but ominous to witness the music of the future propagated so ruthlessly—with the manners of the future.

Nothing is easier than to detect the acid in Wagner's etching and to demonstrate its inaccuracies. In fact, a handful of scholars have tried to rescue Hanslick by separating him from Beckmesser.[5] But two obstacles have stood in the way of Hanslick's full rehabilitation: Wagner's caricature is cruel but it is funny, and it repossesses the general awareness with every performance of the *Meistersinger*. To cavil at this breathing statue to stupid self-importance must seem laborious, humorless. As usual, the sober and complex truth limps helplessly behind the astute, simplistic libel—astute precisely because it is simplistic.

Moreover, Hanslick's defects, though far less crippling than Beckmesser's, are marked enough to invite a less than enthusiastic verdict on his critical performance. All pronouncements about a composer's work are bound to time and place; all are subject to shifts in educated taste. But even allowing for the inescapable changes produced by the passage of the years, it is evident from our twentieth-century perspective that Hanslick's capacity for musical appreciation was relatively constricted. The range of his enthusiasm was bounded on one side by Mozart and on the other by Brahms. Medieval and Renaissance music had little to say to him; even Bach seemed to him often dry, of greater historical than musical interest. Precisely because Hanslick was not merely opinionated but also witty—the apt German adjective, *geistreich*, was often applied to him—his sayings became notorious, and they have haunted his reputation ever since. It is hard to live down remarks like his casual comment that he would "rather see all of Heinrich Schütz go up in flames than the 'German Requiem.' "[6] Even

4. Eduard Hanslick, *Aus meinem Leben* (2 vols., Berlin: Allgemeiner Verein für deutsche Litteratur, 1894), Vol. II, pp. 7–8. For a dignified defense against Wagnerian malice, see pp. 227–234.

5. See especially Stewart Deas, *In Defence of Hanslick* (London: Williams & Northgate, 1940), essentially a pamphlet by a zealous advocate; Friedrich Blume's detailed encyclopedia article in *Musik in Geschichte und Gegenwart*, Vol. V (Kassel and Basel: Bärenreiter-Verlag, 1956), cols. 1,482–1,493, an authoritative treatment, though somewhat marred by an unnecessary "defense" against the "charge" that Hanslick was of Jewish descent; and Werner Abegg, *Musikästhetik und Musikkritik bei Eduard Hanslick* (Regensburg: Bosse, 1974), which takes his ideas seriously.

6. *Aus meinem Leben*, Vol. II, p. 304.

Brahms's most uncritical admirers would nowadays find it embarrassing to accept so compromising a tribute as this. And, just as Hanslick proved deaf to many of the musical glories produced before the 1750s, he was deaf to many of the glories produced in his lifetime. He found Berlioz to be an "odd Romantic—*wunderlichen Romantiker*";[7] he denigrated Liszt as a charlatan, dismissed Bruckner as a madman and warned against Wagner as a grave danger to music.[8]

Hanslick's detractors (except for the implacable Wagner and Bruckner) have felt compelled to admit that he prepared himself conscientiously for his reviewing assignments; he studied the scores of new symphonies and those of revived cantatas with equal diligence. He tried to understand what he could not love. But the point remains that he loved little, and that this is a serious handicap for a reviewer who attends concerts regularly, writes about them copiously and finds his word cited as authoritative. Even if one corrects for Wagner's malice, it seems plausible to hold that his Beckmesser remains in substance a telling, if heartless, depiction of a pedant in power.

Certainly Hanslick was a powerful man in his chosen sphere. Had he been merely ridiculous, Wagner would not have taken the trouble to ridicule him. Contemporary annals are filled with tributes, voluntary and involuntary, to his influence. In 1885, a Dr. Robert Hirschfeld, amateur of *a capella* choirs and of German Renaissance music, issued a pamphlet against "*the adroit moral pressure on the part of a critical authority.*"[9] Critics like Hanslick, he wrote, in measured but resentful tones, could compel or prevent performances of music, and thus shape, or distort, the general taste. Hirschfeld found his readers: he brought out three editions of his pamphlet in the course of a single year. But patently his own courage frightened him: nothing bespeaks his anxiety more eloquently than his continued bows to Hans-

---

7. "Der Berlioz-Cultus," in Hanslick, *Musikalische Stationen* (Berlin: Hofmann, 1880), p. 190.

8. For Liszt, see individual reviews, especially in Hanslick, *Concerte, Componisten und Virtuosen der letzten fünfzehn Jahre. 1870–1885* (Berlin: Allgemeiner Verein für deutsche Litteratur, 1886), pp. 16–17, 39–47, 77–80, 133–134, and others, charmingly supplemented by Hanslick's obituary article reprinted in Hanslick, *Musikalisches Skizzenbuch* (Berlin: Allgemeiner Verein für deutsche Litteratur, 1896), pp. 167–178; for Bruckner, see especially his review of the F-minor Mass, in which he connects Bruckner's musical education with his incoherence, in Hanslick, *Fünf Jahre Musik* (Berlin: Allgemeiner Verein für deutsche Litteratur, 1896), pp. 279–283; and for Wagner, among many essays and reviews, especially those gathered under the rubrics "Richard Wagner," and "Nach Wagners Tod," collected in Hanslick, *Aus dem Opernleben der Gegenwart* (Berlin: Allgemeiner Verein für deutsche Litteratur, 1889), pp. 293–379.

9. *Das kritische Verfahren Ed. Hanslick's* (Vienna: Löwit, 1885), p. 19n.

lick the professor (who, he wrote, is first-rate) in the midst of his attacks on Hanslick the critic (who is merely eighth-rate).[10]

Composers feared Hanslick quite as much as did the amateurs. In the very year, 1885, that Dr. Hirschfeld launched his little assault, Anton Bruckner told his friend and supporter, the conductor Hermann Levi, that it would be better to have his Seventh Symphony printed before it was performed in Vienna, lest "it be ruined by Hl Hanslick etc."[11] It is true that Bruckner was as timid as he was servile, but his pathetic appeal to Levi reflects a reality which Hanslick's admirers cheerfully acknowledged: Hanslick the critic made a difference, often a decisive one, in the musical life of Vienna. And that difference, we can now see, was not always a beneficial one.

If, in the face of such reservations, I offer a plea for Beckmesser, I do so not to deny or to extenuate his flaws, but to place them in perspective. What I want to say is that Hanslick was engaged, and knew himself to be engaged, in a musical campaign in which the stakes were high. All his writings—his innumerable reviews and occasional essays, his informative history of musical life in Vienna and his charming autobiography—bear the mark of alert and unremitting partisanship. My metaphors, drawn from military and political life, are not impositions of my own; it was common in the 1860s to treat musical controversies as a gigantic war (or political struggle) between the forces of innovation and the forces of conservatism.[12] Hanslick was not a purely reactive writer; he early developed reasoned principles which he sometimes neglected and sometimes overstepped under the pressure of an immediate musical experience, but which generally guided his tastes through his long career. Yet these principles found their final definition in response to an adversary. In the 1850s, when Hanslick began to write serious musical criticism and theory, Liszt, Wagner and their allies were moving to engross strategic posts in the musical world: they were beginning to edit respected periodicals, conduct famous orchestras, launch dependable followers. And in the ensuing decades, they took bastion after bastion. The Music of the Future became in Hanslick's lifetime very much the music of the present.

---

10. *Ibid.*, p. 10.

11. April 4, 1885; Handschriftenabteilung, Staatsbibliothek Preussischer Kulturbesitz, Berlin. "Hl" is an abbreviation for the formula "Hochwohlgeboren."

12. For some revealing instances, see selected quotations in Imogen Fellner, "Das Brahms-Bild der *Allgemeinen Musikalischen Zeitung* (1863 bis 1882)," in Heinz Becker, ed., *Beiträge zur Geschichte der Musikkritik* (Regensburg: Bosse, 1965), pp. 30, 41–43.

As politicians and strategists had known for centuries before George Bernard Shaw made his Devil say it: a good slogan is half the battle. Liszt and his disciples made an effective bid for the sympathetic attention of the public by parading their compositions as music that had broken with a dying tradition and was pregnant with new vitality. To be in the camp of Liszt and Wagner was to be original, to be youthful; to be opposed to the *Zukunftsmusiker* was, almost by definition, to be uninventive and hidebound. To be sure, all parties in the combat claimed to respect the past, which is to say, Beethoven: just as Brahms was so much in awe of Beethoven's symphonic achievement that he hesitated for years before he dared to come before the public with a symphony of his own, so Wagner widely advertised his debt to Beethoven, and offered his wilful interpretation of the Ninth Symphony as partial justification for his advocacy of the music-drama.[13] The *Zukunftsmusiker* saw themselves as Beethoven's rightful heirs, their adversaries as mere followers. While *they* were husbanding Beethoven's heritage with just the right mixture of piety and independence, Brahms and Hanslick were mechanically reproducing and thus effectively killing Beethoven's classicism. Hanslick could accept neither of these characterizations. He could not permit the Wagnerites to monopolize the future by monopolizing the past.

The document that most accurately reflects, and most conspicuously reveals, the pressure of partisan combat on Hanslick's musical theory is *Vom Musikalisch-Schönen*, a small treatise first published in 1854 and often reissued and revised; the last edition to appear in Hanslick's lifetime, in 1902, was the tenth. This is a rare tribute to a book, even a short and elegant one, on so recondite a subject as musical aesthetics; its sales are testimony not only to Hanslick's stylistic gifts, but also to the passionate, general interest in the questions to which *Vom Musikalisch-Schönen* addressed itself. The book is a treatise that its readers elevated—or debased—into a manifesto.

Hanslick was the first to recognize the political relevance of *Vom Musikalisch-Schönen*: in the Preface to the ninth edition he acknowledges the "rather sharp and rhapsodic manner" of his presentation, and expresses some regret that the issues of the day had pushed his theoretical principles into the background. In fact, these issues, which had dictated the original distribution of space, only grew more exigent as edition followed edition. His intention, Hanslick noted, had been to place his ideas about musical beauty into the center of his exposition;

---

13. See now Klaus Kropfinger, *Wagner und Beethoven: Untersuchungen zur Beethoven-Rezeption Richard Wagners* (Regensburg: Bosse, 1975).

if "the polemical, negative element" had "gained the upper hand," the public, he hoped, would excuse this. "When I wrote this essay, the spokesmen of the Music of the Future had reached the height of their clamor," and men of his views felt compelled to respond. "When I brought out the second edition, Liszt had just added his program symphonies" to the general repertoire, compositions that "abdicate the independent significance of music" almost completely, and "make the listener swallow them only as a pill designed to promote ideas (*nur mehr als gedankentreibendes Mittel eingeben*). Since then we have had Richard Wagner's *Tristan, Nibelungenlied,* and his doctrine of the 'unending melody,'—that is, formlessness raised to a principle, opium intoxication sung and fiddled, a cult, to which, as we know, a special temple has been opened at Bayreuth."[14]

The text of *Vom Musikalisch-Schönen* confirms the self-diagnosis of this late Preface. From the first edition onward, Hanslick reiterated his objections to what he took to be Wagner's central doctrine: the subordination of music to words.[15] And in later editions, he reiterated his "sharpest possible protest" against such productions as Liszt's symphonic poems.[16] It would be too simple, too personal, to say that Wagner obsessed Hanslick. On the one hand, the structure of Hanslick's argument was complete in 1854, when Wagner was a relatively unknown if promising composer of operas and a relatively uninfluential if provocative writer of manifestos. And on the other hand, Wagner came to obsess his age, not Hanslick alone: Hanslick once wrote a sarcastic little feuilleton from the resort of Karlsbad entitled, "What Do You Think of Wagner?" This, he noted, was the question that dominated the conversation of professional musicians and amateurs alike, disrupted formal dances and intimate suppers, threw christenings, funerals, even the peaceful shower after the steam bath into disarray. If the Holy Spirit were to descend in our time in the shape of a dove, and address the twelve apostles, he would ask them: "Gentlemen, what do you think of Wagner?"[17] What irritated Hanslick almost beyond the bounds of self-control was that Wagner was not merely so wrong, but that he seemed so important.

---

14. Eduard Hanslick, *Vom Musikalisch-Schönen: Ein Beitrag zur Revision der Aesthetik der Tonkunst* (Leipzig: Breitkopf & Härtel, 1910), pp. vi–vii.

15. *Ibid.,* pp. 54–56. See the first edition of 1854, p. 31.

16. *Ibid,* p. 73. This passage does not occur in the first edition. In the same paragraph, Hanslick pays tribute to Berlioz's "dazzling talent."

17. " 'Was denken Sie von Wagner?' " (1889), in Hanslick, *Musikalisches und Litterarisches* (Berlin: Allgemeiner Verein für deutsche Litteratur, 1889), pp. 56–66.

To be sure, political effervescence, no matter how widespread, is no excuse for adopting indefensible theoretical positions or writing myopic reviews; it is precisely in the heat of combat that the rational judge should remain cool. But Hanslick's judgment was neither grossly nor permanently distorted by his detestation of Wagner, nor by memories of his unpleasant encounters with The Master. As I have said, he continued to write appreciative sentences about Wagner's compositions, especially the early ones, and at times publicly revised his first judgment in a favorable direction, even with the *Meistersinger*. Hanslick did not come to think about music as he did because he disliked Wagner. Rather, he came to dislike Wagner because he thought about music as he did. In fact, from the very outset, Hanslick presciently sought to disarm the charge of bias: "The musically beautiful, in the specific signification we have assigned to it, does not restrict itself to the 'classical.' Nor does it imply a preference for the 'classical' over the 'romantic.' It is valid for one school as much as for the other; it dominates Bach as much as Beethoven, Mozart as much as Schumann. Hence, our thesis contains not one hint of partisanship."[18] If it was inappropriate for Hanslick to have stigmatized Wagner's music as "formlessness," it is equally inappropriate for us to stigmatize Hanslick's aesthetics as "formalism." Hanslick was far from denying the place of invention or the power of the imagination; he did not denigrate feeling.[19] On the contrary, he criticized earlier systems of musical aesthetics, notably that of Hegel, for being too much oriented toward ideas and too little awake to "sensuousness-*Sinnlichkeit*."[20] He protested that his "passionate adversaries" had erroneously depicted him as launching a "polemic against everything that is called feeling"; it should have been obvious, he thought, that he was simply objecting to "the unjustified importation of feelings into science." His only real adversaries, to his mind, were "aesthetic enthusiasts who, claiming to enlighten the musician, merely interpret their sounding opium dreams."[21] As an experienced polemicist, he could hardly have expected his indignant disclaimers, justified though they were, to be taken at face value. Yet we are entitled, even obliged, to do so.

Hanslick's cardinal aesthetic principle is the autonomy of musical beauty. The very title of his essay hints at this: just as it is an error to speak of "art" in the singular, since that does injustice to the

---

18. *Vom Musikalisch-Schönen*, p. 80. This passage went through all the editions with only minute verbal changes.

19. See *ibid.*, *passim*, especially pp. 7 and 61.

20. *Ibid.*, pp. 61–62.

21. *Ibid.*, pp. iv–v.

variety of the arts, so one must not fail to differentiate the beauty of music from other types of beauty. To arouse feelings is not the aim of music. Nor are feelings its contents. The feelings of the composer at the moment of production, even when they are known, are irrelevant to the type of beauty he makes as he writes his notes. Music may awaken feelings, mainly through the associations that listeners bring to specific melodies or rhythms, to dances or marches; music can portray ideas and, by swelling or accelerating, represent certain emotional dynamics. Hanslick therefore argues, quite consistently, that one may legitimately assign to music descriptive epithets normally laden with emotional content—"charming, soft, fervent, energetic, delicate, fresh"[22]—as long as one employs these adjectives in their musical connotation alone. But when one insists, as most aestheticians have insisted, that music *expresses* feelings which the listener identifies and may come to share, one misinterprets activity for passivity, mistakes the importation of one's feelings into music for the reception of feelings *from* music. The listener to music and the insufficiently critical aesthetician (Hanslick might have said in Ruskin's words) commit the pathetic fallacy; they (he might have said in Freud's language) project their subjective states into the sounds they hear. The most expressive musical passages, Hanslick shrewdly observes, "are like silhouettes, which we normally recognize only after we have been told whom they represent."[23]

This is a sensible, even penetrating theory, designed to shift the weight of analysis from the producer and the consumer of music to the music itself.[24] It was only Hanslick's unhappy felicity that made him epitomize that theory with a memorable, but far too simple, sentence: "The contents of music are sounding moving forms—*Der Inhalt der Musik sind tönend bewegte Formen.*"[25] Hanslick had no intention of endowing musical beauty with the chilly perfection—frigid, asensual, obscenely chaste—of Canova's Venuses. Musical pleasure was, to him, very potent and very much a matter of feeling. But it was, he insisted, a feeling like no other: its vocabulary, its grammar, its means of expression and modes of communication were all its own. It was to underscore this point that Hanslick emphatically refused to resort to those analogies from architecture and mathematics that writ-

22. *Ibid.*, p. 24.
23. *Ibid.*, p. 39.
24. See, on this point, Abegg, *Musikästhetik und Musikkritik*, Part II, "Allgemeine Probleme der Aesthetik und Kritik," pp. 47–87 *passim*.
25. *Vom Musikalisch-Schönen*, p. 59. In the first edition, this formula is at once more laconic and more dogmatic: "*Sounding moving forms* are, solely and alone, the contents and matter of music" (p. 32).

ers on music, in desperate search for telling description, like to employ. The beauty of music is not architectural or mathematical; it is musical.[26] The point of music, therefore, is to serve nothing and nobody, not even *Stimmung*—indeed, especially not *Stimmung*. One must listen to music, Hanslick wrote, austerely and nobly, "for its own sake."[27] Yet the force of this point, however cogently argued and circumstantially proved, was lost in Hanslick's formula that music is "sounding moving form," probably the phrase among his many good phrases that everyone remembered best. Once Hanslick had launched it, he had launched the myth of his formalism.

Hanslick recognized that his formula, even if correctly understood, did not exhaust what the theorist must say about musical beauty. The music itself, with its ascertainable properties, is central; but the total musical experience, which embraces composer, interpreter and listener in a single, if complex, transaction, requires attention as well. Accordingly, Hanslick devoted a number of pages to the "subjective" side of music. Yet it was always to its objective side—to the structure that can be described, measured, analyzed—that Hanslick returned. "The layman and the man of feeling (*Gefühlsmensch*) like to ask if a piece is cheerful or sad; the musician, if it is good or bad."[28]

Welcome as the complexities are that Hanslick was prepared to introduce into his economical formulations, his combative aesthetics could not escape one potential embarrassment: vocal music. Hanslick did not scant music for the voice—how could he? He reviewed choral performances, Lieder recitals, and operas as extensively as symphonic or chamber music concerts. But the difficulty remains, and Hanslick did not resolve it with the discriminations he introduced for the purpose. Instrumental music alone, he argues, produces unalloyed musical beauty; it alone is the "pure, absolute art of sound—*reine, absolute Tonkunst.*"[29] He protests that this formulation implies no rank order: one may legitimately value vocal music as highly as, or more highly than, instrumental music. But music other than instrumental is an art that derives its total effect from non-musical means like poetry, visual devices, even the suspense of action; opera may be as exalted an art form as a string quartet, but it is another sort of art, calling for another sort of judgment.

Hanslick's solution is more verbal than substantive. It is true, by

---

26. See *ibid.*, pp. 83–87.
27. *Ibid.*, p. 136.
28. *Loc. cit.*
29. *Ibid.*, p. 34. See on this issue, Abegg, *Musikästhetik und Musikkritik*, p. 120.

definition, that the art of pure sound is music without words and without visual action. But the meaning of vocal music, whether Lied or opera, consists precisely in the union of sounds and words, not in their separation. On this union, and on the relation between its two elements, Hanslick has some persuasive things to say. His choice of Gluck's famous aria from *Orfeo*, "Che faró senza Euridice," is adroit: Orfeo's lament for his lost love moves along briskly and could as easily serve a hymn of rejoicing. Its loveliness is independent of its message.[30] Hanslick's discussion of the worldly, erotic duets that Handel borrowed from himself for his sacred oratorio, *The Messiah,* is equally to the point.[31] And his cool comments on the extravagant uses to which Beethoven enthusiasts were putting the choral movement of the Ninth Symphony are worth reading today.[32] Few will dispute Hanslick's dictum that in vocal compositions second-rate words will not spoil first-rate music, while second-rate music will spoil first-rate words. Yet few will find wholly satisfactory the rather offhand conclusion that Hanslick draws from his observations: in opera, the union between music and poetry is a "morganatic marriage," with poetry in the role of the fortunate commoner.[33] The aesthetic experience of opera, which Hanslick sought to capture in many perceptive reviews, is too multifarious to be exhaustively described by such metaphors, charming though they may be.

Yet incoherence in theory should not obscure relevance to practice. Hanslick's skepticism about vocal music was part of the great combat between the "purists" and the "tone-painters" that raged in his lifetime. His defense of "pure" music stood in sharp and unresolvable conscious opposition to Wagner's noisy assertion that in "music-drama" the music is a means and the drama the end. That assertion was, after all, more than an assertion of personal greatness. Wagner meant to claim the glory of a historic achievement: he had restored the true relationship between word and sound—nothing less. The grandiloquence of the claim, and its expression in Wagner's late compositions, were enough to make Hanslick wince and reach for his pen once more.

If Hanslick's significance for the nineteenth-century musical scene is beyond dispute, his long-range importance is a matter of some

---

30. *Vom Musikalisch-Schönen*, pp. 37–39.
31. *Ibid.*, pp. 41–42.
32. *Ibid.*, pp. 90–92n.
33. *Ibid.*, p. 57.

uncertainty. Hanslick, as I have said, lies buried under Beckmesser, and while he remains thus uncomfortably concealed, the general verdict that he is utterly forgettable seems beyond challenge. Nor need one be a fanatical Wagnerian to accept that verdict: all aestheticians convinced in any way by the theory of art-as-expression are bound to find Hanslick's views intolerable. Even so, I am prepared to argue that Hanslick's ideas, despite their time-bound, polemical form, have lasting validity. They are, in significant respects, modern.

To call Hanslick modern, even within narrow limits, must seem perverse. Certainly, the dual quality of Modernism in our age—the openness to all experience coupled with a rage for experiment—was alien to him. He would have wondered at the tendentious traditionalism of the modern sensibility, that selective rummaging through the past, that has characterized Eliot and Joyce, Picasso and Stravinsky. He would have been at a loss to account for the primitivism that punctuates the search for the modern self. To prefer (as Hanslick candidly confessed he did) Goethe to all of Sophocles and Racine, Mendelssohn to Palestrina, Schumann's and Brahms's quartets to Bach's concertos and sonatas,[34] meant that he was what the French moderns approvingly called "de son temps." But while it placed him in the nineteenth century, it scarcely made him a modern for the twentieth. Even if one rejects the Wagnerites' insulting characterization of Hanslick as a timid reactionary, an epigone writing for epigones, one feels safe in calling him a traditionalist, essentially a defensive critic. And it is true that (in contrast to Lincoln Steffens and the Soviet Union) Hanslick had seen the future, and it did not work. Reviewing Bruckner's Eighth Symphony in 1892, he ruefully noted that what he called this "dreamy, confused hangover style—*traumverwirrter Katzenjammerstil*" might well be the style of the future, "a future we do not envy on that account."[35] But we must at least consider Hanslick's appraisal of himself as a critic who could take pride in neither liking nor disliking the new because it was new any more than he liked or disliked the old because it was old. In the "Conversation on Music Criticism" with his friend Billroth, with which he concludes his autobiography, Hanslick looked back on nearly half a century of reviewing music and thought his "receptivity" in the 1890s as fresh as it had been in the 1840s. And he offered as proof of that receptivity contradictory accusations leveled against him: while some had charged him with being a camp follower of the successful, others had charged him with

---

34. See his list of preferences in *Aus meinem Leben*, Vol. II, pp. 303–308.
35. Reprinted in *Fünf Jahre Musik*, p. 191.

a onesided preference for novelty. Whatever the others might say, Hanslick was cheerfully satisfied to call himself a modern.

In this historic movement toward Modernism, intelligent conservatives like Hanslick had their part to play. By sorting out the independent, unique quality of the musically beautiful, he put a considerable measure of wit and learning at the disposal of those forces in the arts, mainy in abstract painting and in "pure" music, which assign a prominent place to the irrational, without permitting it the upper hand. Form—this is the meaning of *Vom Musikalisch-Schönen* and the uncounted articles that accompany Hanslick's treatise like so many grace notes—form has pleasures and, indeed, profundities of its own. Hanslick's vision was limited, and his place in the history of our culture is likely to remain a modest one. But he deserves to be rescued from oblivion or opprobrium for his perceptiveness, his intelligence, his capacity to see the dangers of the unrestricted rule of the id. The army of modern culture cannot be staffed by generals alone.

Erato

LOVE OF LEARNING

MORTIMER ADLER

Teaching and Learning

"Happily there is something stable and clear and useful behind this phantasmagoria of Education—the nature of subject matter and the practice of teaching. . . ."

". . . the whole aim of good teaching is to turn the young learner, by nature a little copycat, into an independent, self-propelling creature, who cannot merely learn but study. . . . This is to turn pupils into students, and it can be done on any rung of the ladder of learning."

JACQUES BARZUN, *Teacher in America*

و§

In the context of these passages, Jacques Barzun observes that we all know, or should know, that it is impossible to "teach" democracy, or citizenship or a happy married life; that not all subjects are teachable; that many who are regarded and probably regard themselves as professional teachers "are merely 'connected with education' "; and that, while teaching "is not a lost art . . . the regard for it is a lost tradition." I hope what I have to say about teaching and learning will confirm and illuminate these observations, especially the point made in the second passage quoted above; namely, that the good teacher should aim to make his tutelage totally dispensable by transforming those he teaches into independent learners.

I would like to dwell for a moment on the contrast which Jacques draws between Education and teaching. In my judgment, Education (with a capital E) is a secondary subject, and a dull one to boot. Countless long and intricate books have been written on the subject, few of them good, none of them great. In contrast, the literature on the art of teaching and the role of the teacher is minuscule. It consists mainly not of books or treatises, but of little gems to be found in the context of discourse on other subjects. It begins with a few passages in the dialogues of Plato and the treatises of Aristotle; it continues with a short tract by Augustine and with a few questions answered by Aquinas in the *Summa Theologica;* and it includes, in modern times, some insights to be found in the writings of Comenius, John Locke, Immanuel Kant, William James and John Dewey.

Contemporary "educational psychology" of the scientific variety may have made contributions to the subject, but I doubt it. At best those contributions will add footnotes to the main points I wish to make about the nature and function of the teacher in the process of human learning. If what I have to say about teaching restores respect for the art, and imparts an understanding of how difficult it is to practice that art effectively, it may also help us to realize how superficial all educational plans, programs and policies must necessarily be when they do not recognize that the number of good teachers available to carry them out will always fall far short of the number required to achieve the appointed objectives.

All learning is either by instruction or by discovery; that is, with or without the aid of teachers. The teachers who serve as instructors may be alive and in direct contact with those whom they instruct, as is always the case in classrooms or tutorials, or they may be present to the learner only in the form of books. The teacher who instructs by his writings cannot engage in discussion with those who are reading his works in order to learn; he can ask them initial questions, but he cannot ask any second questions—questions about the answers they give to his initial questions. He is, therefore, seriously limited in his performance of the art of teaching, though he may have done what he could to apply the rules of that art in his effort to communicate what he knows.

That the effort to communicate what a man knows is not, *in itself,* effective teaching follows from the fact that such efforts are seldom if ever successful and, at best, they succeed only in part. Successful teaching occurs only when the mind of the learner passes from a state of ignorance or error to a state of knowledge. The knowledge acquired may be either something already known by the teacher, or something about which he himself is inquiring. In either case, the transformation effected in the mind of the learner is learning by instruction only if another human being has taken certain deliberate steps to bring about that transformation. What the teacher does must be deliberately calculated to change the mind of the learner. Merely motivating someone to learn is not enough; stimulation is not teaching.

Since whatever can be learned by instruction must necessarily have been learned first by discovery, without the aid of teachers, it follows that teachers are, absolutely speaking, dispensable. Nevertheless, they are useful because most human beings need instruction to learn what they could have learned by discovering it for themselves. If we recognize, as we should, that genuine learning cannot occur without activity on the part of the learner (passive absorption or rote memorization does not deserve to be called learning), then we must also recognize that all learning is a process of discovery on the part of the learner.

This alters our understanding of the distinction between learning by discovery and learning by instruction. If the latter is not to be identified with passive absorption or rote memorization, then the distinction divides all active learning into two kinds—unaided discovery, discovery without the aid of teachers, on the one hand; and aided discovery, or discovery deliberately assisted by teachers, on the other. In both cases, the principal cause of learning is activity on the part of the learner engaged in the process of discovery; when instruction occurs, the teacher is at best only an instrumental cause operating to guide or facilitate the process of discovery on the part of the learner. To suppose that the teacher is ever more than an instrumental cause is to suppose that the activity of a teacher can by itself suffice to cause learning to occur in another person even though the latter remains entirely passive. This would view the learner as a patient being acted upon rather than as an agent whose activity is both primary and indispensable. In contrast, the instrumental activity of the teacher is always secondary and dispensable.

These basic insights are epitomized by Socrates when, in the *Theaetetus*, he describes his role as a teacher by analogy with the service performed by a midwife who does nothing more than assist the pregnant mother to give birth with less pain and more assurance. So, according to Socrates, the teacher assists the inquiring mind of the learner to give birth to knowledge, facilitating the process of discovery on the learner's part. If the learner suffers birth pangs because errors block the way, then, as Socrates tells us in the *Meno*, the teacher may have to take strenuous measures to reduce the learner from a state of error to one of admitted ignorance (by "benumbing" the mind of the learner), so that motion toward learning can proceed unhampered by obstacles.

Before we consider how the good teacher, following the model of Socrates, cooperates with the activity of the learner, which will develop from our understanding of teaching as a cooperative art, let me call attention to two erroneous uses of the word "teach." It is often said

that "experience teaches," but however much we may learn from experience, it teaches us nothing. Only human beings teach. We also frequently say that a man is self-taught—an autodidact—or that he has
taught himself this or that. He may have learned this or that entirely
by himself; all of his learning may have been unaided discovery. But
to say that it occurred without the aid of teachers is not to say that he
taught himself. One individual can be taught only by another.

Teaching, like farming and healing, is a cooperative art. Understanding this, Comenius in *The Great Didactic* again and again compares the cultivation of the mind with the cultivation of the field; so,
too, Plato compares the teacher's art with the physician's.

In arts such as shoemaking and shipbuilding, painting and sculpture (arts which I call "operative" to distinguish them from the three
cooperative arts), the artist is the principal cause of the product produced. Nature may supply the materials to be fashioned or transformed, and may even supply models to imitate, but without the intervention of the artist's skill and causal efficacy, nature would not
produce shoes, ships, paintings or statues.

Unlike the operative artist, who aims either at beauty or utility,
the cooperative artist merely helps nature to produce results that it is
able to produce by its own powers, without the assistance of the artist
—without the intervention of the artist's accessory causality. Fruits
and grains grow naturally; the farmer intervenes merely to assure that
these natural products grow with regularity and, perhaps, to increase
their quantity. The body has the power to heal itself—to maintain
health and regain health; the physician who adopts the Hippocratic
conception of the healing art attempts to support and reinforce the
natural processes of the body. The mind, like the body, has the power
to achieve what is good for itself—knowledge and understanding.
Learning would go on if there were no teachers, just as healing and
growing would go on if there were no physicians and farmers.

Like the farmer and the physician, the teacher must be sensitive
to the natural process that his art should help bring to its fullest
fruition—the natural process of learning. It is the nature of human
learning that determines the strategy and tactics of teaching. Since
learning which results in expanded knowledge and improved understanding (rather than memorized facts) is essentially a process of discovery, the teacher's art consists largely in devices whereby one individual can help another to lift himself up from a state of knowing and
understanding less to knowing and understanding more. Left to his
own devices, the learner would not get very far unless he asked him-

self questions, perceived problems to be solved, suffered puzzlement over dilemmas, put himself under the necessity of following out the implications of this hypothesis or that, made observations and weighed the evidence for alternative hypotheses, and so on. The teacher, aware of these indispensable steps in the process by which he himself has moved his own mind up the ladder of learning, devises ways to help another individual engage in a similar process; and he applies them with sensitivity to the state of that other person's mind and with awareness of whatever special difficulties the other must overcome in order to make headway.

Discipline in the traditional liberal arts imparts the skills by which an individual becomes adept at learning. They are the arts of reading and writing, of speaking and listening, of observing, measuring and calculating—the arts of grammar, rhetoric and logic, the mathematical arts, and the arts of investigation. Without some proficiency in these arts, no one can learn very much, whether assisted or not by the use of books and the tutelage of teachers. Unless the teacher is himself a skilled learner, a master of the liberal arts which are the arts of learning, he cannot help those he attempts to teach acquire the skills of learning; nor can his superior skill in learning provide the learner with the help he needs in the process of discovery. The teacher must put himself sympathetically in the position of a learner who is less advanced than himself, less advanced both in skill and in knowledge or understanding. From that vantage point, he must somehow re-enact—or stimulate—for the learner the activities he himself engaged in to achieve his present state of mind.

The Hippocratic understanding of healing as a cooperative art provides us with analogical insights into the cooperative art of teaching. Hippocrates distinguished between three forms of therapy: control of the patient's regimen, the use of drugs or other forms of medication, and recourse to surgery when that drastic remedy cannot be avoided. He regarded the first of these as the primary technique of the physician as a cooperative artist, for, unlike medication, it introduces no foreign substances into the body and, unlike surgery, it does no violence to it. By controlling the patient's regimen—his diet, his hours, his activities, his environment—the physician helps the body to heal itself by its natural processes.

In the sphere of teaching, the analogue of surgery is indoctrination, the result of which is rote memorization, or some passive absorption of information without any understanding of it. Indoctrination does violence to the mind, as surgery does violence to the body, the only difference being that there is never any excuse for indoctrination, while there can be justification for surgery. The restoration of health may be facilitated by surgery when that drastic remedy is needed, but knowledge and understanding can never be produced by indoctrination. Even so, Hippocrates did not regard the surgeon as a physician, though the physician may find it necessary to have recourse to his services. The physician and the surgeon are distinguished by the line that divides the cooperative from the operative artist. By the same criterion, the indoctrinator is not a teacher.

Lecturing is that form of teaching which is analogous to the use of drugs and medication in the practice of medicine. No violence may be done to the mind if the lecturer eschews any attempt at indoctrination, but the lecture, even when it is attended to with maximum effort on the part of the auditor, is something that the mind must first absorb before it can begin to digest and assimilate what is thus taken in. If passively attended to and passively absorbed by the memory, the lecture has the same effect as indoctrination, even if the lecturer scrupulously intended to avoid that result. At its best, the lecture cannot be more than an occasion for learning, a challenge to the mind of the auditor, an invitation to inquiry. The lecture, in short, is no better than the book as a teacher—an oral rather than a written communication of knowledge. Like the author, the lecturer cannot ask the second and subsequent questions, and unless these are asked, persistently and vigorously, the learner is not aided by a teacher in his own process of discovery. Unlike the indoctrinator, the lecturer may have the same aim as the teacher, but his manner of teaching is at best second-rate.

Analogous to the fully cooperative therapeutic technique of controlling the patient's regimen is the fully cooperative pedagogical technique of engaging the learner in discussion—teaching by asking instead of teaching by telling, asking questions not merely to elicit answers for the sake of grading them (as in a quiz session, which is not teaching at all), but asking questions that challenge the answers elicited, and asking still more questions that open up new avenues of inquiry. Lectures audited and books read may provide the materials for teaching by discussion, and there may be advanced learners, highly skilled in the liberal arts, who can learn from lectures and books without the aid of teachers. But for those who need the help that good teachers can provide, listening to lectures or reading books without discussing them yields little profit to the mind. The help that the good teacher provides takes the form of conducting the needed discussion. Socrates did that without any use of books or lectures, and there may be others who have taught by asking questions without employing any "teaching materials" to ask questions about; yet for the most part even the best teachers find lectures heard and books read useful accessories to teaching by discussion.

Holding up Socrates as the model requires us to consider the one basic issue in the theory of teaching. Like most basic theoretical issues, it first emerged as an apparent difference of opinion between Plato and Aristotle. Their different conceptions of the teacher and of teaching are exemplified in the difference between the Platonic and the Aristotelian styles of philosophical exposition, between the dialogue and the treatise.

For Plato, the teacher is, like Socrates, one who is engaged in the pursuit of truth because he does not possess it, one who is inquiring because he does not know or understand something, to know or understand which is the object of his inquiry. For Aristotle, the teacher is a person like himself, one who knows or understands something and who communicates his knowledge or understanding of it. The mind of the student, according to Aristotle, has the potentiality of knowing or understanding what the mind of the teacher actually knows or understands, and teaching consists in those acts on the part of the teacher by which he reduces the mind of the student from potentiality to actuality in a certain respect.

On the face of it, it would appear that Aristotle conceived of teaching as an operative rather than as a cooperative art, and regarded giving lectures or writing books as effective methods of teaching rather than as second-rate efforts even at their best. However, we have no reason to think that Aristotle rejected the fundamental truth that all learning is a process of discovery involving activity on the part of the learner, which is both primary and indispensable. He would agree that, when learning occurs with the aid of a teacher, the activity of the teacher cannot be more than a secondary and instrumental cause. The teacher who actually knows something must put himself in the position of inquiring to aid inquiry on the part of the learner, who must inquire in order to learn.

That being the case, the lectures that a teacher gives or the treatises he writes may express the knowledge he actually possesses, but they are only the first step in effective teaching. The lecture or treatise by itself will seldom if ever reduce the student's mind from potentially knowing or understanding what the teacher knows or understands to actually knowing or understanding it. To effect that transformation, the teacher must ask questions that probe and move the mind of the learner in a variety of ways. As evidence that Aristotle was aware of this, it should be noted that his treatises are full of questions—questions that are pivotal in his exposition of any subject. The treatises cannot, of course, ask the second and subsequent questions which would emerge in a well-conducted discussion.

It must also be remembered that Socrates' pretension to ignorance is at least partly ironical, the irony itself being employed as a teaching device. Oftentimes in the dialogues, Socrates reveals himself as knowing what, at other moments, he is careful not to claim he knows. That he knows more than those whom he interrogates goes without saying: he knows better than they the object of the inquiry, and he knows better than they how to inquire about it. Such knowledge makes the teacher more competent as a learner or inquirer than those whom he is trying to help in the process of learning. If, in addition, one detects in the Platonic doctrine of learning as reminiscence (exemplified by Socrates' questioning of the slave boy in the *Meno*) something equivalent to the Aristotelian doctrine of learning as the actualization of potential knowledge or understanding, then the one basic issue in the theory of teaching turns out to be an apparent rather than a real disagreement between Platonists and Aristotelians.

Space remains for only a brief statement of some of the implications of the theory of the teacher and of teaching to be found in traditional sources. The reader may perceive other consequences of the theory for educational programs, policies and practices, but the following seem to me to be of prime importance.

1. Just as the physician caring for the health of his patients treats one person at a time, so, too, the teacher operates under ideal conditions only when he cooperates with the learning process of one person at a time. Any increase beyond that in the number of persons being simultaneously served by the teacher reduces the efficacy of his efforts, and when the number exceeds two or three, his efficiency decreases almost to the vanishing point.

2. Many—perhaps most—of the people who are officially engaged in the educational system, in one capacity or another, do very little teaching in the strict sense of that term. In any educational institution, be it school, college or university, the number of those who are teachers in more than name only is relatively small; of those, the amount of time they can devote to teaching is slight, and the conditions under which they teach render their efforts much less effective than they would be under ideal conditions.

3. If, in our educational institutions from grade school through the university, everyone who held the office of teacher were in fact truly a teacher and were afforded optimal conditions for teaching,

many, if not most, of the educational problems that have concerned us in this century would either disappear or become solvable.

4. If, in every hour of teaching, the teacher, even one who is already very learned, were himself to enjoy some increment of learning, the effectiveness of teaching would be maximized. To the extent that those who regard themselves as teachers teach without any increment of learning for themselves, they are likely to fail in their efforts to assist others in the process of learning.

5. In a democratic society, with universal suffrage and universal schooling, the educational system cannot possibly hope to have an adequate number of teachers in the strict sense of that term. To cope with this inadequacy, two remedies may be available. One lies in the fact that the bright students need less help from teachers than those less well endowed; they are better able to learn by unaided discovery. The second remedy is more drastic: that every advanced student should undertake to teach, individually, someone not as far advanced. Not only would this provide every student with a teacher, but it would make every student a better learner, for having to teach a subject to someone else increases one's own understanding of it.

6. Though experience does not teach, it is an aid to learning and, therefore, to teaching. It follows from this that mature persons, of larger and more varied experience, are more teachable than the immature, though the latter may be more trainable. To increase the teachability of students in our educational institutions, policies should be formulated and expedients adopted that would tend to increase their maturity before their schooling is completed. This might be accomplished by some years of non-attendance at schools after the completion of secondary schooling and by provision of facilities for continuing education after the completion of college or university.

7. Since it involves the application of one's highest faculties for the benefit of the mind of another, the gift made by a dedicated and devoted teacher is, as Augustine remarked, "the greatest act of charity."

THEODORE CAPLOW

How Many Books?

"We know—as the saying goes—more than ever before. But who
is 'we' "?

JACQUES BARZUN, *Science: The Glorious Entertainment*

My long pupilship with Jacques Barzun began when I was a sophomore at Columbia College and he was an instructor teaching a course
entitled "The Historical Background of English Literature." We students were asked to read a long series of excerpts from notable authors,
together with Trevelyan's *History of England,* but the class discussions
took an unexpected turn. At the first meeting, as I remember it, Mr.
Barzun introduced Byron's irregular sonnet beginning "She walks in
beauty like the night" to illustrate the method of relating a literary
work to the historical setting in which it was produced. The class flung
itself upon this example with avidity and, with the teacher's encouragement, found so much to consider in the piece that its eighteen lines
and their historical background remained our topic for most of the
term.

The lesson I still retain from that course is that the close, patient
and unhurried reading of a single text is more profitable than the
hasty reading of many. But how does one apply this lesson in the social sciences, where the number of new books and editions published
annually in the world has just passed 100,000 and still rises at a
dizzying rate? Let us suppose that only one in ten of these is worth
reading by anybody and only one in a thousand is interesting to me.
That is still one hundred books a year to read (in addition to all the
papers, monographs and reports that stream unendingly from the
printing presses and the copying machines) or one book every three
days, provided there is no backlog of unread volumes left over from
last year and the year before. Beware of flagging. Next year's books are
already at the printers' and even more numerous.

The problem this poses for the working scholar has no solution that is both personally satisfying and functionally adequate. The founder of my discipline, Auguste Comte, practiced in later life what he called "intellectual hygiene" by refusing to read any writings but his own. One of the most eminent of living sociologists has used the same procedure for some years past, without fanfare. The great drawback of the system is that the scholar who adopts it gradually becomes ignorant of the field in which he professes to be expert.

Specialization is a more conventional solution—learning more and more about less and less, in the old phrase. In some fields, like demography or economic history, the artful savant can arrange to have his field of interest contract at approximately the same rate that its literature expands, so that he stays about even with the game as he regresses from, say, urban growth in the nineteenth century to migration into London during the Napoleonic wars. This strategy relieves the pressure of the literature upon the scholar and has some important incidental advantages from a career standpoint. The number of people interested in the ever-diminishing subject matter being small, they can readily form an invisible college to praise each other's works and advance each other's fortunes. No outsiders are familiar enough with their arcane lore to challenge the high appraisals they put on each other's work. When he undertakes to teach, however, the extreme specialist has the same problem as the intellectual hygienist, namely, ignorance of the subject.

Another strategy for coping with the pressure of the literature is to improve the efficiency whereby we extract information from an existing body of written materials. Devices for this purpose take many different forms, including various systems of speed reading, mechanical note taking, abstracting and data retrieval, and are most useful for sorting through a large mass of written material in order to locate a smaller mass that needs to be read with care. While such devices make it easier to sift through and discard irrelevant material, they also usually increase the number of irrelevant items to be considered. The tests of relevance applied by an abstracting system or a computerized catalogue are necessarily more formal than insightful.

Most working scholars adopt all three of the foregoing strategies for coping with the flood of current writings. They arbitrarily refuse to read some things they ought to read; they read more selectively in any given field as the volume of its literature grows; and they sometimes resort to mechanical devices for extracting information from written materials. Even as they use these strategies, however, they discover them to be palliatives, not solutions. For no matter how much midnight oil we burn, no matter what strategies we use, the mass of writings to be read continues to grow without any regard for our limited mental capacities. This is something the modern scholar must live with, an ugly problem almost sufficient to counterbalance tenure, popular esteem, long vacations and the other advantages of the academic profession.

So much for keeping up with one's field. What about the teaching of it? Which books do we make our students read? The old ones because they have been influential, or the new ones because they are up to date? How closely should each page be read? How much remembered?

In the beginning, of course, formal education consisted only of *explications de texte*, and very few texts at that—Aristotle almost alone in the medieval faculties of philosophy from which all our liberal arts institutions are descended. The habit of defining the curriculum by particular books persisted for many centuries. In William Davies' 1795 plan of education for the University of North Carolina, the Professor of Moral and Political Philosophy and History was to be responsible for four subjects, "Moral and Political Philosophy," "Civil Government and Political Constitutions," "The Law of Nations," and "History," and for each of these subjects, the books to be taught were listed. Paley and Montesquieu sufficed for "Moral and Political Philosophy"; Priestley, Millot and Hume, together with a chronology, for "Ancient and Modern History."[1]

The requirements in literature and languages were set forth in the same fashion. In the physical sciences, however, the subjects to be taught were outlined by topics which seem to refer to a series of classroom demonstrations. The earliest textbooks, as distinct from explicatable texts, were manuals and study guides for such demonstrations. The best of them could be used without a teacher and, in the nineteenth century, often carried such titles as *Chemistry Self-Taught*.

In the social sciences and humanities, textbooks—i.e., works without intellectual pretension, intended to serve both as manuals for teachers and study guides for students—did not appear until much later. The books that attempted to summarize the social sciences in nineteenth-century classrooms, such as Spencer's *Sociology* and Ely's *Economics*, were authoritative and original statements, closer to the philosophical text than to the science textbook. The degeneration of the text into the textbook was a long process. In sociology, the first

---

1. Richard Hofstadter and Wilson Smith, *American Higher Education: A Documentary History* (2 vols., Chicago: Univ. of Chicago Press, 1961), Vol. I, p. 168.

book to be marketed in the modern manner and "adopted" for introductory courses all over the United States—Park and Burgess's *Introduction to the Science of Society*—presented a coherent and original
theory that grounded sociology on botany. It was not until the 1930s
that the first modern textbooks, without minds of their own but
crammed with pictures and teaching aids, began to compete for "shares
of the college market."

The early science textbooks had—and their successors still have—
the understandable function of helping the student to follow the demonstrations the teacher performs on the laboratory table or the black-
board. In the social sciences and humanities, the purposes of textbooks
are more ambiguous. The authors do not ordinarily seek to draw attention to themselves or their own ideas, but provide sensible and non-
committal synopses of the distinctive writings that constitute the intellectual core of these disciplines. The better textbooks summarize
the ideas of Ricardo and Keynes, Marx and Pareto or Shaw and Joyce,
and the viewpoints of their critics, with impersonal neatness and dispatch. (The worst textbooks take the same ideas and garble them.)
The textbook is a substitute for the teacher, not for the text that the
teacher might explicate without a textbook.

What then remains for the teacher to do after he assigns his
students a textbook? If he follows the book in his lectures, students
will soon see that they gain nothing by attending. If he undertakes to
supplement the book's explications of the vital texts with more original
explications of his own, the students' confidence in him and in the
textbook will be undermined by the petty but continual disagreement
between them.

One way out of this dilemma is to assign a book of readings. By
scores and by hundreds, these collections pour off the presses. Five
pages of Marx, seven of Max Weber, two unrelated pieces by Niebuhr,
snippets from *The Village Voice* and the *Wall Street Journal*, twenty
journal articles of various vintages (condensed by the omission of
data), five previously published papers by the editors reproduced in
full, a brief introduction explaining how well the items in this grabbag
fit together, and a briefer conclusion explaining how much the reader
has learned. In sociology, social psychology and—I believe—political
science, books of readings now outnumber the total of all other books
published. In history, economics, philosophy and law, their number is
coming up fast. In literary studies, they have nearly displaced the
serious and useful anthologies that formerly made it possible to sample a large body of literature chronologically.

Averting our eyes from this shambles, let us return to the problem that gave rise to it: how to select the most useful parts of an excessively large literature. When I was very new at college teaching, it seemed to me that the most useful purpose that an undergraduate course could serve would be to give the student so sure a grip on some small body of knowledge that it would stay available to him permanently and give him a private touchstone with which to distinguish information from ignorance. To that end, I proposed a curriculum in which each class would meet daily for a six-week term and cover one circumscribed topic intensively—for example, the first act of *Hamlet*, the distribution of the labor force by occupation in a given census, the battle of Gettysburg, pricing in the soft coal industry or Durkheim's concept of a social fact. Every reading assignment was to be read at least three times, and every writing assignment to be corrected in fine detail. At the end of the six-week term the students were to be given an objective examination in which the lowest passing grade would be 95. Those who failed the course could repeat it as often as necessary. Those who passed were to go on to slightly more difficult topics.

The proposal fell on stony ground originally, but somewhat similar arrangements have recently been adopted here and there. The teacher under this system becomes a tutor and a coach instead of a pronouncer of doctrine *ex cathedra*, and for that reason it probably works best with relatively inexperienced and unjaded teachers.

A more humane version of the short course is recommended in *The American University:*

> Such a course should start with an introductory lecture or two outlining scope and strategy, and commenting on the required reading. Six weeks later the class is examined on the reading. Students who pass are admitted to 8 or 10 lectures, scheduled close together (say within three weeks). The rest of the term provides opportunities for questions and discussions in office hours. In some cases, a short paper —not more than five pages—to show understanding, not scholarship or bulk.[2]

The distinctive feature of the Barzun short course is that the required reading precedes classroom instruction instead of following it, as in most courses. It is probably more suited to graduate students and advanced undergraduates who have already acquired the trick of instructing themselves by independent reading than to the average student whose steps still falter in the library stacks. It should be more comfortable for the teacher than a conventional course because he

---

2. Jacques Barzun, *The American University: How It Runs, Where It Is Going* (New York: Harper & Row, 1968), p. 249.

does not have to struggle with an unevenly prepared audience, but more demanding for the students. My version, as I know by experiment, is uncomfortable for both teacher and student, but rather satisfying in retrospect.

For the time being, however, the short course is unlikely to replace the semester course that corresponds to a specialty within a specialty within a scholarly discipline. Teachers present their credentials and students identify their interests by reference to such specialties. The question of "How Many Books?" must be answered within the framework of the conventional course, and since for most college courses beyond the introductory level we are not likely to find a really suitable textbook, the practical problem is how much reading to assign. To illustrate the problem, and a possible solution to it, I take the example closest to hand, a course in political sociology. It is a trivial example, but not in any way unusual.

The course will be open to advanced undergraduates and graduate students. If the class runs true to form, there will be a considerable range of sociological literacy, from third-year students whose whole acquaintance with social science consists of two or three elementary courses, to doctoral candidates, and I must strike some sort of mean between them in devising assignments.

The specialty of "political sociology" includes two distinct literatures: a long line of analytical and polemical essays about the relationship between polity and society on the one hand; a great mass of contemporary empirical studies of voting patterns, legislative processes and related matters, on the other. Neither of these literatures can be adequately covered in a semester, but we are nevertheless obliged to include them both in a course that purports to familiarize students with political sociology.

Let us consider the analytical-polemical side first. A minimum "comprehensive" reading list might start with Aristotle, the ultimate source of our categories for political institutions, and include Machiavelli, the inventor of the social scientist's split image, as well as Hobbes, Locke, Rousseau, Marx, Engels, Tocqueville, Saint-Simon, Comte, Spencer, Weber, Pareto, Mosca, Michels, Kautsky, Trotsky, Lenin, Mao, Aron, Lippmann, Duverger, Lipset, Nisbet, C. Wright Mills, and perhaps twenty others.

Before we cry Uncle and reach for the book of readings, let us remember that we teachers are paid to sort through difficult books and extract knowledge from them in a form that students can absorb. That there are any number of themes to be pursued is as obvious as that there are a vast number of books to be read. But students are only human, life is short, and what we are trying to do is to give them the experience of learning a few things well so they know what understanding feels like and can eventually replicate that experience by themselves. What we might do, then, is choose a major theme and use it as a selective device.

Suppose we choose as our theme for the course in political sociology the relationship between social stratification and political power. As soon as the theme has been identified, we can see which texts will need to be discussed and interpreted in class: the *Declaration of Independence* and the *Declaration of the Rights of Man*, the *Communist Manifesto* and the *Little Red Book*, the last chapter of Pareto's *General Sociology*, chapter 9 of *Middletown in Transition*, chapters 1–4 of Weber's *Economy and Society*, and a few other pieces of manageable length. Each of them deserves attention by itself, but since I do not propose to read them aloud—we are not in the Middle Ages, to be sure—I had better see that the students have studied them thoroughly *before* the discussion.

So I shall explicate texts, after all—not a single authoritative text as in the good old days of Duns Scotus, but a coherent series of texts linked by a common theme. But what about Aristotle and Aron, Machiavelli and Marcuse, and all the other excluded authors? Thrown out one door, they will return through another, since there is no way of explicating a text except by relating it to other authoritative texts. When we examine Mr. Jefferson's *Declaration*, we can hardly fail to mention its close connection with the *Second Essay on Civil Government* or its remoter connection with *Leviathan*. Nor can we possibly explain the line of development that leads from the *Manifesto* to Mao without attending to the *German Ideology* and *Das Kapital*, Karl Kautsky and the Erfurt Program, the dictator-essayists of the Soviet Union and their critics. The students will want to read some of these out of intellectual curiosity, or in order to write acceptable papers. But not all the students will be choosing the same books or reading them in the same way. I will expect to prepare lists of suggested texts for students who need help with particular lines of inquiry, but having made sure that the books and papers are available, I shall leave the choice of what to read beyond the assigned texts to each student in the privacy of his study.

The other part of political sociology, as we mentioned before, is a body of measurements, statistical calculations, systematic observations and experimental results obtained from empirical studies of various kinds. There is an abundance of empirical evidence about the connection between social stratification and political activity. For example, the relationship between voting patterns and social characteristics has been exhaustively studied in every Presidential election in the United States since 1948, in innumerable local elections, in all the French, German and Dutch national elections of recent years, and to some extent in all the other countries that practice parliamentary democracy. Some of these studies, like Heinz Eulau's *Class and Party in the Eisenhower Years*, speak directly to the theme of our course. Others are peripheral, but still relevant; more than two hundred studies of "community influence" have been published since 1950.

The sheer bulk of this material is almost beyond comprehension. In the physical sciences, the primary job of condensing research papers is accomplished by the abstract journals; Derek Price has shown that the first abstract journal usually appears when about ten research journals have been founded in a scientific specialty, and that abstract journals then increase at about the same rate as research journals. Abstract journals in the social sciences are less numerous and less important. Empirical studies in the social sciences are not easily accommodated to a uniform abstracting procedure. We rely instead on the handbook or research survey, which summarizes the accumulated results of research in narrative form. The best of these are prepared by experts who are actively engaged in research. Summaries of research are also found in journal articles, textbooks and introductions to project proposals. Nearly every student thesis begins with a narrative account of previous research.

These summaries almost always aim to be comprehensive, since omissions are easily detected and criticized, but they are not constrained to be highly accurate. The most important detriment to accuracy is the brute fact that there is little correlation between the significance of a social science study and the space required to summarize it.

To facilitate summary, many journals require authors to prepare abstracts which are published at the head of each paper. In any case, most experienced authors present their conclusions in a section that serves the same purpose. To get the line or paragraph that he needs for his narrative account, the research summarizer need not plow through the whole paper. He will find what he needs in the author's own language.

But there's the rub. Authors' abstracts are not very trustworthy. It is conventional to overgeneralize a little, and the typical abstract is more an advertisement than a critique, so that—at least in the social sciences—a research summary based mainly on authors' abstracts is likely to exaggerate both the extent and the certainty of available knowledge.

A pedagogical alternative to the review of research summaries is to assign a very small number of research reports to be intensively read. The student learns in detail how the data were collected and interpreted. Ideally, he learns enough to replicate parts of the study himself. The studies selected for this close attention ought to be the best studies known to the teacher, works that he himself considers sound, imaginative and significant. It is then his job to explain how these few studies exemplify and illuminate the great formless mass of other empirical studies which only a specialist can undertake to consider en masse, and that only because he has criteria for putting most items aside unread. So we return, even in the demonstrative-scientific part of our subject, to the explication of a valuable text.

I once knew a Greyhound bus driver named O'Mara who thirsted after learning. He obtained a card from the university library and embarked on a long course of reading according to his own system, which consisted of reading six books on one topic, then six books on another topic suggested by the first, then six more on a third topic, and so on. Starting with the defeat of the Spanish Armada, O'Mara was led to Drake's explorations in the Pacific, to the botany of California, and thence to the economics of forest management. He was headed for Henry George and the single tax movement when I lost sight of him.

Most of us omnivorous readers follow the O'Mara system more or less when we read for pleasure. What makes such reading pleasurable is the absence of any ulterior purpose, while the essence of formal education is that it has very definite purposes that go beyond the immediate subject matter—purposes both practical and intellectual. That is why, after long reflection, I propose that *the required reading for a course of academic instruction should be limited to those works which the instructor has time and inclination to explicate.* I would have students read many fewer pages by way of classroom preparation than they generally do now, but read those pages much more attentively.

What about all the other important works that would be found in a more comprehensive reading list? Students will continue to consult them for information or enlightenment on particular points, but will seldom read them from cover to cover. The student will discover for himself that it is easier, more pleasant and more profitable to pursue some well-defined theme through a scholarly literature than to try to swallow that literature whole, and so he may learn to survive and even to prosper under the ceaseless deluge of scholarly writing.

NELL EURICH

Learning in America

"Doubtless we shall have to keep the old pugilistic title of Professor, though I cannot think of Dante in Hell coming upon Brunetto Latini, and exclaiming 'Why, Professor!' But we can and must get rid of 'Educator'! Imagine the daily predicament, someone asks, 'What do you do?'—'I profess and I educate.' It is unspeakable and absurd."

JACQUES BARZUN, *Teacher in America*

The Muses were a mixed-up group of ladies, apparently quite competitive, certainly ubiquitous and obviously highly influential. Virgil called on Erato to inspire an epic poem, Horace asked five of them at one time or another to help him in lyric songs, and Milton chose Urania to bless the creation of *Paradise Lost*. Hesiod tried to straighten out their individual assignments, and sculptors identified each with a lyre, a scroll and so on, but over the years they kept slipping into various roles. Even so, it is a surprise to find Erato here in charge of the art of teaching, and it is a bit overweening on her part if I may say so.

To my knowledge no one of the nine Muses was ever assigned to teaching or learning, probably because that would have been too big a responsibility for one protector alone, albeit a Muse. (The closest exception was Polymatheia, not in Hesiod's list, whose name meant "much learning," but she unfortunately was not one of the regulars and did not appear frequently.)[1] In any case, the point is that all nine Muses together watched over the arts and sciences, indeed all knowledge. While each was supposed to have a particular subject matter such as history, poetry, dance, music or astronomy, they were strongly

---

1. H. J. Rose, *Handbook of Greek Mythology* (6th ed., London: Methuen, 1958), pp. 173–175.

linked as a multidisciplinary group and stood en masse as the foun-
tainhead of learning and inspiration. Homer knew this and as usual
was cleverer than his imitators when he sought the aid of all of them
at once.

For this monstrous task their heritage was suitable: Zeus, the
protector of laws and morals (in his fashion), Power personified, and
Mnemosyne, Memory. It is a good combination to back up learning or
teaching. But no place do I find them concerned with "education." No
chatter about it, no systems promulgated, no commitments to all men.
Their teaching was properly done through powers of inspiration, and
the student-author was free to draw upon their knowledge for his own
purposes. No institutionalized education for the Muses; they were entirely too bright to have fallen into the trap in which we find ourselves.

The word "education" should never have been invented. Then people would not be confused about its meaning, its origin or its use. If
its invention could not be prevented, at least it might have been circumscribed, limited in functions, and not given such a broad mandate
and domain from which to build a huge establishment, an industry. If
learning could have stayed on a porch, under a tree, at a banquet or
in a museum, the world would be a much happier place.

Degrees and certification stamps would not exist, and it would not
be necessary to argue over granting them at birth, so people could get
on about the business of learning. Thirty or forty children would not
be placed in a box with one teacher for a school year. Students would
not be consigned to four years in this level and four in that. In short,
defenseless formulas would not have been devised to please educators'
tastes in structure. It is true that many millions of people would be out
of work, which would aggravate the unemployment rate, but then the
displaced might start learning again, and they might even find some
new answers to old embattled questions, such as how man learns, and
what is really important to know and why.

Perhaps the rigid, quantitative structure was designed to hide the
vacuum inside. If a person does not know what he is doing, it is best to
close the door and keep quiet about it—a protective instinct. Who
wants the world to view the emptiness? If at the same time the operation multiplies and grows, progress is assumed, and size alone upholds
the effort. With extensive public relations to sell the product education, the clients come in larger and larger numbers and the rooms
within the spreading superstructure at least are occupied. But the good
intentions of the people in the rooms do not compensate for a mess of
pottage.

Doubtless a long series of small-minded decisions in the past shaped the present for our generation. Now we are confronted with a huge industry, a conglomerate operating in untold quantities of training areas, inviting unlimited numbers of people to partake of educational fare and charged by society to solve the problems of mankind. The mind boggles at the scope and complexity of the venture into education in the short two hundred years of United States history.

In the early days of our democracy education was the unsung handmaiden. The Constitution and Bill of Rights do not mention it or guarantee an education for all in whatever pursuit. It is not a right like life, liberty and the pursuit of happiness. The documents do not prescribe the means to attain those remarkable goals; they simply put the safeguards on life and liberty insofar as judicial procedures can guarantee them. One is on his own in the pursuit of happiness. If learning emerges as part or all of the pursuit for some of us, then we are free to attempt it, indulge in it, and find joy, even real happiness.

Following the egalitarian principle in democracy, however, since learning was a *privilege* it perforce had to be available to everyone. (And of course, practically speaking, literacy is necessary for a person casting a ballot equal to any other. He had better be able to read and, it is hoped, understand the issue or what the person he is about to elect stands for.) In rapid succession land-grant colleges appeared— taxpayers' money was used to educate for agricultural development— and great state universities emerged. Schooling was legislated for everyone to the age of sixteen. Community colleges added two more years. Mass education moved on to open admission, and today's target is "universal access" to higher education in a "lifelong learning" society. Higher education has become a civil right in people's minds rather than a privilege.

Today's catchwords—universal access and lifelong learning—are silly if not dangerous. Naturally learning goes on for one's life and always has, but those who use the phrase seem to mean that one should go to school at any time in life. That is all right too, if there is a reason. It is sensible to study in or out of school when motivated. So all "lifelong learning" boils down to is that adults should realize they could go to school, and schools should welcome them in more than extension courses. Not very revolutionary unless all adults do it. I am more concerned about universal access, which is certainly a noble idea but a very tall order indeed. Universal, I presume, includes all countries of this world as well as all people. And when I remember that some of them have 80 percent or more of the population illiterate and some have $100 as the per capita annual income, universal access to higher liberal education seems light years away. It may be a false and hollow promise, premature to say the least, and dangerous in raising high expectations that cannot be satisfied.

Both phrases, however, suggest that more and more people should be educated, and at any time in life and any place in the world. The civil right has again been extended: it is a human right beyond the borders of one nation. Now it is the domain of the United Nations (whose Charter, however, does not guarantee it).

What is not sufficiently recognized is each man's responsibility for his own learning and the indisputable fact that one's own learning cannot be given to another. My quarrel is that education seems to operate on the theory that learning *can* be given, and the populace has agreed. So the education industry has mushroomed. It has made a travesty of learning.

An Age of Academic Credit and Credentials (AACC) has been inaugurated with the mass production of courses on any conceivable and many incredible topics. Students expect academic credit for the search for self-identity: there are courses on becoming oneself and how to get along with others. Or, if I want to be creative, you teach me self-expression and creativity. It is latent in me; all you have to do is make it blossom. The apprenticeship is seldom found, and hard, patient, self-critical work is too tiresome. Experience as a way of learning has been superseded by teaching. Credit is awarded for living. We are in the absurd position of teaching people to grow up and rewarding them for being alive. In a society where God is lost, if not dead, people in delirium have turned to degrees.

Universities grant certificates to teachers for taking remedial courses. Institutes promise ever more certificates and—it is true— ombudsmen are trained to "ombuds." Yet such a plethora of paper certificates is patently questionable in value and quality and the recipients may well be deluded. But then, that is also true of the recipients of regular degrees: for many, certificates and degrees on paper have signified money in the bank. When college degrees became a symbol of economic worth, it was the most insidious of all invasions into the purposes of learning. Nevertheless, there it is, and those with more credentials recorded in institutional vaults have, in fact, often been monetarily rewarded and moved up the social scale.

Within the last few years, however, a cataclysmic change has occurred, reversing both trends and results. The social and economic upheaval has hit colleges and universities hard and caused society to re-evaluate its belief in education. A recent front-page story in *The New York Times* announced solemnly that the value of a college degree was declining. The lead sentence:

After generations during which going to college was assumed to be a sure route to the better life, college-educated Americans are losing their economic advantage over those less educated and the value of college as a guarantee of upward social mobility is slipping.[2]

The rate of return on the college investment has fallen dramatically, as a result of the shrinking job market, lower starting salaries and higher costs in tuition and fees. Failure of the economy to expand and provide higher-paying jobs for the increasing numbers of graduates is cited as the root cause. Professional and managerial jobs have begun to level off as a percentage of all jobs.

The *Times* story implies that fewer young people may seek higher education: what is the point of it in time and money if a better position is not awaiting them? The dividend is insufficient. But if this really is the reason that many will not seek advanced education, it is all to the good. For this reason alone, they should not have been there in the first place, and their leaving may help to clean out the ranks for those seeking serious study.

A study makes it official, but the *Times* report only reaffirms what we already know. For at least two years graduates have let us know that they were floundering in a jobless market, and college enrollments generally have been declining. Questioning the value of higher education is now more than parlor conversation: it has reached the masses. In fact, for some time it has been clear that society's faith in more and more education is waning. In many different parts of the country, voters have rejected bond issues for education. Distrust was reinforced by university students' behavior in riots and violent action. Thus the ivory shell has cracked, and public confidence that education would make the world a better place and solve man's many problems has been deeply shaken. The education establishment has felt the results.

Higher education has been caught in a sprawling state of overexpansion, overextended in staff, programs, courses and purposes. Multi-universities embraced additional institutions and added to their purposes, often forgetting what they were all about. Learning and teaching often disappeared in an intricate web of "activities," and odd equations took over, such as the fact that the better known a teacher was off campus, the less he encountered students on campus and taught.

---

2. *The New York Times*, August 14, 1975, pp. 1, 29. The article reports on a study made by Richard Freedman and J. Herbert Hollomon of Harvard University and Massachusetts Institute of Technology, respectively. Another article on the study appeared in the September issue of *Change* magazine, and the full findings will appear in a book, *The Overeducated American*, to be published in 1976 by Harcourt Brace Jovanovich, Inc.

The disease was infectious; students, too, found more to interest and reward them off campus than on. Drugs were more exhilarating and exciting than learning, to march for politics more interesting than to study, and so the spiral spun outward.

Basic purposes were overridden, and institutions sought economic gain, if not survival, in new programs to attract paying customers. Often this was justified as a means of supporting the "heart" of the institution, the liberal arts college for undergraduates, but they were truly forgotten men and women. The language of business became the talk of the educational marketplace. And business practices, management systems and flow charts emanated from administrators' offices. "Accountability" swept the campuses like a strong wind from nearby industry. When the dust settled, procedures were tighter, time was enthroned, numbers were basic, and teacher-student ratios established in every standardized classroom.

If we are not doomed, the present adversity could lead to a cleaning of our house. With fewer dollars and fewer full-time students, especially omitting those who came for the wrong reasons, we could shuffle about and set it in order. Adversity can sharpen analysis, embolden decisions and gird the loins of those who must say yea or nay. Necessary financial cutbacks could force us to slough off nonessentials. Teachers could devote themselves to students and return the focus to teaching—away from the numbers game of the educational entrepreneurs. Achieving these results, however, short of razing the gigantic educational structure and making a fresh start (highly desirable but hardly apt to happen), will confront us with hard decisions that involve many people and therefore the gaping need for strong, enlightened leadership.

Assume for the moment there is a philosopher unafraid of playing king, and make him temporary president of your institution. Then take a negative approach and state clearly what this particular college does *not* offer. This is a method of cleansing the stables, if not the college catalogue, and it is a Herculean task. You might say, for example: "Do not come here for poverty, chastity or obedience. This place opposes the rules of monasteries and convents. But you cannot enter unless endowed by nature with intelligence and gentleness of spirit, and possessed by a well-tried desire to enjoy our fine library, filled with the works of the humanists."

Next, see that the purposes of the institution are openly stated, so no student can claim false promises, and each knows what to expect. As in Rabelais's Abbey of Thélème, publish clearly the rule by which the community will live: "Do as Thou Wilt"—a perfectly safe rule when there are highly selective admissions procedures which require evidence of achievement and motivation before a student is accepted.

Some will violently disagree with the Abbey's purposes, but there they are, spelled out. The example serves: decide and state publicly what the purposes of the institution are. It is the first step toward cleaning up the educational mess, and it is the first step toward differentiation of institutions. Label the package as clearly as if the Pure Food and Drug Act were in effect for education.

And make no apologies to Harvard for all the programs you do not offer. Entirely too many liberal arts colleges and universities have imitated the master to their own detriment. Instead of doing a good job within recognized limits, they ape a model that has its own peculiar history and reasons for being as it is. Similarly, the liberal arts college too often wants to act like a big university and offer graduate degrees, which invariably distorts its focus on undergraduates, drains funds, and leads to second-rate, debased degrees. Worse still, the faculty congratulate themselves on achieving the higher realm of esoteric thought with graduate students and have an inflated sense of their own importance.

Even when clarified and limited by the negative approach, purposes, especially for a liberal arts college, are difficult to explain because the explanations are always attempts to define the indefinable— the immeasurable qualities and abilities that one hopes a successful learning experience will produce. It should be enough simply to say:

> The purpose here is to learn. These are the subjects in which we offer the assistance of teachers, the library and laboratories. Study at your own risk; the college takes no responsibility for the outcome. There is no graduation from this institution because it would mislead you into thinking you had finished learning, whereas you would only have obtained the tools and made a beginning. You may study for as long or short a time as you wish.

That is the catalogue I would like to read and the college I would like to attend. Then in my curriculum vitae years later, I would write: "Attended Ideal College," and simply give the dates.

In that place there existed a group of extraordinary teachers, whom I could find in their offices, which were lovely, quiet, book-filled rooms with a table for papers and comfortable chairs to encourage prolonged thought and conversation—not fast answers from a row of chairs designed for torture and discomfort. There were paintings on walls done in handsome colors, not uniform, hospital beige walls.

The teachers were doctors of learning and students of knowledge. They admitted they learned from students and their own lectures. For them, teaching was not a frontal attack on the less privileged. When I asked one teacher what teaching was, he replied:

> Teaching involves emotions, which cannot be systematically appraised and employed, and human values. . . . "Scientific" teaching, even of scientific subjects, will be inadequate as long as both teachers and pupils are human beings. Teaching is not like inducing a chemical reaction: it is much more like painting a picture or making a piece of music, or on a lower level like planting a garden or writing a friendly letter. You must throw your heart into it, and must realize that it cannot all be done by formulas, or you will spoil your work, and your pupils, and yourself.[3]

I watched the teacher and felt the truth of his statement. Then I asked another the same question. He answered slowly:

> The responsibility of the teacher is so great that a full vision of it can be crushing. He has persons in his charge. The fact should sober him: but he hears in addition that he is responsible for the entire society which these persons represent. The size of the assignment suggests that only madmen would dare to accept it. . . . But it is not as serious as all that. The teacher needs only to remember that he is neither deity nor engine; he is a man, and in proportion as he succeeds at his calling he will be surrounded by more men. He and they are society.[4]

At that point, one of his colleagues joined us (this was a genuine community of scholars) and led the discussion on to *thinking*, as a fitful, incoherent activity, seldom understood, yet vital to the search for knowledge:

> Thinking is messy, repetitious, silly, obtuse, subject to explosions that shatter the crucible and leave darkness behind. Then comes another flash, a new path is seen, trod, lost, broken off, and blazed anew. It leaves the thinker dizzy as well as doubtful: he does not know what he thinks until he has thought it, or better, until he has written and riddled it with a persistence akin to obsession.
>
> Young scholars should believe all this if only in order to overcome their too frequent discouragement at the sight of their first drafts. Too much has been talked about "cold reason" and "orderly processes of mind." . . . The momentary glimpse that shows a relation, a truth, or a method of proof does not come at will. It is watched for like big game, and only when captured and tamed with others like it

---

3. Gilbert Highet, *The Art of Teaching* (New York: Vintage Books, 1961), pp. vii–viii.

4. Mark Van Doren, *Liberal Education* (New York: Henry Holt, 1943), pp. 169–170.

can it be shown off in orderly sequence. All this is unanalyzable interior work. Men of science who feel free to look into themselves and report what they see admit the same thing. "How did you get *that?*" I heard someone ask of a Nobel Prize winner. "I got it by intestinal fiat," was the reply.[5]

It was important to me to learn how these teachers viewed knowledge, its meaning beyond their own special interests, and what a combination of facts in various fields should mean. What was it all about, and what was wrong with our approach? Why could not more people enjoy this talk with us? I put these questions to a man of science, and he said:

> There is only one subject-matter for education, and that is Life in all its manifestations. Instead of this single unity, we offer children— Algebra, from which nothing follows; Geometry, from which nothing follows; Science, from which nothing follows; History . . . a Couple of Languages, never mastered; and lastly, most dreary of all, Literature, represented by the plays of Shakespeare, with philological notes and short analyses of plot and character to be in substance committed to memory. Can such a list be said to represent Life, as it is known in the midst of living it? The best that can be said of it is, that it is a rapid table of contents which a deity might run over in his mind while he was thinking of creating a world, and has not yet determined how to put it together.[6]

So I learned from wise men as well as by myself and for my own pleasure. I argued with Rabelais, took off in flight with Galileo, admired Montaigne until his digressions annoyed me, found Bacon's lucidity splendid but eventually boring; Plato held up better, partly because he was sufficiently vague to support several interpretations; and on I went through many minds. Anyone who says he knows a thing, I learned to doubt and cross-examine. What more can one ask from learning? I shall never get to the end of it.

That is what we should be asking of education for our people. "But nothing is harder to bear than the contrast between what is and what might be."[7] Let us call again upon the Muses. It will take all of them together, their favorite Apollo, and father Zeus as well, to bring us back to our senses.

---

5. Jacques Barzun, *Teacher in America* (Boston: Little, Brown, 1945), p. 307.
6. Alfred North Whitehead, *The Aims of Education* (New York: Macmillan, 1967), pp. 6–7.
7. Jacques Barzun, "The State of Culture Today," in John A. Garraty and Peter Gay, eds., *The Columbia History of the World* (New York: Harper & Row, 1972), p. 1,157.

STEVEN MARCUS

Some Questions in General Education Today

Where are the snows of yesteryear;
or, Is there a light at the bottom of the barrel?

"From a distance the academic grove looks remarkably like Chaos
and Old Night."

JACQUES BARZUN, *Teacher in America*

⌐§

When I was a very young man I read *Teacher in America*. It was—
and remains—a bold, outspoken and confident book, and I read it with
interest, pleasure and considerable excitement. As I recall it now, it
was one of the experiences that influenced me in choosing a vocation.
To put it more precisely, it was one of the experiences that led me to
hope that I might be chosen for a vocation. For whatever the academic
grove might have looked like from a distance, it looked different when
it was seen from the inside. And, the book went on to say, "Happily
there is something stable and clear and useful behind this phantasmagoria of Education—the nature of subject matter and the practice of
teaching." Nevertheless, in the course of its argument, *Teacher in
America* did in fact address itself to questions of education—and particularly to questions of general education in the humanities—and it
found and put forward sturdy if provisional answers to a number of
those questions.

The answers were provisional because they were in the nature of
the case bound to be. If Jacques Barzun, or anyone else, had really
known the answers to such questions, he would certainly not have
been here. He would have been in heaven, along with the sages and
patriarchs who have debated over such matters in our civilization for
the last two and a half millennia. Yet the answers he offered on that
occasion were also sturdy, and they were put with appreciable verve

and force. That was thirty years ago, a historical moment of hopeful expectancy and opportunity, and an appropriate moment at which to ask such questions and venture such answers.

By the same token there may also occur moments when we put such questions to ourselves largely because our ability to approximate formulations that even remotely resemble satisfactory—if temporary—answers is suspiciously low. I expect that this may be such a time. The topic as a whole therefore solicits in me an impulse to try to find and focus attention upon what I take to be one source of the particular feebleness and absence of self-confidence that I sense everywhere about us nowadays. And the topic, properly understood, also directs us to the right place. Although research and graduate study have their share of problems and vexations, the primary troubles are not to be located there, but in undergraduate education. And as with almost all things academic, these troubles are both real enough in themselves and symptomatic of other, probably wider developments. What seems to have happened is that the idea of liberal or general education has expired.[1] It died without anybody killing it, and so it may be said to have died a natural death.

Due exception may be taken to this general statement—which I offer of course only as a hypothesis. Certain undergraduate institutions may be pointed to in which liberal or general education continues to be pursued in a state of rude and vigorous health. That may be true, but it doesn't seem to me to be generally true; moreover, it doesn't seem to me to be generally true of the better or élite undergraduate institutions either, so that we cannot limit or define the situation by such conventional means as stratification. Another objection to my assertion may be voiced in the counterstatement that just as there are no new ideas in education, so too no educational idea ever perishes. It merely leaves the scene for a while and sooner or later reappears in a new guise or costume. This is received wisdom, the lore of our craft or mystery, and we should pay it the regard that its venerable condition

---

1. When I use the term "general" or "liberal education" in this text, I am referring, I realize, to a wide array of phenomena. I am aware of the heterogeneity of kinds of undergraduate programs, how they differ at different levels of the American system of higher education, and how each of them has changed internally over periods of time. Nevertheless, I believe it warranted and useful to discuss the matter as a whole. What I am referring to is *not* any particular program but a series of ideas that have had to do with undergraduate education, and in particular with the first two years of that education. The ideas in question have had to do with certain kinds of study that were not directly connected with pre-professional or pre-technical training, although they were not incompatible with such training. They were also not directly connected with a system of majors, although again they were not incompatible with such a system or systems.

merits. It may be that the eclipse of liberal or general education—and what is equally important, the belief in it—is only temporary, and that if we are patient and bide our time and attend to our duties it will make an appropriate reappearance among us. That may be true. But it is also true that real changes occur, that we live in real time, that cultures and societies and institutions actually alter and develop, and that these alterations and developments have consequences. I will therefore adhere to my hypothesis in a modified form, and say that, in America today, liberal or general education, if it is not extinct, is in a state of decline, that its vital signs are not encouraging, and that it isn't certain that intensive care is going to assist it to survive—or that we know what such survival might entail.

If we mount an inquiry to determine how this state of affairs has come about, there are any number of circumstances, moments of time, occasions and places that may be chosen as points of departure. Unless one goes back at least as far as the *Meno*, there will be something arbitrary in any one choice—as indeed there is something arbitrary in going back as far as the *Meno*. The point of departure that I shall choose, the occasion that seems to me diagnostic, is the first great debate in the modern era that set the tone and framed the terms for much future discussion. I am referring to the spirited exchange that took place in the early 1880s between T. H. Huxley and Matthew Arnold.

In 1880 Huxley delivered an address at the opening of Sir Josiah Mason's Science College at Birmingham. It was printed in 1881 under the title "Science and Culture." In this essay, Huxley attacks with good reason the standard classical education of the period and argues for the intellectual and cultural relevance of the study of science. (He does not of course neglect to mention its practical usefulness as well.) In the spirit of *laissez-faire*, he goes out of his way to deflate "the pretensions of our modern Humanists to the possession of the monopoly of culture," and in a related context in the same essay stigmatizes such humanists as "monopolists of liberal education." In addition to the study of science, he argues for the cultural value of the study of modern languages and literature, and ends with the firm recommendation that the study of Sociology should also be a central part of any first-rate program of education—thereby foreseeing and predicting in one short essay what has become the conventional tripartite disciplinary structure of the modern university.

Although the deadheads of classical education were the chief (and easy) objects of Huxley's attack, he did not stop with them. And at a number of moments he goes out of his way to take aim at the most eminent and high-minded of the apostles of culture of the period. Huxley observes that although it would be mistaken to identify Arnold's opinions with those of the hidebound classical dons and schoolmasters, "yet one may cull from one or another of those epistles to the Philistines, which so much delight all who do not answer to the name, sentences which lend them [i.e., the opinions of the hidebound] some support." And he proceeds to cull.

Arnold was prompt to reply. His famous essay, "Literature and Science," was first delivered as the Rede Lecture at Cambridge University and was then published in the *Nineteenth Century* in 1882. (He subsequently revised it considerably and delivered it as a lecture during his American tour of 1883–84, publishing it in this form in 1885 in the volume *Discourses in America*.) Arnold proceeds according to his custom to take the very highest line. As for the aims of education and "the motives that should govern us in the choice of studies," he does in fact go right back to Plato—significantly, however, not to the *Meno* but to the *Republic*, from which he takes the following sentence: "An intelligent man will prize those studies which result in his soul getting soberness, righteousness, and wisdom, and will less value others." He assumes that there is a consensus on this definition and that it applies universally, "whether we are preparing ourselves for a hereditary seat in the English House of Lords or for the pork trade in Chicago." The line of argument he is going to follow, he characteristically remarks, is "extremely simple." His defense of the primacy of humanistic education is based on something as simple as "the constitution of human nature," and "the instinct of self-preservation in humanity."

Arnold's argument, in brief, is as follows. The largest part of our ordinary or secular education consists in the building up in us of our capacities of intellect and knowledge. Yet we have other fundamental capacities and needs as well, and these have to do with conduct and with pleasure in the form of beauty. Out of these Arnold constructs a paradigm. "Following our instinct for intellect and knowledge," he writes, "we acquire pieces of knowledge; and presently, in the generality of men, there arises the desire to *relate* these pieces of knowledge to our sense for conduct, to our sense for beauty—and there is weariness and dissatisfaction if the desire is baulked" (italics mine). And he goes on to observe how "everyone knows how we seek naturally to combine the pieces of our knowledge together, to bring them under general rules, to relate them to principles; and how unsatisfactory and tiresome it would be to go on for ever learning bits of exceptions, or accumulating items of fact which must stand isolated." Science, for Arnold—however systematic it might be; and I think that Arnold had only a rudimentary awareness of the systematic character of science— remains in the realm of fact and knowledge. But literature—humanistic learning—takes such knowledge and puts it in relation to "our sense for conduct, [and] our sense for beauty." And it does so by reason of its "undeniable power of engaging the emotions," although Arnold is unable to give a precise account of how this comes about. Literature and humanistic study, Arnold continues, have "a fortifying, and elevating, and quickening, and suggestive power." They represent "the criticism of life by gifted men, alive and active with extraordinary power at an unusual number of points"—and they solicit an equal life and power in those who devote themselves to such studies. The effect of humane letters upon its students will be to "call out their being at more points"; indeed, such studies "will make them live more." Hence, he cheerfully concludes, "so long as human nature is what it is," the attractions of humanistic studies

> will remain irresistible. . . . And a poor humanist may possess his soul in patience . . . and still have a happy faith that the nature of things works silently on behalf of the studies which he loves, and that, while we shall all have to acquaint ourselves with the great results reached by modern science, and to give ourselves as much training in its disciplines as we can conveniently carry, yet the majority of men will always require humane letters; and so much the more, as they have the more and the greater results of science to relate to the need in man for conduct, and to the need in him for beauty.

On these grounds, he contends, humanistic studies in general and literature in particular will continue to occupy the center of education.

I do not think it is too much of an exaggeration to remark that there are those of us who were, so to speak, brought up on this essay— or on some modified version of it. To my mind it represents in nuclear form the idea or ideas that were or have been behind most schemes of general or liberal education, although these schemes themselves developed historically along a diversity of related lines.

If we ask ourselves what it is that Arnold is saying in this essay, or how we can translate his utterances into the terminology of contemporary critical discourse, we can derive a number of connected formulations. First, in insisting upon the powers to relate—or the relational powers—that he finds to be of central importance in humanistic education, Arnold is laying stress on what today would be called the integrative functions of such studies. These integrative functions are at work in a number of areas. They are at work in the different domains of knowledge itself, and Arnold regards the humanities as, among other things, functioning to integrate the various separate and vertically developed realms of intellect. Since all these domains and realms exist within living persons, Arnold also notes that humanistic education works to integrate us personally—that is, it answers our inherent needs for structure, wholeness and coherent generality of view. In addition, since all this is taking place in a world, Arnold regards such studies as having an integrative function socially as well; indeed, this complex notion is one of the principal explicit theses advanced in *Culture and Anarchy*.

I do not imagine that anyone will doubt that historically one of the chief and vital purposes of any established system of education has been the purpose of social integration. The ground of contestation in this matter has had to do with such questions as who is being integrated, by whom, by what means and to what ends. Education is, after all, one of the instruments or institutions through which societies and cultures reproduce themselves, and in this context one cannot separate for long the integrative functions of education from the socially reproductive ones. Further, social or cultural reproduction means or includes the reproduction over time of determinate structures, such as classes, élite groups, differential statuses, elaborate arrays of role relationships, and the like.

Second, Arnold singles out one specific form of integration as bearing special weight. What literary or humanistic studies tend to do, he remarks repeatedly, is to relate or integrate all our knowledge "to our sense for conduct, [and] to our sense for beauty." Such studies, in other words, bring knowledge, or knowledges, into integrated relation with certain values or groups of values—or, as we would say today, with certain systems of values. "Values" is a word that is much in currency these days—terms of this sort always tend to be when people or societies begin to become aware that they are living in the midst of a large historical crisis—and the coin has been accordingly both debased and inflated. It remains nonetheless true that Arnold has a point, if not the only point or the whole point or all the points. And it is equally true that some such idea is embedded somewhere in every scheme of liberal or general education.

Third, Arnold specifies the means by which humanistic education will effect this integration. It will do so, he asserts, by reason of the "undeniable power" possessed by humane letters "of engaging the emotions." The logic of this is that humanistic studies will function as religion once did but no longer can. Arnold is quite explicit on this score. "The Middle Age[s]," he replies to one of Huxley's charges, "could do without humane letters, as it could do without the study of nature, because its supposed knowledge was made to engage its emotions so powerfully." Modern science has exploded that supposed knowledge and all that it entailed—revealed religion, special creation, "God's in His heaven," have all become inaccessible and impossible. Only humane letters, only humanistic pursuits, have anything like the comparable power of engaging the emotions. Therefore, according to Arnold, the importance of such studies "in a man's training becomes not less, but greater, in proportion to the success of modern science in extirpating what it calls 'medieval thinking.' "

Arnold has been much chided for putting forth this view. And the chiding has come in from a variety of quarters. He has been accused of trying to sacralize what cannot be sacralized—hence of having committed heresy. (He was anticipated in this forward-looking deviation by Coleridge, who advocated his idea of a clerisy along similar lines.) He has also been charged with encouraging one kind of institution to do something for which it was not designed (at least in its modern forms), and to permit a displacement into it of functions that it cannot perform. In Arnold's scheme, liberal or humanistic education comes to suffer from what today we rather quaintly call functional overload. And our modern secular forms of liberal or general education have as a rule made a studious show of trying to avoid most of Arnold's terminology. Liberal education, for example, aimed to develop "the whole man." Or it was centrally concerned to develop our cognitive but non-quantitative competences in a range of disciplines. Or its primary purpose was to develop in undergraduates a variety of skills in different kinds of inquiry. Or, as it was touchingly put in a document that issued from my own institution, it was meant to "include all studies that contribute to the art of living, as distinct from the channeled preparation for making a living." Or its goal was to expand our cultural horizons, increase our sense of the options in life that are open to us, lead us toward some kind of autonomy. Or its purpose was to develop in us the capacity to appreciate different kinds of experiences and to recognize empathetically in others who seem alien to us "centers of consciousness" as authentic and as human as our own. Or it sought to acquaint us with the canon, the great ideas and the great books, to help us to begin to know—to use a transportable phrase of Arnold's—the best which has been thought and said in the world. There was and there remains something admirable in all of these conceptual formulations and in the efforts and programs that accompanied them, however unevenly they may have each eventually fared. Nevertheless, I am convinced that as soon as we begin to press with moderate force on any one of these formulations, a residuum of Arnold's view pops up. To be sure, that view is more secularized than Arnold's; it tends to be held with greater tentativeness; it is diffuse and sometimes attenuated; when it is articulated it is *sotto voce;* and it is indeed a residuum. Still, it is there, and importantly there.[2] As long as we are talking about that part of organized higher education that is not professional or pre-professional or vocational training, I don't see how it can be avoided. Nor do I think it should be. How it is to be confronted is another matter again.

Finally, there is a fourth connected consideration. This takes the form of a conviction that is both a precondition and a consequence of everything else that Arnold has said, and he puts it out front. Today that conviction, when it is held at all, is held covertly and in silence. It is to be found in the sentence which Arnold annexes from the *Republic*. " 'An intelligent man,' says Pluto, 'will prize those studies which result in his soul getting soberness, righteousness, and wisdom, and will less value the others.' " In other words, there is a moral idea behind it all, a belief in the moral efficacy of education. This belief can be and has been articulated in a diversity of forms. A liberal education, it was said, would make better men or citizens of us. Or, it was once believed, reading good books was good for one's character. Or, it was in part conceded, if virtue could not be taught it could at least be learned. Or, to put it in the idiom of the rationalist-utilitarian mode, education will lead toward the promotion of a better life on earth; it will do so by leading us toward becoming more rational and therefore more wise, more just, more virtuous and more happy than we were before. This idea, I have said, is a moral idea or belief. It is in fact a matter of faith and an article of faith. And it is this faith—I have been implying all along—that is passing, if it has not already been extinguished.

If we ask why this faith is failing, any number of explanations spring quickly to hand. (I am assuming, of course, that there can be no single explanation that is satisfactory for a cultural situation so complex and overdetermined.) For example, it will be said that no one who has lived through the experiences of the twentieth century, and who has learned that an appreciation of Goethe's poetry is by no

---

2. Consider, for example, this passage from the famous Harvard report, *General Education in a Free Society*: "There is doubtless a sense in which religious education, education in the great books, and education in modern democracy may be mutually exclusive. But there is a far more important sense in which they work together to the same end, which is belief in the idea of man and society that we cherish, adapt and pass on."

means incompatible with a predilection for lampshades made out of human skin, is likely henceforth to place much faith in the moral efficacy of humanistic education. A similar observation may be made about what is probably the most important movement in architecture and design in our century, the movement known as the *Bauhaus*. The ideal that directed the practice of this group was that social conduct could be improved and rectified by having it take place within an environmental system of design that was total, rational, pleasant and humane. I have recently read an article characterizing this ideal as a heroic illusion, an *ignis fatuus* of avant-garde thought. And the commentator went on to remark that in any case "no one really becomes less wicked or more rational by living in an International Style building." There is certainly some truth in these observations, but they do not seem to me to account adequately or in themselves for what I have referred to as a failure of faith. After all, history is replete with instances of people continuing to hold faith in ideas and ideals in the face of mountains of disconfirming evidence and disillusioning experience. That's what faith is for—ask any Marxist.

There is another way of coming at these problematical circumstances. At one point in "Science and Culture," Huxley singles out a passage from Arnold as demanding special attention. It comes from Arnold's great essay, "The Function of Criticism at the Present Time," and is one of those many passages in Arnold in which he tries momentarily to define his general position—many and momentarily because Arnold's general position was by intention and necessity insusceptible of being unitarily defined. The kind of culture and the kind of criticism that he is advocating, Arnold writes,

> is a criticism which regards Europe as being, for intellectual and spiritual purposes, one great confederation, bound to a joint action and working to a common result; and whose numbers have, for their proper outfit, a knowledge of Greek, Roman, and Eastern antiquity, and of one another. Special, local, and temporary advantages being put out of account, that modern nation will in the intellectual and spiritual sphere make most progress, which most thoroughly carries out this program. And what is that but saying that we too, all of us, as individuals, the more thoroughly we carry it out, shall make the more progress?

Huxley reproves Arnold for his apparent neglect in this passage of the claims of the modern, and in "Literature and Science" Arnold handily defends himself and convincingly demonstrates that in actuality he meant no such thing.

"The Function of Criticism at the Present Time" was written in

1864, and is almost certainly the most important document of its kind in English written during the latter part of the nineteenth century. Some fifty years later, in "Tradition and the Individual Talent," an essay of comparable importance for the modern period, T. S. Eliot undertook to restate Arnold's notion from a historically altered perspective. His notion of the modern, Eliot argues, was compounded in considerable measure out of an awareness of and a grasp upon tradition. Tradition, however, is not according to Eliot something that can be inherited. Quite the opposite, he asserts: if you want tradition,

> you must obtain it by great labor. It involves, in the first place, the historical sense, which we may call nearly indispensable to anyone who would continue to be a poet beyond his twenty-fifth year; and the historical sense involves a perception, not only of the pastness of the past, but of its presence; the historical sense compels a man to write not merely with his own generation in his bones, but with a feeling that the whole of the literature of Europe from Homer and within it the whole of the literature of his own country has a simultaneous existence and composes a simultaneous order.

This complex historical sense, he goes on to argue, is what makes a writer—particularly a Modernist writer—simultaneously traditional and acutely conscious of his own contemporaneity, difference and uniqueness. When a new work of art or a new cultural creation occurs, Eliot continues, something happens simultaneously to everything that has gone before.

> The existing monuments form an ideal order among themselves, which is modified by the introduction of the new (the really new) work of art among them. The existing order is complete before the new work arrives; for order to persist after the supervention of novelty, the *whole* existing order must be, if ever so slightly, altered; and so the relations, proportions, values of each work of art toward the whole are readjusted; and this is conformity between the old and the new. Whoever has approved this idea of order, of the form of European, of English literature will not find it preposterous that the past should be altered by the present as much as the present is directed by the past.

Prepared by his earlier academic pursuits with a knowledge of Hegel, in part via F. H. Bradley, Eliot is writing with greater theoretical certitude and penetration than Arnold; yet the major point that both are making remains remarkably the same. Eliot, the chief architect in English poetry and literary criticism of that radical movement of departure in culture known as Modernism, is arguing precisely that part of the continuity of tradition is also to be found in the radical breaks and discontinuities within it. Moreover, Eliot is right; for when we look back from the vantage point of the present upon that great cultural movement that is widely and sometimes loosely known as Modernism, we see two things. We see the movement as a whole tending self-consciously to represent itself as radically breaking with the past, as indeed it often did. But we now can see as well—as Eliot warned us we should see—the deep continuities that existed between the chief creative figures of Modernism and the great creative figures who were their predecessors; these continuities were at first invisible to most—so powerful was the impression of newness that the Modernists initially made.

Eliot therefore seems to me to hold firm theoretically, and this holding extends back to and includes Arnold. Yet something else has to be noted as well. Although Eliot, and the passages in question, may hold theoretically, they do not, in my judgment, continue to hold experientially or existentially. Those passages could not, I believe, be written today—nor could anything resembling them in tone. They breathe a self-assurance, a confidence of historical location, and a consciousness of intellectual centrality (even though they were written in the midst of the First World War) that one could not possibly hope to find today. Once again more interpretations of this circumstance are at our disposal than can be possibly brought forward on the present occasion. For example, Eliot is writing in England and from the point of view of a society in which the literary culture had achieved an ascendancy that it never did in America. In addition, since the time in which Eliot wrote, vast changes of every kind have occurred. We all know what some of them are and what powerful influences they have exerted. They include changes in the structure of knowledge, changes in the structure of our institutions of higher education, and changes in the relations of those institutions to both society and culture, whose structures have themselves undergone significant alterations. Higher education at the great American institutions of learning, for instance, is no longer primarily concerned with its functions of integration and social reproduction—though those concerns do continue to persist, and those functions are attended to. The university and higher education as a whole have become auxiliary institutions of production. In this newly emerging context of the university as part of the system of production, the role of liberal or humanistic education becomes increasingly problematic. And we may well ask: What is the essential role of such an education in the production system of a technobureaucratic order whose dominant values are characteristically expressed in forms of utilities and commodities? What is the essential or overriding role of such an education in the culture of such an order? The answers to such questions, I venture to suggest, appear to be about as forthcoming from humanists as the answers to the questions which have provoked these comments.[3]

Yet important and complex as all these circumstances undeniably are—each of them merits extended discussion—they do not, for me, represent by themselves the decisive influences that are involved in the failure of faith, the failure of belief, in the moral efficacy of liberal education that I have been referring to. Perhaps nothing in such an enormous context is decisive, but I should like in closing this section of comments to bring forward two further considerations. When Arnold speaks of "Europe as being, for intellectual and spiritual purposes, one great federation, bound to a joint action and working to a common result," and when Eliot speaks of the poet writing "not merely with his own generation in his bones, but with a feeling that the whole of the literature of Europe from Homer and within it the whole of the literature of his own country has a simultaneous existence and composes a simultaneous order," they are both expressing and referring to an assumption that they hold in common. This assumption has to do with an essentially unquestioned assurance about the hegemony of European culture. In the interval between Eliot's essay and the present that hegemony has been lost. The cultural world that we live in today is presided over by hegemonic powers that are not European in the sense referred to by Arnold or Eliot.[1]

---

3. Let me add parenthetically, however, that efforts are characteristically being made in certain quarters to devise answers. For example, one noted economist has recently written about the pertinent matter of *efficiency* in higher education. "Efficiency in any human endeavor," he writes, "involves a relationship between means and ends. Efficiency is maximised when the end is achieved to the greatest degree possible with given means." In the case "of higher education . . . the ends are multiple . . . [and] include change in people in the form of enlightenment, motivation, values, sensitivity, and effectiveness." Since the means are "labor and capital acquired with money," once we have clearly defined the ends, namely, "enlightenment, motivation, values, sensitivity and effectiveness," we can make a "careful examination . . . from the point of view of cost-effectiveness" to determine whether the means at hand are efficiently producing the ends desired. *There* you have an answer, and the answer in both form and substance is perfectly congruent with the values that are dominant in a technobureaucratic order. That humanists will deny that it represents a valid answer, that it is in fact an evasion rather than an answer, is not, I am afraid, entirely to the point. But this raises another range of questions altogether.

4. We can find an epitome of this superseded hegemonic view in one of Gladstone's utterances. In 1898, the last year of his life, he told Sir Edward Hamilton that he would be perfectly content to stand alone, against the entire world, in defense of the principle that the nations of Europe were a community designed by God to uphold the highest standards of civilization.

The last form in which the hegemony of European culture realized itself is what is known in Europe as bourgeois culture. In America we call and called its equivalent high culture, though they aren't
quite the same thing. And, as I have recently noted elsewhere, what
we have begun to be aware of is that the Modernist movements in art
and thought—now that they are defunct—seem to have been the final
phases of bourgeois or high culture. (It is worth noting in this context
that the Modernist movements were also essentially European in inspiration and composition, although Americans did make significant
contributions to them.) And they were never more so than when they
were most adversary, critical, apparently subversive and élitist—obscure, hieratic, mystagogical, outrageous. They were the positive fruits
of that culture, even when and especially when they were negating it.
Indeed, one can say that at its greatest moments middle-class—or
bourgeois—culture was able to conceive of its own transcendence or
self-transcendence. I am referring to the development and elaboration
on the one hand of the idea of Socialism and on the other of the great
and multifarious projects of Modernist thought and art.

What has occurred since is something else again. When a phase
of culture comes to an end or to a kind of end, it does not simply disappear and leave not a wrack behind. What it usually does is go into
a state of decomposition. It is that state that we are passing through
now. We are, I believe, in the midst of the beginning of the decomposition of bourgeois culture, or of high culture, or whatever it is that
we want to call that phase of culture that accompanied the development of capitalism—industrial and then advanced capitalism—in the
West until 1950 or thereabouts. Since then, as the Modernist phase of
culture began to decompose, what we have been witness to is the increasingly rapid diffusion of the decomposed elements of Modernism
through the larger culture and society. This diffusion has been made
possible by the technologies of mass production and mass consumption characteristic of advanced industrial society. The agent of the
process has been what is known as the culture industry, those large
institutions in modern society which are devoted to the industrial production of culture for mass consumption. The culture industry was
and remains the chief conduit for the further and continuing diffusion
of debased fragments and decomposed remnants of what was once a
great if corrupt bourgeois-modern social and cultural tradition.

In a number of surprising ways, the idea of liberal or general
undergraduate education was in part an analogue (or even at some
moments an expression) within the university system of this last phase
of bourgeois culture. Originally, of course, it functioned to reproduce

a social-cultural élite. And like Modernism, it had a frankly élitist conception of knowledge. Yet it was at its best a liberal élitism, and proposed the possibility that higher education had other purposes than turning out functionaries who would serve the institutional needs of the social world as it exists. Located at the very center of society, it nevertheless provided enough space for young men and women to turn about in and question the dominant social and cultural values of the world they were being prepared to enter. Within this space it was possible to cultivate a spirit of critical inquiry and to begin to imagine a different future. The ambiguities and contradictions of both bourgeois culture and its Modernist phase were reproduced in the ambiguities and contradictions of liberal undergraduate education. On the one hand, it could train and turn out an intellectual and social élite which could be as arrogant and unfeeling as any of the élites that were its predecessors—and at times it did so. On the other, it could stimulate and promote a spirit of critical and intellectual inquiry and of critical doubt of a kind that did not in America previously exist—and at times it did this too. At its best it supported a notion of autonomy, of rigorous intellectual effort which was not in the service of inequities, however stringent and élitist its standards of judgment might be.

I have been suggesting that the failure of faith in the moral efficacy of liberal education, the decline of liberal undergraduate education, and the beginnings of the decomposition of bourgeois culture are entailed in one another. The entailment is complex, and I do not want to propose simple causal sequences or priorities. Nor do I want to rule out influences and developments of other orders and of equal importance—such as those that have to do with economics, social structure and the structure of knowledge. What I want to do is begin to identify a particular historical nexus. This activity should not be construed as a lament for what seems at the moment irretrievably gone; it is not intended to be a swan song for a culture that almost no one of high intelligence was really happy with when it was around; and it will not, I hope, be heard as the disconsolate hooting of the Owl of Minerva, as the world outstrips the thought of the world and passes it by. It is an effort of self-clarification and illumination, an effort that is peculiarly appropriate to the humanistic tradition, whose efforts are always in some part propaedeutic. They are, I would hope, propaedeutic to the answers that others will be able to propose to the questions originally asked.

But I do not want to close this part of my comments on so flat or solemn a note. Let me conclude it therefore by quoting a favorite passage. It comes from the greatest of bourgeois social philosophers, a sometime humanist, and the prophet of doom upon the society and culture out of which he arose and whose nature found idiosyncratic expression in him.

> The ancient conception, in which man always appears (in however narrowly national, religious or political a definition) as the aim of production, seems very much more exalted when contrasted with the modern world, in which production is the aim of man and wealth the aim of production. In fact, however, when the narrow bourgeois form has been peeled away, what is wealth if not the universality of individual needs, capacities, enjoyments, productive powers, etc., created through universal exchange? What, if not the full development of human mastery over the forces of nature—those of humanity's own nature as well as those of so-called "nature." What, if not the absolute working-out of his creative dispositions, without any preconditions other than antecedent historical evolution—i.e. the evolution of all human powers as such, unmeasured by any *previously established* [or predetermined] yardsticks—an end in itself? What is this, if not a situation when man does not reproduce himself in any one determined form, but produces his totality? When he does not strive to remain something formed by the past, and that he has become, but is in the absolute movement of becoming? In bourgeois political economy—and in the epoch of production to which it corresponds—the complete working-out of what lies within man appears as a complete emptying-out, this universal objectification as total alienation, and the destruction of all fixed one-sided purposes as the sacrifice of the human end-in-itself to a wholly external compulsion. Hence on one side the childlike world of the ancients appears to be superior; and this is so in all matters where closed shapes, forms and given limits are sought for. The ancients provide satisfaction from a narrow standpoint; whereas the modern world gives no satisfaction; or, where it appears to be satisfied with itself, it is *vulgar* and *mean.*

It was Marx's faith that even in this darkest hour of dehumanized existence, and even in this abyss of contradictions, mankind was nonetheless closer than it had ever been before to achieving the classical humanist ideal of free individual self-realization. He thought he knew what a good society was. I am not certain about how much thought he devoted to established educational structures. Had a good society, according to his lights, been really in the offing, I suspect he would have had something interesting to say about such structures.

If we turn for the moment from these theoretical considerations to matters of practical interest, to questions that involve possibilities of implementation—of implementing at least *something;* and as

Americans I don't see how we can in good conscience fail to do so—
I find myself drawn back once again to trying to compose what I
have to say from a historical perspective. What I want to suggest has
to do in the first instance with secondary education, and in the second
with dispelling a myth that currently seems to attach to the idea of it,
or to whatever it is supposed to fail to be. If we look back again to the
nineteenth century, one of the more striking things about the institutions of education in America was the weakness of secondary education. For example, as Christopher Jencks and David Riesman have
pointed out in *The Academic Revolution* (1968), in 1870 there were
only 7,064 male high-school graduates in America; yet in 1874, 9,593
male students obtained the B.A. Similarly, "in 1890 the high schools
gave diplomas to 18,549 men, while in 1894 the colleges reported
awarding 17,917 B.A.'s to men." This situation was to continue for
some time; and indeed, "in 1914 male college graduates outnumbered
1910 high school graduates two-to-one." This remarkable structural
imbalance was not eliminated until after the First World War.

What these figures suggest, among many other things, is that
from very early on the United States had failed to develop a system
of secondary education which was in any way comparable to its system of higher education—a system, by the way, which, however inadequate we may judge it to be, is surely the best that has yet existed.
This weakness becomes even clearer when we compare secondary
education in America during this period with the great systems of
secondary education that had been built up in France and Germany,
and, in a different but related context, Great Britain. The strength of
the European systems of secondary education was an expression of
the strength of the bourgeoisie or middle and upper middle classes
as classes. This education aimed to achieve a number of ends. First,
it ensured that the children of the bourgeoisie were safely isolated
from the children of common or working-class people. Second, it
aimed to appropriate for itself the cultural rights, privileges and
prerogatives of the former ruling classes. Third, it prepared the sons
of the middle classes for roles as members of the new ruling order
and for roles that were closely related to the state. One of the results
of this arrangement was the normally strict separation of secondary
and higher education on the one hand from technical training on the
other. It was this separation that Huxley was deploring in his essay.
And it was this separation that did not generally exist in America. In
the American system there has never been a firmly drawn boundary
between higher education and vocational, technical and professional
training. And in America as well, the colleges and universities have—

for at least the last hundred years—been the center of the system of education, while secondary education has not. This has created a much more "open" system of higher education in America—just as American society has been more open than European society—and it has served both the cause and the ideology of social mobility through education as well. What it has not done, and what it can never do as long as our historical circumstances essentially persist, is to create a system of secondary education that is in any way commensurate in quality, force, range, diversity and organization with the American system of higher education. (Hence the nearly universal and quite understandable feelings of status deprivation that high-school teachers in America notably suffer.)

What I am suggesting is that there may be a certain element of cant—or of hot air—in the perennial and current lament that the high schools in America are not doing their job. When did they ever? Due exception must always be made historically for certain special schools both public and private, but we are speaking here about a national cultural problem that exists in similar structural configurations on a variety of levels within the system of higher education. And since a considerable part of the volume of this chorus of lamentations comes from persons like ourselves, members of the professoriate and licensed practitioners of the higher pedagogical arts and crafts, I suggest that we stop bellyaching for a bit and see if we can determine what it is that we might do.

One of the first things we might do is to admit that the work of higher education in America—particularly in the first two years—has always to some extent been reparative. The degree of reparation has varied both historically and according to what level of the system of higher education one is examining; but it has always been there. What has not always been there is the willingness on the part of people like ourselves to admit that this is what we are doing, or that this is proper and legitimate and rewarding work for specialists in medieval literature or French history or the logical theories of signs. If such an admission is made, then a step toward demystification among ourselves will have been taken. And if this step can be followed by the acknowledgment, in all good cheer and with appropriate academic irony and skepticism, that much of the work that has to be done in the first two years is the work that is not done in secondary education and will not be done in secondary education, and that it is our proper work to do, then a step away from demoralization will have been made as well.

A half-step in this direction has in recent years been taken by the University of California. Nearly all freshman students at the University of California campuses come from the top 12.5 percent of their graduating high-school classes. This year, for example, testing revealed that 48 percent of the entering class at Berkeley and 45 percent of the entering freshmen at UCLA needed remedial instruction in English. As a result of such testing the University of California began a few years ago to institute a course to remedy these deficiencies, a course which they delicately named "Subject A." The students cottoned on at once to this euphemism, and in reality the course is widely known as "bonehead English." That the students are correct in their ascription is supported by the fact that the university assesses an extra fee of $45 upon those students who are relegated to taking this course. (I understand that this fee will soon be dropped.) I regard this as a half-step forward for several reasons. The University of California— and there may be others as well—has recognized openly and in public that the problem exists and has begun to make systematic provisions for dealing with it. At the same time, however, it remains stuck with the idea of remedial English or remedial work and what is implied by such a conception. It is this idea that I should like to see banished, if not abolished.

The idea of remedial work throws the substantive onus of failure upon the individual student. It implies that he is personally falling below a norm or standard that his fellows and contemporaries regularly attain. It is in action a punitive notion—witness that extra fee of $45—and in fact a false one. For what we are dealing with in America today is an entire culture that needs work of this kind, and the sooner we bring ourselves to face this circumstance the less harassed and bedeviled we will feel, and the less guilty and bewildered will our students perhaps be. As a result, what I would first propose would be a course— how and at what level it would be taught would, to be sure, vary with the institutional context in which it was set— in which the reading and analysis of selected important and primarily non-literary texts would be accompanied by a great deal of writing: in my mind the two processes are inseparable. And I do not think that this course need be staffed entirely by English Departments; what would be done in such a course does not have an exclusively special relation to the study of literature. It has to do with the study of anything that requires the use of natural language.

I have three further courses that I should like to see tried out in an experimental way on undergraduate students. I should like to have freshmen take a course in history—almost any kind of history will do, as long as it is history. I say this for two reasons: first, because of all the major humanistic disciplines, history seems to me today to be in the least problematical shape, though any historian will, at the drop of a hat, tell you that his professional calling has had its recent share of troubles. My second reason has to do with the circumstance that, after English, history, in my opinion, is the most important foreign language for students—especially American students—to acquire, and that they can make this acquisition most conveniently in a setting in which they have access to historians. I should like to see two further courses experimentally tried out in the second year as provisional requirements. The first would be an introductory course of philosophy. Once again, I would not specify what kind of philosophy, but simply make sure that it was philosophy. The fourth course probably comes out of Utopia or the Utopian future. I would like to see a course instituted in which students are asked to read, discuss, analyze and write about a number of the most important works or documents of social theory. I would say of this course, as I did of its counterpart in the first year, that it ought not to be staffed exclusively by sociologists or social scientists. Indeed, I would make it a requirement that the staffing not be so exclusive.

Such courses, or anything like them, will not save the world, nor will they restore the idea of general or liberal education. They would not be easy to teach or to take; they would be "non-creative," in the current sense of the meaning that is applied to the term "creativity," and they would be meant to be. They might even on occasion be dull. They would not, however, visit upon students the indignities of taking non-courses in non-subjects in an institution that has on occasion appeared to be a supermarket for the mass consumption of poorly packaged intellectual goods. And they would not treat the individual student as an object that requires personal or idiosyncratic remedial intervention and attention. The remedy would be directed at the culture in which we all perforce live.

And there, alas, is the sticking point. At the risk of hyperbole, I will now undertake to say directly what I have been implying all along, which brings us back to where we started. It seems to me that there exists today a widespread if quasi-conscious doubt among humanists in particular about whether in fact they have a culture to transmit. This doubt may be only partly articulated, but it is not to be confused with the poised and critical skepticism that characterizes the humanist tradition at its moments of strength. This kind of doubt may express itself differently at different levels of the system of higher education and in the society and culture at large, but it is distinctly perceptible among the élite groups at the great universities and the larger cultural enclaves with which they are symbiotically connected.

If in fact humanists cannot sustain their belief in the value of the culture they have inherited—and which is professionally within their care—or in the value of its values both immanent and overt, then it seems to me to follow that they will be severely hindered in arriving at judgments and decisions about priorities within their own disciplines and judgments and decisions about allocations of resources in both research and teaching—about curriculum, the structure of advanced degrees and other internal matters—not to speak about judgments and decisions that pertain to the substance of their own continuing work and vocation.

The belief that seems to be passing, as I have said, is the belief in the intrinsic or transcendent value of a historical culture and in the intrinsic and transcendent values that attach to the activities by which it is sustained, transmitted, reproduced, internalized and modified. The erosion of such beliefs undermines the humanities in particular, if for no other reason than that in them the teaching function is extremely intimate and peculiarly vital. And that function is most vital and most demanding in the first two years of higher education. The problematic of those first two years, then, remains inseparable from the larger problematics I have touched upon in these comments. That theoretical inseparability does not, however, mean that nothing can be done. It does mean, I think, that we should remain aware of the character and magnitude of what it is that we are facing.

Let me finally conclude by referring to how another of our great humanist ancestors tried at one moment to realize his awareness of the character and magnitude of what it was that he in his time thought had to be faced. The passage I have in mind comes from the text, "On Fortune and Misfortune in History." It was the last in a series of lectures that Jacob Burckhardt gave at the University of Basle between 1869 and 1871, and reappears in revised form as the last chapter of his *Reflections on World History*. Burckhardt looks out on the European scene and finds himself driven to these remarks:

> Everything depends on how our generation stands the test. It may well be that frightful times are ahead, and an age of deepest misery. We should like to know on which wave we are driving forward—only we form part of it. But mankind is not destined to perish yet, and nature creates as liberally as before. But if happiness is to be found in the midst of our misfortunes, it can only be a spiritual one: to be turned facing the past so as to save the culture of former times, and facing the future so as to give an example of the spiritual in an age which might otherwise succumb entirely to the material.

Well, the frightful times were indeed ahead, more frightful than even
Burckhardt could have imagined. And we learned through those frightful times that everything does *not* depend on how one generation
stands the test, although each generation must stand the test on its
own and do what it can for those who come after it. And if the suc-
cumbing to the "material" that Burckhardt refers to has also taken
place to a degree and in a depth that even he was quite unable to
foresee, yet the idea of the "example" that he sets forward, and that
his own being and career in life embodied, is still in large measure
the idea by which humanists justify their vocation. For although it is
probably not true that being a professor at Basle is preferable to being
God, yet it remains true that being a humanist means that one has a
vocation. And that it is a vocation is what constitutes its justification,
or such justification as it may, even in these advanced times, continue to claim.

ROSEMARY PARK

Liberal Education: A Chameleon

"Vae diebus nostris, quia periit studium litterarum a nobis. . . ."
Gregory of Tours, *Historiae I, praefatio prima.*
See JACQUES BARZUN, *House of Intellect,* p. 243, for comment.

For the ancients a chameleon had many strange powers, including its capacity to entrap a hawk, to cure headaches or to signal through its appearance in dreams imminent and extraordinary dangers.[1] Aristotle, who apparently dissected a specimen, reported that its change in color took place when it was inflated with air.[2] In making a comparison between liberal education and this unusual small beast, I am suggesting that liberal education, whether inflated or not, has a similar capacity to change, even to entrap the high-flying and to warn of coming dangers. In the course of its more than 2,000 years of history, liberal education has been at times an educational ideal of great richness and substance reflecting the common understandings and aspirations of a society. It has led to the idea of the philosopher king and to the more humanistic concept of the wise man. At other times liberal education has supplied the basis for Scriptural interpretation or the preliminary training for the established and aspiring professions. It has been attacked as the useless foppery of an outmoded social structure and subsequently praised as the only means of providing society with men trained to cope with the rapid pace of national development. These varying claims have been made for liberal education over the centuries and only the term itself appears to have any constancy. In modern times especially, the components of the concept have shifted so that

---

1. Pliny, *Natural History,* 28, 29, 113 ff.; Artemidorus, *Oneirocritica,* 2, 13 *ad fin.*; Aulus *Gellius, Attic Nights,* 10, 12, 1 ff.
2. Aristotle, *Historia Animalium,* 2, 11, 503B, 2 ff.

it would be difficult indeed to define with any exactitude today what is included in and what is excluded from liberal education.

Why has the term, however defined, had such persistence through history? And what particular educational insight can be discovered in its many manifestations which could justify the continued use of the word "liberal" to describe such different processes and goals? A simple response might point to the fact that initially the term was used to describe the education of the upper class in a given society, a class which consisted of free men, not slaves or serfs, and a class whose education constituted evidence of high rank. Liberal education according to this diagnosis implied status. Whatever the process may actually have consisted of at any given time was less important than that society agreed to call the education liberal.

The idea that the status adhering to liberal education also makes it a vehicle for social ascent did not appear until the mid-nineteenth-century in America. Previous centuries which used the term did not construe it as a channel for social mobility since their social structures were essentially feudal, with fixed class boundaries. For those societies the concept had other meanings which could, with equal justification, be characterized as liberating or liberal, though not in a social sense. To discover some of these interpretations may help to explain why this chameleon-like term has continued to be educational tender over so many centuries.

In some ways ancient Greek society might be said to resemble our own in its concerns for the process and problems of education. The Greek philosophers revert continually to the need to form a younger generation of citizens with more profound understandings of politics and ethics. One of the earliest uses of the phrase "liberal education" can be derived from a passage in Plato's *Laws* in which two kinds of education are being contrasted. The first, the narrower kind, says the Athenian speaker, concerns itself with vocational pursuits, e.g., the retail trade or shipping; while the second, the only one deserving of the name, he maintains, studies virtue, the perfection of citizenship. The first aims at wealth or bodily strength or mere cleverness and is "mean and illiberal" (Βάναυσον . . . καὶ ἀνελεύθερον). The second, however, seeks to form good men, and is "the first and fairest thing that the best of men can ever have."[3] Since the first is specifically called "illiberal," "unfree," it is clear that in the second, "liberal" education is being described.

The components of this type of education are analyzed at various

---

3. Plato, *Laws*, I, 644.

places in the Platonic Dialogues, the most famous perhaps being the seventh book of the *Republic*, which includes the parable of the Cave and the description of the education of the Guardians upon whom the ideal state will depend for its welfare and happiness. For these leaders and protectors of the state, Plato planned an education which began with grammar, music and gymnastics, "nerving and sustaining the reason with noble words and lessons and moderating and soothing and civilizing the wildness of passion by harmony and rhythm."[4] The students then advanced through several increasing levels of abstraction, through arithmetic, geometry, astronomy, and the science of harmony to dialectics, and having mastered this, and only then, to the idea of the Good. In the final, ultimate goal of education, intellect and ethical insight are conjoined. In this conjuncture are reflected the first Socratic judgments, which had equated Virtue and Knowledge. The relationship between Virtue and Knowledge gains in profundity in Plato by being associated with his theory of Ideas. But without regard to that aspect of his philosophy, the process of education he describes is worthy of careful examination. He recommends that the leadership of the state rest with those whose education has brought them through the mastery of abstractions to the greatest of these, the most necessary of all, the Idea of the Good. Intellect and Virtue are not separate products of separate processes, but are the joint result of prescribed learning. Most significant of all, as it is told in the parable, those who are attaining this ethical insight through education return to commune with their brethren still chained in the darkness of the Cave. Implied is that this extraordinary process of education not only cultivates ethical and intellectual achievement but fosters as well a profound sense of social obligation. Moreover, the stages of education are a public sequence, not a totally private experience, although some moments of unique elevation may be associated with it, as in other aspects of Plato's thought. Plato's description is, of course, of an ideal state, but it makes clear, nevertheless, what he intends by "real education" when he contrasts the "mean" and "illiberal" with "liberal" in the passage quoted from the *Laws*. The concept of liberal education for him unites ethical insight, intellectual discipline and social obligation in its goal, and the three aspects are not thought of as separate but as facets of a unified process. One is always conscious of its unity, though at times, like the chameleon, it may appear to be of different hues.

Through Cicero and his circle the Greek tradition in philosophy and in education was interpreted for the Roman world. Liberal studies

---

4. Plato, *Republic*, IV, 441 f.

were for Cicero the *cibus humanitatis;*[5] they were at once a discipline,
a solace in adversity and a joy at home (*adversis perfugium ac so-
lacium praebent, delectant domi*).[6] Though he looked upon these studies as necessary to the orator, he valued them equally as cultivating a
true humanism which perceived man as the measure of all things. The
word *"humanus,"* the favorite complimentary attribute of that society,
meant much the same as our term "urbane," in the best sense—being
possessed of a self-confident inner freedom. Cicero argues that Cato
had studied these liberal arts as an aid to virtue; he, however, finds
them a noble form of recreation for the mind (*hanc animi remis-
sionem humanissimam ac liberalissimam iudicaretis*).[7] From time to
time he lists these studies: geometry, music, literature, and those
which concern the nature of things and the customs of men (*quae de
naturis rerum, quae de hominum moribus*).[8] Cicero's definition of liberal education is reminiscent of Plato's preparatory education in geometry, music and grammar, the last of these being, of course, an
inclusive term which comprised for Plato acquaintance with the historical myths and literature. The similarity in the selection of preparatory studies in both Plato and Cicero does not imply a coincidence of
goals, though both envisage this educational process as training for
public responsibility—Plato in the formation of the Guardian and
Cicero of the orator. For Cicero, however, the pleasures attendant on
liberal studies seem at times to be almost ends in themselves, although
philosophically, he perceives the goal of the process to be the creation
of the wise man who, in the Stoic sense, combines Virtue and Knowledge. In varying degrees of emphasis, then, the ancient world in these
two great exemplars understood that education addressed itself simultaneously to both Knowledge and Virtue, and that the process consisted of learnings of a selected and, as it were, a prescribed kind.

It was a contemporary of Cicero, M. Terentius Varro, who apparently established what was to become the traditional list of subjects
which constituted liberal education.[9] Four were being taught in his
day in the schools of Greece: geometry, arithmetic, astronomy and
music. Three were found in the schools of Italy, but came, of course,

---

5. Cicero, *De Finibus*, 5, 54.
6. Cicero, *Pro Archia*, 7, 16, 10–11.
7. *Ibid.*, 7, 16, 7–8.
8. Cicero, *De Oratore*, 3, 32, 127.
9. *Paulys Realencyclopädie der classischen Altertumswissenschaft, Supple-
mentband* VI (Stuttgart: Metzler, 1935), pp. 1,255 ff.; and Martin Schanz, *Geschichte der römischen Literatur*, Vol. I. 4th ed. Carl Hosius, ed. (*Handbuch der
Altertumswissenschaft*, Vol. VIII, 1 [Munich: C. H. Beck, 1927, reprinted 1959]),
p. 567.

originally from Greece: grammar, rhetoric and dialectic.[10] After Varro, who added medicine and architecture, making nine subjects in all, the list stood until the fifth century A.D. when Martianus Capella, in his *Marriage of Philology and Mercury*, dropped medicine and architecture again and gave final form to the liberal arts as seven—a number which persisted through Cassidorus, Isidore and St. Augustine into modern times.[11] Some three hundred years after Martianus, the divisions implicit in Varro were being commonly called the trivium and quadrivium, the first consisting of grammar, rhetoric and dialectic, the second and then more advanced, of arithmetic, geometry, astronomy and music.[12] However divided or denominated, the sense of the ancients was preserved that these subjects were not concerned with trivialities or occupational skills but prepared the mind to receive Virtue, as Seneca had said.[13]

Through the bridge of the Stoics the conjunction of Virtue and Knowledge was to penetrate the Christian tradition. Where Cicero and the Stoics spoke of *humanitas* as the goal of liberal education, the Christian aspired to the salvation of the soul, but both used the liberal arts as a path under certain circumstances. Among the literate clergy there were popular beliefs to the effect that David and Plato were acquainted and that Plato knew Moses.[14] And St. Jerome relates a dream in which, on his asserting that he is a Christian, he is rebuked with the words: "Mentiris, . . . Ciceronianus es."[15] Even later in the twelfth century, Honorius of Autun writes: "Liberales quippe artes sunt utiles, quia sunt instrumenta sacrae Scripturae, ut mallei fabro, et arma contra haereticos."[16]

The efficacy of the liberal arts in leading to salvation is reflected in artistic representations like the one in the banquet hall of St. Gall, which was said in the ninth century to be a portrayal of Divine Wis-

10. R. M. Martin, "Arts libéraux (sept)," in *Dictionnaire d'histoire et de géographie ecclésiastiques*, Vol. IV (Paris: Letouzey & Ané, 1930), p. 830.

11. Schanz, ed. Hosius, *op. cit.*, p. 567.

12. Hastings Rashdall, *The Universities of Europe in the Middle Ages*, F. M. Powicke and A. B. Emden, eds. (3 vols., Oxford: Clarendon Press, 1936), Vol. I, p. 34n. "Quadrivium" as a term first appeared in Boethius, *De Institutione Arithmetica*, I. 1 (ed. Friedlein [1867], pp. 7. 25 and 9. 28); "trivium" first in scholium on Horace, *Ars Poetica*, 307, in *Codex Vindobonensis* (ed. Zechmeister [Vienna, 1877], p. 37); see P. Rajna, "Le denominazioni *trivium* e *quadrivium*," *Studi medievali*, n. s. 1 (1928), pp. 4 ff., nota bene 8.

13. Seneca, *Epistolae Morales*, 88, 20: "non quia virtutem dare possunt, sed quia animam ad accipiendam virtutem praeparant."

14. Johannes Stelzenberger, *Die Beziehungen der frühchristlichen Sittenlehre zur Ethik der Stoa* (Munich: Max Hueber, 1933), p. 74.

15. Jerome, *Epistolae*, 22, 20.

16. Jacques-Paul Migne, *Patrologia Latina*, Vol. 172, p. 362A.

dom surrounded by her daughters, the seven liberal arts.[17] This symbiosis between Christian and classical continued in many artistic forms, in cloisters and palaces, in miniatures and statuary, until by the thirteenth and fourteenth centuries work in the liberal arts had become the necessary preparation for specialized study in theology and in medicine.[18] But whereas for the ancients there had tended to be a conjunction of ethical and intellectual education, the Christian tradition, with its foundation in revelation, separated the two kinds of learning into the purely intellectual and that which (as in the ethical and some aspects of the religious realms) depends not on reason alone but on the experience of love or grace. The theologians came to rely on Aristotle and the Stoics in formalizing the orthodox teaching of the Church. For the faithful, however, it was not necessary to be able to argue logically or master geometry in order to accept the teaching of the Church. The trivium and quadrivium were no longer required as preparation for dialectics which could lead on to some perception of first principles; rather, these liberal studies were the means by which the higher clergy and the theologians sought to systematize matters of faith first revealed through the Gospels and the Fathers. Increasingly the ancient tradition, which had looked upon the study of the liberal arts as preparation of the mind to receive Virtue, came to accent instead the preparation of the mind to become a lawyer, a doctor or a priest and, sometimes, a humanistic scholar. Instruction in first principles, in theology and ethics, became separate concerns and were no longer to be achieved by the process of liberal education alone. The chameleon had brought down the high-flying hawk.

When the Reformation enlarged the participation of the laity in the Church, in both its services and in the interpretation of the Gospels and the Fathers, education gained a new and broader significance. This was particularly true among the English Puritans and their American descendants. The Puritan was required not only to believe in his heart but in addition to formulate his belief in his mind. As Perry Miller says, the average church member in New England "respected the prerogatives of the liberal arts and never questioned that the rules of grammar, of logic, and of rhetoric should determine the

17. Karl Künstle, *Ikonographie der christlichen Kunst* (2 vols., Freiburg-i.-Br.: Herder, 1928), Vol. I, p. 147. Cf. Adolf Katzenellenbogen, "The Representation of the Seven Liberal Arts," in Marshall Clagett, Gaines Post and Robert Reynolds, eds., *Twelfth-Century Europe and the Foundations of Modern Society* (Madison, Wis.: Univ. of Wisconsin Press, 1966), pp. 39–55.
18. Rashdall, *The Universities of Europe . . .* , Vol. I, p. 325, note 2, p. 329, note 2, p. 475, note 1; and Vol. III, p. 68.

interpretation of the Scripture."[19] Some five centuries before, it will be remembered, Honorius of Autun was expressing a similar respect for the liberal arts as the defense of the faith. Strangely enough, that Church Father would have partially understood Charles Chauncy, the second president of Harvard, when he insisted upon a knowledge of the tongues for a true understanding of Scripture and of the liberal arts for a correct interpretation.[20]

What form had the liberal arts now assumed that they were required in Puritan New England for a correct understanding of the Scripture? We know that Chauncy had prescribed that "in the teaching of all Arts, such Authors bee read as doe best agree with the Scripture truths."[21] The course of study under Chauncy shows the continuing influence of Martianus Capella and his interpretation of liberal education: in preparation for life in the Protestant outpost of New England, the student was required to take grammar, rhetoric, logic and physics in the first year; rhetoric and grammar among other subjects in the second; and rhetoric, arithmetic, geometry and astronomy in the third year. The quadrivium and trivium were still living educational forms, though with a difference. Grammar, for instance, did not mean what it meant to Plato, an inclusive concern for literature and history as well as the structure of language. In seventeenth-century Cambridge, Massachusetts, grammar meant the actual forms of specific languages, namely, Greek, Hebrew, Aramaic and Syriac. Latin was the language of instruction, known to the student before he entered college. Rhetoric, with its analysis of classical authors and the extraction of their *flores*, as Morison describes the process,[22] furnished an introduction to the practice of oratory as well as the development of a tolerable Latin style, both useful for a man expecting to enter public life. This kind of preparation was furthered by the study of logic—a prime requisite for the public disputation or refutation and rejection of heretical beliefs. Astronomy, part of the old quadrivium, had, like physics and geometry at Harvard, a practical cast, though we know that the theories of Copernicus, Galileo and Kepler were accepted.[23]

In effect, the first collegiate program in America maintained a respect for the liberal arts not as means of reaching first principles,

---

19. Perry Miller, *The New England Mind: The Seventeenth Century* (New York: Macmillan, 1939; reprinted with new Preface, 1961), p. 87.

20. *Ibid.*, p. 85.

21. Samuel Eliot Morison, *Harvard College in the Seventeenth Century* (2 vols., Cambridge, Mass.: Harvard Univ. Press, 1936), Vol. I, p. 145.

22. *Ibid.*, p. 174.

23. *Ibid.*, p. 216.

but rather as means of equipping an élite for public service, whether in Church or civil state. And thus in seventeenth-century America the liberal arts were thought of as the education given to the élite, though this term did not always coincide with an economically or socially privileged class. There was still attached to this constellation of studies that faint association of liberal learning with ethical insight which had prevailed in ancient times. Consequently, these studies were preferred for the younger generation, especially for those who aspired to leadership in the community. But what had been an accepted outcome of the study of the quadrivium and trivium was now separated from these subjects and instead formed the substance of the president's course in Natural or Moral Philosophy, a course which was characteristic of all early American colleges. Here the orthodox religious system was reinforced and doctrinal soundness assured, while behavior in the college was controlled in valiant attempts to teach decorum, if not ethical standards. Both the president's course and dormitory and campus regulations were specific measures to attain what an earlier education had held to be the results of disciplined, abstract learning. The liberal arts lent status to the learner, but they were no longer expected to prepare the mind to receive Virtue. That aim was achieved, if at all, by direct instruction and control. The result of the symbiosis of theology and the liberal arts was to make the latter the servant of the queen of sciences and to separate instruction in theology from instruction in the liberal arts, a separation which became more necessary with the rise of Protestant sectarianism and its varying doctrines. Yet even in the area of religion, as the Puritan colleges show, the liberal arts maintained some of the basic contribution to understanding and commitment which Honorius had phrased in the twelfth century as "instrumenta sacrae Scripturae."

From their seventeenth-century institutionalization in the New World, the liberal arts continued to constitute the essence of liberal education. But as the nineteenth century approached, and throughout that period, two other factors began to affect the traditional interpretation of liberal education. One was the egalitarian mood of the country, and the other was associated with those intellectual developments described as the rise of science. Science was hardly new in the educational process; one remembers the components of the quadrivium: arithmetic, geometry, astronomy and the science of harmony. What was new was the method of experimentation and the increasing conviction that some problems of society had technical solutions. In a developing country, as the United States then was, there existed an increasing need for engineers to build transportation and communication networks and for agricultural experts to increase the yield of crops. Experimental science was expensive in instruments and the colleges were always poor. Even with the interest and generosity of men such as Rensselaer, Abbott Lawrence and Sheffield, the colleges proceeded, but slowly, in relation to this need. Their reluctance can be attributed partly to the lack of trained faculty and instructional materials, but also partly to the undefined relation between the slowly accumulating new scientific knowledge and the existing liberal arts. The question of how to define that relationship was especially acute when it became clear after the middle of the century that in the Darwinian hypothesis a challenge to the sectarian basis of most higher education had emerged.

As if to prepare for this fundamental attack, a classic statement in defense of the liberal education of the time had been presented to the Yale Corporation in the Faculty-Administrative Report of 1828. From the sentiments expressed in the Report, it is apparent that the new science was not perceived as an outgrowth of the concern for science in the ancient tradition of liberal education, but that the literary and philosophical aspects of accepted liberal studies now constituted the *depositum fidei* of the liberal arts. In defending itself against the charge that the college is unresponsive to the needs of the age and that its curriculum never changes, the faculty states that "whole sciences have *for the first time* been introduced; chemistry, mineralogy, geology, and political economy"[24] (italics mine). The aim of liberal education is regarded as "the discipline and the furniture of mind,"[25] and is characteristically discussed apart from the college's responsibility for ethical and behavioral standards (in the analysis of which appears the somewhat forbidding conclusion, "there may be those whom nothing but the arm of law can reach").[26] Throughout the Report references are made to the proper symmetry and balance of character,[27] which is to be achieved by breadth of intellectual training and which does not appear to connote the self-confident urbanity of the Ciceronian humanists. The eloquent defense of studying the ancient classics in the original tongues reveals the interesting way in which these studies had come to represent the liberal arts as a whole. There are echoes, too, of the public responsibility which the student of Plato's

---

24. See Document 11 in Richard Hofstadter and Wilson Smith, *American Higher Education: A Documentary History*, 2 vols. (Chicago: Univ. of Chicago Press, 1961); Vol. I, Part 4, p. 277.
25. *Ibid.*, p. 278.
26. *Ibid.*, p. 280.
27. *Ibid.*, p. 279.

liberal education assumed when the Report describes the successful graduate: "He who is not only eminent in professional life but has also a mind richly stored with general knowledge, has an elevation and dignity of character which gives him a commanding influence in society and a widely extended sphere of usefulness. His situation enables him to diffuse the light of science among all classes of the community."[28] Here the ancient conjunction of Knowledge and Virtue seems to be intended, though it arises from the scope of knowledge acquired rather than from the grasp of first principles. Nowhere is there a theoretical consideration of a possible contribution of experimental science to liberal education; Yale, in fact, preferred to keep the students of the Sheffield School separated from the other undergraduates.

Despite Yale's defense of the literary interpretation of the liberal arts, the need of the developing country for applied scientists and for the results of their research, as well as the gradual application of the scientific method in other fields, began gradually to prevail. Both Henry Tappan, first president of the University of Michigan, and Francis Wayland of Brown tried to introduce agricultural courses in their institutions in mid-century, though without much success. Twenty years before, Eliphalet Nott had succeeded at Union College and a course in applied science was offered at Amherst as well. That no attempt was made to regard advances in natural science as consonant with at least some of the components of liberal education, however, meant that the literary interpretation of the liberal arts tended to be pitted against the more practical concerns of the developing experimental sciences. This dichotomy was weakened, however, by the egalitarian demands of groups in the population who had not before participated in liberal education to any extent. By mid-century these citizens were making successful attempts to direct higher education's attention to their needs and to what they considered society's limited definition of liberal education.

The most obvious proof of this challenge to liberal education as defined in the colleges was the passage of the Morrill Act in 1862, which by the use of federal land enabled the states to establish colleges in which not only scientific and classical studies but also work in agriculture and the mechanic arts should be offered, "in order to promote the liberal and practical education of the industrial classes in the several pursuits and professions of life." This historic federal intervention in education took place only after much debate and exhorta-

---

28. *Ibid.*, p. 282.

tion. Speaking in 1854 on the fiftieth anniversary of Eliphalet Nott's inauguration as president of Union College, Francis Wayland of Brown urged that "the farmer when he goes home from his work ought to be conversant with just as good books as his minister, or his lawyer, or his physician."[29] To that end, Wayland stressed the obligation of the colleges to be useful to what he called "the middling interests," i.e., the mechanic, merchant and manufacturer, those, he said, "who unite intelligence with muscular strength."[30] In his Report to the Brown Corporation in 1850, he had observed that "our colleges are not filled because we do not furnish the education desired by the people."[31]

Another reformer, Jonathan Baldwin Turner, agitated through the Middle West for "a system of industrial universities which would develop a more liberal and practical education among the people, tend the more to intellectualize the rising generation and eminently conduce to the virtue, intelligence, and true glory of our common country."[32] His plan would have afforded the industrial classes "precisely the same principles of mental discipline and thorough scientific practical instruction in all their pursuits and interests which are now applied to the professional and military classes."[33] The sponsor of the congressional measure authorizing the land-grant colleges, Justin Morrill, saw them as a means of breaking the exclusive control of education now vested in the already educated, who were "most sure to educate their sons," and thereby to perpetuate a monopoly "inconsistent with the welfare and complete prosperity of American institutions."[34] In the land-grant movement, then, the egalitarian mood of the country and the need for applied scientific training were united and were not totally divorced from what the Morrill Act called "scientific and classical studies." It was the combination that was seen as necessary "to promote the liberal and practical education of the industrial classes."

The land-grant institutions, in view of the lack of instructional materials and trained faculty for agricultural and mechanic arts, tended, in fact, to duplicate the curricula of existing colleges. As Wilson Smith remarks, "There was little study of cows in public 'cow

29. Theodore Crane, *Francis Wayland: Political Economist as Educator* (Providence, R. I.: Brown Univ. Press, 1962), p. 45.

30. *Ibid.*, p. 8.

31. Quoted in Hofstadter and Smith, *American Higher Education*, Vol. II, Part Six, pp. 478 ff.

32. Mary Turner Carriel, *Life of Jonathan Baldwin Turner* (Urbana, Ill.: Univ. of Illinois Press, 1961), p. 115.

33. *Ibid.*, p. 114.

34. William B. Parker, *Life and Public Services of Justin Smith Morrill* (Boston and New York: Houghton Mifflin, 1924), p. 263.

colleges' until almost a half century after most of them began."[35] The first achievement of these colleges was therefore not so much the introduction of applied sciences in the university as the promotion of social equality. As the Joint Select Committee of the Wisconsin legislature stated in 1858: "It is by the proper establishment of the State University alone, that the industrial classes of the State are to find their position advanced and industry placed side by side with the so-called learned professions."[36] Through the second half of the nineteenth century, the industrial classes laid claim to liberal education via the land-grant colleges and thereby participated in the status which adhered to students of the liberal arts. At the same time, these "new" students and their parents supported instructional consideration of applied sciences, and these practical subjects depended for their scope on the successful expansion of that theoretical experimental science which grew in uneasy proximity with traditional classical studies and liberal arts in the first American universities.

As the results of research accumulated both in scientific and nonscientific areas, pressure for new subjects and courses and against the required curriculum, which the Yale Report had confidently assumed to be the basis of every influential man's education, mounted. Since Thomas Jefferson's day as chancellor of the University of Virginia there had, from time to time, been educators who doubted the efficacy of the required curriculum, holding that the individual and therefore society were best served when the student followed his own interests and capacities in the choice of his studies. This free-elective system received its most dramatic and thorough demonstration at Harvard under Charles W. Eliot, who believed that education must be constantly adjusted to the spirit of the age,[37] and that "no subject of human inquiry can be out of place in the programme of a real university."[38]

Starting from the premise that "it is not the proper business of universities to force subjects of study or particular kinds of mental discipline upon unwilling generations,"[39] Eliot presided over the conse-

---

35. Wilson Smith, "Cow College Mythology and Social History," *Agricultural History*, XLIV, No. 3 (July 1970), p. 302.

36. Quoted in Merle Curti and Vernon Carstensen, *The University of Wisconsin* (2 vols., Madison, Wis.: Univ. of Wisconsin Press, 1949), p. 100.

37. Henry James, *Charles William Eliot* (2 vols., Boston and New York: Houghton Mifflin, 1930), Vol. I, p. 361.

38. Charles W. Eliot, "The New Education," *Atlantic Monthly* (February 1869), p. 216.

39. Charles W. Eliot, *Educational Reform* (New York: The Century Co., 1889), p. 120.

quent enlargement of the curriculum. He urged a redefinition of liberal education to include such subjects as history, economics[40] and natural science, and commented that "to make a scrupulously accurate statement of a fact observed, with all needed qualifications and limitations, is as good a training of conscience as a secular education can furnish."[41] This may seem an echo, at least, of the ancient conjunction of Virtue and Knowledge, but contrary to Eliot's judgment was the negative opinion of George Herbert Palmer, the Harvard philosopher, who denied that instruction could unite moral and intellectual culture.[42] "Liberal studies," maintained Eliot, "are those which are pursued in the scientific spirit for truth's sake,"[43] and since all the options offered at Harvard are liberal,[44] a student, whatever he chooses, will have had a liberal education. Clearly, any concept of liberal education as excluding certain subjects on principle and including others which are prescribed for all students, has quite withered away.

More than a generation and two world wars later, James Bryant Conant as president of Harvard, in the Preface to the Harvard study *General Education and a Free Society*, observes the same lack of precision in defining liberal education. He suggests the use of the term "general education" to indicate that both secondary schools and colleges are struggling to find a balance to the educational specialization which developed out of the free-elective system and the rise of research and graduate education. The aim of general education is "effective thinking, communication, the making of relevant judgments, and the discrimination of values."[45] The goal is familiar enough in the history of liberal education. But without some philosophic abilities on the part of both student and faculty, one may wonder whether the synthesizing courses created by the movement served this projected end.

In the student unrest of the last decade the unanswered question of what constitutes liberal education was raised again, as Joseph J. Schwab's recent study, *College Curriculum and Student Protest*, demonstrates. His proposals for reintroducing an ethical concern into the process of higher education involve no mere resurrection of the presidential course in Moral Philosophy, but rather the careful study of

---

40. *Ibid.*, pp. 104–112.

41. Charles W. Eliot, "Wherein Popular Education Has Failed," *Forum* (December 1892), p. 419.

42. George Herbert Palmer, "Can Moral Conduct Be Taught in Schools?" *Forum* (September 1892), p. 675.

43. James, *Charles William Eliot*, Vol. I, p. 105.

44. Eliot, *Educational Reform*, p. 139.

45. *General Education in a Free Society* (Cambridge, Mass.: Harvard Univ. Press, 1945), p. 73.

legal cases and the creation of deliberative situations, as well as the examination of great ethical theorists, "so that discovered structures of meaning illuminate the knowledge gained in education."[46] The word "liberal" is not used to describe this educational plan; indeed, as these pages have shown, the term has been exhausted in attempts to adapt it to its surroundings. Under pressure from religion, from democracy, from the professions and from the élites, it has served each in turn by adding or subtracting components. In all fairness, we should now let it rest until we have devised ways to make its original insight, the conjunction of Knowledge and Virtue, a modern reality, or at least until we have reinflated or reinstated our useful chameleon.

---

46. Joseph J. Schwab, *College Curriculum and Student Protest* (Chicago: Univ. of Chicago Press, 1969), p. 202.

Polyhymnia

CRITICISM AND LANGUAGE

ৼড়

SHIRLEY HAZZARD

A Jaded Muse

"Magnitude creates its own space."
JACQUES BARZUN, in conversation.

⋙

A jaded Muse. The phrase is from Rochester, who would have been entertained to see his Lyric Muse jaded under new duties towards "Criticism and Language." Other designations raise their own questions here, in particular the suspect terms of "artist" and "critic" whose use will be convenient to this essay. "Artist" has a debased or precious or pretentious knell to it these days, but no other single word immediately distinguishes the creative writer from the literary commentator, or embraces practitioners of all the arts.

While the title of "artist" is not conferred simply for the claiming of it, a degree of quality is assumed in creative writers who merit critical discussion. "Critic," on the other hand, suggests large discrepancies of quality, and areas of disagreement over qualifications. ("I do not agree with what you say," Stravinsky wrote to a musical journalist, "and I dispute to the death your right to say it.") This word "critic" is recklessly bandied about, and I only once heard a writer of criticism—a capable one—repudiate it and ask to be called a reviewer instead.

Stuart Hampshire has described literary criticism as "a light science which should not be asked to carry heavy burdens" of complex ideas. Whether it is, or even could be, a science at all is debatable; but among literary forms it is probably the least durable and certainly, in retrospect, the least pleasurable and most ludicrously exposed. I do not refer to the exceptional instances where literary commentary transcends its form, to become—as philosophy, history, biography or literature itself—an inalienable part of the life of learning. Critical talent of that order is found, in our language, in a tiny handful of eccentric personalities in a generation, and is too uncommon for the present discussion, as are the highly individual approaches that, on rare occasions, can create their own categories.

Two other classes of criticism are also excluded here: that produced by poets or creative writers—Coleridge or James, for instance, or in our time Auden, Empson, Jarrell; and the work of the regular or occasional reviewer who sees his task as making honest, modest, and, as far as possible, intelligent indications to a modern reading public bedevilled by the inundation of new books. Of this last and respectable profession some members remain, though they are very sparse in a large metropolis.

It must be recalled that all other criticism is without a readily demonstrable function. Author and reader are in direct communication, and might profitably remain so were the vast apparatus of modern criticism to be obliterated: good writers do not write as if through an intermediary. It has become the accepted business of the modern critic less to draw reader and writer together than to "try and come between them"—to borrow a phrase employed by, appropriately enough, Lytton Strachey. The critic of course maintains that he interposes himself and his interpolations for the benefit of literature; but this again is a claim not made valid by the mere asserting of it.

The industrial revolution, as it might be called, that has overtaken American criticism in recent decades, interwoven as it is with accelerating social convulsion and a concentration of intellectual effort into topical, provocative, and ultimately disposable forms, may still be traced in some distinct outlines; even as may, indeed, the larger pattern of American political and social life with which it often confuses itself and whose vocabulary of coercion—of "power" and "influence"— it has adopted.

In 1928 Edmund Wilson was writing in *The New Republic* that "What we lack . . . in the United States, is not writers . . . but simply serious criticism." Calling for "hard-hitting polemics" (with the—one feels—quite unheeded aside that "I do not of course mean to assert that . . . any criticism, however able, could make or unmake artists"), Wilson held that "contemporary writing would benefit by a genuine literary criticism that should deal expertly with ideas and art."

A creative writer, Saul Bellow, looks back differently at that period of spontaneous "artistic" life in the Eastern United States:

> For a time [in the 1920s] New York really was the center of the country for certain rare and valuable qualities. Its free versers, free lovers, elegant boozers, its rich ninnies and eccentrics, its artists and revolutionists charmed and heartened the younger generation.

Bellow goes on to survey the situation in 1970, after the critical order advocated by Wilson had presumably been imposed:

> All that, of course, is over. New York is now the business center of American culture. . . . It has no independent and original intellectual life. It provides no equilibrium, it offers no mental space to artists. The present leaders of culture in New York are its publicity intellectuals. These are college-educated men and women who have never lived as poets, painters, composers or thinkers, but who have successfully organized writing, art, thought and science. . . . All these things have been made to pay and pay handsomely.

On the same theme Bellow speaks elsewhere of "those professionals of culture . . . creating enormous cultural bureaucracies within the universities, the media. . . . As a younger writer it was made quite explicit to me that if I wrote in an approved way—in the way, that is, that *they* approved—I would have their support. I didn't, and subsequently lost them."

"They," to authors, are the aptly named "literary circles" that endlessly circle literature and are almost never themselves engaged in creative activity. Like the figures in the lunettes and spandrels of the Sistine Chapel, they stand round the verge of Creation.

Distinguished mentors cannot always choose, and do not always deserve, their disciples. Wilson—some of whose own writings reflect productive disturbance, rather than undirected stagnation, in the 1920s—could not foresee huge transformations of event and outlook that would convert even his justified strictures into an inadvertent invitation to the forces of gross opportunism, self-importance and the pestilential modern mania for classification.

Wilson's call, in 1928, was for what is "systematic," "methodical," "authoritative"; writers were to "readjust themselves" under the corrective of "a competent criticism." In Bellow, the recurring word is "free." Wilson depicts creative writers isolated "in their solitary labors." Bellow sees them engaged in the vital disorder of random experience. With Wilson, the theme is regulation; with Bellow, life.

In another part of the 1920s forest, Evelyn Waugh was writing of twentieth-century criticism: "One day the critics will realise that by their rigid restriction of artistic scope they are making bores of all but the very greatest." Of all, that is, but those whose creative gifts and convictions carry them beyond the reach of critical intimidation.

When Hesiod observed that trouble[1] is good for work, he was not

---

1. I.e., "trouble" in the sense of "care." Hesiod, *Works and Days*, line 412.

referring to harassment. Whatever literature may have suffered through critical laxity, it has never responded favourably to exhortation or safeguards. By insisting on their monitory role, critics are now getting what they have asked for: a large body of creative work that, in all the arts, looks to its reception and interpretation instead of deriving its strength from the sensations and assumptions in which it is formed.

In painting, the loss of creative independence has been described by the art historian Douglas Cooper as resulting in the production of art "in a rarefied, bloodless atmosphere too much divorced from everyday life." Contrasting the present climate with that in which, for example, the Cubist paintings were created, Cooper has said, of works by Picasso in his possession:

> Look at these pictures. They've *lived*. They've probably had innumerable glasses of wine thrown at them in their time, they've been used to stop draughts in doors, they've been used to pay for meals, they've taken part in ordinary human lives. Modern paintings have never been allowed to live. Museums are becoming instant graveyards for canvases.

It was in analogous tribute to the "accidental" nurturing of genius that Alexander Fleming remarked of an immaculate laboratory visited in the United States that if he had worked there he would never have discovered penicillin.

Unhealthy self-consciousness in all the arts arises also from the artist's awareness that his work will generally be regarded by critics either as a series of efforts at concealment, which the enterprising specialist may unmask, or as an exercise in what one writer has called "the cult of the Involuntary." It is not hard to find examples of artists either covering their traces, in response to such pressures, with fashionable ambiguities, or even planting plums in the Christmas pie so that some incipient Jack Horner may have the satisfaction of extracting them and exclaiming, "What a good boy am I."

This absurd state of affairs inevitably leads, as many artists have unavailingly attested, to critical obtuseness towards manifest and essential aspects of creative works.

In a posthumously published essay the late Elizabeth Bowen pointed out that, in their assiduous delvings into her presumed underlying literary motives, interpreters of her novels have without exception passed over the large, consequential, and overt role of locality in her books: "On the subject of my symbology, if any, or psychology . . . I have occasionally been run ragged; but as to the *where* of my stories, its importance in them and for me, and the reasons for that, a negative apathy persists." Noting that "lengthy critical studies, theses are perpetually being written about writers," and that a number of these have been addressed to her own work, Miss Bowen forbearingly reports: "I have found some of them wildly off the mark."

Like any person who presumes to instruct, the critic has special duties towards civilisation. Beyond these he has, like any teacher, an opportunity to inspire. In this respect it must be noted how rarely in modern criticism one encounters outright admissions to, or recommendations of, pleasure. "Pleasure," as Auden has written, "is by no means an infallible critical guide, but it is the least fallible." It is also, in the assertive context of contemporary criticism, the least likely to be employed towards living artists. Pleasure is in part an act of submission, akin to generosity or love; and confession to it, through praise, is a commitment to a private "unauthorized" response. Not only critics but human beings in general have always feared the exposure that candid enjoyment of particular works of art might bring upon them; and it is a rare enthusiasm that comes unqualified by a battery of knowing reservations or is not subject to retraction under the pressures of "authority" and fashion.

Artists are familiar with this melancholy phenomenon, and resigned to it. The painter Constable recounts in a letter his journey by coach with "two gentlemen and myself, all strangers to each other. In passing the vale of Dedham, one of them remarked, on my saying it was beautiful, 'Yes, sir, this is Constable's country.' I then told him who I was, lest he should spoil it."

The public is furthermore conditioned to renounce its rights to personal opinions, and to look to a leadership that "deals expertly"—in Wilson's words—in these as in other modern matters, relieving readers of time-consuming burdens of independent choice. Referring to literary appreciation, a foremost American critic has declared in conversation that "a person can be trained in literature just as he is trained to be a doctor or an engineer." Here again is the concept of art as a discipline to be contained within consistent laws, the seductive promise of a technology to be mastered by those who will then be equipped to dictate taste. A more unsettling view would reintroduce the element of submission to art—as an endless access to revelatory states of mind, and a means of pondering these; as a vast extension of living experience, and a way of communing with the dead; or as an intimacy with the truth, through which, however much instruction is provided and absorbed, each of us must pass alone.

The degradation of language inevitable to the "clinical" or "technological" approach takes dehumanised and pretentious forms. (A reputation becomes "canonical status," a life together is a "symbiotic relationship," and so on.) A richly literate, concisely expressive vocabulary is neither at the command, nor in the interest, of the modern critical method.

No climate outside actual repression could be less invigorating or less conducive to nonconformist inventions and discoveries than the literary atmospheric conditions we are examining here. Year after year we are led by critics through the same approved or disputed names, or bludgeoned with the one or two highly publicised newcomers; but almost never surprised by having our attention drawn to a neglected or unfashionable talent in contemporary writing, or a voice that speaks in unsanctioned registers. Indeed, it is by dwelling on established celebrity that critics can command the prominent space and attention necessary to their self-esteem.

Such a critical attitude may hold dominion only for a limited time and over a territory of manageable dimensions. It is significant that no American periodical of appreciable circulation regularly—or even intermittently—draws attention to literary developments throughout the English-speaking world (a service long provided in Britain by the *Times Literary Supplement*), and that novels published only outside the United States are virtually never noticed or mentioned by American critics. (New novels are in any case receiving steadily less attention from reviewers in the United States.) Critical incuriosity, or, rather, an order of approved curiosity only, is contagious to readers and to authors themselves. James Jones echoed a prevalent belief when he recently told the press, "I got the feeling that the only real cultural excitement is happening in the U.S."

Readers, and Mr. Jones, are in a sense victims of a defective critical apparatus which, by categorically assuming responsibility for directing our aesthetic attentions, gives rise to an unfounded assumption that if anything interesting were happening in the world of English-speaking letters we would have been "told" of it. The narcissism of modern critics makes it difficult for most of them to imagine that there are significant works of whose existence they are ignorant, or whose importance they cannot adequately assess. In this ambiance the main body of intelligent American readers has been deprived of contact with extraordinary artists in every field whose work, even when published or exhibited in the United States, has been generally ignored by American critics as falling outside their target and their control, and lacking the cachet of publicised recognition.

The work of Patrick White, a foremost talent of the century, was only cursorily mentioned in the United States until, in his sixties, he was awarded the Nobel Prize for Literature. The novels of Christina Stead and the poetry of A. D. Hope were similarly neglected until both writers were in their sixties. It is to be hoped a like fate does not await the remarkable work of Randolph Stow. An outburst of literary vitality among younger Australians has gone totally disregarded in America. I recall the consternation when Edmund Wilson himself uncovered literary talent in Canada—arousing critical interest that quickly waned. American critics have not, since then, found it necessary to draw our attention to such a figure as Irving Layton. Jean Rhys was in her seventies before her reputation in Britain forced itself on unadventurous critical attention. Ivy Compton-Burnett has never had an appreciable public in the United States; neither has William Gerhardi. American readers encountered Muriel Spark not through the critical apparatus but in the pages of *The New Yorker*—where they have discovered the work of good writers from South Africa, India, New Zealand. The remarkable novels of British writers like Nicholas Mosley and Frank Tuohy remain almost unknown in America. One might give many other examples. There are also the examples of which, because of the excluding nature of modern criticism, we cannot yet know.

It is by no coincidence that many of the writers neglected or belatedly recognised by American critics have shown themselves indifferent or impervious to crude forms of "success," and are practitioners of outlawed forms—the novel of manners or of high satire, the art of narration itself or of visual imagery, the *roman psychologique*.

Parochialism—or imperialism—in literary commentary comes about when critics begin to address themselves to an audience they can readily identify: to their cronies and *copains*, to the faces in their classrooms and lecture halls, to readers of the periodicals where their articles appear. Even that limited range cannot be maintained if one does not set one's private sights beyond it. Lasting enlargements of public taste and knowledge, as distinct from fads, may disseminate from individuals but not, I think, from cliques.

While it would seem curious to call Jacques Barzun "a man of the people," his work is addressed to the responsive elements dispersed throughout a nation and an entire culture, rather than to the promptly attested notice of a predetermined segment. In the case, for example, of his writings on Hector Berlioz, a profound "influence" has truly been wielded, not for passing self-aggrandisement but for the extension of human perceptions and solaces. It is in such a spirit that we might understand Oscar Wilde's decree that "Art should never try to be popular; the public should try to make itself artistic." There is laughter in that remark, but the root of it is generosity.

Barzun has said that "magnitude creates its own space." And, at the opposite extreme, minor abilities will feel insecure and fiercely competitive in their narrow, overcrowded compound. Like all persons who openly pride themselves on the possession of analytical powers—or perhaps like all persons who openly pride themselves on anything—contemporary critics are in general disinclined to analyse themselves. Academic and journalistic mills grind small over "the creative impulse," but the impulses of critics have understandably attracted less attention. The restless Unconscious of the critical body deserves some exploration, if only to elucidate its effects on the life of the imagination.

We have already noted the need among modern critics for the touchstone of the familiar—familiarity of tone and attitude, of material, of personalities and auditors. There are few individual voices in contemporary criticism, and virtually no eccentrics. This craving for familiar association has been converted from an intellectual or private weakness into a method of regarding literature. Like the fearful traveller who is irresistibly put in mind of Lake Tahoe at Trasimeno, or perceives in the Pyrenees the reassuring profile of the Appalachians, the modern critic compulsively sees an individual work of literature as a decoy over which a net of allusion and analogy may be cast. The inter-action—the "ecology"—of reading and general culture that prepares us to discern and enjoy each singular work is thus dissipated, in the name of the ominous oxymoron "comparative literature," in distracting correlations fortifying to the critic's uncertainty but exhaustingly burdensome to literary appreciation.

In examining this method of criticism we must again notice how rarely the pleasure of a given work is made present to us; and how seldom, if ever, the critic steps aside to allow art to speak, inimitably, for itself. In this regard we might recall Auden's observation on the poetry of C. P. Cavafy—that Cavafy's "unique tone of voice [leaves] nothing for a critic to say, for criticism can only make comparisons."

How little accounting has been required of this ideology. Should we not enquire of its academic exponents—who are often also the journalists of modern criticism—why the literary doctoral dissertation has been reduced under their tutelage to a byword for witless pretension and bureaucratic self-advancement? What explains the lack of issue from the "schools of creative writing" where many critics ply their trade? Why for instance should the post-graduate student of an eminent critic pass an afternoon propounding to me his mentor's view of the "ancestral" development of literature, but be incapable of accurately reciting a single line of the celebrated short poem central to his own doctoral thesis? Why does conversation with the advocates of such methods provide so little enlightenment or plain pleasure? And why, above all, has literature been for centuries delighted in and generated by persons unversed in the present approaches?

A related and painful search for public and social acceptance colours much contemporary critical writing. While a "realism" of the self-serving and selective kind against which Plato cautions is rigorously enjoined by critics upon artists, their own vocabulary is dense with embarrassing homage to what is "patrician," "aristocratic," "exquisite," "august," "prestigious," "gracious," "towering," and even "upper-class" —expressions ingenuously exposing a hankering either after feudal bondage or for a naïvely conceived and apparently unattainable worldliness. The modest activities of colleagues are rashly pronounced "major" or "brilliant"; and the very word "sophisticated," at the best of times an uneasy adjective, has developed a parvenu ring.

The same trend to *cafonaggine* presumably accounts for the introduction into a number of modern critical studies of what one reviewer has politely called "unfocussed erudition"—a profusion of learned references having little or no relation to the text. Such indications of insecurity remain, so far as I know, unexplored. Might not the critic urging "tough-mindedness" be encouraged to develop a version of it that would include honesty towards his own contradictions, vanities, prejudices and worldly ambitions?

"From this day painting is dead." That greeting—offered to early photography—has often been exultantly quoted in recent years. (And no clearer illustration could be given of the delusion that revelations made to us, in this case visually, through imaginative art can be made more "efficient," and in fact superseded, by "improved techniques.") As it is patently to the benefit of all that as many forms of expression as possible should be encouraged to coexist, it would be recreant to ignore the competitive and destructive view that delights in such a remark. We are continually hearing—though not from novelists—that the novel is dead; the death of the theatre is acclaimed with undisguised satisfaction each Sunday. One literary journalist proclaims that every novel is guilty until it proves itself innocent, while another writes of "loving to hate" literary prizegivings. An eminent critic tells us that reading is itself "an art of defensive warfare," and that modern poetry is doomed, "self-slain, murdered." Indicatively violent phrases and images, along with the inevitable "hard-hitting" talisman, abound in modern criticism, whether employed in self-praise or to extol approved authors, or in blatant aggression against art itself; the whole more suggestive of a mugging than of the writing and reading of books. To disregard the hatred and envy overt and even explicit in such utterances is to be "unrealistic" in the extreme.

The intentions of a novelist or poet are important, but he must be judged on talents of expression that may not be commensurate with them. The intentions of the critic, on the other hand, necessarily form the basis of our judgement of his writings, whatever his abilities or deficiencies of communication.

Such then is the climate of criticism in which creative writers in the United States, and to an increasing degree throughout the English-speaking world, have been at work for more than a generation. Its effects on content and style are evident enough, and through these we may guess at more subtle repercussions on the central nervous system of literature.

As always where there is intimidation, attempts to neutralise or appease it become confused for lack of firm conviction; while combativeness is merely another unhelpful distraction in the case of art. The contemporary artist already labours under social, political and cultural conditions to which he may well feel antagonistic or alien; and modern criticism, in blindly aligning itself with these, has come to be an exacerbation of his difficulties.

Much contemporary fiction pays tribute to the critic's restrictive range of reference, or to his view of "reality" in repetitive fantasies of violence or of absolute action and belief bearing little relation to the living experience of most writers or their critics. Only a handful of serious modern novelists—among them Evelyn Waugh, Graham Greene, Anthony Powell, Nicholas Mosley—have treated the "developed" society where it is rifest: inside the offices, professions, bureaucracies and industries that are daily life for tens of millions. As heroes of Victorian novels died of immaculate "wasting" diseases, modern characters, when gainfully employed at all, are in the main assigned blameless or "interesting" professions—are writers themselves or, more vaguely, painters or architects seldom discovered at easel or drawing board.

The vast contingent loss to fiction can be briefly illustrated not only by reflecting on the richness contributed by worldly professional experience in an extraordinary case like Conrad's, but by considering the validity of such a character as Lydgate in *Middlemarch*, whose medical career, meticulously studied by George Eliot, is yet brought forth in a complete and human naturalness; or by recalling the multi-dimensional creation of a painter's life in Patrick White's *The Vivisector*.

The retreat, in most modern fiction, from the raging occupational diseases of our era is one of those "light planks over a dark abyss" which Henry James bravely deplored in a work of his own. Few writers, and fewer reviewers, in fact now possess, or take pains to acquire, intimate knowledge of a livelihood outside the enclosures of academic life, journalism, publishing, or authorship itself. Yet the realism—and here I wish to give the word a rightful meaning—of Flaubert was precisely the ability to confront us with our daily human condition and proclaim it in what Barzun has called "the rhetoric of actuality." While ignoring the abyss of daily occupation, critical trends have paradoxically and insistently called upon artists to become chroniclers of, and even spokesmen for, the events rather than the experiences of our era.

Barzun has said, speaking of Auden, that "it is very difficult for an artist to be intelligent." This ancient and complex question, which has undergone great transformations of context since it exercised Socrates, acquires new force in an epoch when there is heightened temptation, and high critical provocation, for the artist to deliver a "message," persuading himself it is intrinsic to his vision. In the critic's lexicon, the word "committed"—formerly used to denote consignment to a madhouse—has come to refer in commendation to the author who in his creative work makes specific, topical intervention towards some immediate public end. This demand presupposes not only that art must be serviceable, but that "pure" art, left to its own artifices, will necessarily be detached, tame, and in fact "artistic." There is nothing in the history of literature to suggest any such puerile outcome.

It is not the business of the artist to give functional satisfaction as if he were some sort of home appliance, but to enlarge our sensation and perception of life. He is not simply a reflector to be judged by distinctness of received impression, but a source of insight and consolation. We can only transcend a fate we can reveal and express—in that sense realism itself is a means of spiritualising experience; and society, forced back to the wall of essentials, will require not mere vivid bulletins on its afflictions but the coherence and redemption that a great articulation can by complex means provide.

Auden's reiterated assertion that "Poetry makes nothing happen" can neither be demonstrated nor disproved. We need not in any case assume that General Wolfe took Quebec *in spite of* having read Gray's *Elegy*. What is certain is that the poet or novelist must be free of the constricting desire to cause events. "Universality" itself—or a self-indulgent insistence on crude representations of it by author or critic —can be a retreat from larger themes and more demanding forms of disclosure.

One sympathises with Auden's anxiety that poetry not be perverted into a "useful" instrument. In a larger sense, however, the nature of poetry has been differently regarded by other societies and eras; and, even in the view of poets themselves, its "function" has not been agreed or constant. In his *Paideia,* the classicist Werner Jaeger comments that "the modern belief in art for art's sake" cannot be applied to the study of Greek poetry, and goes on to say:

> The idea that poetry is not useful to life first appears among the ancient theorists of poetics; and it was the Christians who finally taught men to appraise poetry by a purely aesthetic standard—a standard which enabled them to reject most of the moral and religious teaching of the classical poets as false and ungodly, while accepting the formal elements in their work as instructive and aesthetically delightful.

*

Asked to justify his employment of "fine allusions, bright images, and elegant phrases," Dr. Johnson responded with a definition of "style":

> Why, Sir, all these ornaments are useful, because they obtain an easier reception for the truth.

A recurring error of criticism is to treat "style" as an insubstantial literary contrivance distinct from the author's "material." In no form of serious creative expression is such a divorce possible. Style is a context, as well as a deployment of words and phrases. It is a tone in which the writer proclaims and maintains his independence, and establishes affinities with his reader. In books, as in human relations themselves, style may be developed almost imperceptibly or fixed in an instant. One has been aware of style as providing animation or, simply and splendidly, ease of reading. Or one has seen a comma placed like a stone in a Japanese garden.

Literalness, and the preference for comparables over distinctions, have not favoured the apprehension of context that Proust was assuming in his readers when he told us, through his Narrator:

> I recognise that Dostoevsky's preoccupation with murder is something extraordinary that makes me feel quite alien to him. I am stupefied enough when I hear Baudelaire say:

> *Si le viol, le poison, le poignard, l'incendie . . .*
> *C'est que notre âme, hélas! n'est pas assez hardie.*

But I can at least assume that Baudelaire is not sincere.

Proust was not of course accusing Baudelaire of expressing false sentiments, but acknowledging a gulf between sentiment and commitment, and a distance between an environment of deadly earnests and one in which a poet might explore sensation in the knowledge, shared with his reader, that none of his exercises need be conclusive.

The ultimate function of style is not to deliver successive new effects but to refresh and acclimatise perpetual truth. It is through art that this continuity of our existence is given both coherence and mystery, and that even as children we recognise and learn about our lives before we live them. The task of the writer is to find an inspired means of striking truth afresh and releasing its regenerative powers. "The thousandth time," Robert Frost says, "may prove the charm." Even the greatest artists, or great movements in the arts, cannot exhaust fundamental truths: they can only draw out aspects of them. Thus Stravinsky on the music of Wagner: "Wagner did much harm to certain things in music. Everyone who creates does harm to something. *But that something must defend itself.*"

The reclamation through style of a recurring human discovery may be illustrated with three disparate and relatively recent literary renderings of the same emotion:

In a brief passage in Graham Greene's novel *The Heart of the Matter* (1948), the death of his daughter is, through a confusion of telegrams, first announced to the central character at his wartime post in Africa, and then "mitigated" by a subsequently delivered message that there is still hope.

> For a moment until I realised what had happened, I was—disappointed. That was the terrible thing. I thought "now the anxiety begins, and the pain," but when I realised what had happened, then it was all right, she was dead, I could begin to forget her.

The Dr. Watsons of literary detection may easily connect this passage to Greene's description in his autobiography (1971) of the "two telegrams delivered in the wrong order," which during his own wartime service in Sierra Leone brought him news of, respectively, his father's death and illness.

An analogous experience is treated, in great length, subtlety and beauty, by Proust in the death of Albertine—through letters, mistimed attempts at reconciliation, and, ultimately, a misconception concern-

ing a telegram received at Venice that evokes, in the recipient-Narra-
tor, sensations of resistance and disappointment closely similar to
those recounted by Greene.

Lastly, in *The Importance of Being Earnest,* yet another imbro-
glio of the telegraph office finds Miss Prism expressing, in a single
sentence, her uneasiness at the resurrection of the supposedly defunct
Ernest:

> After we had all been resigned to his loss, his sudden return seems to
> me peculiarly distressing.

It is experience that is "comparative" here, not literature.

*

In the Italian hill town of Cortona there is a painting on wood
of which the official *Guida d'Italia* has this to say:

> The Muse Polyhymnia: according to some, an original classical work
> from the first or second century A.D. According to others, a fabrication
> from the 18th or 19th century.

No doubt the experts have the matter in hand . . .

C. BRIAN COX

The Editing of *Critical Quarterly*

". . . the conquest of the public imagination by the arts, by 'art
as a way of life,' has reinforced the natural resistance of the
mind to ordinary logic, order, and precision, without replacing
these with any strong dose of artistic logic, order, and precision.
The arts have simply given universal warrant for the offbeat, the
unintelligible, the defiant without purpose. The schools have
soaked up this heady brew. Anything new, obscure, implausible,
self-willed is worth trying out, is an educational experiment. As
such, it is validated by both science and art. Soon the pupil
comes to think that anything unformed, obscure, slovenly *he*
may do is validated by art's contempt for tradition, correctness,
and sense."

JACQUES BARZUN, *The Centrality of Reading*

In August 1958, Tony Dyson and I were lecturing at a British Council
summer course in Cambridge. One pleasant afternoon we walked to
Grantchester, and our talk was about literary criticism and the changes
we should like to see in the teaching of English. We contemplated a
book to be written jointly on the subject, and then later in the afternoon we considered starting a new literary journal.

F. R. Leavis's *Scrutiny* had died in 1953, and since then the need
for a replacement had become a common university topic of conversation. In 1958 Dyson and I were lecturers at provincial universities,
both under thirty years of age. There was no hope of financial backing,
and from our own money we knew we would have difficulty raising
even £50 to launch the project. Our conversation moved forwards and
backwards between our literary values and questions of administration
and finance. We were full of ideas and enthusiasm. At the end of the
day we had a scheme for promotion of the new journal fully worked
out.

Many young writers dream of starting a new literary journal, but in most cases their unconscious purpose is solipsistic self-expression, and they do not think about their readership. Dyson and I were determined to reach a large audience, and this had an important influence on the characteristic values of our journal. For the next fifteen years we were to spend much time at editorial meetings discussing money. This incentive to find subscribers, to be aware of the needs of our readers, contributed significantly to the early success of *Critical Quarterly*. To lie in bed at dawn thinking of an unpaid printer's bill for £300 forces an editor to reflect carefully on the realities of communication, on how his journal can become a living, active agency in society. This preoccupation with communication and audience also fitted in with our ideas about the function of literary criticism; it put *Critical Quarterly* in tune with the most interesting developments in recent English writing. Just as *Scrutiny*, started in 1932, by and large reflected the literary values established by Eliot and the moderns, so our journal was influenced by the assumptions of Philip Larkin, Donald Davie and the Movement poetry of the 1950s.

Our plan was to move forward in stages, and to leave ourselves the possibility of withdrawal if anything went wrong. We decided that first we must associate with ourselves a number of writers whose work we admired. This would provide a group of useful contributors; it would also persuade prospective buyers that this was not to be a young man's folly, but a major new literary magazine. We started by asking two friends to work as editorial advisers. These were John Danby, an excellent literary critic, author of *Shakespeare's Doctrine of Nature*, and Richard Hoggart, well known for his *The Uses of Literacy*. Both were generous and warm-hearted, willing to offer assistance while leaving final decisions to Dyson and myself. Danby was Dyson's professor at Bangor, and Hoggart was at that time teaching in the Extra-Mural Department at my university at Hull, so consultation was easy. Dyson had the use of a flat in London, where we met for editorial meetings, and there were many long telephone calls. We had a simple agreement that in selection of material both of us had the right of veto.

The first problem was to choose a name for our journal. Should it be "Bastion" (too pompous), "Horizon" (used before), "Ariel" (not distinctive enough), "Bridge" (a card game) or "Communication" (sounds dull)? In the end Danby proposed *Critical Quarterly*. "It sounds as if it has existed for a hundred years," he argued.

The next stage in our plan was to write to several friends to invite them to join an honorary committee. These included the poets Philip Larkin and R. S. Thomas, the novelist Angus Wilson, and university teachers such as John Jump, David Daiches and Graham Hough. We sent out sixteen invitations hoping for five or six favourable replies. Within a few days we received acceptances from all sixteen. We found ourselves in an embarrassing position, for our list now looked distinctly odd. If all these people had been selected, why had others not been asked? We decided to invite every Professor of English in Britain. Again the response was good, with this time just a few refusals. We ended up with an honorary committee of thirty-five. After our first issue was published we were assisted by an American associate editor, R. J. Kaufmann, and he added eleven American names to the list, including Saul Bellow and Richard Wilbur.

Meanwhile we had been obtaining estimates from printers for an eighty- or ninety-six-page octavo size quarterly journal. The best estimate came from Hull Printers Ltd., just a couple of miles from my home; the opportunity to drop in regularly to discuss problems proved invaluable. Our next step was to print stationery with a large letterhead listing ourselves, our advisers, and our honorary committee.

The time had come to risk our £50. We could not afford to advertise in the *Times Literary Supplement* or similar journals, and this was fortunate. In later years, when we were more affluent, we discovered that such advertisements do not bring in many subscriptions. Our plan was to duplicate descriptions of our journal on our printed notepaper and to send these through the post to selected groups of people. Our market would be teachers of English in universities, colleges of education and schools. In addition to our circulars we enclosed a business reply card, which could be returned free of charge. On this the subscriber promised either to buy the first issue at 3 shillings, including postage, or to pay an annual subscription of 12 shillings. We trusted that a policy of order now, pay later, would be attractive, and that our audience of professional teachers would not produce many bad debts.

By October we were ready to send out the circulars. In 1958 postage for advertisements cost only twopence, and so for £30 it was possible to dispatch our material to 3,600 people. The only additional costs were for paper and envelopes. Parties were held at my home, with neighbours enlisted with bribes of wine to write addresses and put circulars in envelopes. Eventually the posting was completed, and we awaited results. The first day there were seven cards returned. The next day we were jubilant when a pile of thirty-two arrived. Although we did not realise it, our success was assured. Over the years, during which we repeated these circularisations regularly, we discovered that a good initial response inevitably continues for several weeks. Many subscribers ordered for the year, and we were encouraged to send out further circulars, particularly to libraries all over the world. We were also bullying our friends to subscribe, and soon we had enough money promised to cover our first printing bill, with a good deal left over for the second. We had only obtained three and a half pages of advertising at £10 a page, but this was to improve after our first issue when our circulation figures became known.

The stages we had planned in Cambridge in August were complete. By Christmas 1958, we were editors of a non-existent journal with an impressive honorary committee and over 1,000 subscribers. The total cost to our own pockets was not much more than our original allocation of £50. The first issue was due out in Spring 1959. We were about to learn that although our financial problems were temporarily solved, it would not be so easy to fulfil our literary ideals.

In 1955 Philip Larkin had been appointed university librarian at Hull. I had completed one year at Hull, and he was to have an important influence on my literary values and on the policy of *Critical Quarterly*. Larkin, an admirer of Thomas Hardy, disliked both the obscurity of modern verse and the aridity of much professional literary criticism. He felt that "poetry, like all art, is inextricably bound up with giving pleasure, and if a poet loses his pleasure-seeking audience he has lost the only audience worth having, for which the dutiful mob that signs on every September is no substitute." In October 1955, he published *The Less Deceived*, which made him famous. In 1956 Robert Conquest's anthology, *New Lines*, firmly established Larkin and the "Movement" as the main development in British poetry of the 1950s. *Critical Quarterly* included an article on Larkin in its first issue, and was particularly influential in publishing Movement poetry. (Our journal was to publish new poetry as well as literary criticism, and perhaps its principal success was that so many well-known poems first appeared in its pages—Larkin's "Love Songs in Age," Ted Hughes's "Hawk Roosting," Thom Gunn's "Back to Life," R. S. Thomas's "Here," Sylvia Plath's "A Birthday Present," Louis Simpson's "On the Eve.")

This policy immediately brought a split between the editors and some of their *Scrutiny* supporters. Dyson and I had both been taught at Cambridge, and for one term had attended F. R. Leavis's practical criticism seminar. During our years at Pembroke College from 1949 onwards we had been typical of many fellow undergraduates reading English in taking little interest in contemporary verse. We read Dylan Thomas, of course, but our attitude towards new poets tended to be one of contempt. We were swayed by Leavis, whose denunciations of contemporary writers such as Auden were naturally popular with youthful, immature audiences. There was a puritanical narrowness of spirit in the Cambridge English school which led us to confine our attention exclusively to Leavis's great tradition, and which left us unresponsive to the pleasures of games with words, or to the small felicities of diction which grace even minor poems. Ted Hughes, also at Pembroke at this time, wisely abandoned the English Tripos after Part One, and transferred his attention to archaeology and anthropology. I saw him regularly for three years; it is a sign of the Cambridge atmosphere that I never discovered he was writing poetry.

During the 1950s, Dyson and I had become increasingly critical of our Cambridge training. As editors we were in tune with George Steiner's views as expressed in 1974 in an open letter to the first issue of *The New Review:* "One trusts critical ferocity when it has behind it either a manifest creative achievement or a parallel impulse to advocacy. . . . It is an open question whether it is *ever* productive to discard courtesy, humaneness, a complete alertness to the vulnerabilities involved, when one is writing criticism." Dyson and I felt that the *Scrutiny* tradition, so full of vitality in the 1930s, had lost this impulse to advocacy. We wanted to turn literary criticism away from puritanism towards intelligent celebration of creative achievements. As editors we committed ourselves to advocacy by printing new poems in each issue, often by unknowns, and by our choice of recent writers to be featured.

In 1958 we felt optimistically confident that we could assist the development of an expanding élite. We believed that it is worth devoting a life to presenting, teaching, and celebrating great art, of both past and present, and that academic criticism can be of benefit to the general reader. The aim of *Critical Quarterly* was to promote high standards in common educated discourse, to make literature accessible to any student with goodwill, and, in Northrop Frye's words, to prevent it from "stagnating among groups of mutually unintelligible élites." We opposed the tendency to introduce specialised jargon into literary criticism, and could see no reason why a Ph.D. dissertation should not be written in clear English. The style of our articles, like that of Movement poetry, was to be intelligible to any educated reader.

Donald Davie contributed a poem to our first issue and became a regular contributor. Our ideas as editors were influenced by his books, *Purity of Diction in English Verse* (1952) and *Articulate Energy* (1957), which in many ways served as an apologia for the Movement. Davie argues that words should be part of a contract entered into tacitly by speaker and hearer, writer and reader, a convention

which they both observe. The poet should communicate with his readers in terms of contracts to which they are accustomed. If a reader
knows that a poem is to be an elegy or a pastoral or a satire, then he
is prepared to give it a certain kind of attention. Both genre and syntax are forms of contract which assist the poet to communicate with
the reader. Words themselves are another type of contract, and, if
civilised communication is to be achieved, it is essential that words
should keep their relation to everyday meanings, and not be transformed into a private language by the poet himself.

Davie requires poets to mean what they say, and to relate their
poems to common experience. These ideas impose a clearly defined
role upon poet and critic, different from that held by Leavis and the
Scrutiny critics. The poet is no longer seen as the guardian of T. S.
Eliot's "unified sensibility," uttering fine sentiments to a small élite of
initiates. He is a man speaking to men. And the critic no longer claims
special insights beyond the comprehension of the common reader. He
is concerned not just with a small number of great works that satisfy
his rigorous ethical demands, but with all the rich varieties of response
offered by literature. He thinks of himself not as a member of an
Elect, but as scholar and teacher.

Davie argues that systems of syntax are part of the heritable property of past civilisation, and to hold firm to them is to be traditional
in the best and most important sense. The abandonment of syntax
testifies to a failure of the poet's nerve, a loss of confidence in the intelligible structure of the conscious mind and the validity of its activity. Eliot's theory of the objective correlative implies a loss of faith
in conceptual thought, and much subsequent analysis of poetry is
grounded on the delusion that what cannot be imagined cannot be
conceived. In fact, abstract language can often be more concrete, more
adequate as an articulation of experience, than imagery.

This emphasis on orthodox syntax and clarity of meaning was a
strong influence on the idea of an educated community which inspired
the early years of *Critical Quarterly.* Our aim was to ensure that high
standards of lucid English and a wide appreciation of great literature
remained powerful elements of our common culture.

Each issue of *Critical Quarterly* was to include regular features,
with emphasis on recent literature. We were also determined to print
only short articles of up to 4,000 words, but under pressure from our
contributors this policy had to be abandoned. We have always tried,
however, to include short articles, as a help to the reader and because
a good argument often needs only 2,000 or 3,000 words for clear

elucidation. In our opening year we had articles on living authors (myself on Larkin, Dyson on Hughes, Danby on Empson), on recent literature (Dyson on *Look Back in Anger*, Raymond Williams on *Under Milk Wood*), analyses of poems, symposia on the teaching of English, "Our Debt to Dr Leavis" and Dickens, reviews of new books, and surveys of recent literary criticism on major works or writers (G. K. Hunter on *Hamlet*, Rosemary Woolf on Chaucer). We were accused of riding two horses. We were publishing new poems and engaging in controversial assessments of new writing; at the same time we had an educational aim. The main response to our circulars had come from school teachers cut off from first-class libraries, and we had to keep their needs in mind. In my opinion this double role gave vitality to the early years of *Critical Quarterly;* by introducing new poetry and criticism into schools it had a major influence on the teaching of English.

We printed 2,000 copies of the first issue. It sold out quickly, and we had to order a reprint of 1,000. Our circulation crept up steadily towards 5,000, where it stuck for the next twelve years. We discovered that we could derive little financial benefit from sales through bookshops. Famous shops such as Dillon's in London or Blackwell's in Oxford might sell ten or twenty over the counter, but all shops demanded a 25 percent or 33 ⅓ percent or even 50 percent discount, which we could not afford. W. H. Smith took twelve copies of the first issue at their Hull bookshop, put them on display for three days, sold one, and, according to their custom, tore the covers off the remaining eleven for return to us to prove they had been unsold. We received 1s 3d from the deal. Although advertisements increased to about ten to twelve pages per issue, our income came largely from direct subscriptions through the post.

At the beginning of our second year, Oxford University Press agreed to administer our subscriptions for a payment of 10 percent of the money collected. This removed a major burden of work, but until 1973, when Manchester University Press took over, Dyson and I retained final responsibility for balancing the books and paying the bills. In 1962 the Calouste Gulbenkian Foundation provided a grant for a full-time secretary for three years, but previously almost all the work was done by the editors. It is not too difficult to bring out a quarterly journal once, but when the thirteen-week cycle is completed it starts again immediately, and there is no rest period.

I had always imagined that material of high quality would come through the post from unknown writers. This is not so. Very soon we were receiving an average of twenty manuscripts per week; today the number is sometimes as high as forty. Unfortunately almost all are useless to us. Most of the verse is childlike in technique; it is an interesting phenomenon that so many people write and try to publish bad verse. Many critical articles are from the United States and presumably have already been rejected by major American journals.

All selection is carried out by Dyson and myself, and we rarely refer manuscripts to experts. We believe we ourselves must determine the identity of the journal. Most material has to be specially solicited. At our editorial meetings a regular feature is the compilation of lists of people to whom we might write for an article or poems. What does an editor do if the solicited material proves poor? Our view is that the editor's duty must always be to his audience, and that in no circumstances must he publish material of unsatisfactory quality. A commercial journal can pay the fee and not publish; we cannot afford to. The results may be unfortunate. Editing a literary magazine is an effective method of making enemies.

Our success persuaded us to bring out further publications, and to organise conferences for our subscribers. In 1960 we published a twenty-four-page poetry supplement, intended as a selection of the best recent poems. We also organised a poetry competition and included the two winning poems in the supplement. Philip Larkin assisted us with the judging, and the prize was shared between Alan Brownjohn and Sylvia Plath. We sold 12,000 copies, and so began an annual series which continues to the present day.

In our second year we published "The Sediment" by Thomas Blackburn, which won the Guinness prize of £300 for the best poem of the year. At the Guinness party to celebrate the awards I first met Sylvia Plath. She was gratified to hear that our prize had been awarded to her before we knew she was married to Ted Hughes. During the next two years Dyson and I had dinner on various occasions with Ted Hughes and Sylvia, and we persuaded her to edit our second anthology, *American Poetry Now*, a collection of new writing. This too sold thousands of copies.

In 1961 we organised a five-day course at Bangor for over 150 of our subscribers. We repeated this the following year when Ted Hughes and Sylvia Plath read their poetry. We turned ourselves into a Society and started a new journal, *Critical Survey*, with special emphasis on the educational needs of the schools. We began a series of four-day courses for sixth-formers, with all the main sessions devoted to academic discussion of literature. These still continue, and are regularly attended by audiences of over four hundred. We also arranged an annual dinner, and invited all our regular contributors. We had an excellent younger group (Bernard Bergonzi, A. R. Jones, Barbara Everett, David Lodge, Malcolm Bradbury, Tony Tanner, G. D. Josipovici) and also support from established writers such as Helen Gardner, John Wain, Graham Hough, Raymond Williams and William Empson.

In the mid-1960s we were confidently expanding our activities, with little idea of the problems soon to assail our enterprise. We were already aware that the Movement had been supplanted by new developments in poetry. In 1964 we published "After the Tranquillised Fifties," by A. R. Jones and myself, in which we acknowledged that the most startling poetry since Conquest's *New Lines* had been Robert Lowell's *Life Studies* (1959) and Sylvia Plath's last poems, eventually collected in *Ariel* (1965). We ourselves had published Plath's "A Birthday Present," one of the extraordinary poems written in the months before she died. We were also publishing Anne Sexton's confessional poems and printing articles on Harold Pinter and Samuel Beckett.

Jones and I argued that the return to orthodox syntax and conventional stanza forms in Movement poetry had often accompanied a withdrawal from certain difficult areas of experience. The result was thinness of content. It was as if the 1939–45 war had produced a relapse among many English writers, a psychological return to Edwardian modes of art, as a means of avoiding the terrifying implications of war. Many Movement poets had been young men during the war. Their writing appeared to represent a denial of the horror of such facts as Dachau, Belsen and Hiroshima, a refusal to be contaminated by the chaos in which their youth had been involved. They withdrew from politics and fighting, and tried to celebrate the inviolate quality of their personal emotions in orderly, disciplined verse. Larkin's *The Whitsun Weddings* (1964) included some of the best poems in this mode, combining lucidity and compression of meaning with orthodox metres and rhyme. Larkin often makes the point that for him withdrawal from life is necessary for the preservation of the self, though in poems such as "Dockery and Son," "Self's the Man" and "Send No Money" he explores with subtlety his own doubts and the price he has had to pay.

In contrast, much European and American literature of the 1950s remained experimental, only too conscious of the irrational anarchy by which the individual was threatened. In the early 1960s these influences began to dominate the English literary scene, particularly the theatre. Pinter's new plays, with their verbal brilliance, their lack of paraphrasable rational content and their atmosphere of menace, clearly had more in common with *The Waste Land* than with the poetry of the Movement. Similarly, the poetry of Lowell and Plath was moving into new and disturbingly unusual territories of mind.

As editors of *Critical Quarterly* could we welcome the subversive quality of this new modern writing with the same enthusiasm as we had greeted poets such as Larkin and Davie? Was it right to promote literature whose tendencies were anti-rational and even suicidal? We were confronted with the dilemma which Lionel Trilling explores in his own rather different terms in *Beyond Culture*.

"After the Tranquillised Fifties" was attacked by Movement sup- porters, such as Bernard Bergonzi and John Wain, who felt we were betraying the cause. Our answer was that both *Life Studies* and *Ariel* are extraordinary because of their success in articulating the poet's personal conflicts. In this way the new poetry had kinships with that of Larkin himself, who is also concerned to express the vulnerability of the individual consciousness. As editors we were prepared to pub- licise this poetry as a form of aesthetic truth. But in the years after 1964 we became more and more disturbed by current phenomena in the arts, and we had to agree with Bergonzi and Wain that these could be dangerous. As editors we could no longer feel optimistic that by promoting rational discussion of new literature we were contributing to a gradual and inevitable enlargement of a civilised community. We had to accept that we were increasingly in the position of a be- leaguered minority, and that our duty in the future would involve more emphasis on the transmission of great literature of the past into the consciousness of present-day readers.

In 1966 we published an article by David Lodge entitled "Objec- tions to William Burroughs" which began: "Have we come to handle the *avant-garde* too gently?" He condemned the *Naked Lunch* as "dull." We ourselves responded in a similar manner to much of the neo-Modernistic ferment, the growth of neo-Dada, for example, in the late 1960s. In *Innovations*, Bergonzi suggests that what is most notice- able about neo-Modernist art is its anti-teleological quality, its lack of concern with overall order, with goals or ends. Its main function is simply to exist, to catch a perceiver's attention, and not to move in any particular direction, or manifest any ultimate purpose. For the neo-Modernist artist the past is irrelevant; art must be random, inde- terminate, and precise communication is deemed impossible. This is directly opposed to *Critical Quarterly*'s belief in the value of rational articulation. In editorials in the early 1970s we opposed the new avant-garde, which seemed to us committed to a reduced sense of human possibilities.

The major impact of our ideas was to be in the field of education. We had observed in the schools the growing influence of progressive education in breaking down faith in high culture, in reason and disciplined learning. Emphasis on activity and self-expression easily became associated with the immediacy and sensationalism of neo-modern art. As Jacques Barzun says in the epigraph to this article, the schools had soaked up this heady brew. In March 1969, we devoted a whole issue of our second journal, *Critical Survey*, to an attack on major abuses in education. We called this a Black Paper, in contrast to government White Papers which deal with future policy.

We opposed student sit-ins, and argued that students should not participate in the organisation of courses. Kingsley Amis's article in the first Black Paper began:

> A student being (if anything) engaged in the acquiring of knowledge, is not in a position to decide which bits of knowledge it is best for him to acquire, or how his performance in the acquisition of knowledge can most properly be assessed, or who is qualified to help him in this activity.

We also criticised the destruction of grammar schools in favour of large comprehensives, and we analysed the ill-effects of progressive education, particularly in the primary schools.

The first Black Paper included articles by Robert Conquest, John Gross, William Walsh and Bryan Wilson. A free copy was sent to every M.P., and we held a press conference. The pamphlet occasioned leading articles in *The Times* and the *Daily Telegraph*, and lengthy reviews in other journals.

On April 8 Mr. Short, the Labour Secretary of State for Education and Science, was due to give his major speech of the year to the annual conference of the National Union of Teachers. He chose the Black Paper as his theme, and described its publication as "one of the blackest days for education in the past 100 years." The situation created by this "backlash" against progressive education, he said, had provoked "the crisis of this century."

The result was very large coverage by the mass media and even debate in the House of Commons. The Black Paper became a best seller, and we found ourselves leading a national campaign against the excesses of progressive education. In 1969, we published a second Black Paper, perhaps the best of the sequence, in which quotations from Barzun's *The House of Intellect* were interwoven with the text. Again there was wide publicity, with coverage in all the media continuing for several weeks. Since then two further Black Papers have appeared. The most recent, *Black Paper 1975*, includes a new article by Jacques Barzun, together with contributions from Iris Murdoch, Geoffrey Bantock and H. J. Eysenck. It achieved the distinction of being listed number six in the *Sunday Times* chart of bestselling paperbacks.

And so our decision in 1958 to start a literary journal has ended in a political campaign, with the editors speaking at meetings up and down the country, contributing articles to newspapers, appearing on radio and television, giving evidence to government committees. We have proved in a unique manner that there can be no divorce between literature and politics.

JOHN SIMON

Translation or Adaptation?

". . . The worldly way to disguise that bitter pill, Shakespeare, is
to stage him with lyrics and music by Cole Porter, to direct him
out of recognition à la Webster (Margaret, not John), or to trans-
moviefy him under a coating of Freud and philosophy spoken
sepulchrally by Laurence Olivier."

> JACQUES BARZUN, "Three Memoranda on
> the New Arden Shakespeare," *The Mid-Century*, 1961.

Jacques Barzun's inquiring mind—having the unidentical twin aspects
of all truly inquiring minds, restless curiosity and calm incisiveness—
has at times also addressed itself to the theatre. Though it is unfortunate that this happened relatively infrequently, it is fortunate that
it happened at all. On one such occasion Barzun turned his attention
in *The Mid-Century* to what he called "the comedy of comedies,"
Molière's *Le Misanthrope*, and, concomitantly, to Richard Wilbur's
verse translation of it. Here, as also in the Preface to his own accomplished English version of Beaumarchais's *Figaro's Marriage*, Barzun
made some pertinent and suggestive comments on translation and
adaptation. This encourages me to hope that the following discussion
of the most important translation of *The Misanthrope*, by Wilbur, and
its most prominent adaptation, by Tony Harrison, may harmonize with
some of his concerns, whether or not it earns his approbation.

In that miniature essay about *The Misanthrope*, Barzun remarks
poignantly, after dismissing the Arnoldian notion of literary touchstones, that "if there *were* touchstones, this masterpiece would be one
of them." Yet, as he points out, the work has never been especially
popular on stage, either in France or abroad, where "for lack of proper
translations, it has tended to seem thin and dry." But the lack of an
adequate English translation was, for Barzun as also for me, remedied
with the publication, in 1955, of Richard Wilbur's splendid English

Misanthrope. It has since been performed with deserved success on numerous stages, and had no serious challenger until the British poet Tony Harrison brought out his adaptation of the play, commissioned by the National Theatre of Great Britain and first performed there under John Dexter's direction in 1973. This updating of the play to 1966 was highly successful in England, and did almost equally well on a subsequent tour of the United States; it has since been performed by other companies on this continent, notably at Canada's Shaw Festival at Niagara-on-the-Lake.

The intentions of the two poets are made clear in the respective Forewords. The one point on which Wilbur and Harrison agree is that formal verse is necessary to convey in English the effects of Molière's original. For Wilbur, the reasons are "the parody-tragic effect," "the constant of rhythm and rhyme . . . for bridging great gaps between high comedy and farce," and the assumption that "words . . . dancing within [strict] patterns are not their prosaic selves, but have a wholly different mood and meaning." Harrison explains it this way: " . . . the effect of the rhyming couplet is like that of a time-bomb ticking away behind the desperation of Alceste, and Célimène's fear of loneliness. The relentless rhythm helps to create the tensions and panics of high comedy. . . . The explosion never comes. But the silence, when the ticking stops, is almost as deafening. There is an almost Chekhovian tension between farce and anguish." Allowing for certain differences of emphasis, Wilbur's and Harrison's arguments are distinctly similar.

But whereas Wilbur announces that his is "a line-for-line verse translation quite as faithful as any . . . in prose," Harrison explains his updating as being inspired by André Ribaud's articles in the satirical paper *Le Canard enchaîné*, in which De Gaulle's régime was likened to that of Louis XIV, both of them allegedly centered on an identical "Court." Between 1959 and 1966, when Harrison's version takes place, there were, it seems, over three hundred convictions based on an ancient law that made it a crime "to insult the Head of State"; this, of course, parallels the offense of the subversive pamphlet Oronte and others attribute to Alceste. So Harrison feels that his version "has the advantage of anchoring in a more accessible society some of the more far-reaching and complex implications of Alceste's dilemma, personal, social, ethical, political."

The general merits of adaptation and updating versus those of maximal faithfulness can best be debated after a close examination of specific passages in Wilbur and Harrison. It is immediately apparent, however, that Harrison has involved himself in certain damaging

contradictions. Wilbur admits that he has made some small concessions in his diction, which "mediates between then and now, suggesting no one period." Fair enough, especially if the archaisms are no
worse than, as Wilbur says, "spleen" and "phlegm," and nothing like
"the zounds sort of thing." But here now is Harrison about his compromises in versification (in diction, where he boldly modernized, no
compromise was considered): "I have made use of a couplet . . . running lines over, breaking up sentences, sometimes using the odd
half-rhyme to subdue the chime [curious that Harrison, in this of all
places, should commit the jingle rhyme-chime!]. . . . My floating 's
is a way of linking the couplet at the joint and speeding up the pace
by making the speaker deliver it as almost one line. . . ." He mentions
also his occasional use of the Drydenian triplet and the "switchback"
rhyme derived from the comedian George Formby, where a somewhat
off-color rhyming word, though easily guessable, is deliberately superseded by a harmless non-rhyming one. And, peculiarly, he has tried
"to orchestrate certain coughs, kisses, sighs and hesitation mechanisms
into the iambic line," sometimes indicating them "by a (/) in the text."

Now, I wonder: take this many formal liberties, and what becomes of your inexorable time-bomb ticking away in the background?
Does a time-bomb make elisions, enjambments, half rhymes and
switchbacks, to say nothing of allowances for coughs, kisses and hesi-
tations? Or doesn't the tension Harrison is after depend on the greatest
strictness of metrical form being played off against the emotional,
intellectual, moral untidiness of the characters out of Molière, and
the various modernizing touches out of Harrison? But let us now see
how Wilbur's and Harrison's methods work out in characteristic
instances.

Consider, in Act I, Scene i, Philinte's "Ce chagrin philosophe est
un peu trop sauvage./ Je ris des noirs accès ou je vous envisage . . ."
Here Wilbur's "This philosophic rage is a bit extreme;/ You've no idea
how comical you seem," is perhaps less felicitous and faithful than
Harrison's "Your dark philosophy's too bleak by half./ Your moods of
black despair just make me laugh." Wilbur's "comical" seems to carry
its last syllable deliberately for the sake of the scansion, and his "philosophic rage" comes less close to *chagrin philosophe* than does Harrison's "dark philosophy." But now take the following outburst of Alceste's from the same scene:

> On sait que ce pied plat, digne qu'on le confonde,
> Par de sales emplois s'est poussé dans le monde,
> Et que par eux son sort, de splendeur revêtu,
> Fait gronder le mérite et rougir la vertu.

> The whole world knows the shady means by which
> The low-brow's grown so powerful and rich,
> And risen to a rank so bright and high
> That virtue can but blush, and merit sigh.   (Wilbur)

> The guttersnipe! There's no one who can't guess
> the tricks he's stooped to for his quick success.
> The niche he's carved himself, in padded plush,
> makes talent vomit and real virtue blush.   (Harrison)

Neither Wilbur nor Harrison conveys the original image of the flat foot that pushes its way into high society, though "guttersnipe" seems even more inappropriate than "low-brow." But the fourth line works much better in Wilbur: Harrison's "real" is mere deadwood for the sake of scansion and weakens the parallelism ("talent" remains unmodified); moreover, "vomit" is far too strong a word to counterpose to "blush"—even if Wilbur's "sigh" may be a bit too weak for *gronder*.

Take now, a few lines later, Philinte's "Il faut, parmi le monde, une vertu traitable;/ A force de sagesse on peut être blamable;" which Wilbur renders with "This world requires a pliant rectitude;/ Too stern a virtue makes one stiff and rude," and Harrison with "Moderation's where true wisdom lies./ What we should be is *reasonably* wise." Harrison has said that he has let "the occasional couplet leap out as an epigram in moments of devastation or wit." This must be such an occasion, and he has certainly aimed at being gnomic and lapidary beyond the original itself. The pun on "reasonably" works handily for him, but why must he spoil it all by inverting the first line into catalectic trochaic pentameter: "Mŏdĕrátiŏn's whĕre trúe wísdŏm líes"? Even if we scan the third foot as an iamb (rather than as the spondee it really is), the overwhelmingly trochaic movement, clashing excessively with the iambic norm, trips up that epigrammatic "leaping out" Harrison desires. Actually, the original, with its facile rhyming of *traitable* and *blamable*, is less than Molière's best, and Wilbur's translation here might almost be an improvement over it but for that vaguely redundant "stiff and rude." But "pliant rectitude" is a very handsome rendering of *vertu traitable*, heightening a quasi-euphemism into a near-oxymoron.

Here it becomes incumbent on us to examine some of Harrison's modernizations independently of comparisons with Wilbur. For example: "And Dorilas how much he bores us all/ with how-I-won-back-France for Charles de Gaulle,/the Maquis mastermind who saved the war . . . " There would be no great harm in this if the very Molièresque *Dorilas* did not ring anachronistic in the context. Again: "In social intercourse the golden rule/ 's not curse, like you, but, like me, 'keep one's cool.' " This, too, would be clever if it were not for that awkward shift from "me" to "one's." In any case, the formal "one" is out of the question—it should be "keep your cool"; but that would get the impersonal "your" into the hair of the "you" that is specifically Alceste. This is the sort of tangle modernizers get themselves into.

But there is worse. Take "That's your humanity. There's no escape./ These are the antics of the 'naked ape.' " The reference to Desmond Morris's anthropological best seller, itself a piece of vulgarization, becomes even more questionable when you consider that the place is Paris and the time before the publication of *The Naked Ape*. In that respect, " . . . in spite of all,/ *La Belle Dame Sans Merci* has me in thrall" is better—Keats rather than Desmond Morris, and no anachronism (though, perhaps, something that could be called anatopism, for Frenchmen don't go around quoting English poetry). But is it in character for Alceste to make such literary allusions? He takes himself and his grievances extremely—excessively—seriously, and such a conversational strategy is already a kind of joking, indeed a safety valve—which is precisely what Alceste fatally lacks.

When Oronte enters, I, ii, he affirms his devotion to Alceste by saying, "if there's anything at all that I can do,/ Elyséewise, a place, an interview,/ just say the word." Now, this is simply bad English, this "Elyséewise," and no one in Molière speaks bad French; and it is particularly out of character for Harrison's Oronte, who seems to be on the fringe of the literary set, to speak like that. Harrison consistently goes in for something that, on the rare occasions when Wilbur uses it, is a blot on his version too, namely, macaronic verse, as in Harrison's "There can't be many men much more *au fait*/ with all that happens at the Elysée." Again, Oronte is made to say: "Perhaps you could suggest (I know it's cheek)/ which editors you know are *sympathique*."

This kind of language-mongering thoroughly undermines the dignity of the versification. For one thing, it presupposes an Englishy mispronunciation of French words: *fait* and *Elysée*, which do not remotely rhyme in French, have to be transmogrified into "fay" and "Elysay." But beyond versification and language, character itself gets distorted. Britishers and Americans who pepper their English with such French phrases (and that is how these translated personages affect us) are at best pretentious, at worst phonies. But Molière's characters are not—at least not all of them—obvious fakes, otherwise the whole profound meaning of the play would be lost. Even Oronte must not fall into this category; in the original, he does not ask Alceste with such obvious cheek for pull with an editor or publisher. What he asks is whether he should publish his sonnet at all, an option always available to an affluent and well-placed seventeenth-century gentleman. The trouble with modernization, then, is that what looks like an equivalent is nevertheless subtly different, and so manages to distort essential meanings.

To return now to our comparative investigation: there are a few times when Harrison's version works better than Wilbur's. Thus at the conclusion of Oronte's recitation, after Philinte praises the poem's *chute*, Alceste murmurs: "La peste de ta chute! Empoisonneur au diable,/ En eusses-tu fait une à te casser le nez!" In Harrison, Philinte exclaims: "That 'dying fall!' It closes beautifully!" To which Alceste: "I wish he'd fall and break his neck and die . . . " Wilbur has Philinte praise the poem's "close," upon which Alceste remarks: "Oh, blast the close; you'd better close your face . . ." Clearly, a literary pun is called for, and Harrison gets it, exactly as in Molière; Wilbur's pun is non-literary and somewhat lowbrow. On the other hand, Wilbur would never tolerate an ear-grater like Harrison's "to end up laughing stock and *salon* martyr,/ all for some private press's *imprimatur*," which is equally painful when, in high British, it is pronounced as an identity rather than a rhyme, and when, in some lower parlance, it becomes one of those near-rhymes too close for comfort. (With similar cacophony, Harrison will rhyme Célimène-regimen.) The original here reads: "Pour prendre de la main d'un avide imprimeur,/ Celui [i.e., ce nom] de ridicule et misérable auteur," which Wilbur renders aptly with "To purchase at a greedy printer's shop/ The name of silly author and scribbling fop."

But let us consider a few more instances of Harrison's extreme, often modernizing, cleverness actually doing him harm. Here is Célimène, in II, i, justifying her male retinue:

> Des amants que je fais me rendez-vous coupable?
> Puis-je empêcher les gens de me trouver aimable?
> Et lorsque pour me voir ils font de doux efforts,
> Dois-je prendre un bâton pour les mettre dehors?

> Is it my fault that all these men pursue me?
> Am I to blame if they're attracted to me?
> And when they gently beg an audience,
> Ought I to take a stick and drive them hence?   (Wilbur)

> Am I to blame if men can't keep away?
> I'm not the one who's leading them astray.
> They're sweet. They visit. What do you suggest?
> A mounted sentry, or an entrance test?   (Harrison)

Wilbur's rendering is correct down to the rather weak feminine rhyme of the first couplet; Harrison's moves along with nice briskness until the last verse (though one might question the two caesuras in the third line), but then he makes Célimène into a smart aleck by giving her not one but two sarcastically provocative suggestions. Even getting a mounted sentry is more of a hyperbole than just picking up a stick; the entrance test, however, is a real and uncalled-for bit of impudence. It is, moreover, beside the point; Alceste would resent erudite rivals as much as ignorant ones, perhaps even more.

When Alceste scornfully wonders by what means Clitandre has endeared himself to Célimène, Molière has: "Est-ce par l'ongle long qu'il porte au petit doigt/ Qu'il s'est acquis chez vous l'estime où l'on le voit?/ Vous êtes-vous rendue, avec tout le beau monde,/ Au mérite éclatant de sa perruque blonde?" This presents problems for a translation meant to be performed: how is a contemporary English-speaking audience to understand that a very long nail on the little finger and blond wigs were both current fads among fops? Wilbur translates admirably, conveying the implications without, as it were, incorporating footnotes in his text: "Is it that your admiring glances linger/ On the splendidly long nail of his little finger?/ Or do you share the general deep respect/ For the blond wig he chooses to affect?" Note how the second verse, though still in pentameter, is lengthened by two initial anapaests, followed by a trochee that creates a tumescent spondaic effect, "lóng|náil," followed in turn by an iamb and amphibrach. Truly, the scansion lingers, without, however, becoming hypertrophic. (Conversely, Harrison will fall, perhaps inadvertently, into hexameters, as in "Ah, you're diabolical! You take a man's weak spots . . .") Here is Harrison's version of the foregoing: "I'm at a loss. Now let me see. *I know!/* It's his little finger like a *croissant*, so,/ crooked at *Angelina's* where he sips his tea/ among the titled queens of 'gay' Paree!" Later Harrison gets around to "those golden blow-wave curls (that aren't his own)," but, beforehand, he cannot resist the vulgarity of "the titled queens of 'gay' Paree," where the homosexual reference is gratuitous, and "Paree" is what a crude American tourist, not Alceste, might say.

Things get worse whenever Harrison inserts a whole passage of his own invention. Thus Clitandre's first speech, four lines in Molière, is accurately translated by Wilbur, but Harrison prefaces it by four verses all his own: "We've been at a lateish evening 'over there.'/ Hilarious (*kiss-kiss*), the whole affair!/ I was absolutely helpless. Who'd've thought/ Elysée functions could provide such sport?" Notice that the Marquis is made more ridiculous and contemptible if he launches directly into his backbiting, as in the original and in Wilbur,

than if, as here, he first sets the scene, however effetely and inter-
larded with blown kisses. In this scene, II, iv, Harrison pulls out all
stops. Consider the passage about young Cléon, which Wilbur trans-
lates as follows:

> CELIMENE: His cook has made him popular, not he:
>   It's Cléon's table that people come to see.
> ELIANTE: He gives a splendid dinner, you must admit.
> CELIMENE: But must he serve himself along with it?
>   For my taste he's a most insipid dish
>   Whose presence sours the wine and spoils the fish.

And Harrison:

> CELIMENE: But they only go to Cléon's for the food.
> ELIANTE: Cléon's cuisine though 's not to be pooh-poohed.
> CELIMENE: The dinner turns to sawdust on one's lips
>   when Cléon's served with everything, like chips.
>   He tells a boring story and you'd swear
>   the Château Mouton Rothschild's ordinaire.

Note first how inappropriate it is for the sober Eliante to use a cute
expression like "pooh-poohed." Even more out of key are those very
British "chips," after which the ordinaire sounds like a sweaty bit of
overcompensation. The "floating 's" is overdone—three instances in
five lines—and coming before another, non-floating 's in "Cléon's
served," it creates undue sibilance on top of the customary confusion
of meaning—an audience in the theatre might well wonder "Cléon's
what is served?" By contrast, how neat and classic is Wilbur's "But
must he serve himself along with it?"—rather better, or at least clearer
on a stage, than Molière's original.

Finally, as an example of cleverness totally defeating itself, let
me adduce a speech of Eliante's (II, iv) in which, to be sure, Molière
allows that thoroughly good woman to join in the general obloquy,
but makes her do it (as Wilbur does also) with a certain reticence and
ladylike poise. In Harrison, however, we get verses like these:

> . . . the girl whose face is pinched and deathly white
> 's not plain anaemic, she's "pre-Raphaelite."
> The loved one's figure's like Venus de Milo's—
> even the girl who weighs a 100 kilos!
> "Earth Mother" 's how some doting lover dubs
> his monstrous mistress with enormous bubs.
> "A touch of tarbrush?" No, that's healthy tan.
> The one called "Junoesque" 's more like a man.
> The slut's "Bohemian," the dwarf's virtue
> 's multum in parvo like a good haiku . . .

Sheer absurdity. To begin with, the whole speech is attributed to Lucretius—Harrison starts out "How does that bit in old Lucretius go"—which makes it an anachronism within an anachronism when Lucretius speaks of pre-Raphaelites and haiku, the former, once again, a term that does not belong in France—why not Puvis de Chavannes or Maurice Denis? The tone, throughout, is unsuited to Eliante, who would not say "old Lucretius" either. In Molière, the last two verses of the speech are indeed part of a lost fragment from Lucretius he translated; but Lucretius' name is not mentioned, and, ironically, those closing lines that really are Lucretian are missing from Harrison's translation. The "touch of tarbrush" smacks of racism, inconceivable in the worthy Eliante; the "enormous bubs" is vulgar, and equally wrong for her. But consider the total chaos of the last couplet I quoted. First, "virtue" and "haiku" do not rhyme by the remotest stretch of the imagination—not unless both words are utterly mispronounced. Then, the first line of the couplet is in tetrameter, a frequent lapse in Harrison, and always uneuphonious. To make it come out right, the scansion would have to be: "The slút's|'Bŏhé|mǐán,'|the dwárf's|vǐr-túe," which is impossible, and the couplet ends up a shambles.

I have given sufficient examples, I trust, of Harrison's loose versification, exaggerated cleverness, and excessive modernization, and the damages done by them. There are, however, two cases where the updating results in utter nonsense, and seriously endangers the very plausibility of the action. One is the business of the Marshals' Tribunal set up to prevent dueling, which commands Alceste and Oronte to appear before it so as to forestall a potential duel. Harrison changes this into a midnight meeting at Maxim's of the members of the French Academy (a likely story!) to which the feuding poetaster and his critic are summoned for the settling of their literary dispute (an even likelier story!). But Harrison compounds the preposterousness when (as reported by Philinte) he has Alceste ask the academicians about Oronte: "What is it that he wants my praises for?/ Recommendation for the Prix Goncourt?" Not even the tactless Alceste could be such an oaf as to bring up the rival academy, the Goncourt, to the Académie Française, a gaffe of the first order. And Philinte's account ends: "On that the two shook hands. M. Malraux/ seemed heartily relieved to see him go." I seriously question the taste of bringing in Malraux as a topical reference to lend authenticity to all this specious, tone-traducing hocus-pocus. It smacks of the vaudevillian who, coming to play a new town, quickly throws into his stock material a few jocular local references. And so sloppy is Harrison that he keeps referring to Oronte's poem as a sonnet, which in Molière and in Harrison's own first draft it was indeed. But Harrison changed it in his final version into "something closer to . . . today's poetaster," as he says—to wit, a piece of free verse. But nowhere else in the text has the necessary emendation been made. To return to my basic point, though: Free verse for sonnet, why not? But a literary debate with academicians for an urgent summons by a high court is not maintaining the tone and implications of Molière's *Misanthrope*.

The other serious lapse is that of the intercepting of Célimène's self-incriminating letters. Today, a prudent coquette would obviously use the telephone for such potentially damaging utterances. (Come to think of it, why didn't Harrison go all the way and introduce tape recordings made of Célimène's telephonic declarations?) Then again, no amount of champagne-guzzling (indicated in the stage directions) and pot-smoking (not in the Harrison text, but inserted by Dexter into his production) can make us quite forget that these people who keep rushing in to tell one another things that they could have communicated telephonically belong to a much earlier age than Charles de Gaulle's.

What then are we to make of Harrison's already quoted contention—which is served up to us by all good adapters, transposers, updaters and, especially, such modernizing directors as Peter Brook—that there is an advantage in "anchoring" a play "in a more accessible society"? Does *The Misanthrope* profit from setting its clock three hundred years ahead by way of a supposed Daylight Shedding Time? The measure strikes me as counterproductive. "Least of all do practical readers," wrote Jacques Barzun in a review of *The Ages of Man*, "require their Shakespeare instructively updated—Hamlet in love with his mother, Coriolanus as a Fascist, Macbeth the victim of matriarchy, and *The Tempest* an allegory of nuclear science." Yet in all of those cases there is at least a governing idea, however absurd; in Harrison and Dexter's updating of *The Misanthrope* there is only the discovery—or manufacture—of modern analogues of a random sort. But, surely, that is not news: great plays are eternal—in doublets and hose, ruffs and periwigs, farthingales and bloomers, their characters are still people, and so related to ourselves. What makes these plays magnanimous and consoling is that they permit us to reflect that humanity has not changed much, if at all, over the centuries; that our faults and follies are but variations on a theme; that our sufferings and defeats have been experienced before us, as they will be after us. We are alone, but we are not alone—someone has been there ahead of us. This quality, this comfort, is lost if the play is updated and seems to refer to our own muddles exclusively.

It is imperative, therefore, that an Englishing of *The Misanthrope*, along with possible concessions to the present, retain the timeless, old-and-new quality of a classic. Look, for example, at a passage that Harrison has translated—or, rather, updated—brilliantly. Here is how Célimène loses Alceste in the original: "ALCESTE: . . . Vos désirs avec moi ne sont-ils pas contents? CELIMENE: La solitude effraie une âme de vingt ans . . ." Harrison improves on this; his Célimène answers: "I'm only twenty. I'd be terrified!/ Just you and me, and all that countryside." This is extremely droll—rather like Oscar Wilde's Lady Bracknell asking Jack, after he has mentioned his country house and land, "You have a town house, I hope? A girl with a simple unspoiled nature, like Gwendolen, could hardly be expected to reside in the country." There is, in other words, a very modern cynicism to this "all that countryside," where the hyperbolically magnifying "all that" is made to subvert the intimate, idyllic concept of "countryside."

But the end of *The Misanthrope*, that supreme comedy that transcends comedy, should not be cleverly cynical. Rather, it should have that which it retains in Wilbur's translation, and which Barzun has labeled as nearly accurately as it can be: "Molière's mysterious ability to endue the language of Descartes with such passion and sense of fatality as to produce the sublime." That is the very thing Harrison loses, say, in Alceste's final words to Célimène: "This last humiliation's set me free/ from love's degrading tyranny." The switch from pentameter to tetrameter gives the utterance a jauntiness that is out of Alceste's and the play's character. How much more sober, weighty, and correct is Wilbur's: "Go! I reject your hand and disenthrall/ My heart from your enchantments, once for all." The regular scansion, the mildly archaic diction, and the heavy, dark, almost assonant monosyllables "once for all"—these convey the high seriousness of this great comic play.

Clio

CULTURAL HISTORY

DORA B. WEINER

Three Champions of the Handicapped
in Revolutionary France

> "The ways of cultural history are devious and uncertain to the
> degree that there can never be a handbook which will list all the
> valuable facts, and no short cut to arrive at an understanding of
> relationships . . . cultural life is both intricate and emotionally
> complex. One must be steeped in the trivia of a period, one must
> be a virtual intimate of its principal figures, to pass judgment
> on who knew what, who influenced whom, how far an idea was
> strange or commonplace, or so fundamental and obvious as to
> pass unnoticed. . . .
>
> "When we scan [our cultural heritage] and its growth at
> any given stretch of time, one of the plainest sights afforded the
> observer is the extraordinary coherence and striking family like-
> ness among the products of the age. This might in fact be made
> the test of the cultural historian's knowledge—not how much
> bibliography he can remember but how infallibly he recognizes
> a sample of prose, music or painting, or even a particular deed.
> For acts too carry their dates engraved upon them, regardless
> of the motives which, abstractly considered, are eternal."
>
> JACQUES BARZUN, "Cultural History: A Synthesis,"
> in Fritz Stern, ed., The Varieties of History, 1956.

When eighteenth-century reformers promised "equality" in the "pursuit of happiness," they gave little thought to the deaf, the blind, or
the insane. Yet the promise was soon applied to these handicapped
citizens and interpreted to imply their right to special assistance. In
France, the ferment of reform and humanitarian activity stimulated
the lifelong dedication of three leaders: the abbé Roch-Ambroise-
Cucurron Sicard (1742–1822), head of the National Institution for the

Deaf-Mute from 1790 until his death;[1] Valentin Haüy (1745–1822), founder of a school for the blind in 1785, and headmaster of their National Institution until political intrigue forced him into exile in 1806; and Dr. Philippe Pinel (1745–1826), physician-in-chief of Bicêtre in 1793, and of the Salpêtrière from 1795 to 1822, when politics felled him too. Each of these three contemporaries wrote books of fundamental importance, devised a novel method of instruction or therapy, championed a cause.

As teachers, they encountered a varied reception: Pinel and his student J. E. D. Esquirol (1772–1840) found a readier acceptance than Haüy and more lasting admiration from posterity than Sicard. Their therapy differed also: Pinel, the physician, mixed psychological treatment with modern medical methods; Haüy and Sicard, ignorant of contemporary advances in ophthalmology and oto-laryngology,[2] remained restricted to developing compensatory skills in their students. The competitive efforts of these two men were highlighted by a lifelong, fratricidal hatred.

Their work was timely. The eighteenth century perceived the deaf, the blind and the insane as freaks to ignore or ridicule, or as beasts and criminals to incarcerate and torture. True, some philosophers became fascinated with the problem of sensory deprivation; persons with impaired perception or faulty reasoning capacity intrigued them. Diderot's *Letters* on the blind and the deaf exemplify the brilliant analysis and practical concerns of philosophers. His humane thoughtfulness foreshadows the active involvement of academies and governments.[3]

But philanthropy, scientific curiosity and therapeutic devices alone did not suffice to advance the cause of the handicapped. It was the doctrine of the "Rights of Man" that secured their claim to assistance as citizens shortchanged by nature. Under the Old Régime, champions of the disadvantaged like Sicard, Haüy and Pinel drew support from the Church, the court, the Philanthropic Society, the medical profession. The French Revolution challenged, dispossessed and dis-

---

1. The notion of mutism as a necessary consequence of deafness began to be widely questioned in the mid-nineteenth century, and the term "deaf-mute" has now fallen into total disrepute. In this paper, usage will vary with the context.

2. The terms "ophthalmology," "oto-laryngology" and hereafter "psychiatry" are used for the sake of clarity even though they were not current at the time.

3. See D. Diderot, "Lettre sur les aveugles à l'usage de ceux qui voient," in *Oeuvres* (20 vols., Paris: Brière, 1821), Vol. I, pp. 283–382; and D. Diderot, "Lettre sur les sourds-muets à l'usage de ceux qui entendent et qui parlent," in *Diderot Studies*, VII (Geneva: Droz, 1965).

banded these institutions to create a more egalitarian society. Now the handicapped had to rely on the government only.

The abbé Sicard, a realist and a showman with an uncanny sense of timing, succeeded before Haüy or Pinel in using favorable circumstance and powerful connections. When, in February 1790, the Poverty Committee of the French National Assembly began to investigate sickness and disability as causes of destitution, Sicard brought some of his deaf students before the legislature where they faced written questions such as "What is an aristocrat?" Jean Massieu, Sicard's star pupil, answered in writing: "An aristocrat is a man critical of good laws who wants to be Sovereign Master and very rich." Skeptics might have noticed that Massieu (aged twenty-seven) was hardly a child and that they had witnessed a well-staged performance.[4]

Such demonstrations were familiar to contemporary Frenchmen. The abbé Charles-Michel de l'Epée (1712–1789), founder of the school that Sicard took over in 1790, had used regular public sessions to popularize sign language. He preferred this to lip reading and speech therapy which he judged unsuitable for his large classes. Sicard would in addition teach grammatical structure and logical thought to his deaf students. Both abbés considered religious instruction to be their essential goal.[5]

Sicard's political intervention brought quick reward. On July 21, 1791, the rapporteur of a bill to aid the deaf, Prieur de la Marne, pre-

---

4. The handwritten answers are preserved in the Archives nationales (henceforth referred to as AN), F[15], 2584. Among the usual participants in these public demonstrations was Laurent Clerc, later a teacher at the school. In 1816 Dr. Thomas Hopkins Gallaudet came to Paris from the United States to inquire into European methods of instructing the deaf. Clerc followed him to Hartford, Conn., to head the American Asylum for the Deaf.

5. Abbé C.-M. de l'Epée, *La véritable manière d'instruire les sourds-muets, confirmée par une longue expérience* (Paris: Nyon, 1784).

Sicard's writings pertain to three fields, all of which remained lifelong interests that often overlapped. The earliest dealt with instruction of the deaf, eventually leading to his most famous book, the account of how he taught Jean Massieu. Soon after the fall of Robespierre he produced two catechisms, one for normal children and one for the deaf, and the devotional theme reappears under the Empire and Restoration. A list of these writings follows: abbé R. A. C. Sicard, *Mémoires sur l'art d'instruire les sourds-muets de naissance* (Bordeaux, 1789); *Cours d'instruction d'un sourd-muet de naissance, pour servir à l'éducation des sourds-muets* (Paris: Le Clerc, An VIII; 2nd ed., 1803); *Manuel de l'enfance, contenant des éléments de lecture et des dialogues instructifs et moraux* (Paris: n.p., 1796); *Catéchisme, ou instruction chrétienne à l'usage des sourds-muets* (Paris: Institution nationale des sourds-muets, 1796); *Journée chrétienne d'un sourd-muet* (Paris: n.p., 1803); *Théorie des signes pour l'instruction des sourds-muets, dédiée à S.M. l'Empereur et Roi* (2 vols., Paris: Imprimerie des sourds-muets, 1808); and *Vie de Mme la Dauphine, Mère de S.M. Louis XVIII* (Lyon: Rolland, 1819).

sented to the Assembly an appealing picture of Sicard's institution.[6] He praised sign language as the proper means of communication with, and among, the deaf, especially if used in conjunction with written "conversation." He described the school's printshop, where deaf workers produced the *Journal des savants* and the *Journal d'agriculture,* earning 3,000 livres a year. Skilled volunteers taught classes in mechanical arts, drawing, sculpture, engraving and botany. A few years' support from the Assembly, and the deaf would be self-sustaining!

Prieur's bill, with an annual budget of 12,700 livres for ten staff members and twenty-four scholarships, became law. The Assembly proclaimed its "belief that it owed special protection to the establishment for the deaf-mute," afflicted with what Prieur called "a sad mistake of nature." The Assembly emphasized that the institution should become a "training school for teachers throughout the nation," and decreed that its founder, the abbé de l'Epée, be "ranked among those citizens who deserved the special thanks of humanity and of the fatherland."[7]

While Sicard thus sought national aid, Haüy appealed to the citizenry of Paris. In September 1789, for example, Haüy arranged to present to the City Council the special edition of a patriotic speech that his blind students had printed.[8] Haüy

> entered the Hôtel de Ville, escorted by a battalion of National Guards. . . . The Assembly [of the Paris Commune] moved to the great hall to receive him. The two leaders of the Commune [J.-S. Bailly, the mayor, and the Marquis de Lafayette, the commander of the National Guard] soon arrived. They entered to the sound of military music performed by Haüy's children.[9]

---

6. "Rapport sur l'établissement de l'Institution des sourds-muets de naissance, fait au nom des Comités de l'extinction de la mendicité, d'aliénation des biens nationaux, des finances, et de constitution, par M. Prieur, député de Châlons, département de la Marne, à l'assemblée nationale, imprimé par les sourds-muets," in C. Bloch and A. Tuetey (eds.), *Procès-verbaux et rapports du Comité de mendicité de la constituante, 1790–1791* (Paris: Imprimerie nationale, 1911), pp. 736–745. Archival evidence indicates that Sicard coached Prieur assiduously. See especially two letters dated June 26 and 29, 1791, from Sicard to Prieur, in AN, F[15], 2584.

7. "Rapport . . . ," in Bloch and Tuetey, *Procés-verbaux*, p. 744. The school that the Archbishop of Bordeaux, Champion de Cicé, had founded in 1783 and Sicard had headed became part of this project in 1793. Eventually, in 1859, all deaf girls were sent to Bordeaux, and the Paris establishment was reserved for boys.

8. Le Vacher de Charnois, *Discours sur le patriotisme prononcé le mardi, 1er septembre 1789, à la suite d'une messe célébrée par les Enfants aveugles, à l'occasion de l'Octave de St. Louis* (Paris: Clousier, 1789).

9. S. Lacroix, ed., *Actes de la Commune de Paris pendant la révolution* (7 vols., Paris: Cerf & Noblet, 1894–1909), Vol. I, pp. 508–509.

Observing a similar demonstration, Sébastien Mercier, in his *Tableau de Paris*, found "nothing more touching than to watch [Haüy] in the midst of his students, whose sight he seems to restore by perfecting their other senses."[10]

Haüy sought publicity to protect the future of his establishment. To make money, his workshops sold visiting cards, formal announcements and programs, and even musical notation and maps. These were printed, by a process he had perfected, as embossed text which the blind could read with their fingertips and which, when blackened, produced handsome print for the sighted.[11] His lifelong preoccupation with the mechanical and practical details of type, presses, tools and machines as teaching devices identifies Haüy as the contemporary not only of Rousseau's theories in the *Emile*, but of the plates for Diderot's *Encyclopédie* as well. Yet he had not, like Sicard, secured the right to print any official journal or review, and he was worried. With the progress of the Revolution, contributions diminished and wealthy patrons began to emigrate. "In order to help support themselves, the blind children sang masses in various churches [in 1790]," reports Galliod, one of the participants, "and afterward a collection was made on behalf of the institution."[12] Government assistance would be needed if this school was to survive.

Only after Sicard's successful appeal to the National Assembly, the source of political power, did Haüy realize that the blind, too, had rights. The legislators bowed to his claim—and, to save money, de-

---

10. *Ibid*, Vol. IV, p. 477. The quotation is from L. S. Mercier, *Tableau de Paris* (12 vols., Amsterdam: n.p., 1783), Vol. XII, p. 179.

11. V. Haüy, *Essai sur l'éducation des aveugles ou Exposé de différents moyens vérifiés par l'expérience pour les mettre en état de lire à l'aide du tact, d'imprimer des livres dans lesquels ils puissent prendre des connaissances de langue, d'histoire, de géographie, de musique, etc., d'exécuter différents travaux aux métiers, etc.* (Paris: Imprimé par les enfants aveugles, 1786). *Dédié au Roi.* More detailed treatment may be found in D. B. Weiner, "The Blind Man and the French Revolution," *Bulletin of the History of Medicine*, Vol. XL (1974), pp. 60–89.

12. [?] Galliod, *Notice historique sur l'établissement des jeunes aveugles* (Paris: Imprimé aux Quinze-Vingts, 1828), [10]. [Page references are to the longhand transcript in my possession kindly undertaken by M. Gautrot, librarian at the Institution Valentin Haüy.] This is the only account of Haüy's institution written by a participant. A search for the document at the Bibliothèque nationale, the Archives nationales, the Quinze-Vingts archives, the Institution nationale des jeunes aveugles, or the Institution Valentin Haüy pour l'aide aux aveugles all proved fruitless. Finally, a cardboard-bound volume by Galliod, dated 1828, was located. Though said to be in Braille, and therefore not previously consulted, it was printed on blank paper in relief letters—that is, by Haüy's method, preceding Braille. The unusual method of production of this text accounts for its absence from the catalogues of printed books, manuscripts or books in Braille.

creed that both institutions be lodged together in the vacant Célestins Convent.

The possibility of merging the institutions for the blind and the deaf had first been mentioned in the Assembly on August 26, 1790.[13] In fact, the idea of associating a blind man with a deaf-mute so that they might, together, have eyes and ears, was not novel; Diderot mentions it in his "Letter on the Blind."[14] However appealing initially, the arrangement does not, upon reflection, appear promising. But reflection was no longer possible in September 1791 when the Constituent Assembly faced adjournment and the hard-pressed deputies welcomed a money-saving proposal:

> "Yes, gentlemen," the rapporteur exclaimed, "the deaf-mute will understand the blind man's conversation and the blind will learn the sign-language of the deaf-mute. . . .
> Two souls locked into imperfect prisons will overcome the insuperable obstacle that nature has placed between them."[15]

This idyllic picture was further enhanced by the proposal that the needed funds should be provided by the Quinze-Vingts Hospital, "whose income shows an annual profit more than sufficient for the new establishment."[16] Nationalization of hospital property, however, would soon invalidate these calculations.

To defray the enormous cost, Haüy himself, together with L.-F.-J. Alhoy (1755–1826), headmaster of the school for the deaf in 1797–99 while Sicard was imprisoned as a dangerous rightist, elaborated a tax proposal whereby every grateful godfather would, at the birth of a healthy baby, contribute 50 centimes to aid the handicapped.[17] The legislature discussed this far-sighted and humane idea in the fall of 1799, but Bonaparte's *coup d'état* swept it away.

The Institution nationale des jeunes aveugles had a complicated early history, largely as a result of Valentin Haüy's extreme republican fervor, his limited administrative talents and his lifelong rivalry with the abbé Sicard. When the two men were enjoined to share the Célestins Convent in the fall of 1791, they already nursed a mutual

13. By Périsse du Luc, a member of the Poverty Committee. Bloch and Tuetey, *Procès-verbaux*, p. 120.

14. D. Diderot, "Lettre sur les aveugles . . . ," *Oeuvres*, Vol. I, p. 295.

15. Bloch and Tuetey, *Procès-verbaux*, p. 756.

16. *Ibid.*, p. 757. The decree of September 28, 1791 provided for the merger; see *Archives parlementaires, 1ère série*, Vol. XXXI, p. 532. The Hospice national des Quinze-Vingts, founded in 1260 by King St. Louis, is still functioning today.

17. L.-F.-J. Alhoy, [with Valentin Haüy], *Eclaircissements sur le projet d'assurance des écoles nationales des sourds-muets et aveugles-nés, fournis par les instituteurs-en-chef de ces écoles à Paris* (Paris: Institution des sourds-muets, An VIII [1799]).

resentment dating back to their apprenticeship with the abbé de l'Epée in the 1780s. In fact, manuscript autograph documents have just come to light in which the aged and bitter Haüy pinpoints "this intrigue which has persecuted me ever since December 5, 1784."[18] That date appears on an Open Letter addressed by the abbé de l'Epée to the *Journal de Paris,* in which he claimed that he could successfully teach a child *both* deaf and blind. This aroused Haüy's indignation. One may assume that the abbé Sicard sided with the abbé de l'Epée and that Haüy eventually blamed the extravagant claim on Sicard alone.

Reading the *Journal de Paris* two hundred years later, one senses a keen competitiveness between the teachers of the deaf and the blind; Haüy felt that his expertise had been challenged.[19] At the Célestins Convent in the 1790s, the two men faced each other with increasing hostility: a Catholic abbé now shared quarters and administrative authority with a married man, the father of two daughters, whose political convictions had veered sharply toward the Left.

After the declaration of war in the spring of 1792 and the fall of the monarchy in August, the situation grew more tense for Sicard, especially since the Célestins Convent was located in the populous, radical Arsenal Section of Paris, near the fallen Bastille. Haüy, the layman, emerged as an active member of revolutionary committees, while Sicard the priest aroused suspicion among the local inhabitants. Despite his great personal prestige, Sicard was arrested. "I had only one enemy," he wrote, "whose name and intrigues I shall not mention and who owed me more than one favor. . . . They came to get me on August 26, 1792."[20] Transferred to the Abbaye, Sicard rightly feared for his life, in those notorious days of the September Massacres when the rabble emptied the prisons of priests and "traitors" and killed them.

---

18. See manuscript autograph letter from Valentin Haüy to Dr. A.-R. Pignier (then Director of the National Institution for the Blind), dated October 10, 1821. Musée Braille, Institution Valentin Haüy pour le bien des aveugles, Paris.

19. See *Journal de Paris,* Dec. 20, 1783, Apr. 20, Sept. 11, 20, Nov. 23, Dec. 5, 15, 1784.

20. This quotation is taken from the ultra-conservative *Annales catholiques,* whose chief contributor and probable editor, Sicard, was then in hiding. The accounts were first "published in separate and isolated articles; they are collated to make a coherent story, *supervised and authorized by the abbé Sicard himself."* (italics mine). A. Serieys, ed., *La mort de Robespierre, tragédie en trois actes et en vers. Avec des Notes où se trouvent des particularités inconnues, relatives aux journées de septembre et au régime intérieur des prisons; notamment une relation complète de l'Abbé Sicard, et des anecdotes . . .* (Paris: Monory, 9 Thermidor, An IX [1801]). Sicard's articles in the *Annales catholiques* are often signed with the anagram "Dracis."

But Sicard was rescued by the watchmaker Monnod and hastened to reassure the National Assembly about his fate: "All hearts expected me there, and general applause announced my arrival. All deputies rushed to the rostrum to embrace me, tears flowed from all eyes when, inspired by the strongest feelings, I spoke to thank my liberators."[21] The *Moniteur universel* duly printed this address of September 4, delivered while foreign troops were invading France and the Assembly feared loss of control over a populace giddy from the recent bloodbath. But Sicard's respite lasted only one year, for he was again denounced —unquestionably by Haüy—and briefly imprisoned.[22] In 1797, the government prosecuted Sicard together with other right-wing subversives, deprived him of his headmastership and of his seat in the French Academy,[23] and condemned him to deportation to Guiana. He hid "underground" near the Boulevard Saint-Marceau.

The location suggests he might have stayed in touch with his school, which had been moved in 1794 to what is now 254, rue Saint-Jacques. After the unworkable arrangement at the Célestins had been dissolved—by a fortunate coincidence, the entire convent had been needed to enlarge the adjoining Arsenal barracks—Sicard, understandably eager to remove himself from the radical heart of Paris, had sought some spacious building with fresh air and ample grounds for his handicapped wards. His negotiating skill and political and ecclesiastic connections had procured the transfer of the deaf, in the spring of 1794, to the former Magloire Seminary, high on the Montagne Sainte-Geneviève, with magnificent gardens, orchards, nurseries and greenhouses (a location modern readers may recall from François Truffaut's film, *L'enfant sauvage*). Thus, while they shared the terrible hardships of a nation at war and in social turmoil, the deaf children, always adept at gardening, could at least grow some of their own food.

Haüy, in contrast, and for reasons of patriotic parsimony and political preference, requested on May 30, 1794 that the Committee of

---

21. Article "Sicard" by Durozoir in *Biographie Michaud*. See also *Moniteur universel*, séances du 2 et 4 septembre 1792.

22. *Procès verbal et interrogatoire de l'abbé Sicard par le Comité de surveillance et de sûreté générale dit Comité révolutionnaire de la Section de l'Arsenal, le 10 octobre 1793*. At a meeting of this Arsenal Section, of which Haüy was a member, someone challenged him to "repeat in public what he had asserted in several private conversations regarding Sicard. . . ." Cf. *Divers renseignements fournis au comité révolutionnaire de la Section de l'Arsenal sur le compte de Sicard prêtre, instituteur des sourds-muets, successeur de feu l'abbé de l'Epée*, p. 3. Both documents are to be found in AN, F[15], 782.

23. Institut national. Académie française. Archives. *Procès-verbaux*, An VI, A 2, 2.

Public Safety transfer his establishment to the vacant Maison des Filles Sainte-Catherine, on the rue des Lombards. He argued that

> the working blind and their teachers are true *sans-culottes* and ene-
> mies of luxury. They like to be housed in classrooms and workshops.
> And may I add that this building is perhaps the only one in Paris that
> would require no expense to adapt it to the uses of the National Insti-
> tution for the Working Blind.[24]

He envisioned a highly productive, self-sustaining school in the bustling, densely populated center of Paris, regardless of narrow quarters
that lacked air and sunshine and were surely inappropriate for children
in poor health. His proposal proved irresistible to the legislators, hard-
pressed at the height of the Terror.

After the fall of Robespierre, it was Haüy's turn to be "incar-
cerated three times as a terrorist." Sicard's responsibility for at least
one of these episodes can be documented.[25]

Under the Directory, both schools struggled on the edge of destitution.[26] Haüy and Sicard (or his replacement Alhoy) evidently attempted to run their establishments according to the Spartan regulations. These bear the unmistakable stamp of the duc de La Roche-
foucauld-Liancourt, their author —ever humane, idealistic, yet practical. He stipulated, for example, that:

> 19. Each student must, before leaving the establishment, have learned
> a useful trade that will enable him to earn a living . . . *The teachers
> should never forget that this is the essential goal of the . . . institution*
> [italics mine].
> 20. [Teachers get two months' vacation].
> 21. Teachers will see to it that their time of rest profits the institution
> by acquainting various parts of the kingdom with the special programs
> and explaining their purpose. They shall try to stimulate the creation
> of similar establishments in their native provinces.[27]

These precarious experiments in democratic philanthropy were
rudely shaken by General Bonaparte's *coup d'état* of November 9,
1799, which resulted in a complete reorganization of hospitals and
hospices, especially in Paris. It brought new men to power, among
them two of Sicard's old friends: André Daniel Laffon de Ladébat

---

24. AN, F[15], 231, letter dated 11 Prairial, An II.

25. AN, F[7], 4775–18.

26. See a government report dated September 1, 1797, in AN, F[15], 2459. The disorganization and scarcity prevailing in charitable institutions is abundantly documented. See, e.g., F. Rocquain, *L'état de la France au 18 Brumaire* (Paris: Didier, 1874), or L. Lallemand, *Histoire de la charité*, Vol. IV: *Les temps modernes* (Paris: Picard, 1910).

27. AN, F[17], 1145.

(1746–1829), a career civil servant who admired Sicard's work; and especially Jean-Antoine Chaptal (1756–1832), the physician and chemist who was also Pinel's friend, and who would serve as Bonaparte's Minister of Interior from 1801 to 1804. And of course the *coup d'état* brought the abbé out of hiding and back to his school, doubtless eager to get even with Haüy. The results came swiftly.

At the beginning of the Consulate, on October 8, 1800, Lucien Bonaparte, then Minister of Interior, ordered the removal of Haüy's students to the Quinze-Vingts Hospital. Youngsters who had been taught a trade and given an education were to join three hundred aged beggars. Haüy protested passionately, in three "Notes" published and posted on November 9.[28] "Why has Citizen Haüy addressed a complaint to the Tribunate?" asked Lucien Bonaparte of his deputy, Chaptal. In answer he received a copy of Chaptal's stern letter to Haüy expressing "surprise" at Haüy's public protest. When Napoleon heard of the delay, he "voiced his displeasure in the liveliest manner," Chaptal wrote to the hospital administrators. "He wishes the transfer completed within twenty-four hours." Chaptal added: "Do realize, Citizens, that the First Consul is most insistent. . . . Give me the assurance that the transfer will be accomplished by the deadline he has indicated. . . ."[29] The frightened officials complied and, on February 15, 1801, some sixty blind children were carted off to the Quinze-Vingts, whose forbidding walls surrounded former army barracks. No preparation had been made for the young guests.

This shocking episode seems even stranger when contrasted with the enlightened policies that the same Chaptal was simultaneously pursuing in hospital reform, the training of midwives and the restoration of the nursing orders. Reasons more compelling than a temper tantrum of the First Consul must account for this cruel, reactionary decision.

The archives reveal three possible explanations, the first two being the need for economy[30] and the shift in administrative power. Indeed, the relevant decree stipulates: "The trustees of the Deaf-Mute will henceforth be responsible for the administration of the Quinze-Vingts." The fact that Sicard was appointed to this board of trustees

---

28. V. Haüy, *Première (seconde, troisième) note du Citoyen Haüy, auteur de la manière d'instruire les aveugles, en réponse aux insinuations défavorables répandues dans la société, sur sa conduite politique* (Paris: Institut des aveugles travailleurs, 19 Brumaire, An IX), pp. 15–16. Found only at the British Museum and at Institut national. Académie française. Archives. Pièces annexes aux Procès-verbaux, "Dossier Sicard."

29. These various documents in AN, F[15], 2576.

30. *Ibid.*

on October 26, 1804, makes one suspect his influence on a decision that crushed his rival.[31] But the third and main cause of Haüy's downfall was his role as a founder of the revolutionary religious sect of theophilanthropy, one of those civil cults that worshipped the Supreme Being.[32] The sect's public enthusiasm for Robespierre and radical activity at the height of the Terror naturally made Haüy suspect to the Directory and to Bonaparte, although the young general attended at least one theophilanthropic meeting.[33] The theophilanthropists had rated police surveillance since 1797.[34] On 12 Vendémiaire, Year X (October 4, 1801), Bonaparte's Minister of Police, Joseph Fouché, decreed: "The Societies known by the name of Theophilanthropists shall no longer meet in public buildings."[35] This measure destroyed the Society, just as the earlier decree had eliminated Haüy's school and workshops.

Finally, on February 16, 1802, the government abolished Haüy's position of Chief Instructor of the Blind. Chaptal's terse letter to Bouret, the administrator of the Quinze-Vingts, stated: "Please inform Citizen Haüy of this decision and convey my regrets that the need for economy precludes retaining the post that had been entrusted to him."[36] A modicum of decency did impel the government to award the patron saint of blind children an annual pension of 2,000 francs.

Angry and unemployed, Haüy eventually opted for exile. In 1806, he accepted the invitation of Czar Alexander I and founded a school for the blind at St. Petersburg.[37] After eleven years he returned to Paris, where he died in 1822. His National Institution for the Blind,

---

31. Cf. *Almanach national de France* (Paris: Testu, 1806).

32. Haüy is often described as the chief founder of this cult—see, e.g., L. M. de La Revellière-Lépeaux, *Mémoires* (3 vols., Paris: Plon Nourrit, 1895), Vol. II, pp. 166–167. The consistently biased French historian Albert Mathiez admires Haüy for having the "soul of an apostle, enchanted with ideals, incapable of self-doubt, at ease in vast, moral, and intrepid undertakings." *La théophilanthropie et le culte décadaire, 1796–1801; essai sur l'histoire religieuse de la révolution* (Paris: Durand, 1904), p. 90.

33. See *La visite de Bonaparte aux théophilanthropes; sa prière à l'Eternel, et le détail de la liste de tous ceux qui assisteront au banquet civil donné à Bonaparte* [n.p., n.d.]. Bibliothèque nationale, L^b 42 1702 8°.

34. AN, F⁷, 7338.

35. [J. Fouché], *Lettre du Ministre de la police générale de la république qui fait défense aux Théophilanthropes de s'assembler davantage dans les endroits ci-dessus indiqués par ordre du gouvernement. Arrêté du 12 Vendémiaire, An X.* Bibliothèque nationale, LD 188³³.

36. Hospice des Quinze-Vingts. Archives. Série B 109, 6715.

37. The only published account of this establishment is that of A. Skrebitzki, *Valentin Haüy à St. Pétersbourg* (Paris: Noizette, 1884). A "Fond" concerning Haüy's school in St. Petersburg has been located in the Leningrad State Archives and negotiations to obtain microfilm have been initiated.

which languished during the Napoleonic era, was revived by Louis XVIII and, in 1843, moved into its present palatial home at 56, Boulevard des Invalides.

While the deaf and the blind had profited as early as 1791 from the arousal of the national conscience, the mentally ill came into the government's purview somewhat later, perhaps because "alienation" was only gradually distinguished from criminality, the first "psychiatrists" were just emerging, and vast funds were needed. Even Philippe Pinel, that psychiatric pioneer, discovered his calling late in life. For almost twenty years he languished in pre-revolutionary Parisian medical circles, gave lessons, translated Cullen, Baglivi and four volumes of the *Philosophical Transactions* of the Royal Society, edited the *Gazette de santé,* and frequented the salon of Madame Helvétius, where he shared in the elaboration of "ideologue" thought. The mental illness of a friend turned his attention to deranged patients, and in 1792 he won a prize for an essay on mental alienation.[38] Finally, in December 1794, his friends A.-F. de Fourcroy, the chemist, and M.-A. Thouret, the future director of the Paris Health School, obtained his appointment as Professor of Hygiene at the Paris medical faculty. As physician-in-chief at Bicêtre, Pinel learned psychiatric practices from Jean-Baptiste Pussin, who had been the lay "administrator" of the insane since 1784. His appointment as physician-in-chief at the Salpêtrière in 1795 placed the finest French clinician in the world's largest hospital.

Pinel brought to his work with the insane a conceptual framework that set him apart from Sicard and Haüy. After all, sign language and embossed print are but techniques, whereas the categorizing of mental illness according to etiology and pathogenesis requires a philosophy of medicine. Haüy, it is true, resembled Pinel in that he sensed psychological needs: he provided sighted as well as blind playmates and teachers, and encouraged his wards to marry and have children of their own. Sicard, in contrast, remained enthralled by grammar and continued to rely on logic and syntax.

---

38. W. Cullen, *Institutions de médecine pratique,* trans. by Philippe Pinel (2 vols., Paris: Duplain, 1785); G. Baglivi, *Opera omnia medico-practica,* trans. and annot. by Philippe Pinel (2 vols., Paris: Duplain, 1788); and P. Pinel, *Abrégé des transactions philosophiques de la Société royale de Londres, 5ème–8ème partie* (Paris: Buisson, 1790–91).

The Société royale de médecine had proposed the question: "Indiquer les moyens les plus efficaces de traiter les malades dont l'esprit est devenu aliéné avant l'âge de vieillesse." The unpublished *Plumitif* [minute book] of this Society indicates that, according to custom, Pinel's prizewinning essay was read aloud to the membership in the fall of 1792. (Académie de médecine de Paris. Archives, *Plumitif,* vol. 11bis, folio 286 verso.) It has so far been impossible to locate this essay. Although Pinel's early years are well documented, his biography remains to be written.

Pinel had a unique opportunity because the revolutionary government was in the process of completely reorganizing the hospitals of Paris. This enabled him to apply his *Philosophic Nosography* of 1798 to the actual situation at Bicêtre and at the Salpêtrière. He viewed insanity as illness and, like another Linnaeus, labeled his patients manic, melancholic, demented or imbecile. Classification and grouping, in true Baconian manner, he deemed essential.[39] His books testify to the benefits he derived from good relations with the Paris Hospital Council that his old friend Jean-Antoine Chaptal, the Minister of Interior, had created in 1801.[40] Pinel could now assign patients to special wards according to their illnesses and thus use the hospital as a therapeutic instrument. He taught his "moral" method for thirty years, convinced that psychological control is preferable to physical coercion and that the dignity of the individual justifies each patient's right to health care.

Owing to the nationalization of hospital property, the government had acquired the seventeenth-century château of Charenton, and reopened it as a "Maison nationale" in 1797. Unfortunately, the ex-Premonstrant priest F.-S. de Coulmiers (1741–1818) was appointed director of this mental hospital. There ensued an interlude of almost thirty years of mismanagement and therapeutic aberration, compounded by political hostility, which prevented the introduction of the modern methods Pinel was so successfully pursuing at the Salpêtrière. Not until Pinel's student Esquirol was appointed psychiatrist-in-chief at Charenton in 1826 could a model psychiatric facility be created. This was achieved by applying the method of "moral" persuasion in therapy and by the imaginative use of the *carré isolé* in architecture.[41]

---

39. P. Pinel, *Nosographie philosophique, ou Méthode de l'analyse appliquée à la médecine* (Paris: Brosson, 1798; 2nd ed., 3 vols., 1802–3; 3rd ed., 3 vols., 1807); *Traité médico-philosophique sur l'aliénation mentale* (Paris: Brosson, 1801; 2nd ed., 1809); and *La médecine clinique rendue plus précise et plus exacte par l'application de l'analyse ou Recueil et résultat d'observations sur les maladies aigües, faites à la Salpêtrière* (Paris: Brosson, 1802; 2nd ed., 1804; 3rd ed. 1815).

40. See *Paris. Conseil général d'administration des hôpitaux et hospices de Paris et du département de la Seine. Rapports . . . sur les hôpitaux et hospices, les secours à domicile, et la direction des nourrices* (Paris: Imprimerie des hospices civils, An XI [1803]), and *Rapport . . . sur l'état des hôpitaux, des hospices, et des secours à domicile, à Paris, depuis le 1er janvier 1804 jusqu'au 1er janvier 1814* (Paris: Huzard, 1816). See also D. B. Weiner, "Public Health Under Napoleon: The *Conseil de salubrité de Paris, 1802–1815*," *Clio Medica*, Vol. IX (1974), pp. 271–284.

41. The *carré isolé* is a U-shaped architectural module which can be adapted to open and isolation wards. On hospital architecture in France, see D. Jetter, *Zur Typologie des Irrenhauses in Frankreich und Deutschland (1780–1840)* (Wiesbaden: Franz Steiner, 1971). The documents concerning Charenton are in as-

The worldwide renown that Charenton earned under Esquirol's expert stewardship gradually erased the notoriety it had gained during the Revolution and Empire. Esquirol himself gives us the most informative critique of that period. Besides waste and cruelty, he decried the lack of financial guidelines in the reorganization of 1797 because it left the director "absolute master." De Coulmiers interpreted "moral treatment" to consist of dancing, plays and musical entertainment, with the "all too famous de Sade" serving as choreographer. Esquirol commented:

> This spectacle was a pretense, the madmen were not playacting, rather, the director played with people's gullibility and hoodwinked the public; old and young, knowledgeable and ignorant, all wished to attend a performance given by the insane of Charenton; for several years, "tout Paris" rushed in. Some were curious, others wanted to ascertain the prodigious results of this admirable therapy for the insane. The truth is: playacting cured no one.[42]

De Coulmiers's methods doubled the number of patients, but indigents, who had numbered seventy after the regulations of 1802 had gone into effect, were permanently excluded in 1807, and sent to Bicêtre and the Salpêtrière—where Pinel continued to treat them, but in a huge, multi-purpose institution.

Charenton, rescued for progressive psychiatry in the 1820s, can be compared to the schools led by Sicard and Haüy because of its experimental, modern nature. Small, and directly controlled by the Ministry of the Interior, it opened vistas of therapy to reclaim ill and handicapped patients—but at crushing public expense. Here, too, the revolutionary era spurred the analysis and definition of a problem whose solution would take centuries.

It is tempting to speculate whether Pinel, Esquirol, Sicard and Haüy all knew each other. The two psychiatrists must have been familiar with the current methods for teaching the handicapped, since these resemble psychiatric rehabilitation. We know that Pinel and Sicard came face to face when the famous *enfant sauvage*, the "Wild

---

tonishingly good order at the Archives nationales (Série AJ²); however, they reveal a disappointing paucity of fact.

42. J. E. D. Esquirol, "Mémoire historique et statistique sur la Maison royale de Charenton," *Annales d'hygiène publique et de médecine légale*, XIII (1835), pp. 5–192. The quotation is from p. 46. A recently discovered manuscript confirms Esquirol's harsh judgment. See Marquis de Sade, *Journal inédit. Deux cahiers retrouvés du Journal inédit du Marquis de Sade (1801, 1808, 1814), suivis en appendice d'une notice sur l'Hospice de Charenton par Hippolyte de Colins* (Gallimard: Nouvelle revue française, 1970).

Boy from Aveyron," was brought to Sicard's institution in 1800. The attending physician, Dr. J. M. G. Itard (1775–1838), and Dr. Pinel examined and observed "Victor"; finally Pinel pronounced him an incurable idiot, a verdict with which Sicard agreed. For ten years Victor lived at the rue Saint-Jacques, with Itard trying to teach him speech and manners. He failed, but gained invaluable insights into speech therapy—the alternative that has proved preferable to Sicard's sign language.[43] Indeed, visitors to Sicard's public demonstrations had long wondered whether lip reading and speech were not superior to sign language, which confines the deaf to communication with their comrades and teachers. In England and Germany these methods had been widely adopted,[44] but in France the prestige of the kindly abbé de l'Epée, and the power of Sicard, his pupil, for many years precluded experiment with alternative methods.

Whereas Sicard's fame as teacher of the deaf thus appears, in retrospect, as the artifact of political publicity, Haüy emerges as a man of genius, the tragic victim of his own suspiciousness and of a vengeful rival. Sicard wrongly relied on gestures instead of speech; Haüy rightly used the sense of touch as a substitute for sight. He not only perfected embossed print but recognized the potential of the semaphore. His "Moyens nouveaux, si l'on ne s'abuse, à étendre et même à perfectionner le service du télégraphe" was presumably published in St. Petersburg in 1810. Had Haüy still been headmaster when the young Louis Braille (1809–1852) elaborated his new system, it would not have taken the student ten years to change the school's method of instruction.[45]

43. J. M. G. Itard, *Rapports et mémoires sur le Sauvage de l'Aveyron, l'idiotie et la surdi-mutité* (Paris: Alcan, 1894). The volume begins with an "éloge" of Itard and contains: "Premiers développements du jeune sauvage de l'Aveyron"; "Second rapport fait au Ministre de l'Intérieur sur les nouveaux développements et l'état actuel du sauvage de l'Aveyron"; "Mémoire sur le mutisme produit par la lésion des fonctions intellectuelles lu à la première séance publique de l'Académie royale de médecine."

44. See J. P. Seigel, "The Enlightenment and the Evolution of a Language of Signs in France and in England," *Journal of the History of Ideas*, XXX (1969), pp. 96–115. That some experimentation was going on in France in Sicard's time can be documented, for example, from V. R. T. Lebouvyer-Desmortiers, *Mémoires ou considérations sur les sourds-muets de naissance, et sur les moyens de donner l'ouïe et la parole à ceux qui en sont susceptibles* (Paris: Buisson, An VIII [1799–1800]). The author "almost cured" a deaf girl with the help of electricity.

45. L. Braille, *Procédé pour écrire les paroles, la musique, et le plain-chant au moyen de points, à l'usage des aveugles et disposé pour eux* (Paris: Imprimé à l'Institution nationale des aveugles, 1829). The musical notation apparently is based on the system Jean-Jacques Rousseau had devised in the 1740s. (Cf. P. Henri, *La vie et l'oeuvre de Louis Braille, inventeur de l'alphabet des aveugles*

Pinel alone, among the three, achieved lasting worldwide fame. His work, like that of Haüy, was of permanent value. Pinel even succeeded in curing numerous psychiatric patients. Moreover, his appointment to a position of power represented, like that of Sicard, the choice of the political establishment. All three men helped show that disabilities such as insanity, deafness and blindness are treatable by specialists, but that treatment requires onerous public funding.

Beyond the similarities and differences in personalities, careers, methods and posthumous reputations, it seems noteworthy that these three pioneers were Frenchmen. France was the first country on the European continent to reject the strictures of the Old Régime and face fundamental social, moral and therapeutic questions in their national context. And the equal right to health care, whether ignored or heeded, was unmistakably a part—as Barzun implies in the passage quoted at the head of this essay—of the eighteenth-century humanitarian credo.

(*1809–1852*) (Paris: Presses universitaires de France, 1952). Professor Samuel Baud-Bovy of the University of Geneva offers the following explanation: "The reference is to Rousseau's *Projet concernant de nouveaux signes pour la musique*, where the notes of the scale are represented by numbers, thus eliminating the staff and which could therefore be adapted to Braille's alphabet." [Letter to the author]

ALAN B. SPITZER

Victor Cousin and the French Generation of 1820

"[T]he one thing that unifies men in a given age is not their individual philosophies but the dominant problem that these philosophies are designed to solve."

JACQUES BARZUN, *Classic, Romantic and Modern*

⋙

All systems of philosophy, Stendhal once remarked, are addressed to the young. As examples he cited the success of Plato, Abelard, and the contemporary hero of the Paris youth, Victor Cousin.[1] He was certainly right about Cousin. In the early years of the Restoration, the largest and most enthusiastic audience for a new system of philosophy was young—young as students usually are, but not exclusively a student youth. Between 1815 and 1820 an intelligentsia under the age of thirty rallied to Cousin's lectures at the Sorbonne as to a standard. In a manner strikingly similar to the cult of Henri Bergson before the First World War, attendance at the lectures of the young philosopher functioned as the defiant expression of a distinct generational identity. The defiance was directed against established élites and their worn-out ideologies; the identity lay in a shared sense of millennial potential.

There is general agreement on the importance of the phenomenon.[2] Cousin contributed decisively to the ideological formation of the talented and self-confident generation that would dominate French

---

1. [Stendhal], *Courrier anglais* (Paris: Le Divan, 1936), Vol. I, pp. 328–329. (Originally published in the *Paris Monthly Review*, June 5, 1822.) Stendhal continues: "Les philosophes, d'un amour-propre peu délicat, sous le nom de *systèmes de philosophie*, adressent des *romans* à cette bonne jeunesse, et ils sont sûrs d'en être applaudis avec toute la chaleur que l'on a à vingt ans pour les romans."
2. The question of Cousin's influence on the youth of the Restoration has received considerable attention in such nineteenth-century works as: Hippolyte Taine, *Les Philosophes classiques du XIXᵉ siècle en France* (7th ed., Paris:

culture until at least mid-century.[3] There is also considerable agreement on the historical existence if not the precise chronological boundaries of the generation.[4] By the historical existence of a genera-

Hachette, 1895), pp. 79–202, 289–315; Jules Barthélemy-Saint Hilaire, *M. Victor Cousin, sa vie et sa correspondance* (Paris: Hachette, 1895), Vol. I, pp. 49–50; Jules Simon, *Victor Cousin* (Paris: Hachette, 1891), pp. 7–8, 16–19; Paul Janet, *Victor Cousin et son oeuvre* (Paris: Calmann-Lévy, 1885), pp. 15–31; and Charles Dejob, *L'Instruction publique en France et en Italie au dix-neuvième siècle* (Paris: Armand Colin, 1894), pp. 333–336.

It has been taken up again in several useful recent studies: W. M. Simon, "The 'Two Cultures' in Nineteenth-Century France: Victor Cousin and Auguste Comte," Journal of the History of Ideas, XXVI (January–March 1965), pp. 45–58; Doris S. Goldstein, "Official Philosophies in Modern France: The Example of Victor Cousin," *Journal of Social History*, I (Spring 1968), pp. 259–279; André Canivez, *Jules Lagneau, professor de philosophie* (Paris: Les Belles Lettres, 1965), Vol. I, pp. 144–177, 203–222; Lucien Sève, *Philosophie française contemporaine* (Paris: Editions sociales, 1962), pp. 95–96; Armand Hoog, "Un Intercesseur du romantisme. Victor Cousin vu par Stendhal," *Revue des sciences humaines*, Nouvelle Série, 62–63 (April–September 1951), pp. 184–200; Pierre Barbéris, *Balzac et le mal du siècle* (Paris: Gallimard, 1970), Vol. I, pp. 240–243; and D. G. Charlton, *Secular Religions in France, 1815–1870* (London: Oxford Univ. Press, 1963), pp. 97–99. I will discuss the testimony of Cousin's contemporaries below.

3. On the generation of 1820, see Paul Thureau-Dangin, "Une Génération nouvelle," chap. III of *Le Parti libéral sous la Restauration* (Paris: Plon, 1888), pp. 191–264; Sébastien Charléty, "L'Avènement d'une génération nouvelle," chap. III of *La Restauration*, in *Histoire de France contemporaine*, ed. E. Lavisse (Paris: Hachette, 1920–22), Vol. IV, pp. 197–228; Charles Bruneau, "La Génération de 1820," chap. I, book II of Ferdinand Brunot, ed., *Histoire de la langue française des origines à nos jours* (Paris: Armand Colin, 1948), Vol. XII, pp. 103–115; Albert Thibaudet, "La Génération de 1820," second part of *Histoire de la littérature française* (Paris: Editions Stock, 1936), pp. 105–292; Louis Liard, *L'Enseignement supérieur en France* (Paris: Armand Colin, 1888–94), Vol. II, pp. 142–144, 162–165; Henri Peyre, *Les Générations littéraires* (Paris: Boivin, 1948), pp. 136–138; F. A. Isambert, *De la Charbonnerie au Saint-Simonisme. Etude sur la jeunesse de Buchez* (Paris: Les Editions de minuit, 1966), pp. 59–69.

The key primary material for the history and self-image of the generation is the scattered reminiscences of the ex-normalien Carbonarist, and editor of *Le Globe*, Paul-François Dubois, some of which have been collected and published by Adolphe Lair: Paul Dubois, *Cousin, Jouffroy, Damiron* (Paris: Perrin, 1902); Adolphe Lair, "Les Souvenirs de M. Dubois," *La Quinzaine*, 43 (November 1, 1901), pp. 74–87; (December 1, 1901), pp. 305–318; (December 16, 1901), pp. 462–477; and "Souvenirs inédits," in fourteen issues of *Revue bleue* between September 21, 1907, and December 26, 1908. See the recent biography, Paul Gerbod, *Paul-François Dubois, universitaire, journaliste et homme politique, 1793–1874* (Paris: Klincksieck, 1967), which cites various unpublished sources, the most important of which were deposited by Gerbod in the Archives nationales. *Archives privées*, Papiers de Paul-François Dubois, 319 A 1–3.

4. I agree with Sainte-Beuve that the generation of 1820 should be distinguished from those born after 1802 or 1803 who comprised a *jeunesse* in 1830. C. A. Sainte-Beuve, *Portraits littéraires* (Paris: Garnier, 1862), Vol. I, p. 296, and

tion, I mean that it was historically significant with reference to age rather than some other variable.

This is not to exclude the relevance of other variables. In this case we are concerned with a group of educated, predominantly middle-class French males, born between 1791 and 1803, whose collective behavior set them apart from other age cohorts. They constituted what the classic article of Karl Mannheim has characterized as a "generation unit":

> Youth experiencing the same concrete historical problems may be said to be part of the same historical generation; while those groups within the same actual generation which work up the material of their common experiences in different specific ways, constitute separate generation units.[5]

A significant product of the common experience of the generation unit of the early Restoration was the articulation of a "youth ideology" —an affirmation of youth culture as a distinct type of social and cultural life.[6] As in all such cases, the Restoration *jeunesse* assumed that the attributes of this emerging culture would persist to transform the entire society. This is not to say that there was a systematic claboration of a new unified ideology to which most young intellectuals adhered, but that various concepts were repeatedly affirmed as peculiarly appropriate to the historical moment and generational location of those growing into maturity out of the wreck of the First Empire. A notable but puzzling element in the formulation of this amorphous but distinct world view is the extent to which it reflected the influence of Victor Cousin.[7] At least, the extent of that influence has posed a puzzle for later generations. Cousin enjoyed one of those in-

Causeries du Lundi (Paris: Garnier, 1883), Vol. XII, p. 7. See also Peyre, *Les Générations littéraires*, p. 138; Emile Deschamps, *Oeuvres complètes* (Paris: A. Lemerre, 1873), Vol. IV, p. 302. For an authoritative treatment that fuses both groups into one "generation," see Thibaudet, *Histoire de la littérature française*, p. 105. I have discussed the general problems of distinguishing and delimiting historical generations in Alan B. Spitzer, "The Historical Problem of Generations," *American Historical Review*, 78 (December 1973), pp. 1,353–1,385.

5. Karl Mannheim, "The Problem of Generations," in *Essays in the Sociology of Knowledge* (London: Routledge & Kegan Paul, 1959), p. 304.

6. See S. N. Eisenstadt, *From Generation to Generation: Age Groups and Social Structure* (Glencoe, Ill.: Free Press, 1956), pp. 102, 311.

7. I am here concerned with Cousin's influence over those who were exposed to his philosophy during the first years of the Restoration, 1815–1820, and agree with Janet's view that "ce qui nous paraît le plus important à signaler et à étudier, c'est l'impression produite par ce premier enseignement intérieur de l'Ecole sur ceux qui l'ont entendu; c'est l'appréciation qu'ils en ont donée, le caractère qu'ils lui ont attribué." Janet, *Victor Cousin*, p. 15.

flated reputations so decisively, so devastatingly, so wittily deflated (by Taine above all) that its real merits and the nature of its original appeal seem lost to the historical imagination.[8]

However, various solutions to the problem of Cousin's appeal have been imagined. Among the most influential are: the circular solution —to the effect that Cousin was the incarnation of his era;[9] the Marxian characterization of Cousin as the first of the "great ideological functionaries of the bourgeoisie in power";[10] the theory of generational alternation, in which skeptical fathers are succeeded by sons in search of a faith, conveniently provided by Cousin.[11] But there remains the question of why just such a philosophy would inspire the militant youth of the early Restoration. As Armand Hoog cogently inquires, "What special quality drew the public to Cousin, rather than to someone else?"[12]

Hoog's question requires two answers: the identification of the specific elements in Cousin's lectures and early writings that appealed to his young public; and an explanation for the receptivity of that public to Cousin's particular arguments. I believe that the answer to the second question is to be sought in the historical location of the generation of 1820, and in the preoccupations that its historical situation imposed.

It is not difficult to identify specific elements in Cousin's first course of lectures that might appeal to an educated audience in the early years of the Second Restoration. Doris Goldstein has provided a clear summary of the salient points:

> To the University youth who applauded him Cousin's philosophy stood for the ability of reason to arrive at truth unaided by theology and, in politics, for Constitutional monarchy. In short, by 1830 Cousin had

---

8. There is a long list of those who have consigned Cousin to the philosophical scrapheap, starting with such contemporary critics as Armand Marrast in *Examen critique du cours de philosophie de M. Cousin* (Paris: J. Corréard jeune, 1829); and *Examen critique du cours de philosophie de M. Cousin (leçon par leçon)* (Paris: J. Corréard jeune, 1828–29); also Pierre Leroux in *Réfutation de l'éclectisme* (Paris: C. Gosselin, 1839). For characteristic negative evaluations of Cousin, see Taine, *Les Philosophes classiques*, pp. 129–178; Félix Ravaisson, *La Philosophie en France au XIXᵉ siècle* (Paris: Hachette, 1904), pp. 32–34; George Boas, *French Philosophies of the Romantic Period* (Baltimore, Md.: The Johns Hopkins Press, 1925), pp. 197–233; and Emile Brehier, *The History of Philosophy*. Vol. VI. *The Nineteenth Century: Period of Systems, 1800–1850* (Chicago: Univ. of Chicago Press, 1968), pp. 74–91.

9. Hoog, "Un Intercesseur du romantisme," pp. 186, 192.

10. Sève, *Philosophie française contemporaine*, pp. 105, 111.

11. Taine, *Les Philosophes classiques*, pp. 290–296.

12. Hoog, "Un Intercesseur du romantisme," p. 188.

attained prominence with a philosophy which was secular and yet not irreligious, liberal and yet not revolutionary.[13]

Yet, in 1820, Cousin's philosophy *was* considered revolutionary by students and other young admirers, and by the authorities. The problem lies in relating the anodyne content of "this nice, relaxing tepid bath into which fathers dip their children as a healthful precaution"[14] to its bracing effect. It seems scarcely revolutionary to send off a student body convinced that rigorous introspection guarantees the existence of the self, the soul, the external world, God, immortality and universal objective criteria of truth and beauty; that good and evil receive their eternal rewards; that liberty is an inviolable element of human nature and property a sacred component of liberty; that sovereignty is not to be found in the hands of despots or in the whims of the masses but in the absolute idea of justice; and that a constitutional monarchy is the best of all régimes.

One cannot separate the effect of Cousin's doctrine from his personal impact on students only a few years younger than their charismatic instructor.[15] His dynamism radiated out beyond the walls of the university to stimulate a large circle of admirers and to influence the young militants who enlisted in the secret societies of 1820–22. Despite the denials of Cousin and his biographers, there is considerable evidence for his clandestine role in recruiting members of the aborted conspiracies of August 1820 and the Carbonari.[16]

However, Cousin's major impact was public, delivered from the platform. Here too it had to do with personality and manner of delivery as well as with philosophic content. As Royer-Collard's substitute, Cousin recapitulated that high seriousness in the exposition of philo-

---

13. Goldstein, "Official Philosophies in Modern France," p. 261.

14. Taine, *Les Philosophes classiques*, p. 311.

15. Cousin's magnetism and the stimulating informality of his relations with his pupils at the Ecole Normale were fondly recalled. See, e.g., Philippe Damiron, *Essai sur l'histoire de la philosophie en France du dix-neuvième siècle* (Paris: Ponthieu, 1828), p. 324, and *Souvenirs de vingt ans d'enseignement à la Faculté des lettres de Paris* (Paris: A. Durand, 1859), XLII; Paul Dubois in A. Lair, "Les Souvenirs de M. Dubois," *La Quinzaine*, 43 (December 16, 1901), p. 476. See also the contemporary testimony of Théodore Jouffroy in *Correspondance de Théodore Jouffroy. Publiée avec une étude sur Jouffroy par Adolphe Lair* (Paris: Perrin, 1901), Jouffroy to Damiron, March 5 [1817], pp. 115–116: "je tomberais si Cousin ne me ranimait et ne me réchauffait de la chaleur de son zèle philosophique. . . . Cet homme-là a une ferveur qui se communique, et une seule de ses conversations vous donne des forces inconnues et une vigueur toute nouvelle."

16. I present and evaluate the evidence on this question in Alan B. Spitzer, *Old Hatreds and Young Hopes* (Cambridge, Mass: Harvard Univ. Press, 1971), pp. 221, 227–228, 240, and 268.

sophic problems which had captivated the audience for his predecessor's first course in 1811. In contrast to the urbane lectures of an autumnal ideologue such as Laromiguière—"occasional *causeries* full of nostalgic charm"[17]—Cousin's course was perceived as an intense personal statement, expressing "the gravity of a moral commitment contracted in public and under the authority of science."[18] The moral intensity of Cousin's delivery helped to impart a provocative quality to essentially moderate propositions,[19] and even to convey an impression that the lecturer's health was threatened by his pedagogical devotion.[20]

By Cousin's second series of lectures in 1828—again a personal triumph—a hostile young critic such as Armand Marrast was able to identify the studied oratorical effects and to characterize him as "the most artful actor of the faculty."[21] The response to Cousin's brand of oratorical delivery eventually became a matter of taste and philosophic temperament. But in the beginning his facile eloquence was the perfect medium for the message his audience wanted to hear.

Following Stendhal, Armand Hoog emphasizes the emotional effect of Cousin's virtuoso performance, which conveyed "less a system of thought than a system of fascination," but in a manner perfectly suited to the content of the lectures. According to Hoog, Stendhal was the only contemporary to identify the philosopher's appeal with the fact that he was the aesthetician of a nascent Romantic sensibility. Cousin did not articulate a full-fledged Romanticism, but he did suggest that many of the Romantic themes derived from the premise of the supremacy of the imagination over reality. It was Stendhal's great merit to see that "the vast majority of well-bred youth had been converted to Romanticism by the eloquence of M. Cousin."[22]

---

17. [Paul Dubois], "Les Souvenirs de M. Dubois," p. 471.
18. Augustin Thierry, *Dix Ans d'études historiques* (Paris: Firmin-Didot, 1883), p. 203. On the effect of Cousin's eloquence, see Dubois, *Cousin, Jouffroy, Damiron*, p. 38; Louis de Carné, *Souvenirs de ma jeunesse au temps de la Restauration* (Paris: Didier, 1872), p. 15; Charles Rémusat, *Séance de l'Académie Française du 23 avril 1868. Discours de réception de Jules Favre. Réponse de M. De Rémusat* (Paris: Firmin-Didot, 1868), pp. 64–65; [H. J. G. Patin], *Discours de M. S. de Sacy . . . prononcé aux funérailles de M. V. Cousin le 24 janvier 1867, et discours de MM. de Parien et Patin* (Paris: Firmin-Didot, 1867), p. 16.
19. This is the insight of Canivez, *Jules Lagneau*, pp. 157–158.
20. Thierry, *Dix ans d'études historiques*, pp. 221–222.
21. Marrast, *Examen critique*, p. 7; Cousin was characterized as "le comédien le plus désagréablement grimacier que j'aie jamais rencontré" by an older contemporary, Etienne Delécluze, in *Journal de Delécluze, 1824–1828* (Paris: Bernard Grasset, 1948), p. 226.
22. Hoog, "Un Intercesseur du romantisme," p. 194, quoting, somewhat out of context, Stendhal's *Racine et Shakespeare*, Vol. 37 of *Oeuvres Complètes* (Paris: Cercle du Bibliophile, 1970), p. 123. Lucien Lévy-Bruhl makes a similar case in

There are many elements in Cousin's lectures that can be subsumed under the various definitions of Romanticism. However, we cannot explain the influence of a particular thinker on a particular audience merely by identifying aspects of his thought that happen to coincide with our prior assumptions about the climate of opinion. Any definition of a Romanticism to which Cousin *then* appealed would have to include such terms as "severe," "rigorous," "the experimental method," "founded on incontestable facts," and above all, "scientific," because they adumbrate the contributions that were most admired by his public.[23] Augustin Thierry, who managed to admire Cousin and Saint-Simon simultaneously, characterized Cousin in exact contradiction to his subsequent reputation: "the same mental rigor which made him reject vaguely liberal theories without practical application, also excluded from his lessons everything that he did not perceive as rational and scientific."[24]

Some of Cousin's critics even accused him of the defects of these alleged scientific virtues. As late as 1839, Pierre Leroux attacked Cousin for excluding sentiment from philosophy, thereby reducing the discipline to "a science of observation analogous to geometry or physics" that did not speak to human feelings or human needs.[25]

But Cousin convinced his first audience that precisely in that science of observation lay the answers to all of the big questions, the questions of how to live and what to believe that history had forced on a generation coming to maturity during the collapse of one régime and the rebirth of another. The commitment to the science was perceived as the affirmation of a morality, and in many recollections Cousin's

his lucid summary of Cousin's philosophy, arguing that Cousin's introduction of German metaphysics constituted a philosophic Romanticism that accounts for his enthusiastic reception by contemporary youth. Lucien Lévy-Bruhl, *History of Modern Philosophy in France* (La Salle, Ill.: The Open Court Publishing Co., 1899), p. 341. For the relation of Cousin's aesthetics to Romanticism, see Frederic Will, *Flumen Historicum, Victor Cousin's Aesthetic and Its Sources* (Chapel Hill, N.C.: The Univ. of North Carolina Press, 1965).

23. E.g., Damiron, *Essai sur l'histoire de la philosophie*, p. 362; Théodore Jouffroy, *Nouveaux mélanges philosophiques* (Paris: Joubert, 1842), pp. 122–128; F. A.-A. Mignet, *Notice historique sur la vie et les travaux de M. Victor Cousin* (Paris: Firmin-Didot, 1869), p. 9; and Charles Rémusat, *Séance de l'Académie Française*, p. 56. For the Romantics' positive attitude toward science, see Jacques Barzun, *Classic, Romantic and Modern* (Boston: Little, Brown, 1961), pp. 64–66.

24. Thierry, *Dix ans d'études historiques*, p. 213.

25. Leroux, *Réfutation de l'eclectisme*, p. 266; Alfred de Vigny characterized eclecticism as "une lumière sans doute, mais une lumière comme celle de la lune, qui éclaire sans réchauffer. On peut distinguer les objets à sa clarté, mais toute sa force ne produirait pas la plus légère étincelle." Alfred de Vigny, *Le Journal d'un poète* (Paris: Bibliothèque Larousse, 1913), p. 34.

greatest contribution was to have begun the moral education of his audience. He seemed, in his unsparing dedication to the life of reason, to personify "the austere alliance of patriotism and science"[26] that might provide the foundation for a personal ethic and public morality.

This admirable science did not require laboratories, observatories or field expeditions, but could be practiced on the podium. With occasional reference to actual practice in the physical sciences, Cousin would demonstrate how to proceed from meticulous particular observations to the discovery of general laws and those fixed and absolute principles "which were the goal and justification of any science." These principles could only be attained through Reason, which for Cousin was quite distinct from mere "raisonnement" or "raison appliquée."[27] Thus Cousin stands with those who distinguish the absolute intelligible order of the universe from a particular way of putting questions to it.

Yet Cousin believed that there was a particular way of putting questions to reality, one that solved the essential scientific problem of how to unite reason with observation.[28] This method was psychological and constituted a science of self-observation. The analysis of thought was thus the point of departure for any philosophic (which is to say scientific) research.[29] For this analysis to be empirical rather than arbitrary or hypothetical, it had to be applied to the self with meticulous objectivity.

The great appeal of this science of self-observation was that it carried the necessary empirical credentials while charting a path out of the swamps of skepticism. It was the method through which the insights of the Scottish philosophers of common sense and Kant's critical idealism could be brought to bear against the sensationalism of the ideologues and the other pernicious variants of Lockean em-

---

26. Thierry, *Dix ans d'études historiques*, p. 215. Less enthusiastic commentators have seen this as an alliance for the defense of Cousin's science through appeals to his public's patriotism. On Cousin's tendency to evaluate philosophic arguments in the light of their presumed moral and social consequences, see Taine, *Les Philosophes classiques*, pp. 148–151, and Boas, *French Philosophies of the Romantic Period*, p. 201.

27. Victor Cousin, *Cours de l'histoire de la philosophie moderne* (Paris: Didier, 1846), Vol. II, p. 36. There is no literal text of the first lecture series. The several published versions are lecture notes put into publishable form by former students, but somewhat revised by Cousin in successive editions. For a comparison of the various editions, see Janet, *Victor Cousin*, pp. 13, 60–61. The most useful summary of Cousin's early ideas is in the Preface to the first edition of Victor Cousin, *Fragments philosophiques*, drafted in 1826.

28. Cousin, *Cours de l'histoire de la philosophie moderne*, Vol. II, p. 37.

29. *Ibid.*, Vol. III, p. 4.

piricism. Cousin's elaboration of the classic principles of contemporary anti-empiricism—his assimilation and fusion of ideas borrowed from Thomas Reid, Kant, Schelling and Maine de Biran—enabled him to demonstrate how to proceed, "by way of irreproachable inductions, to metaphysical affirmations which thus assume a character as scientific as physical laws."[30] The presentation of these technical and abstruse arguments in the form of an oratorical *tour de force* made an impression on Cousin's contemporaries that would not be felt by subsequent critics of his printed word.

In justice to Cousin it must be remarked that he was presenting to a large Parisian audience the first systematic public exposition of the major issues of modern philosophy. Perhaps this is to say that we have merely situated Cousin in the great international campaign to rescue metaphysics from the specter of David Hume.[31] Seen from this perspective, he was not so much satisfying a particular age group as expressing the philosophic preoccupations of an entire age. Like contemporary audiences for philosophy throughout Europe, the French desired a refutation of materialism and skepticism that did not depend on the reiteration of outworn pieties but proceeded from the most rigorous application of the successful principles of scientific investigation. However, in presenting his version of the standard arguments of the Scottish and German critics of empiricism, Cousin also articulated the special preoccupations of the French generation to, and for, which he spoke.

To understand why this was so one must locate historically the generation, or that minority of it sufficiently educated to benefit from university lectures. Its historical location is suggested by Charles Rémusat's recollection that Cousin's approach to education was in striking contrast to "the narrow intellectual discipline of the imperial régime."[32] Those who emerged from the hardened authority of the late Empire to face manhood in the early years of the Restoration have been identified as the "first post-revolutionary generation,"[33] but were

---

30. Brehier, *The History of Philosophy*, Vol. VI, p. 85.

31. Hume's works were scarcely known to the French, who were more concerned to refute Condillac. However, see Théodore Jouffroy, "Préface du traducteur," in *Oeuvres complètes de Thomas Reid* (Paris: V. Masson, 1836), Vol. I, p. ccxiv.

32. Rémusat, *Séance de l'Académie Française*, p. 51; Paul Dubois, *Fragments littéraires* (Paris: E. Thouin, 1878), Vol. II, p. 302: "Sous l'Empire l'enseignement rétrograda vers la discipline du moyen-âge, renforcée de la discipline des camps"; Joseph-Daniel Guigniaut, *Notice historique sur la vie et les travaux de M. Augustin Thierry* (Paris: Firmin-Didot, 1863), p. 5.

33. Isambert, *De La Charbonnerie au Saint-Simonisme*, p. 67.

more specifically the first generation formed in the *lycées* and *grandes écoles* of the new Imperial University. The historical trauma that stamped their collective character was not the Revolution but the collapse of the Empire. They struggled into maturity out of the wreck of the assumptions by which they had been raised, hopeful but confused, wondering what standards to follow and whether they were forever to be the victims of circumstance.[34] They shared a thirst to understand their own place in the cataclysmic course of events, desiring, said Dubois, "to emerge from the profound ignorance of history, in which the Imperial University had kept its pupils."[35]

This desire, which was to be expressed in the formation of a great historical school, was first gratified in the popular historical lectures of Guizot at the Sorbonne, but perhaps even more by Cousin's historical approach to the teaching of philosophy. For Cousin, any study of philosophy was a history of philosophy. His task as he saw it was "to carry out the reform of philosophical studies in France, clarifying the history of philosophy by a system, and demonstrating this system by the entire history of philosophy."[36]

Out of this historical justification of his philosophical system, Cousin developed his philosophy of eclecticism. Using a method which he supposed to be that of the physical sciences, he selected the correct elements from all previous philosophies to arrive at a complete philosophy, uniting all of the truths to be found in the preceding doctrines in a higher synthesis. These truths were to be winnowed out of past philosophies through meticulous analysis, and above all, in the early lectures, through a critical evaluation of the great contributions and fatal flaws of eighteenth-century sensationalism and empiricism.

In his version of the transition from a critical to an organic epoch, Cousin granted to the eighteenth century an indispensable role in clearing the ground, or rather littering the ground with the wreck of old prejudices and obsolete authorities, thus freeing humanity for its irreversible advance across the debris. It had left to its heirs in the nineteenth century the legacy of an "energetic and fertile love of liberty," and the task of "filling in the chasm and replacing what had been destroyed."[37]

---

34. Rémusat, *Séance de l'Académie Française*, p. 54.

35. Dubois, *Fragments littéraires*, Vol. II, p. 303; Barbéris, *Balzac et le mal du siècle*, Vol. I, p. 243: "Cet effort de *compréhension* du passé est l'un de ceux qui distinguent le plus nettement la génération nouvelle de la génération impériale," and *ibid.*, pp. 123–124.

36. Victor Cousin, "Préface de la première édition," *Fragments philosophiques* (Paris: Ladrange, 1938), Vol. 1, p. 83.

37. Cousin, *Cours de l'histoire de la philosophie moderne*, Vol. II, pp. 10–11.

Again, one might argue that Cousin struck notes already in the air, and played on themes whose appeal was scarcely confined to a Parisian youth. The characterization of the post-revolutionary era as an age of reconstruction was a contemporary commonplace; the oft-repeated metaphors of "ruins" or "debris" delineate what Jacques Barzun has called the dominant problem of the Romantic era, the need "to create a new world on the ruins of the old."[38]

In fact, that virtually universal assumption was not precisely congruent with reality. That is to say, the year 1815 was not 1795. The Restoration régime did not occupy ruins, but moved into a vast institutional complex vacated by Napoleon, with, admittedly, some sections incomplete and others in a state of considerable disrepair. The metaphor of post-revolutionary ruins is most persuasive when applied to the intellectual debris of churches and philosophies. Daily life and the business of the state went on; what lay in ruins were the old verities and the old authorities as yet replaced—it seemed to many—by nothing.

Cousin's assumption that this situation was intolerable and transitory was the commonplace conviction of his circle of students, and widely shared—by the Saint-Simonians and Auguste Comte among others.[39] They all believed that society could not live by the obsolete conceptions of the Old Régime nor by the negative ideas of its opponents, and that the first task on the intellectual agenda of the nineteenth century was the formulation of a new unifying doctrine.

Such prescriptions implied heavy obligations and magnificent opportunities for those who had inherited the task of ideological reconstruction. In the Introduction to his first course of lectures in 1815, Cousin presented this task as the patriotic obligation of the young, whose destiny was to re-establish liberty in France by repudiating the pernicious philosophies of their predecessors:

> It is to those of you whose age is close to mine that I dare to speak at this moment; to you who will form the emerging generation; to you the sole support, the last hope of our dear and unfortunate country.

---

38. Barzun, *Classic, Romantic and Modern*, p. 64.
39. Claude-Henri de Saint-Simon [and A. Thierry], *L'Industrie* (first published in 1817), in *Oeuvres de Claude-Henri de Saint-Simon* (Paris: Editions Anthropos, 1966), Vol. I, pp 206–214; Claude-Henri de Saint-Simon, *Du Système Industriel*, Vol. II (first published in 1821), in *Oeuvres de Claude-Henri de Saint-Simon* (Paris: Editions Anthropos, 1966), Vol. III, pp. 50–51; Auguste Comte, "Plan des travaux scientifiques nécessaires pour réorganiser la société," in *Ecrits de Jeunesse, 1816–1828* (Paris: Mouton, 1952), pp. 246–249; Saint-Amand Bazard, "Des Partisans du passé et de ceux de la liberté de conscience," *Le Producteur*, 1 (September–December 1825), pp. 399–412.

> Gentlemen, you passionately love your fatherland; if you wish to save
> it, espouse our noble doctrines.[40]

Taine quotes the passage in full, emphasizing the irresistible effects
of the demagogic appeal to patriotism.[41] It is also unlikely that Cousin's
audience could resist the appeal to its generational solidarity and collective *amour-propre*.

What Cousin presented as a challenge, his young admirers accepted as a birthright. His conception of their providential role in the
history of philosophy and the history of France reinforced their belief,
as Frank Manuel has put it, that history was bifurcated by their generation.[42] A corollary to the assumption that history had assigned a
unique destiny to the new generation was the belief that preceding
generations, still very much on the scene, were no longer adequate to
the realities they themselves had created. And this conviction unified
those who grew up in the waning years of the Empire, irrespective of
political loyalties or aesthetic preferences.

It is certainly true that by 1820 or 1821 a majority of young people who publicly expressed their political attitudes were hostile to the
ultra-royalist government and the Catholic Church militant. What the
minority of the articulate *jeunesse* whose loyalties lay with Church
and King shared with their disaffected coevals is suggested by some
strictly literary remarks appearing in 1825 in the first issue of *La
Muse française*. Although *La Muse* professed political neutrality, it
was put together by a group of young romantics whose politics were
predominantly royalist. The Foreword to the first issue of their journal
identified obligations imposed on literary criticism by recent events,
and in which *les pères de la critique* had little interest.

> As the French Revolution has launched society along unfamiliar paths
> and into unprecedented relationships, literature *which is the expres-
> sion of society* has been profoundly affected by these violent shocks
> and strange innovations. Criticism, purposefully or out of habit, seems
> to lag somewhat behind the general movement. Thus it is not always
> sufficiently relevant to contemporary literature; for in order to guide
> it one must march along with it. To consolidate and not to paralyze
> such youthful, untrammeled progress the *Muse française* will devote
> its efforts and its solicitude.[43]

---

40. Cousin, *Cours de l'histoire de la philosophie*, Vol. I, pp. 22–23.
41. Taine, *Les Philosophes classiques*, pp. 301–302.
42. Frank Manuel, *The Prophets of Paris* (Cambridge, Mass.: Harvard Univ.
Press, 1962), p. 168.
43. [Jules Marsan], *La Muse française* (Paris: E. Cornély, 1907), Vol. I, p. 5.

The mild suggestion that the "fathers of criticism" suffered from a sort of historical sclerosis illustrates an attitude so widely shared by young intellectuals as to constitute a generational ideology. The romanticism of the young royalists of *La Muse française,* and the romanticism of the young liberals of *Le Globe,* was conceived in opposition to the fossilized classicism of literary dignitaries of all camps.[44] The *raison d'être* for the neo-liberalism of *Le Globe* lay in its refusal to parrot the shop-worn doctrines of *La Minerve française* or *Le Constitutionnel.* Paul Dubois, founder of the *Globe,* indignantly repudiated Guizot's patronizing recollection that the *Globistes* were junior Doctrinaires.[45] Indeed, the journal owed its success to the generational autonomy of its board of editors.

> It was young and free of all ties to the past. Among us there was not one old or well-known writer. Come, so to speak, from the four points of the compass—Carbonari, liberals of every type, we constituted, out of our various opinions and temperaments, a brand new army.[46]

The young Saint-Simonians who introduced *Le Producteur* in 1825 had even less reason to defer to age. The generation of their predecessors consisted of Saint-Simon, whose legacy contained the assumption that history had created conditions for which all previous systems of thought were inappropriate. The first issue of *Le Producteur* proclaimed the goals of the journal in the light of the situation of *la génération actuelle:*

> Our efforts will be fruitless, useless, and inglorious to the extent that we attack or defend a past which survives only for a few timid minds and obsolete interests. The struggle is over, there is no point in further combat, liberty has been won, we must profit from it. This particular generation has been summoned to prepare the organization of the new system; our task will be to help it comprehend the valid application of its talents, to persuade it to drop pointless debates in order to undertake the tasks required by the present state of knowledge and civilization.[47]

---

44. Charléty, *La Restauration,* pp. 197–215, emphasizes the refusal of the Restoration youth of all political tendencies to be patronized by their elders. See also C. M. des Granges, *La Presse littéraire sous la Restauration* (Paris: Société du Mercure de France, 1907), pp. 42–50, and Christian A. E. Jensen, *L'Evolution du romantisme* (Paris: Minard, 1959), pp. 52–57.

45. See François P. G. Guizot, *Mémoires pour servir à l'histoire de mon temps* (Paris: Michel-Lévy, 1858), Vol. I, pp. 324–325.

46. Quoted in Adolphe Lair, " 'Le Globe.' Sa fondation—sa rédaction—son influence," *Académie des sciences morales et politiques,* 161 (May 1904), p. 588.

47. *Le Producteur,* October 1, 1825.

These notes were repeatedly struck by self-elected spokesmen for their generation. A unique destiny had been bestowed on them, not by some inborn merit but by history—above all by the gigantic historical divide of the Revolution. It was not particularly to their credit that they had had the good fortune to inherit the Revolution without having made it; but because this legacy was received with spotless hands, "contemporary youth combined all of the attributes of a generation destined to establish the public weal on firm foundations."[48]

The works already published by those "precocious writers formed by the new century" revealed their superiority to a crabbed and prejudiced older generation.[49] They were better equipped than their elders to understand the recent past because their vision was unclouded by the prejudice of personal recollection. Therefore, as Paul Dubois remarked in his review of Thiers's work on the French Revolution, only someone who had not experienced the Revolution was sufficiently disinterested and objective to write its history.[50] When Charles Rémusat boldly identified himself and his contemporaries as "born of the Revolution," completely and irrevocably steeped in its principles and its consequences, he carefully distinguished the acceptance of this legacy from the actions of those who had handed it down. The mission of the fathers was to destroy, that of the sons to conserve. The *esprit révolutionnaire* was not to be confounded with the *esprit né de la révolution* —what the former undertook the latter was to consolidate.[51]

Even the very best of those who had survived the heroic epoch of the Revolution were frozen in its old hatreds,[52] or had been stained by

---

48. [A. F. Carrion-Nisas] *De la Jeunesse française* (Paris: DeLaunay, 1820), p. 6. In a pamphlet defending the students involved in the riots of June 1820, the law student Senemaud inquired "quel nom, selon les hommes sages, doit mériter une jeunesse dont les mains sont pures de sang, dont les années n'ont point été souillées, de qui le coeur n'est point noir et coupable, mais franc, sensible, généreux, et toujours ému aux noms sacrés de Patrie et d'Honneur. . . ?" [Senemaud], *Détails historiques sur les évènements de la première quinzaine de juin 1820, par M. Senemaud, élève de la Faculté de droit de Paris* (Paris: Corréard, 1820), p. 8. Reflecting on the events of June 1820, Michelet expressed his admiration for the courageous youth facing the sabers of the gendarmerie and wondered if its destiny was to deliver a new revolution. "Quelle gloire pour la jeunesse française si, seule, elle faisait cette sublime révolution!" Jules Michelet, *Ecrits de jeunesse* (Paris: Gallimard, 1959), p. 84.

49. *Le Surveillant politique et littéraire* (1818), p. 71. This journal was published by the young admirer of Victor Cousin, J. J. Darmaing.

50. Dubois, *Fragments littéraires*, Vol. I, p. 46.

51. Charles Rémusat, "La Révolution française," *Passé et présent* (Paris: Ladrange, 1847), Vol. I, pp. 109–111 (first written in 1818).

52. See Auguste de Staël Holstein, *Du Nombre et de l'âge des députés* (Paris: Delaunay, 1819), pp. 55–60.

the compromises required for survival, or had been so disillusioned by
the failure of grandiose ideals as to fall easy prey to the meretricious
rewards of the Empire. "We on the other hand," Rémusat concludes,
"should be proof against false promises, prestige or power."[53]

The most confident and influential assertion of the unique identity and destiny of that fortunate generation was in Théodore Jouffroy's much praised essay, *Comment les dogmes finissent*, drafted in
1823 and published in *Le Globe* in 1825. We can understand the contemporary acclaim for this mediocre tract[54] in the light of the general
acceptance of its assumptions, not only by Jouffroy's coevals, but by
many members of the older generation. The essay is cast in the form
of a universal history of the circulation of dogmas but unmistakably
speaks to the immediate French past.

It contains the familiar representations of a degenerate Old Régime destined to be swept away, and of the revolutionary generation
whose task it was to wield the iron broom but whose destructive accomplishments rendered it incapable of reconstruction. Its ultimate
failure is intellectual because it has found no truths to replace the
falsehoods it has destroyed. Nevertheless the first soldiers of reform
have not fought in vain. They have broken the spell, and on their
young and enlightened successors this spell can never be cast again.
The revolutionary fathers, burned out in the cosmic struggle, have
necessarily to be outstripped by their fresh and unscarred heirs, who

> have already gone beyond their fathers and perceived the emptiness of
> their doctrines. A new faith appears before them, they advance toward
> this enchanting prospect with enthusiasm, conviction and resolution,
> the hope of the new era rests in them, they are its predestined apos-
> tles, and in their hands rests the salvation of the world.[55]

What Jouffroy has identified is a world-historical generation. The
self-image is scarcely that of De Musset's anxious youth come upon
a world in ruins, or of the victims of a pervasive *mal du siècle*. The

---

53. Rémusat, *Passé et présent*, Vol. I, pp. 115-116.
54. I agree with Henri Peyre, *Les Générations littéraires*, p. 59, that Jouffroy's
essay was "peut-être trop loué." There is an eloquent affirmation of the impression
that the essay made on Jouffroy's contemporaries in the *Papiers de Paul-François
Dubois* at the Archives nationales. *Archives privées*, 319 AP 3, Dossier 1.
55. Théodore Jouffroy, "Comment les dogmes finissent," in *Mélanges philosophiques* (Paris: Paulin, 1833), p. 20. Cf. the passage in De Staël Holstein, *Du
Nombre et de l'âge des députés*, p. 58: "Les révolutions politiques ont, comme les
maladies du corps humain, un terme qu'il est jusqu'à un certain point possible de
fixer d'une manière générale. Ce terme est celui où les combattants qui ont ouvert
la lutte commencent à se retirer de la carrière, et où une génération nouvelle vient
les remplacer."

attributes of that peculiar disease were certainly manifest, but they were accompanied, and in the first years of the Restoration dominated, by a robust sense of collective superiority. That phenomenon was the product of the historical experience and the social situation of those age cohorts old enough to have begun their education under the Empire and young enough to look forward to new careers in the early Restoration.

The complex question of the extent to which a historically significant generational identity is a phenomenon of social class deserves systematic investigation, but in the confines of this essay I shall merely comment on certain issues suggested by Georg Lukács and Pierre Barbéris in their brilliant Marxist interpretations of the world of Balzac.

Lukács and Barbéris have persuasively argued that one cannot understand the history of Balzac's generation without relating it to the general history of the bourgeoisie. However, to understand the actual behavior of those particular sons of the bourgeoisie, one must narrow the historical focus to the specific circumstances in which they confronted the challenge of the new century.

According to Lukács, they confronted this challenge burdened with illusions which they had to shed in order to survive. The heroic eras of the French Revolution and the First Empire had allowed the best elements of the bourgeoisie to translate their ideals into reality; but that age had passed with the Empire, to be succeeded by a period of petty calculation and the cash nexus. "It was the tragedy of a whole generation . . . that bourgeois society would not let it realize the ideals that society itself had given them but forced them to shed their illusions to survive."[56]

In extending the heroic age of the bourgeoisie to the end of the Empire, Lukács blurs the actual experience of the generation that would make the transition from the restrictions of the authoritarian Empire to the ambiguous potentialities of the Restoration. The heroism allotted to Napoleon's last cohorts lay in the opportunity to be decimated in lost battles; the earlier glory of concrete accomplishment in administrative construction, legal reform, and institution building had degenerated into the tangible rewards available to servile functionaries. Professional and intellectual opportunities seemed congealed in the narrow authoritarianism of the late Empire.

In his more detailed analysis, Pierre Barbéris suggests some of the

---

56. Georg Lukács, *Studies in European Realism* (London: Hillway, 1950), pp. 47–64.

ephemeral but historically significant social consequences of the transition from Empire to constitutional monarchy. Of particular relevance to the theme of this essay is his observation that the imperial educational system had, for the first time, postponed the entrance of a significant segment of the population into the adult world and enabled it to assume "an idealistic demanding mentality as yet untempered by responsibility."[57] The mentality of these first products of imperial secondary and higher education was also conditioned by a system which taught them that they constituted an élite, as it accepted and advanced them on the basis of competitive success. They did not universally perceive the Empire in its last frozen phase as providing the scope for their potentialities. Many experienced its collapse as a personal trauma, but simultaneously welcomed the intellectual and occupational possibilities of a less disciplined, less militarized society.[58]

The career of Victor Cousin seemed to incarnate these possibilities.[59] His legendary ascent from humble origins by way of an unrivaled series of triumphs in scholastic prize competitions made him the first great athlete of the meritocracy, star of the first *promotion* of the Ecole Normale. His decision in 1810 to refuse a position of *auditeur* on the Napoleonic Conseil d'état in order to enter the Ecole might be thought of as the first signpost on the highroad of mobility for the brightest competitors in the new generation. His appointment as university lecturer at the age of twenty-three indicated the promise of early rewards for distinguished talents. The suspension of Cousin's course in 1820 was understood as a frustration of that promise by an increasingly reactionary régime. And the triumphant reconstitution of the course in 1828 was celebrated as a concomitant of the defeat of ultra-royalism in the election of 1827.

The history of the Restoration régime's relationship with its most promising young philosopher is bound up with the contemporary reception of Cousin's essentially moderate message as the trumpet call of his generation. The manifest political content of his lectures was perfectly compatible with the moderate royalist version of a constitu-

---

57. Barbéris, *Balzac et le mal du siècle*, pp. 237–238.

58. For an example of the standard view (against which I will argue elsewhere) that the transition from Empire to Restoration frustrated youthful aspirations for social and economic mobility, see Pierre Barbéris, "Mal du siècle, ou d'un romantisme de droite à un romantisme de gauche," in *Romantisme et politique, 1815–1851*. Colloque de l'Ecole Normale Supérieure de Saint-Cloud (1966) (Paris: Armand Colin, 1969), pp. 171, 174–175, 193–194.

59. See the insightful analysis of Cousin's popularity in Canivez, *Jules Lagneau*, Vol. I, p. 158: "Il est jeune, il est d'origine populaire, il semble être le fils de ses oeuvres, sorti de néant par l'énergique impulsion de son génie."

tional monarchy, but the vast philosophic, moral and essentially theological pretensions of a pedagogy directed beyond the classroom to a general public seemed to threaten the precarious equilibrium of the preservers of the faith and the guardians of the state. And the youthful arrogance and self-assertiveness of Cousin's extended audience was not appreciated by those committed to the reconstruction of a stable order on old foundations. The official response to youthful "turbulence" —the tight surveillance of the student population and the paranoid harassment of the university system—greatly contributed to the identification of the educated youth with the politics of the opposition. This conflict of youthful aspirations and conservative anxieties made it impossible for the restored monarchy to assimilate the ideological pretensions of a Victor Cousin, whose destiny would be to apologize for régimes, not to subvert them. In this regard, as in others, the Bourbon régime helped to produce its own gravediggers.

WILLIAM R. KEYLOR

Clio on Trial: Charles Péguy as Historical Critic

> "What is to be the end of revision and refutation and substitution, if the building of the edifice out of the small parts is always left to other ages? Actually, the desire to make the single brick indestructible conceals a vast indifference to its utility, an indifference that the whole organization of academic and scholarly life tacitly supports. The printing press relieves everybody of the need to contemplate what has been found. History, which was once the sum of collective and individual memories, is now delegated: we let the bookshelves remember for us. What has taken so much pains to dig out and package will surely last forever—nobody will care to touch it."
>
> JACQUES BARZUN, *Clio and the Doctors*

Ever since his death on the battlefield at the beginning of the First World War, Charles Péguy has inspired a remarkable degree of scholarly interest. This contrasts with the relative indifference his works encountered from all but a small circle of admirers and detractors during his lifetime. His posthumous renown is attributable to the tendency of modern commentators to treat him as the personification of a critical period in modern French history. He emerges from the pages of a number of recent studies as a thinker who continually wrestled with the three principal challenges that confronted France between 1870 and 1914: the restoration of national self-confidence after the débacle of the Franco-Prussian War; the establishment of a durable political ideology appropriate to the new régime of the Third Republic; and the resolution of the century-long conflict between Church and state which threatened to rip apart the fragile fabric of French society.[1]

---

1. See, for example, Marjorie Villiers, *Charles Péguy: A Study in Integrity*

But by focusing on Péguy's contribution to the patriotic, political and religious debates which buffeted France at the turn of the century, modern scholars have tended to overlook a fourth aspect of his influence. Though closely related to these three concerns, his historical criticism deserves separate consideration. Péguy had reached the conclusion early in his career that historical consciousness was a necessary condition for the spiritual rehabilitation of his nation, humiliated in war and divided in politics. After his premature withdrawal from the Ecole Normale Supérieure in 1897, he deposited at the Sorbonne a prospectus for a thesis topic which announced his intention to explore the paramount influence of historical writing on nineteenth-century thought.[2] Though he never returned to the university to fulfill that ambitious commitment, he published a number of articles which constituted fragmentary attempts to redeem his earlier pledge in the *Cahiers de la quinzaine*, the literary journal that he founded at the beginning of the twentieth century. His last important work, the posthumously published *Clio*, signified that this interest in history had remained with him to the end of his life.[3]

What is most striking about these historical writings is that they reveal Péguy as critic rather than creator, iconoclast rather than prophet. They constitute a full-scale assault on the school of historical writing formed at the Sorbonne and the Ecole Normale during the last quarter of the nineteenth century by scholars such as Ernest Lavisse, Charles Seignobos, Charles Victor Langlois, Alphonse Aulard and Gustave Lanson. Historical writing was then transformed from a gentlemanly pastime of freelance writers into an academic discipline practiced by professional historians. Research methods were (at least in theory) modeled after the exact sciences, and the lessons of the past were employed for political proselytism in the educational system of the newly established Third Republic.[4] It was against these three trends—the scientific methodology, the republican ideology, and the professional character of historical writing—that Péguy directed the brunt of his historical criticism.

Heading Péguy's indictment of the academic historical method in

---

(London: Collins, 1965); Hans A. Schmitt, *Charles Péguy: The Decline of an Idealist* (Baton Rouge, La.: Louisiana State Univ. Press, 1967); and André Robinet, *Péguy entre Jaurès, Bergson, et l'Eglise* (Paris: Seghers, 1968).

2. The thesis topic was ambitiously entitled: "De la Situation faite à l'histoire dans la philosophie générale du XIXᵉ siècle." See "Sur les Thèses en Sorbonne de Péguy," *Amitié Charles Péguy, feuillets mensuels*, 76 (1960), p. 29.

3. See Charles Péguy, *Clio* (Paris: Gallimard, 1932).

4. I have examined these multifarious developments in my *Academy and Community: The Foundation of the French Historical Profession* (Cambridge, Mass.: Harvard Univ. Press, 1975).

France was his criticism of what he called its "presumptuousness." He complained that most professional historians harbored the conviction that since *la science historique* possessed the methodological key that could unlock the secrets of social life, it deserved to become the pre-eminent intellectual discipline in French higher learning.[5] He ridiculed the scientific pretensions of the French historical profession and its ill-founded confidence in the capacity of the human mind to establish a set of incontestable verities about the past.[6] He remarked that such an undertaking would require of the historian intellectual qualities normally reserved for the immortals. That historians could imagine themselves capable of mastering the infinite detail which forms the material of history suggested to Péguy a lack of appreciation for the limits of historical scholarship. On the contrary, the modern historian had become "an eternal, absolute, all powerful, totally just, omniscient God."[7]

Péguy bluntly stigmatized this ambition to comprehend the totality of human history as a doomed enterprise. He argued that even if such an exhaustive familiarity with the documentary evidence were possible, it would by no means automatically yield the type of knowledge that constitutes the ultimate objective of historical study. So long as the historian mines the archives for factual evidence, he can remain loyal to his ideal of scientific objectivity, though at the cost of producing little of recognizable value. But as soon as he reassembles the results of his research in comprehensible form, he betrays the methods of scientific historical scholarship. For the process of distillation requires that he interrupt the indiscriminate pursuit of detail and select out certain facts on the basis of some criterion that is extrinsic to the historical data.[8] Péguy cited this epistemological constraint as an insurmountable obstacle to the attainment of the scientific objectivity which represented the professed goal of the academic historians.

This academic dropout enjoyed catching the most prominent historians in the act of violating the rigorous methodological canons of scholarship they themselves had promulgated. When Gustave Lanson —founder of the new school of scientific literary history, and the man

5. Charles Péguy, "De la Situation faite au parti intellectuel dans le monde moderne," *Oeuvres complètes* (hereafter cited as *OC*), Vol. III (Paris: Editions de la Nouvelle Revue française, 1927), pp. 118–133.

6. Charles Péguy, "De la Situation faite au parti intellectuel devant les accidents de gloire temporelle," *OC*, Vol. III, p. 212.

7. Charles Péguy, "Zangwill," *OC*, Vol. II (Paris: Editions de la Nouvelle Revue française, 1922), p. 200.

8. *Ibid.*, pp. 269–270.

who had been Péguy's nemesis at the Ecole Normale[9]—published a work describing his impressions of America gathered during a three-month sojourn, Péguy applied Lanson's own methodological criteria to the work in order to expose its scholarly shortcomings. Lanson was not entitled to comment on such a complex subject as American life, Péguy facetiously declared, until he had "exhausted all the documentation and literature on America from the Incas to the present."[10] In a more serious vein, Péguy suggested that Ernest Lavisse, the illustrious dean of the Sorbonne historians, who had produced dozens of discursive works that could scarcely be considered models of scientific erudition, would have to be relegated to the status of "an insipid man of letters" were he to be judged according to the inordinately stringent standards of the historical profession.[11]

A rather caustic attack on Péguy's style by Charles Victor Langlois, the leading proponent of scientific historical methodology at the Sorbonne, elicited from the victim his most stinging parody of the modern historical methods and what he called the "maniacs of erudition" who employed them.[12] Langlois's denunciation of his stylistic eccentricities as egregious violations of scholarly regulations drew from Péguy a response in a *Cahier* carefully subdivided into numbered sections in mock deference to the accepted scholarly format. Péguy playfully labeled the distinguished historiographer an "amateur" for presuming to evaluate literary works with which he was unfamiliar and for neglecting to furnish sufficient documentation for his assertions. Describing himself as a good pupil of Langlois who appreciated the importance of source criticism, Péguy treated the offensive article as a historical document and claimed to have spent eighteen months determining its precise publication date. Feigning astonishment that the date he had arrived at in his research coincided with the one that appeared on the title page, he justified the detective work as a necessary exercise in scholarly corroboration.[13]

What particularly outraged Péguy was the tendency of these "hypocritical" proponents of scientific history to require of their stu-

9. See Daniel Halévy, *Charles Péguy and Les Cahiers de la Quinzaine*, trans. Ruth Bethell (London: Dobson, 1946), pp. 27–28.

10. Charles Péguy, "L'Argent suite," *OC*, Vol. XIV (Paris: Editions de la Nouvelle Revue française, 1932), pp. 11–12.

11. Charles Péguy, "Langlois tel qu'on le parle," *OC*, Vol. XIII (Paris: Editions de la Nouvelle Revue française, 1931), pp. 300–301.

12. Charles Péguy, "De la Situation faite à l'histoire et à la sociologie dans les temps modernes," *Cahiers de la quinzaine* (8th series, 3rd cahier, 1906), p. 24.

13. Péguy, "Langlois tel qu'on le parle," pp. 291–294, 305–307, 311–312.

dents strict adherence to professional standards which they violated with impunity in their own writings. At doctoral dissertation defenses they invariably chided the candidate for having failed to exhaust the available documentary evidence before drawing conclusions from his investigation. They treated historical research as an open-ended exercise in methodological procedures, as though the means were more important than the end itself. Péguy complained that modern historians were so constrained by scholarly requirements that they were obliged, before reading a particular text, to trace its genesis and familiarize themselves with the totality of historical influences that operated upon society at the time it was produced. This perpetual effort to refine the procedures of archival research, as well as the obsession with tracking down every last shred of documentary evidence of a particular historical period, tended to divert attention from the reality that the scholar was seeking to understand.[14]

The scientific historical method served as an object of ridicule not only because Péguy considered it an unnecessary waste of time and effort, but also because of what he deemed its destructive effect on its subject. By carving up the historical record into a disjointed mosaic for the purposes of monographic analysis, the historian destroys the organic totality of the past. The historian's task is not to disentangle, denature and analyze, but rather to reconstruct, reintegrate and conserve. "How," Péguy asked, "can he conserve what he cuts up?"[15]

The endless pursuit of historical documents appeared to Péguy as a wild goose chase in search of the superficial manifestations of historical reality. The historian who averts his attention from the present and immerses himself in the documentary evidence of the past blinds himself to the continuity of past and present that only intuition can apprehend. The preoccupation with amassing data and perfecting the critical method discourages the scholar from addressing the important problems of modern life which historical understanding might illumine and which, conversely, might shed light on the past. Péguy complained that the academic historians' emphasis on methodological rigor had produced a generation of pedants skilled in research methods but lacking in the sense of continuity, who behaved as though "ignorance of the present were an indispensable condition for gaining access to knowledge of the past."[16] Reacting to the oft-quoted dictum of Langlois and his fellow specialist in methodology, Charles Seignobos,

---

14. Péguy, "Zangwill," pp. 190, 215 ff.
15. *Ibid.*, pp. 212–214.
16. Péguy, "De la Situation faite à l'histoire," pp. 15–17.

that "History is made with the documents,"[17] Péguy retorted that history is made *against* the documents." Elaborating on this rather cryptic contention, he distinguished between the concepts of "history" and "memory." History is an indirect method of grasping the external meaning of the event recorded in the document. It is incapable of penetrating those "interior articulations" of past occurrences that are accessible only to the memory of living man.[18]

Maurice Barrès once remarked that Péguy's own writings on Jeanne d'Arc constituted a masterly effort to re-experience a historical reality of which the surviving documents were merely indirect reflections. Péguy's conception of historical knowledge coincided with Barrès's own notion of the invisible bond that stretches across the ages to link successive generations in a common consciousness of their heritage. "We have a secret memory of our history," he declared, which can be reactivated only by a process of sympathetic imagination. The individual best suited to appreciate the historical significance of the maid of Orléans was not some erudite scholar steeped in the latest methods of paleography and armed with a myriad of manuscripts, but rather an inhabitant of her native province who personally shared the peasant mentality of his subject.[19]

The rather unorthodox treatment accorded this important historical figure by Péguy in his *Mystère de la charité de Jeanne d'Arc* may have satisfied Barrès, but it prompted harsh criticism from observers less inclined to the mystical view of things. One critic, in what he described as an attempt to "introduce the scientific process and method to the Péguy school," accused Péguy of confusing history with legend by presenting a simplistic portrait of the holy heroine which was familiar to every schoolchild but anathema to serious scholars. Péguy's defense of his work emphasized that his objective had been to intuit the inner experience of the saint, while historians customarily address only her external, historical significance.[20] He remained convinced that the deeper realities of the past, whose essence could never be recorded in historical manuscripts, were accessible only to the intuitive grasp of a sympathetic mind, regardless of previous scholarly training. He frequently hailed the untutored capabilities of his grandmother as

17. This familiar phrase appeared in Langlois's and Seignobos's influential manual of historical methodology, *Introduction aux études historiques* (Paris: Hachette, 1898), which served as the breviary for generations of history students in France.

18. Péguy, *Clio*, p. 195.

19. Maurice Barrès, Preface to Charles Péguy, *OC*, Vol. II, p. 32.

20. Charles Péguy, "Un nouveau théologien, M. Fernand Laudet," *OC*, Vol. XIII, pp. 11–12, 281.

a storyteller, always adding that she was incapable of reading a news-paper, let alone an archival manuscript. He described his own method as that of "never writing anything except that which we experience ourselves,"[21] and later defined the ideal historian as "a man who re-members."[22]

This unconventional conception of historical understanding had been formed not in the scholarly seminars of the Ecole Normale or the Sorbonne, but rather in the spacious amphitheatre of the Collège de France, where Péguy went each Friday afternoon to receive his philo-sophical edification from Henri Bergson. Péguy came to believe that the inability of Clio, the Muse of Scientific History, to grasp the pro-found realities of the past which lay beneath their superficial, transient manifestations necessitated the intervention of her half-sister Minerva. It was from Bergson that he appropriated the philosophical scaffolding for his methodological critique of the putative "science" of professional history.[23]

Péguy learned from Bergson that the chronological approach to human history was a misguided attempt to apply temporal categories to a subject which properly belonged to the realm of eternal duration. He maintained that the scholar was too often led astray by his relent-less effort to record the events of the past without understanding their underlying, eternal significance. He charged that most modern histori-ans erroneously viewed history as a linear, chronological progression of events to be classified as curiosity pieces. Whereas his own Muse, Clio, striving to embrace the fluid reality of the living past, announces that "I, history, temporality, time, transcience itself, have my source deep in eternity,"[24] the scientific Clio of the academic historians declares that she is "not a Bergsonian" but rather, "a woman who notes things down. All I need is a little *guichet* and some pidgeon holes. I am the chief clerk of all those employed in cataloguing, filing, and regis-tration. Movement and reality are not my business."[25] The eternal significance of past events eludes this queen of the temporal world. When her scribes approach her throne for instructions, she does not demand of them a direct, intuitive reconstruction of the past, but

21. Charles Péguy, "Notre jeunesse," in *Temporal and Eternal*, trans. Alex-ander Dru (New York: Harper & Row, 1958), p. 44. See also Schmitt, *op. cit.*, pp. 113–114.

22. Charles Péguy, "Discours pour la liberté," *OC*, Vol. II, p. 32.

23. See Villiers, *op. cit.*, p. 73.

24. Charles Péguy, "Clio I," in *Temporal and Eternal*, p. iii. See also his de-nunciation of the "philosophy of history" and its religion of progress in his "De la Situation . . . gloire temporelle," pp. 209–211.

25. Péguy, "Clio I," p. 114.

inquires instead: "Where are your documents, your monuments, your proofs, your testimonies?" "Do you have your papers?" she asks, warning them that she recognizes only scholars who possess "those papers that fill the archives."[26] These masters of erudition were, in Péguy's eyes, nothing but the "trustees and guardians" of historical evidence.[27]

Péguy saw in the contemporary attitude toward the Dreyfus Affair the confirmation of his suspicion that the historical record inevitably reduces the living drama of the past to dry-as-dust commentary. He was deeply discouraged by the disparity he observed between his personal recollection of the Affair from the vantage point of an active participant and the recorded history of the event. This discrepancy was so blatant as to move him to predict that the Affair's essential meaning would never be understood by the future historian who had access only to the written record.[28] He seemed to be implying that the eternal meaning of a historical event can survive only in the form of a perpetually revived memory.[29] The historian who equated the Dreyfus Affair with the collection of contemporary newspaper clippings, official documents and personal testimonies that recorded it was committing a grave error of omission. For the documentary evidence presented merely a single perspective on past reality, and was destined to be incomplete even if it embraced all the relevant facts.[30] Péguy never forgave Daniel Halévy, his former comrade in the Dreyfusard cause, for what he regarded as the insufficiently reverential tone of the brief history of the Affair that Péguy had persuaded him to write for the *Cahiers*.[31] Halévy subsequently explained that he could no longer see anything sacred about the Affair, remarking that while he approached the events as a historian, Péguy approached them as a poet.[32]

Bergsonian philosophy had taught Péguy that a documentary reconstruction of the past produces only discontinuous, fragmentary traces of a few memorable dates, names and events which have little to do with the real existence of past peoples.[33] He noted that the term "history" had always had a double meaning, denoting both "the past" and "the written record of the past," and argued that the modern historian's preoccupation with producing the second had progressively

---

26. Charles Péguy, "A Nos amis, à nos abonnés, *OC*, Vol. III, p. 335.
27. Péguy, "L'Argent suite," p. 80.
28. Péguy, "Clio," *OC*, Vol. III, pp. 330–331.
29. Villiers, *op. cit.*, pp. 233–234.
30. See *ibid.*, p. 232, and Péguy, "A Nos amis," pp. 346, 354.
31. Péguy, "Notre jeunesse," p. 45.
32. Halévy, *op. cit.*, p. 110.
33. Péguy, "A Nos amis," pp. 351–352.

separated him from the first. Historical reality enjoys an independent existence apart from its residual manifestations, which represent nothing more than what is commemorated. The historical observer must seize historical reality directly in order to achieve a direct communion with the past, instead of "always touching it lightly with those circumlocutory glances" which characterize the scholarly method.[34]

Péguy's mordant criticism of the *methods* employed by the academic historians was accompanied by an equally vociferous attack on their historical *interpretations*. These, he believed, dissolved the traditional certainties which had inspired respect for France's heritage among successive generations of Frenchmen. He repeatedly insisted that a people can remain optimistic about its nation's future only if it retains reverence for its past. It is a serious matter when a society begins to "cut itself off from its ancient roots," because these latent historical connections preserve the sense of continuity that represents the lifeblood of a healthy civilization.[35] Péguy accused the university historians of jeopardizing this fragile link to the past. He denounced their irreverent treatment of those historical institutions which they judged incompatible with the political ideology of Radical Republicanism they had embraced during the Dreyfus Affair.[36]

The first such traditional social institution to come under attack by the Sorbonne scholars was the Church. Péguy's spirited defense of the Catholic tradition was inspired by an ardent admiration for its decisive contribution to the foundation of French national identity. By denigrating France's religious heritage in their writings and lectures, Péguy argued, the professional historians were poisoning the minds of Frenchmen against an integral part of their history. This left them floundering in a spiritual void with nothing to sustain them but the bare bones of secular republicanism.[37] If modern Frenchmen could no longer believe in the saints for whom they named their offspring nor derive spiritual sustenance from the established traditions of their faith, he warned, they would lose contact with their entire national heritage.

Péguy also reproached the university historians for contributing to the emasculation of the second bulwark of French tradition: classical humanism. The revision of the classical curriculum of French secondary education in 1902, which placed modern subjects such

---

34. *Ibid.*, p. 232, and Péguy, "L'Argent suite," p. 80.

35. Péguy, "De la Situation faite au parti intellectuel dans le monde moderne," p. 138.

36. *Ibid.*, p. 165, and Charles Péguy, "L'Argent," *OC*, Vol. III, pp. 426–433.

37. Villiers, *op cit.*, p. 165.

as science and living languages on an equal footing with Greek and Latin, alarmed Péguy as much as the contemporaneous campaign against the parochial schools. He regarded Catholicism and Greco-Latinism as mutually reinforcing traditions whose confluence had produced the grandeur of French civilization. His compatriots were privileged to inhabit the geographical intersection of these two eternal traditions. They ought to defend their pre-eminence in French culture instead of treating them historically, as obsolete vestiges of a bygone age.[38] Péguy regarded the system of secondary education as the last oasis of classical culture amidst a desert of secular, scientific, utilitarian values. By seeking to replace Christian ethics and classical humanism with so-called modern subjects in the schools, the "little clan at the Sorbonne" was threatening to destroy the pedagogical tradition that had protected France's pious, patriotic youth from the menace of barbarism.[39]

This effort to rehabilitate the classical and Catholic traditions did not in itself violate the spirit of French republicanism. The synthesis of the classical and republican traditions had been a common theme during the Revolution, and the concept of Catholic republicanism had gained currency during the 1890s through the encouragement of the liberal Pope Leo XIII. But when Péguy dared to utter kind words about the third "eternal" tradition of French history, the monarchy, he plunged into dangerous waters. French republicans, who might have been willing to accept an interpretation of French history which praised the religious and pedagogical practices of the Ancien Régime, could hardly have been expected to welcome a defense of its political system, particularly during a period when the neo-royalist movement, L'Action Française, was launching a violent crusade against the Third Republic. Péguy's defense of France's monarchical institutions threatened to identify him with the newly revived forces of reaction which had emerged during the Dreyfus Affair, thereby disqualifying him as an authentic republican.

But Péguy had never been known for his willingness to permit the fear of guilt by association to divert him from his chosen path. He protected his republican reputation by denouncing the modern royalists for reducing the complex history of France to a rigidly mechanistic doctrine in order to bolster their indictment of the French Revolution and its modern offshoot, the Third Republic. But he then proceeded

---

38. Péguy, "Clio I," p. 158, and "De la Situation . . . gloire temporelle," pp. 225–226.
39. Péguy, "L'Argent," pp. 435–436, and "L'Argent suite," p. 78.

to accuse the university historians of the converse sin of defaming ten centuries of French history by disseminating the mistaken notion that France had been instantaneously transformed in 1789 from an abyss of ignorance and backwardness into an enlightened, modern nation.[40] That this crude operation of historical oversimplification was camouflaged in the pseudo-scientific doctrines of historical evolution imported from Germany offended Péguy's Bergsonian sense of eternal duration. When would the readers of this nonsense learn about the profound continuities underlying the superficial political transformations described by the proponents of scientific history, he wondered. When would they realize that France possessed a glorious history predating the year 1789, which had not disappeared overnight and could not be dismissed by a stroke of the ideologically biased historian's pen?[41]

The most serious consequence of this official effort of historical falsification in Péguy's eyes was its damaging effect on the average Frenchman's faith in the historic symbols—whether royal, classical, or Christian—of national grandeur. He accused the Sorbonne scholars of denigrating the heroes of antiquity, the saints of Christendom, and the rulers of the Ancien Régime, reducing them to the status of historical subjects and thereby depriving them of their eternal significance. He denounced the "party of intellectual degradation" for constantly seeking to belittle France's past heroes in a spirit of envy that invariably resulted in a corrosive iconoclasm. "They are like water, for they produce a perpetual erosion," he complained. "They spend their time reducing everything that outstrips them," undermining popular respect for the traditions that produced the greatness of French civilization.[42]

As the likelihood of war with Germany increased after the first Moroccan crisis of 1905, Péguy became concerned less about the intellectual subversion of French traditions than about the immediate military threat to the fatherland. But when he surveyed the attitudes of the French academic intelligentsia toward the impending crisis, he concluded that certain historians were guilty of treasonable be-

---

40. Péguy, "Notre jeunesse," pp. 33, 74–75.

41. Péguy, "De la situation . . . gloire temporelle," pp. 209–211, 219–222, and "L'Argent suite," pp. 127–128.

42. Péguy, "L'Argent suite," pp. 50–52, 176; "Un nouveau théologien," pp. 177–178, 236; and Villiers, *op cit.*, p. 312. Péguy also blamed this spirit of jealousy for the rancor displayed by academic historians toward the luminaries of their own profession. He noted that most academics, and particularly historians, "despise genius and works of genius," preferring to conceive of scholarship as a collaborative enterprise of monographic researchers. Péguy, "De la situation faite à l'histoire," pp. 33, 35.

havior: the very same men who had been criticizing classicism in the name of moderism and Catholicism in the name of secularism were also spearheading a campaign against patriotism. Under the banner of a spurious brand of internationalism and anti-militarism they undermined the fatherland, both in their scholarly writings and in their political activities.[43] To Péguy, the devout republican patriot, the most precious legacy of the French Revolution was the tradition of the *levée en masse*—the citizen militia that spontaneously rose to defend the republic against the invading armies of the autocratic empires of Eastern Europe. With this in mind he lashed out at the "conspiracy" of the Sorbonne historians who would purge the revolutionary republican tradition of its patriotic character in order to adapt French history to the needs of the ideology of anti-militarist internationalism which they had recently embraced.

To Péguy, the Declaration of the Rights of Man constituted a ringing call to arms which had inspired the revolutionary crusade of the First Republic.[44] Such a conception of the Revolutionary war as an inevitable consequence of the principles of 1789 clashed with the official interpretation of the French Revolution propounded by Alphonse Aulard, the first occupant of the Sorbonne chair in the history of the Revolution. Aulard portrayed that central event in modern French history as an internationalist movement to liberate all of humanity from the yoke of absolutism rather than as a catalyst of narrow French nationalism.[45] Burning whatever bridges that remained between himself and such protégés of Aulard as Albert Mathiez (his former study-mate at the rue d'Ulm) and Philippe Sagnac and Pierre Caron (whose *Revue d'histoire moderne* he had once housed in his tiny bookshop), Péguy reproached the Aulard school of Radical Republican historians for falsifying the meaning of the Revolution in order to accommodate the international Socialists, its newly acquired allies in the campaign of republican defense.[46] He charged that the French Revolution's conception of national liberation had been perverted by modern historians. In their hands it had come to signify

---

43. Many of the leading historians at the Sorbonne and the Ecole Normale had been active in the abortive campaign to prevent the extension of the term of military service from two to three years in the years immediately preceding the First World War.

44. Péguy, "L'Argent suite," pp. 137–141.

45. See François Aulard, *Polémique et histoire* (Paris: Cornély, 1904) and *Histoire politique de la Révolution française* (Paris: Colin, 1901).

46. See Paul Farmer, *France Reviews Its Revolutionary Origins: Social Politics and Historical Opinion in the Third Republic* (New York: Octagon Books, 1963), pp. 89–97, for a discussion of this development.

a dangerous sort of cosmopolitanism which threatened to weaken French security at a time of great peril. When the Germanophile, internationalist Socialists and their Radical Republican friends betrayed the interests of the French fatherland, he declared, they were simultaneously betraying the very revolutionary heritage they professed to revere. Had they been acting in such a manner in 1793, they would have been suppressed by the Convention, which would never have tolerated their pacifist fulminations.[47]

Péguy warned his readers that the Sorbonne historians were employing specious historical arguments to soften up the French people for a repetition of the disaster of 1870. Their predictions of international reconciliation and perpetual peace were illusory. With Socialist politician-historians like Jaurès mouthing empty platitudes about the solidarity of the working classes of Europe, and Radical Republican historian-politicians like Aulard prematurely hailing the advent of détente with Germany as a guarantee against war, the French intelligentsia was diverting public attention from the ominous policies of the Kaiser. French patriots needed to be reminded that, "contrary to all the teachings of our modern historians, and notably of the professional anti-militarists," national defense was an imperative Frenchmen could ill afford to ignore.[48]

Foremost among these professorial culprits was Charles Seignobos, whom Péguy denounced for failing to profit from the lessons of his own historical instruction. Seignobos had demonstrated in his lectures how the German universities had led the movement of national liberation during the Napoleonic wars, yet a century later this eminent historian was actively participating in the French university's effort to undermine France's military preparedness. After reading a series of articles in which Seignobos predicted a decline in German belligerence, Péguy felt obliged to deliver to this celebrated expert on German history a stern lecture on the folly of basing predictions of future trends upon knowledge of the past. He complained that only professors of history would dare to pontificate with such self-assurance on conjectural matters of national importance because of their mistaken conviction that their experience in identifying the causal connections between historical events qualified them to predict the future consequences of present developments.[49]

What disturbed Péguy most of all about the corrosive criticism of

---

47. Péguy, "L'Argent suite," pp. 119–123, 137, 152–158.
48. Péguy, "A Nos amis," p. 360.
49. *Ibid.*, pp. 95, 102–107.

French traditions by the practitioners of scientific history was that it emanated not from some shadowy *cénacle* of discontented Bohemians, but rather from the lofty platform of the state university. Having systematically distorted French history in order to make it serve the interests of the regnant ideology of Radical Republicanism—which Péguy labeled the metaphysic of positivism, materialism and the religion of progress—the professoriate was able to transmit it to the next generation through the monolithic, centralized educational apparatus of the republican state.[50] The rewards which it reaped for these services—professorial chairs, lavish salaries, academic honors,[51] control of professional periodicals and predominant influence over the recruitment and promotion of successors, awarding of scholarships and granting of degrees[52]—enabled this academic coterie to institutionalize, professionalize and centralize the writing of history under its auspices. From this position of power it could reshape the historical thinking of an entire nation.

Péguy's indictment of the methods, doctrines and professional orientation of French academic history expressed the mounting resentments of those amateur, freelance writers of history among the non-academic literary intelligentsia, the successors of Lamartine, Tocqueville and Thiers, who had seen their traditional function usurped and monopolized by the prophets of scientific history in the centers of higher learning. By raising the standard of the Republic of Letters against the encroachments of the Republic of Professors, he was embracing a cause for which many members of the French intellectual élite were prepared to do battle.

---

50. Péguy, "L'Argent," pp. 426, 433, and "De la Situation faite au parti intellectuel dans le monde moderne," p. 165.

51. Péguy, "De la Situation . . . gloire temporelle," pp. 171–177. Lavisse, the czar of French academic history, was "swollen with incomes, pensions, salaries, and honors." Péguy, "Un Nouveau Théologien," p. 136.

52. Lanson engineered the promotion of his protégés on the basis of favoritism rather than merit (Péguy, "Un Nouveau Théologien," pp. 143–147). Aulard and Langlois shamelessly extended their intellectual hegemony by influencing the dispensation of scholarships and degrees (Péguy, "De la Situation . . . gloire temporelle," p. 200).

FRITZ STERN

Capitalism and the Cultural Historian

> ". . . [W]e must assert what no one questions in theory and every-
> body violates in practice, namely that the complexity of life,
> taken both quantitatively and qualitatively, is greater than our
> documentary, chronological, and critical schemes allow for. The
> clues and witnesses are, to begin with, very numerous, taken as
> brute facts by themselves. But they are, even so, a vast over-
> simplification of the past. . . . But huge as this harvest of clues
> may seem, it is not enough. The Ariadne's thread is missing. It is
> found in no letter, no archive, no encyclopedia. It must be spun
> from one's inner consciousness, at great risk of error and on
> guard against cocksure superiority. Hence the need for *a priori*
> sympathy, in the exact meaning of that term: *feeling with.*
>
> " 'Feeling against' is sure falsification, for life is lived by
> everyone on the assumption that it has meaning, that he who
> lives it is a rational being, honest, worthy, and human."
>
> JACQUES BARZUN, "Truth in Biography: Berlioz,"
> *The University Review: A Journal of the
> University of Kansas* (Summer 1939)
> and in *Biography as Art*, ed. by
> James L. Clifford (1962).

Talk of capitalism is endemic and in most areas of the world contemptuous. The detractors of capitalism are legion, its defenders few
and uncertain. Stereotypes prevail: capitalism involves alienation, exploitation, class conflict. Historically it is seen as the triumph of a
corrupt and spineless bourgeoisie, ruthless in its pursuit of profit and
in its repression of the class it lives off; faithful followers of Marx still
expect that this same class, the proletariat, will some day inherit the
earth and establish at last a just and egalitarian society. Such is the
simplified drama, as suggested by compressed accounts and sweeping

systems and as believed in by a multitude of people. Increasingly, historians have dealt with discrete, often highly technical aspects of capitalism so that the simpler version could prevail.

It is paradoxical that the longer we live in capitalism the less we seem to understand it. In the nineteenth century, when capitalists promoted and profited from the ever greater application of industrial power, the understanding of the dynamism of capitalism—of its immense power, of its revolutionary character—was deeper than it is today. In the first half of the last century, poets, novelists and critics understood the magnitude of the upheaval and saw in it a force that was changing the physiognomy of the world, most notably through the railroads, and transforming the social and moral conditions of life. They perceived man's changed relation to nature, to one another and to the self; his painful mobility; the "purse-proud impertinence" of the bourgeoisie, as Balzac called it—the psychic vulnerability and the vulgarity of the newly risen and their monumental callousness; and new class antagonisms exemplified not by the clash of abstract classes but by the lives and sufferings of individuals. They wrote of peasant sons seeking their fortune in a Paris that was at once enticing and corrupt; of love denied by convention or economic calculation (how vivid are the torments of love and class for Bradley Headstone, infatuated with Lizzie Hexam); of aristocrats who saw their world denied and bourgeois who saw theirs sumptuous but empty, and who had to pay for their achievements with repression and denial of self. (The antagonism between Thomas and Christian Buddenbrook is fed by their contradictory responses to the demands of repression and to the psychic cost of success.)[1]

The artists and writers of the last century not only understood the nature of the new society but inveighed against the greed and the hypocrisy of the new age. They felt the changes, and hence their accounts are memorable, whereas "value-free" renditions, once again in vogue today, are neither vivid nor memorable. Jacques Barzun has often referred to the impact of the earlier generation: "Carlyle," he wrote, " . . . denounced the mounting tide of poverty, disease, squalor, and vice in words which make Marx's sneers look boyish in comparison." Or again: "The swearing and cursing against the burgher-at-large by Beethoven, Berlioz, Liszt, Flaubert, and Shaw are simply peacetime

---

1. I am told that a German social historian has recently "quantified" the results of the *Buddenbrooks*; he studied and found that indeed a large percentage of family enterprises in Germany faltered in the third generation, as happened in the *Buddenbrooks*. Are such "verifications" likely to enhance or impoverish our understanding of either the novel or reality? Perhaps another study can "quantify" how many British armament magnates left their enterprises to foundlings?

bombs and bayonets.''[2] Marx converted the moral outrage of his predecessors and his own into a system which, so ran the promise, would
lay bare the laws of capitalist development with the same objectivity
as obtained for the laws of nature, and these would likewise operate
independently from human intentionality. Marx's laws also signaled
the direction of capitalism: mankind would move forward to a preordained stage of Socialist equality. In the wake of Marx and Marxism,
the analysis of capitalist society lost some of its subtlety and acquired
a harsh, lifeless quality which at times falsified Marx's own complex
thought and brilliant insights into the interconnectedness of social
phenomena.

At present, capitalism is mostly studied by economists and economic historians who develop ever finer abstractions and mathematical
models for the behavior of the market but who tend to forget in print
what they know in fact: that the economic order and the social and
cultural realms are linked in countless vital and non-quantifiable ways.
The one important book of our time which is fully cognizant of this
interplay is characteristically entitled *The Unbound Prometheus*, the
very title harking back to ancient myth and poetic truth.[3]

I came to understand the impact of capitalism—and some of
the inadequacies of general abstractions—in a study of Gerson Bleichröder, born in Berlin in 1822. He was the son of a Jewish money jobber,
a trader in foreign currencies, who only gradually came to be known
as a banker. Gerson was the first of the family to have been born into a
world that no longer imposed legal restrictions on Jews. In 1830,
Gerson's father became an agent of the Rothschilds, that fabled
dynasty which by the 1820s already was recognized as the embodiment of a new power. (Heine, an occasional guest at Baron James de
Rothschild's, proclaimed that "Money is the God of our age, and Rothschild is his prophet.") From 1830 to 1855, the Bleichröder Bank prospered, by virtue of its ever closer ties to the Rothschilds and its own

---

2. Jacques Barzun, *Darwin, Marx, Wagner: Critique of a Heritage* (2nd ed.,
New York: Anchor Books, 1958), p. 154; and *Berlioz and the Romantic Century*
(2 vols., Boston: Little, Brown, 1950), Vol. 1, p. 530.

3. David S. Landes, *The Unbound Prometheus: Technological Change and
Industrial Development in Western Europe from 1750 to the Present* (London:
Cambridge Univ. Press, 1969), who frequently reminds the reader that "attitude
is more decisive than law or fiat," that "ideology has roots of its own, and the
economy is as much its servant as its master," and that "too often it is assumed
that non-economic obstacles simply melt in the face of economic opportunity,"
pp. 129, 541, 550. On this general subject, see also the earlier, rather biased collection, F. A. Hayek, ed., *Capitalism and the Historians* (Chicago: Univ. of Chicago
Press, 1954).

shrewd exploitation of the railroad boom. By 1859, the Frankfurt Rothschilds recommended Gerson to the departing Prussian minister, Otto von Bismarck, and thus began a relationship which ended with Gerson's death in 1893. Bleichröder became Bismarck's private banker and counselor, his *homme de confiance* and secret agent at home and abroad. Because of his many roles in Bismarck's life, Bleichröder had immediate access to him; with no one else outside his family did Bismarck have an equally long or close relationship. Bismarck and Bleichröder: an unlikely combination, representing an old and a new world, and yet their collaboration was symptomatic of the energies that shaped the new Germany.[4]

I was attracted to the prospect of writing on Bleichröder by two considerations: the lure of an unexploited Bleichröder archive, which on first inspection seemed to promise a new perspective on Bismarck and his era; and the cooperation of an economic historian who would handle the story of the great banking house, a story which I would have been incapable of writing. The archive proved a tantalizing beginning, but no more; it contained private letters to Gerson but almost none from him, and hence was inadequate as a guide to his career. It had to be supplemented by material from the most diverse private and public archives of Europe. After a few years, the economic expert vanished as well, and the task of writing about Bismarck and Bleichröder fell on me alone.

My first day of work in the Rothschild Archives on the rue Laffitte I came across a receipt for 1,000 taler, debited by Bleichröder on the Rothschild account, and signed by Cosima von Bülow, née Liszt. A few years later, of course, Cosima was to become Wagner's mistress, later mother to his children, even wife, and, after his death, guardian and exploiter of his heritage, musical and ideological. I had once written an essay on this formidable creature, so noble, so greedy, so idealistically anti-Semitic, for a seminar given by Jacques Barzun, and through many years of labor, I remembered Cosima's draft as a talisman, a sign that even a cultural historian could find sustenance in the complicated travails of a banker.

Bleichröder was a representative man, an exemplar of the *homo novus* who shaped the life of the nineteenth century. His beginnings were modest; he died the richest man in Berlin. He demonstrated the enormous power of wealth—and all the limitations and ambiguities of wealth as well. A close study of his life offers insights into the

---

4. For details on Bleichröder, see my *Gold and Iron: Bismarck and His Banker Bleichröder*, to be published early in 1977 by Alfred A. Knopf.

mentality—the ambitions, values and fears—of the capitalist class in Germany, and his intimate relations with Bismarck, with Bismarck's entourage, and with the old aristocracy reveal something of the complicated response that the older class, based on birth and honor, had to the new class, based on wealth alone.

Bleichröder amassed a fortune; this was the obvious condition for his success, but it was never enough. He was indefatigable in ferreting out economic opportunities; he came to have an intuitive sense of where to place his funds, on what terms, with what associates and against what rivals. He cultivated his close ties with officialdom and had important clients among the fourth estate. He was not a demonic entrepreneur but a prudent banker who knew how to play the market; he financed railroads, helped build the St. Gotthard tunnel, floated companies, served foreign governments as banker, and made a profit on every transaction.[5] And yet he was anything but an "economic man," that abstraction of the textbooks which would lead us to believe that businessmen, with lightning speed, are able to gauge the opportunities of the market and make their decisions accordingly, rationally, and with an eye to maximum profit. For Bleichröder that activity became routine; he excelled at it, even if in his later years he may have eschewed profitable risks for the sake of respectable security. But his incessant striving showed that the accumulation of wealth, which no doubt at a certain stage of his life had been an end in itself, became essentially a means. He knew how to make money, but money could not buy—at least not entirely—what he most desired: a recognized place in society, prominence and influence.

The social ambition of the bourgeois is one of the great themes of the nineteenth century. In Bleichröder's case we have the documentation of this ambition and can reconstruct the maneuvers by which he sought to realize it. In a few cultures, notably in North America, the epithet "self-made man" became a badge of distinction. Not so in Europe, and least of all perhaps in Germany. Traditional society defined a man by his birth and bearing, by his honor. Wealth was rarely considered as a moral asset; more likely it bespoke character traits of dubious morality. In the face of such prejudice against Mammon—prejudice that was at once moral, religious and self-serving

---

5. Relevant here are Joseph Schumpeter's remarks about the motivation of entrepreneurs: "First of all, there is the dream and the will to found a private kingdom, usually, though not necessarily, also a dynasty. . . . The sensation of power and independence loses nothing by the fact that both are largely illusions" —*The Theory of Economic Development* (New York: Oxford Univ. Press, 1961), p. 93.

since it was a defense precisely against the presumptions of a Bleich-röder—it was hard to gain acceptance. Money talks—but it talks in different tongues in different countries and at different times.

Bleichröder's struggle for acceptance was an extreme instance of a common experience. It was made extreme by his Jewishness—he had to contend with prejudice not only against Mammon but also against a race that for long had been suspected of being uniquely gifted in materialistic, that is, evil, pursuits. His special ties with Bismarck gave him a unique advantage which, in turn, quickened his desire for admission and status. A Bleichröder had to forge his own role, as his old identity as a marginal man in society and a pariah became invalid. For Bleichröder, this search for a new identity was made even more imperative when in 1872, at Bismarck's personal behest and for services rendered to the state and its financially embarrassed paladins, he was formally ennobled. No other unconverted Jew had had such an honor bestowed on him in Prussia. Now Bleichröder had to fashion a life that would be consonant with his new position as Herr von Bleichröder, or Baron von Bleichröder, as he was often called.

It called forth an extraordinary effort. By dint of great feasts at which the diplomatic corps and the local élite, including the Princess Bismarck and her sons, dined and danced in the company of handsome officers from the best regiments, Bleichröder established his social presence in Berlin. The feasts were opulent—and painstakingly prepared. One enjoyed at Bleichröder's the best food, the most celebrated musicians, and always and above all the choicest company; fellow Jews or fellow financiers were usually excluded, as were Bleichröder's relations. Neither host nor guests could have felt at home. Bleichröder's social role—so solid on the outside and so fragile in reality—caused endless tongue-wagging. As Princess Radziwill once wrote: "Berlin society is divided into two camps—those who go to Bleichröder while mocking him, and those who mock him but do not go."[6]

But most went, because social gatherings had long since ceased to be celebrations of congeniality; they had become a reflection of the market. Likewise, Bleichröder was assured of the gratitude and friendship of many leading figures, and the protestations marked the decline of the ideal of friendship. Bleichröder craved acceptance and his social fortunes epitomized the triumph of utility—he was a presence because of his unsurpassed usefulness and because, as an intimate of Bismarck's, he was a dangerous man to snub. The Bismarck entourage,

6. Comte Paul Vasili, *La Société de Berlin* (Paris: Nouvelle Revue, 1884), p. 158.

suffering under the moody inconstancy of the genius-autocrat, suspected Bleichröder of having a mysterious hold over the chancellor
and of having the power to make and break careers. Since Bismarck
had to be humored, Bleichröder had to be humored and the élite had
to go to his house, vilifying him the more as it went.

Bleichröder also "modernized" impoverished members of the old
élite, seeking to salvage the fortunes of men who had fallen on evil
days. He helped men who had succumbed to the great capitalistic
greed of the time by placing them in lucrative directorships. His services were legion—quite aside from providing the routine advantages
of a reliable and accommodating banking house with the most excellent connections in Europe.

In his search for acceptance, Bleichröder sought to impress
the world by his intimate knowledge of all that went on in Europe.
Everybody came to Bleichröder—officials, diplomats and fellow magnates—to solicit his advice and receive his news. Like the Rothschilds,
he discovered the usefulness of instant intelligence, and he built up
a network of informers so that he was probably the most knowledgeable man in Berlin. He was especially knowledgeable about Bismarck,
whose fortune he invested and who therefore had to keep him properly informed. Bleichröder collected secrets as other plutocrats collected *objets d'art*, and for the same reason—to dazzle people and to
exalt his own importance. As in most things Bleichröder did, the functional and the psychological coincided: being in the know was an in-
estimable advantage in the market and in society, and served as well
to augment self-esteem.

The drive for acceptance was the lodestar of his later life. In the
pursuit of it, he distanced himself from his own people. He still inter-
ceded for the Jews and used his power in Berlin to lobby for his co-
religionists in Eastern Europe; had he done less than that, his valuable
connections with the Rothschilds would probably have snapped. But
gradually he moved away from the Jewish community; at most, he
served as a kind of ambassador of Jewry to the dominant culture. The
police report of 1874—two years after his ennoblement—may have
maliciously exaggerated, but it has a ring of authenticity, and many
variations on the theme were current in Berlin in the 1870s:

> Mr. von Bleichröder, who since his elevation to nobility almost bursts
> with pride and who publicly no longer entertains his former friends
> and associates, keeps himself apart from them even in his walks: on
> his promenades in the Sieges-Allee [Berlin's fashionable avenue along
> the Tiergarten] he walks on the western side, instead of on the eastern
> with the great majority of promenaders, who are almost all Jews.

Asked why he walked on the other side, he is supposed to have answered that the eastern side smelled too much of garlic. Several of Bleichröder's former acquaintances heard of this remark and a few days ago took him to task for it on the promenade, and things did not go too smoothly then.[7]

The police report depicts the classic case of the *arriviste*—who never arrives. Bleichröder's life was an attenuated form of deferential dissembling; as such it brings to mind Lionel Trilling's observation that there were societies that seem to favor dissembling:

> We cannot establish by actual count that there were more villains in real life at one time than another, but we can say that there was at one time better reason, more practical use, for villainous dissembling than at another. Tartuffe, Blifil, *la cousine* Bette, Mme Marneffe, Uriah Heep, Blandois, Becky Sharp—these wolves in sheep's clothing are not free fantasies, and it is a misapprehension to think of them as such. The possibility of their actual existence is underwritten by social fact.[8]

Bleichröder's social climbing was a form of dissembling and forced a similar dissembling on the élite he sought to emulate, for the latter had to conceal its true feelings. Most aristocrats, contemptuous of such climbing and such disloyalty, were bemused at Bleichröder's efforts to emulate them. And he tried hard. Shortly after his ennoblement, he purchased the large estate of Field Marshal Roon, an old landed seat near Potsdam, which in the early nineteenth century had been remodeled by the great Prussian architect David Gilly. Here he led the quiet life of the landed élite. But if it was a genuine retreat for him, it was also the spot where his royal neighbor, William I, once called on him after the most intricate preparations for the event.

Bleichröder had decorations, titles, connections. Yet nothing—not even a royal parchment—could prevail against ancient prejudice. The Junker nobility still drew its living and its dignity from the land, but agrarian pursuits were threatened by overseas competition and by the rise of new wealth at home. The Junker feared that the new plutocracy would buy up their mortgaged estates, that wolf or Jew was forever waiting at the door. They thought themselves in a mortal struggle for survival, and in that struggle they were not about to give up their ancient prejudices against business and unproductive wealth, or their traditional sense that honor, service, and unpretentious living and piety defined human worth.

---

7. Police Report, January 16, 1874, in Bismarck Archive, Friedrichsruh.
8. Lionel Trilling, *Sincerity and Authenticity* (Cambridge, Mass.: Harvard Univ. Press, 1972), p. 15.

Money, so the saying went, was something one had, but did not talk about. Under the new system, exemplified by Bleichröder, the Junker stood in danger of not having money, and so they were condemned to talk about it, at least in private, while publicly maintaining their stance against Mammon. The more capitalism altered the social physiognomy of Germany, the more the Junker were forced to do battle in the material arena, to mobilize their political power in order to defend their declining economic interests. All of this hardened their prejudices against the grasping money-man who had but one value, that of ruthless profiteering. If only there had been a Marxism for nobles. As it was, they had to make do with their own harsh mixture of the idealization of rural life and the denunciation of urban, rootless capitalism, for which Jews seemed to have a most uncommon penchant.

It is not surprising that by the end of the century the old classes were trying to reassert their higher status, their more honest and authentic life, their superiority in virtues that were decisive for the state, such as self-denial. (These virtues came generally into vogue as the military spirit spread through society, aided by universal conscription and chauvinism.) What was less predictable—and certainly ran counter to the expectations of Marx and liberals alike—was the willing submission of the upper bourgeoisie to these same values. That submission Bleichröder exemplified in a hundred ways, perhaps none more poignant than his carefully orchestrated petition to William I to restore his son, Hans, to his position as a reserve officer (lost when, on the day the emperor was shot, he appeared at the royal castle with a *cocotte* at his side). In his petition Bleichröder begged for his son's reinstatement, because the continued humiliation might drive the father to leave Germany; not all his millions, not all his proximity to eminence, could balance the shame of having a demoted, denuded son. The emperor showed some clemency, and Bleichröder's other sons fared somewhat better. But the descent of Bleichröder's progeny into sloth demonstrates the terrible risks of success. The father's labors paid for the children's license. Spoiled from the beginning and also desirous of belonging, they converted to Protestantism, while abandoning the Protestant ethic. They lived a life of decadence, and Thomas Mann's "Blood of the Walsungs" conjures up something of the suffocating atmosphere.

Bleichröder's career demonstrated the lure of wealth and the yearning for what has been called "status," but the term does not suggest the anguish that the long climb involved. Quantifying or latter-day scientific historians tend to neglect this side of capitalist striving.

Adam Smith, who discovered "economic man," also knew that there was no such reality. "The rich man," he wrote,

> glories in his riches, because he feels that they naturally draw upon him the attention of the world, and that mankind are disposed to go along with him in all those agreeable emotions with which the advantages of his situation so readily inspire him. At the thought of this, his heart seems to swell and dilate itself within him, and he is fonder of his wealth, upon this account, than for all the other advantages it procures him.[9]

A recent critic, aware of the discomfort that terms like "fame" and "honor" would cause his scientific brethren, has jestingly spoken of such "ultimate desires" as "obituary-enhancing activities."[10] The rich have always striven for more than wealth: the more may have been ostentation or pomp, may have been morally and aesthetically less creditable, less genuine than their search for wealth; but the yearnings have existed and have further unsettled society.

In Imperial Germany, the striving for these "higher things" was both peculiarly necessary and peculiarly arduous. If Bleichröder's life shows anything, it is the strength and dynamism of capitalism in practice and the pervasive power of anti-capitalism in spirit. The aristocratic classes—but not only they—looked upon the new system and its profiteers as an insidious evil. Capitalism offended their code and their social standing, and however much they may secretly have embraced capitalistic techniques or capitalistic greed, their public stance and private views were still contemptuous. (In this, as in so much else, Bismarck was the exception. But although he was a modern Junker, quick to recognize the utility of capitalism for the state and for the individual Junker, his unease at his link with Bleichröder can be gauged by the fact that his memoirs mention his banker and long-time confidant only once, and then in an inconsequential role.)

---

9. Adam Smith, *The Theory of Moral Sentiments* (London: Cadell & Davies, 1801), Vol. I, p. 99.

10. Albert O. Hirschman, "An Alternative Explanation of Contemporary Harriedness," *Quarterly Journal of Economics*, LXXXVII (November 1973), pp. 634–637. I am grateful to Professor Hirschman for a discussion of "economic man," and for calling my attention to this passage from Adam Smith: "But the principle which prompts to save, is the desire of bettering our condition, a desire which, though generally calm and dispassionate, comes with us from the womb, and never leaves us till we go into the grave. In the whole interval which separates those moments, there is scarce perhaps a single instant in which any man is so perfectly and completely satisfied with his situation, as to be without any wish of alteration or improvement of any kind. An augmentation of fortune is the means by which the greater part of men propose and wish to better their condition"—*An Inquiry Into the Nature and Causes of The Wealth of Nations* (New York: The Modern Library, 1937), pp. 324–325.

The social disdain of the aristocracy was matched by the anger and resentment of the lower classes, whose lives had been placed in jeopardy and whose self-esteem had been destroyed by the relentless pressures of "a free economic society." Artisans who had once found their economic security and their dignity in guilds felt themselves estranged and disadvantaged in the new society. In the late 1870s, these groups were attracted to a new ideology which blamed their lot on Jews because Jews had fastened an alien economic system on unwitting Germans. The proof of the charge was Bleichröder: his wealth and pretensions, his connections with men of power, his widespread and pernicious influence over press and parliament. The early anti-Semitic movement was also anti-capitalistic, and Bleichröder was the chief witness to the validity of its assertions. If he had not existed, it would have been impossible to invent him; he found, moreover, that it was impossible to defend himself against charges that combined the obvious with the venomously fanciful. The proletariat, imbued with the Marxist faith, held not the Jews but the capitalistic system as such culpable, and lived and worked in the confidence that the eventual overthrow of exploitative capitalism and its replacement by a humane Socialism was historically preordained.

Imperial Germany, as seen through Bleichröder, affords the extraordinary picture of a triumphant capitalism spiritually devalued. The psychological premises of capitalism were obviously incompatible with the pretensions of German idealism and nationalism: the German ideal of self-cultivation was hardly consonant with an insistence on material self-aggrandizement, and the glorification of state authority in German nationalism can be seen as a rebuke to economic selfishness. Capitalism became widely discredited in the 1870s, when a great boom, fueled in part by speculation and corruption, gave way to a great collapse, and when serious economic dislocation was followed by Bismarck's abandonment of free trade—that classic ingredient of early capitalism or Manchesterism—and his adoption of protectionism. By the end of that decade, unfettered capitalism was thought morally bankrupt, and gradually a new kind of cartelized capitalism, at times in collusion with the government, replaced it, while popular sentiment continued to denounce a system of private greed.[11]

The notion of devalued capitalism may also help us to understand the prevalent hypocrisy of Imperial society. The new system was

---

11. I developed this theme in an earlier essay, "Money, Morals, and the Pillars of Society," in *The Failure of Illiberalism: Essays on the Political Culture of Modern Germany* (New York: Knopf, 1972), and in a lecture on "Der Krach der Werte" at the Berlin Akademie der Künste in September 1974.

a special spur to dissemblance. It condemned everyone to hide or deny his true role: the *Bürger* sought the trappings of nobility and the nobleman, so contemptuous of any system that assigned rank by wealth, needed to modernize his ways or lose his ancestral seat. It is customary to speak of the alliance between upper bourgeoisie and nobility which governed Germany after 1879, and in a political sense there was an alliance between landowner and industrialist; but like most alliances between unequals, common interests and common foes barely hid a deep suspicion and antagonism.

The life of Bleichröder makes this clear. Everybody used him and nobody acknowledged him—Bismarck partly excepted. A list of his clientele reads like a selection from the Almanach de Gotha; but these clients came to him stealthily or wrote him letters about their material needs with the injunction, "to be burned." Perhaps it has always been so, yet the degree of involvement and concealment seems to have been unusual: Thorstein Veblen commented on the discrepancy in Germany between capitalistic reality and older cultural survivals long ago in his *Imperial Germany*. But it is only fair to add that the German reaction to capitalism—a subject so infinitely complicated that it still deserves to be examined in all its aspects—was conditioned by more than the survival of pre-modern customs. The hostility to this bustling, ever innovative and restless force was also affected by a collective nostalgia, part genuine and part nurtured, for "The World We Lost," for a pre-industrial world of communitarian harmony in smaller cities and amidst guild structures that regulated morality and economic pursuit in one insulated system. Wagner was the greediest of artists; his people were uplifted by the *Meistersinger von Nürnberg*, which they took to be the epitome of their true heritage.[12]

For many Germans of the mid- to late-nineteenth century, the dance around the Golden Calf was the more revolting because it coincided with a falling away from true worship. None of this was unique to Germany; churchmen—and not only churchmen—of the nineteenth century railed against the replacement of God by Mammon, of faith by indifference and greed, of duty by utility. In Germany, however, the degree of resistance—and hypocrisy—may have been greater than elsewhere; the unrecognized social reality poisoned the political atmosphere for decades. (It has of course always been

---

12. One of the most striking of contemporary works on German history, Mack Walker's *German Home Towns: Community, State, and General Estate, 1648–1871* (Ithaca, N.Y.: Cornell Univ. Press, 1971), analyzes and evokes the real experience of communitarian life and briefly sketches its transformation into retrospective ideology.

thought that devotion to material objects would diminish devotion to spiritual commands: "Having food and raiment, let us therewith be content. But they that will be rich fall into temptation and a snare and into many foolish and hurtful lusts which drown men in destruction and perdition. For the love of money is the root of all evil" [I Timothy, 6:7–10]. But the race after the goods of the world has mobilized human energies and the race itself constituted a goal. In contemporary society, the dance around the Golden Calf is once again in great disrepute, but what other dance will mobilize the same energies? Or will an increasing number of affluent young devote their energies to subduing that drive in order to embrace what Nietzsche warned against as the worst form of nihilism: European Buddhism?)

Bleichröder's desire for acceptance manifested itself in ways other than the emulation of the forms and values of the older classes. He also embraced the new secular faith, nationalism, and did so with the special passion that so many Jews, hitherto homeless, displayed. Bleichröder's special tie to Bismarck proved a kind of personal bridge to patriotism, which by the late 1860s and early 1870s had taken on the emotional hue of a new, exuberant nationalism. At times he exuded this overweening pride in the new Germany even to the Rothschilds, who reacted with predictable chill. As a banker, he remained a man of pacific and cosmopolitan leanings; like most bankers, he thought himself an instrument of peace. But for the rest he cherished a demonstrative loyalty to the new nation—and for his estate, ordered a collection of stones from all the battlefields in France where German troops had fought victoriously. It was a bizarre demonstration of faith and taste, but not out of keeping with the monumental architecture which at the time glorified German arms and unity.

The rich needed to show their munificence in many ways, and Bleichröder became a patron of the arts and sciences. He commissioned Germany's foremost portrait painter, Franz von Lenbach, to paint a portrait of Bismarck; years later, he asked Lenbach to paint his own portrait as well—which Lenbach did, at twice the fee. As Bismarck liked to tell the story, Lenbach, when asked about the discrepancy, explained that he had *enjoyed* painting Bismarck. For his own portrait, Bleichröder had to pay 30,000 marks.[13] One is reminded of Jacques Barzun's apt definition: ". . . the really paying patron of art in our society [is] the passionate snob—C. Snobius Maecenas."[14] Bleich-

---

13. Otto von Bismarck, *Die Gesammelten Werke* (15 vols., Berlin: Stollberg, 1924–35), Vol. IX, p. 476, and Lenbach receipt, August 10, 1882, Bleichröder Archive.

14. Barzun, *Berlioz and the Romantic Century*, Vol. I, p. 538.

röder also commissioned Reinhold Begas, the most celebrated sculptor of the day, and the perpetrator of many a monstrosity in Berlin, to design a family mausoleum. Begas suggested a large, ornate structure in Carrara marble, at a cost of 75,000 marks.[15]

But Bleichröder had also to show his largesse while alive, and his giving was truly ecumenical. He contributed to the poor and sick of all denominations—from Catholic hospitals to the Hebrew Orphan Asylum in New York. He helped to build an Anglican church in Berlin, a synagogue in Ostende, a Protestant church in a Rhenish village. He was endlessly solicited. Toward the end of his life, anonymously but in memory of his parents, he gave Robert Koch, the discoverer of the tubercle bacillus, a choice plot of 16 acres in Berlin and 1 million marks, for the construction of a new hospital and for the treatment of destitute patients.[16]

Neither Bleichröder's achievements nor his munificence shielded him from growing attack. On the contrary, his prominence made him the perfect target. The polemics began in the 1870s, when Germans first became conscious that they had been engulfed by a new economic system. Their hostility to the system was personified by branding the Jews (who did play a major role in promoting capitalism in Germany) as the culprits of subversion. In the beginning, Bleichröder was cited as the proof of racist charges: he was cunning, corrupt and powerful—and so were all his fellow Jews. In the turmoil of that first decade after unification, when exultation over foreign victories gradually gave way to concern over domestic divisions and depressions, the charges against Jews—validated as it were by Bleichröder's known role—confirmed what Barzun has written about racism generally: ". . . it satisfies a need common in complex societies—the need to give body to vague hostility, to find excuses for what goes wrong, to fear aliens or neighbors and curse them, while enjoying self-approval from within the shelter of one's own group. . . . It satisfies the starved sense of kinship and it promises a vast supernational community."[17] In Germany, this combined anti-Semitism and anti-capitalism remained a powerful subterranean current, ready to burst forth when the dams of social order and moral restraint weakened.

The life of Bleichröder exemplifies the many faces of capitalism in nineteenth-century Germany and the many interconnections between

---

15. Reinhold Begas to Bleichröder, Bleichröder Archive.

16. Gossler to Bleichröder, Robert Koch to Bleichröder, and *Norddeutsche Allgemeine Zeitung*, December 2, 1890, Bleichröder Archive.

17. Jacques Barzun, *Race: A Study in Superstition* (rev. ed., New York: Harper & Row, 1965), pp. x, xix.

realms that historians all too often keep in separate compartments. To speak of "the triumph of capitalism in Germany" is much too simple—and yet among economic historians the principal debate focuses on when this putative event took place.[18] Bleichröder should be a reminder that the triumph was but partial, that the animus of economically, socially and psychologically aggrieved groups against the new economic order remained strong, as did the nostalgia for a pre-capitalistic and pre-industrial world. For many decades, anti-capitalism was a sentiment that informed both the Right and the Left, though it could be argued that until recently it was a stronger force on the Right than on the Left. Balance sheets of capitalism beyond market fluctuations, production rates and cost-accounting are subject matter for a book that still needs to be written; the culture of capitalism remains a subject worthy of study and reflection.[19]

Capitalism is too serious a subject to be left to the economic historians alone. It is too subtle and elusive a subject to be captured by the rigorous specialist in the laws of the market or in the stages of economic growth; it does not yield to statistics. Put differently, capitalism is so much more than economics, so much more than collusion with government or class conflict. It expresses itself in changing attitudes and sentiments, in different self-perceptions and masks, in dress and painting and furniture, in a spreading rationality and a recoiling from it—in short, in all the aspects of a culture. The cultural historian, often so heedless of the transformations wrought by material changes, needs to rescue a subject which cuts so deeply into modern history, which tells us so much about human motives and achievement, about social reality and thought. "Nothing but the fullest and clearest—which is not the same as the simplest—view of our cultural past and present should satisfy us," wrote Jacques Barzun nearly twenty years ago, and the injunction has become even more timely.[20]

Capitalism has ever been suspect. In our own day, when the corruptibility of capitalism appears as an everyday headline, and when the traditional justification for capitalism—its successful functioning —seems once more threatened, we might do well to ponder the para-

---

18. See the very useful summary by Karl W. Hardach, "Some Remarks on German Economic Historiography and Its Understanding of the Industrial Revolution in Germany," *Journal of European Economic History*, I: 1 (Spring 1972), pp. 37–99.

19. A quite unsatisfactory beginning was made by two German sociologists, Dieter and Karin Claessens, in *Kapitalismus als Kultur. Entstehung und Grundlagen der Bürgerlichen Gesellschaft* (Düsseldorf: Diederichs, 1973), but it does at least raise the question "whether in Germany 'capitalism' has ever existed," p. 200.

20. Barzun, "Preface to the Second Edition," *Darwin, Marx, Wagner*, p. xvi.

dox that one of the most valuable and insidious consequences of capitalism is anti-capitalism: valuable because of its reformist impulse, and insidious because beneath it often lurks a Utopian illusion that social evil springs from capitalism and that some, often nebulous, alternative would usher in a period of human brotherhood and goodness. As with all great themes of past and present, the study of capitalism is at once a command of our craft and a dictate of our social existence. Capitalism has brought misery and degradation; it has also brought freedom, mobility and rationality. It is a subject worthy of study, for it involves not only the functioning of a worldwide market but the minds and habits of men. In an age that speaks of late capitalism or post-capitalist society, perhaps we need to ponder as well the likely consequences of a withering of capitalism. To paraphrase the title of an essay that Jacques Barzun long ago recognized as portentous, we may need to think of "The Moral Equivalent of Capitalism," for the Faustian impulse will reassert itself—in our understanding of the past and in the shaping of some future.

Melpomene

DRAMA IN LITERATURE

&

CAROLYN G. HEILBRUN

Axiothea's Grief: The Disability
of the Female Imagination

> "Stendhal would very likely say that woman should be brilliant
> if unable to be beautiful."
>
> JACQUES BARZUN, *The Energies of Art*

Woman's most persistent problem has been to discover for herself an
identity not limited by custom or defined by attachment to some man.
Remarkably, her search for identity has been even less successful
within the world of fiction than outside it, leaving us today with a
situation largely unchanged for more than two millennia: men writers
have created women characters with autonomy, with a self which is
not ancillary, not described by a relationship—wife, mother, daughter,
mistress, chief assistant. Women writers, however, when they wish
to create an individual filling more than a symbiotic role, have projected their ideal of autonomy onto a male character, leaving the
heroines to find their role in subservience, or change of name, or both.

This revelation, flatly stated, is both revolutionary and provocative. Do we not know, after all, as one of our best critics has put it,
that the novel found "its subject in the desire for women and money
which has ruled storytelling from *The Iliad* to *The Wings of the Dove*"?
Yet examine carefully these two examples. In *The Iliad*, women may
be an excuse for the Trojan War and for Achilles' quarrel with Aga-
memnon; honor and the love of men are, nonetheless, more important
for Trojans and Greeks. Neither money nor women propel Hector to his
death; they fail even to protect him from it, being of only secondary
importance. In *The Wings of the Dove*, love of money is a motive, yet
we must substitute "men" for "women" in the phrase quoted. Two
of the protagonists in this novel are women, and their varied abilities
to rise above the accepted female roles, using a man in the process,

may be called the theme of the book, if not its subject. Both *The Iliad* and *The Wings of the Dove* were written by men and encompass, in goddesses and heroines, autonomous women. Women writers have never achieved this.

The meaning of "identity," and the general failure of women to discover it for themselves, can now be fruitfully defined and examined in the light of several recent revisions in psychoanalytic theory. These new interpretations have made little headway in the culture generally; they are, however, profoundly useful in revealing the central disability in the imaginative life of women writers.

Freud's discovery, not only of the patterns of the unconscious, but of the stages of early development culminating in the oedipal phase as well, made apparent the process by which the child, from birth onward, undergoes and survives the tensions between himself, his parents and the society as a whole. The magnificence of Freud's discovery lay in his recognition of this process. The terrible, and terribly different, burdens he cast upon males and females, however, evolved from an inevitably male-centered view of the human condition which he did not, of course, invent: it lay, from his infancy, all about him. He saw the male child as able to accomplish successfully that passage known as the oedipal crisis precisely because—and this was of greatest importance to later interpretations—he believed the male child to be in the correct, or ideal relation to the mother. Of the opposite sex from his mother, the boy was able to consider himself as her lover and, potentially, as the lover of women.[1] Freud went astray, as we now know, not in his observations of the data, but in his interpretations. The unfortunate consequences have followed not from Freud's misinterpretations alone (these were certainly understandable in a man of Victorian origins), but from the persistence with which succeeding generations have, with the tenacity of Aristotelians, insisted upon the literal accuracy of Freud's *particular* interpretations rather than upon the brilliance with which he revealed previously unimagined processes in human development. Nor has the Freudian establishment yet found itself ready to incorporate the new findings in a meaningful way. Their special "Catch-22"—if you cannot believe the

---

1. The most recent defense of Freud's doctrine, and a detailed explication of it, is Juliet Mitchell's *Psychoanalysis and Feminism* (New York: Pantheon, 1974). Mitchell believes that Freud presented the patriarchal structure without bias, and she defends him from feminist criticism. She has, however, neglected to take into account the objections to Freud's understanding of women by men who are not necessarily feminist: David Riesman, Stanley Edgar Hyman, Philip Rieff, Erik Erikson. Mitchell looks to Marxism and structuralism to counter the Freudian pattern.

classical Freudian interpretation, that is because you are neurotic—
has saved them the bother of confronting new ideas.

Four discoveries have, nonetheless, brought the problem of
female identification closer to our understanding. One is the realization that the so-called basic sex is not male, as Freud thought, but
female: every fetus starts out female. The second is the discovery
that sexual identity for a child—what has come to be termed "core
gender identity"— is not biological, but assigned. If the child has not
been able to conceive of itself as definitely one sex or the other by the
age of three, nothing but disaster can follow; it is the assignment, however, that is important, not the biological sex.[2] The third is the realization that the male child, not the female, has the harder adjustment
in maturation: the infant's first desire is to be the mother, to identify
with her. For a girl child, this first, overpowering infant identity need
never shift; for a boy child that shift will be essential. This leads, in
my view, to a fourth set of insights. The problem for the boy, as
analysts now recognize, is that the shift in gender identification is
not easily made. The male, therefore, suffers many forms of sexual
dysfunction as a direct result of this switch: extreme homosexuality,
transvestitism, fetishism, sado-masochism, etc. The female, secure
in her sexual identity, suffers few if any of these. Her problems, I believe, arise precisely from the lack of struggle, from the fact that she
need never undergo an identity crisis, and indeed, is almost incapable
of one.

All societies, from the earliest and most primitive to today's, have
ceremoniously taken the boy from the female domain and urged upon
him his identity as a male, as a responsible unfeminine individual.
The girl undergoes no such ceremony, but she pays for serenity of
passage with a lack of selfhood and of the will to autonomy which only
the struggle for identity can confer. The male undergoes a profound
struggle, but often pays for it with sexual dysfunction.

The girl thus passes all too easily from infantile identity with the
mother to complete identity with her. If she comes to hate this mother

---

2. The phrase "core gender identity" was coined by Robert J. Stoller. See his
Sex and Gender (New York: Jason Aronson, Inc., 1968). It is important to note
that "core gender identity" and gender are not the same. Male homosexuals and
transvestites have an especially strong "core gender identity." For studies in sex
assignment, see J. Money and A. A. Ehrhardt, *Man and Woman, Boy and Girl*
(Baltimore, Md.: The Johns Hopkins Univ. Press, 1973), and Ehrhardt's description of her recent work in Buffalo. A clear account of these new developments
can be found in Ethel Person, "Some New Observations on the Origins of Femininity," in Jean Strouse, ed., *Women and Analysis* (New York: Grossman, 1974),
pp. 250–261.

she may, as an adult, suffer a dislike of women, postpartum depression, or frigidity. These conditions need not, however, affect her entire personality adjustment as a man's sexual dysfunction must affect his. But the price of this personality adjustment is high: her autonomy. Robert J. Stoller, expressing the classical Freudian view, tells us that biological bisexuality "produces an unalterable part of human psychology, which leads in men to a fear of not being manly, and in women to an urge to be manly."[3] To the classical analyst, this means that a man fears the loss of his penis, while the woman desires one. To the modern, non-classical Freudian, it can mean that the man struggles through to an identity at high cost, while the woman, her struggle called improperly feminine, recognizes the need for an identity crisis, but cannot discover a way to achieve it, nor even the form it is likely to take: society has provided her with no model but the nurturing, ultimately deserted mother.

The woman writer, then, casting about her for a fictional character in whom to embody the search for identity, is as bereft in her creative imagination as in life of a knowledge of the process by which a woman could achieve identity, or of what the result might be. Indeed, her creative imagination will fail her even when life does not. The woman writer, therefore, projects upon a male character the identity and experience for which she searches. Male writers, meanwhile, having had the passage to identity made mandatory by society and their sex, struggle rather for a role in which the pains of sexual dysfunction may be mitigated. Often they create female characters who have achieved the identity crisis, but upon whom the pains of male sexual function are not imposed.

Not all male writers, it need hardly be said, create "women heroes." The American male writer eschews this altogether, as do American men generally: the fear of the loss of masculinity is so extreme that any recognition of a feminine self is unbearably threatening. Among major American writers, only one male, Hawthorne, ever achieved the creation of an autonomous female character, and he was so terrified by what he had done that he spent the rest of his life in fear.[4] European male writers do not all, of course, create great women characters, any more than all women writers are concerned with identity or the challenging of the conventional female role. Yet it is ex-

---

3. Robert J. Stoller, *Perversion* (New York: Pantheon, 1975), p. 18.
4. "We seldom meet with women, nowadays and in this country, who impress us as being women at all—their sex fades away and goes for nothing in ordinary intercourse." Nathaniel Hawthorne, *The Blithedale Romance*, quoted in Jacques Barzun, *The Energies of Art* (New York: Random House, 1962), p. 120 n.

traordinary how many male writers have created autonomous women characters and how few women writers, awake to the question, have found it possible to resist the creation of men instead. We scarcely need the fingers of one hand to tick off the women writers who were able to create autonomous female characters, and to present men as "sex objects": Colette, Virginia Woolf, Rose Macaulay, Doris Lessing. The fingers of the other hand would probably suffice for those unmentioned or unthought of here. Contemporary women writers still reflect the struggle, rather than succeeding in creating women who have surmounted it. Franker now, they continue to tell the old familiar story of women's passivity and dependence.

An extremely successful and popular woman novelist whose career perfectly demonstates the woman writer's deep need to affirm the patriarchal structure is Mary Renault. Like other women writers, but more openly and to a wider audience, she reveals an author fascinated with male wholeness, unable to conceive of power as passing from males in fiction as it has not passed in life. Renault's early novels, written before her discovery of the all-male Greek world, display awareness of the problem of female autonomy. Yet the struggle is apparently too fundamental for a woman writer, requiring too much of the imagination.

Renault is commonly mentioned as a writer with a strong interest in homosexuality; certainly her concern with this subject has been present from the beginning and honestly handled in advance of the new permissiveness. But the history of her novels is, more profoundly, the history of a woman writer's struggle to present ideal loves and destinies without the terrible burden of female dependence.

Her six earliest novels had contemporary English settings. The first, *Promise of Love*,[5] is, like many to follow, set in a hospital: Renault, after Oxford, trained to be a nurse. Lookalike brother and sister, with ambiguous names in the manner of Rose Macaulay, are loved by the same man. In the end the brother dies, the sister marries the man and conventionally longs for a baby and her husband's professional success. Renault's second novel, *Kind Are Her Answers*, embarrassingly bad, is also dull because trite; the women are tiresome stereotypes. The third novel, *The Middle Mist*, frankly and courageously presents female homosexuality; yet any chance for female autonomy

---

5. Titled *Purposes of Love* in England; *The Middle Mist* was entitled *The Friendly Young Ladies* in England. Her other novels, all in print, have the same titles in both countries. (Her publisher in the United States is Pantheon Books in New York City.)

in these characters is muted. The central male character is hopelessly idealized, and the women are not, as he is, devoted to their professions; they are merely competent, seeing their jobs as compromises.

Return to Night is, at first, more promising. The central character is a woman doctor, ambitious and willing to face the demands of her profession, higher for a woman. She falls in love with a much younger man, however, and discovers a need to sacrifice herself to him: " 'You're not suggesting I should give up my work? It means as much to me as acting does to you.' As she spoke she realized, with a muffled astonishment, that this statement had become wholly untrue." Her final capitulation to *his* destiny and her love for him are absolute, even though she knows he will eventually tire of her:

> Hilary, for her part, was recalling the ambitions and the indignations which had seemed important to her a year or two ago. It was as if somebody had repeated to her a very old joke, of which she had only just seen the point. How anxious she had been to prove that she could get an appointment over David's head! To do this, it had seemed, would prove something or other about women and men. It was excruciatingly funny to think she might have got it—or the presidency of the College of Surgeons, for that matter—only to find herself exactly where she now was. The hard core for a feminist to bite on had, after all, been something as simple as this. . . . Now for the first time it was borne in on her, like a piece of news, that being a woman was a fact about which absolutely nothing could be done. She had spent so long in battle with non-essentials; the essential had stolen up on her unaware.

Is it any wonder that, with such a view of woman's inevitable destiny as subservient passion, Renault should have looked for action to the world of men alone? Especially since she tended to see men as victimized by the love of women.

North Face, the fifth novel, is again conventional, with stereotyped women (to which the "old maid" figure has been added) and intense friendships between men. These friendships turn to sexual love in *The Charioteer*, her final English novel. Taking its title from the *Phaedrus*, this novel abandons annoying women characters to minor roles, and explores problems of relationships with a cast of males. The hero thinks of women as Nazis and dreams of Athens. Deciding not to live with his lover, he thinks: "He wants to be brave for me too; and no one can do that." Every woman should aspire to that sentence, but Renault could not imagine one doing so.

The Last of the Wine, set in ancient Greece, freed her imagination from the necessity of sex stereotypes, not because women had different roles in ancient Greece, but because they could be conceived as having no roles at all. The lovers in this book refer to women simply as property, as in the Ten Commandments. Renault found herself free to play out ideals of love and destiny with no concessions to the troublesome female struggle for identity. Oddly, boys took the place of the girls of pre-First World War England, with tutors instead of governesses to protect them from lascivious males. Xantippe is twice confirmed in her shrewishness, though neither Plato nor Xenophon gives any basis for this tradition. Like the brilliant women who worked with Freud, like women Freudian analysts since, like most successful women in past years, Renault became an apologist for female subservience. The lovers speak to one another:

> "Tell me this, Lysis; where do you think the soul goes when we die?"
>
> "Who has come back to tell us? Perhaps, as Pythagoras taught, into the womb again. Into a philosopher if we deserved it, or a woman if we were weak; or a beast or bird if we failed altogether to be men."

The King Must Die reaches back to the legend of Theseus, who sets out deliberately to overthrow women rulers, the worship of female gods and the male role of consort to the Queen. Yet when Theseus sails for Crete with his team of boy and girl bull dancers, he conceives of the girls as an integral, essential part of the team's success; they achieve equality and even esteem as athletes. Renault seems to move, given the possibility within her material of such an interpretation, toward the creation of women of achievement.

The Bull from the Sea, the sequel, provides Renault's only attempt at a major autonomous woman character. The myth of the Amazons gives her Hippolyte. Yet the equality Hippolyte finds as Theseus' consort is a gift from him; their "marriage" is one of equals, which he can allow since his male dominance has been established. This may seem a prophetic scheme, looking forward with hope toward a possible future when men would no longer have to prove themselves, and women might develop high skills. Alas, Hippolyte ends as "a woman to the last," sacrificing herself in the place of her husband with an insistence upon self-immolation which he recognizes is in conflict with his destiny. Here again, the creation of a woman hero is deflected; the unusual destiny of an individual refusing the stereotyped role is given to Hippolytus, who is safely male. Interestingly, Antigone is twice deprecated in this novel, as Xantippe had earlier been.

The Mask of Apollo, recreating the acting profession in the third century B.C., demonstrates prophetically for literature that the creation of women's roles, that high art, is the proper work of men. Again there is, between actors, what would have been between a man and a woman an idealized "marriage." The only female is one of two women students known to have been in Plato's academy. Axiothea confides to the hero her grief at not being able to go to war with the male students:

> "I must have done wrong in my last life on earth, and this is the punishment I chose when my eyes were opened. So I ought to bear it patiently, and hope for better next time. But, oh, it is hard."

Renault finds it easy to agree with Plato in his epigraph to Dion, that all women are "spun into the dark web on the day of their birth."

The novels about Alexander, *Fire from Heaven* and *The Persian Boy*, return again to an all-male world of armies, where women are raped and murdered. The role of "female" lover is played by the Persian eunuch who, though idealized in the degree of servitude he offers Alexander, can assert his manliness by accompanying the army on the campaigns.

It is, obviously, ungrateful to criticize Renault in the face of her considerable accomplishment. Her novels are readable and intelligent, and they create with great imagination a past world. Should we ask that she create a possible future world also? Yet we cannot help but notice that many women novelists, Renault among them, have themselves achieved an autonomy they deny their heroines. Why does this identity crisis so strongly resist imaginative recreation? As a recent critic has observed about an earlier, greater woman novelist:

> What is fatally hampering to George Eliot's heroines is not society, not even provincial society, but their own lack of creativity, which includes creative intellectual powers. Obstacles of all kinds are put in their way, it is true, and George Eliot makes us feel so sorry for them that we overlook the fact that in real life, given the motivation and the talent, women could and did overcome them. George Eliot herself triumphed over greater handicaps than any of her women characters are faced with.[6]

So women analysts, from Helene Deutsch and Marie Bonaparte onward, have used the result of their own successful search for identity to persuade women patients cheerfully to accept the conventional female role. To overcome oppression has occasionally been possible, but to imagine a pattern for the terrible burden of freedom and choice has always been harder for the oppressed than to defend their oppression.

---

6. Patricia Beer, *Reader I Married Him* (London: Macmillan, 1974), p. 181.

The English detective novel shows women writers tiptoeing toward an interesting compromise. Unlike the American Dashiell Hammett-Raymond Chandler "private eye," the English fictional detective was, from the beginning, not aggressively manly. If anything, he tended to be mild-mannered, over-educated, sensitive and devoted to conversation, the arts, violin playing or the cultivation of roses. When the great women detective story writers entered the field, they found ready for them detective models who were not likely to indulge in *macho* orgies, who might even dare to appear effete. Then, fame achieved, these novelists—Sayers, Christie, Marsh, Tey—began to create women companions for, or counterparts to, their male investigators, and to explore the possibility of employing a female detective. This tendency, we cannot now be surprised to learn, was fraught with imaginative dangers, and was abandoned in many cases. Most recently, P. D. James, having produced the delightful and revolutionary *An Unsuitable Job for a Woman*, retreated in her next novel, *The Black Tower*, to her gentle male detective and to women characters from central casting. Amanda Cross, an American detective novelist, exhibits the greatest falling off of all. Having begun with a woman detective who solved her first case, Cross almost immediately provided her with a lover (later husband) who is called in upon every occasion to rescue her or solve the case himself.

Colette, Rose Macaulay, Woolf, Lessing—these are among the few women writers who have created major women characters who struggle for an identity as themselves and make it. Today women have begun more frankly and openly to explore their condition of servitude and exploitation. Perhaps from this some imaginative daring may follow. The marvelously skilled younger contemporary English writers, such as Margaret Drabble and Gillian Tindall, have begun to create women characters not completely immersed in love and motherhood. Iris Murdoch, after all, gave us, in *A Severed Head*, one professional woman character in a cast of six.

Yet, as Samuel Johnson remarked about second marriages, such optimism must rest more upon hope than experience. Experience shows us how many contemporary novelists have chosen male protagonists for their first novels: Iris Murdoch, Susan Sontag, May Sarton. Most of their women have been presented in conventional roles if not, as in Sontag's novels, actually mutilated. Alone of these, May Sarton has imagined, in fiction, the life of an autonomous woman artist. How unconventional, at the same time how frankly in search of identity, have been the female protagonists of some male novelists since the novel's beginnings: Becky Sharp, Kate Croy, Gissing's heroines, Meredith's heroines, Hardy's heroines—these are only the most blatant examples. They do, however, suggest the sparsity of their counterparts in the works of women writers. Elizabeth Bennet may delight us, but not because she ever questions marriage as her only and chief destiny (although her creator did), not because she conceives of a wifely role as other than the preservation of her husband's *amour-propre*: Darcy, she knew, was not ready to be laughed at. Rather, by writing about the ordinary female destiny with infinite talent, women writers have struggled, often with brilliant results, to impose meaning upon it.

Women writers today, like other women not enamored of the patriarchal society, have so far devoted themselves to consciousness raising: a necessary step. But the achievement of identity, imaginatively perceived, still lies ahead. Adrienne Rich once said: "The awakening of consciousness is not like the crossing of a frontier—one step and you are in another country."[7] But the discovery of the possibility of autonomy *is* like the crossing of the frontier: the step *is* into another country. Until women writers can take that step across that frontier, into that country, the Muse of Fiction must remain either a counselor in the household arts or in the service only of male artists and male characters.

---

7. Adrienne Rich, "When We Dead Awaken," in B. C. and A. Gelp, eds., *Adrienne Rich's Poetry* (New York: Norton, 1975), p. 98.

MORRIS PHILIPSON

Virginia Woolf's *Orlando:*
Biography as a Work of Fiction

> "The critic's ultimate hope is that he may facilitate the beholder's
> pleasure by indicating its kind and by associating it with tenable
> meanings, emotions, and experiences. Association is what every-
> thing lives by in the memory, hence the *data* of the work, right
> down to points of factual information and right up to images of
> transcendence, may all have importance. The fused cluster of
> perceptions and associations is The Work in as full a sense as it
> is given anyone to possess it. Its actual shape and force in a
> living mind depend on the individual sensorium, which, despite
> all the journal articles written and to be written, is beyond the
> *control* of the critic. He wields no scientific club with which to
> coerce. He can only point and give reasons as he flashes a beam
> here or there."
>
> JACQUES BARZUN, "Biography and Criticism—
A Misalliance Disputed," Critical Inquiry, 1975

If one is fortunate to live long enough, one comes to see the faces
of relatives and friends who were old when one was young reappear
as the faces of their grandchildren. Such similarities contribute to
a sense of the continuity of life with a unique forcefulness. For it
feeds not an intellectual hunger for comprehending the means of
biological transmission, but a much more primitive emotional need
for belief in inheritance labeled, as it has been from ancient times,
with the image of "blood relationship"—for which seeing is believing.

Readers of the first edition of *Orlando* had an advantage over
readers of almost all subsequent editions published between 1928 and
1973, for only the original edition was correctly illustrated. It is easy
to suppose that reproductions of the paintings and photographs were
dropped later by publishers in order to save money, but surely not by

someone with an intimate knowledge of the book. Those pictures must be reckoned with as elements of the text. They help move the argument forward, they contribute to the cumulative effect of conviction or accession of belief on the part of the reader. If photographs illustrating a factual biography are considered valuable, then the portraits which appear in this fictional biography must be recognized as invaluable: first because they are the internal evidence that this novel is a "biography" of V. Sackville-West, for it is pictures of her that represent Orlando as a woman; and because the images of Orlando as a boy and as a man are taken from the collection of portraits of her ancestors. They are, in effect, the only equivalent in this work of fiction to the documentary evidence used in an actual biography. Without them, as without the subtitle or the dedication, there is no injunction to the reader to think of this novel as a true story.

Nearly fifty years after the publication of *Orlando*, conventional biographies of both Virginia Woolf and V. Sackville-West have now appeared. In the much more engaging of the two, Quentin Bell describes an incident that occurred at the end of 1925:

> The Woolfs spent Christmas that year with the Bells at Charleston. Vita drove over from Long Barn to lunch on Boxing Day. "How beautiful she is," said Clive to Virginia after the guests had left. "An aristocrat of ancient race," said Virginia to Clive. Leonard turned to Julian, then a freshman at King's. "What snobs they are," he said. This remark unleashed, as it was intended to unleash, furious expostulations and an argument which lasted the rest of the evening.[1]

Snobbery of that sort expresses an excess of admiration and desire for association, when respect and enjoyment may be mutual but where there is no possibility of equality or genuinely shared experience. Virginia Woolf could never become what she herself was not—"an aristocrat of ancient race." It is not that the admiration is misplaced but that an excess of it would appear to be misleading to such a vigorously pragmatic mind as Leonard Woolf's, for it might seem more an expression of self-pity than a means to any useful end. But in this he was wrong because—and this is always the difference between the factual mind and the visionary—it was not the character or the performance of V. Sackville-West's life that fascinated Virginia Woolf; it was the idea of her life, not what she alone was but what she represented. As with Proust's experience of his contemporary French aristocrats, the imaginative power sees through the individual

---

1. Quentin Bell, *Virginia Woolf: A Biography* (New York: Harcourt Brace Jovanovich, 1972), Vol. II, p. 120.

and is engaged also by a class embodying a kind of historically determined experience which is of a different order in its social nature. "Now, the truth is that when one has been in a state of mind (as nurses call it) . . . the thing one is looking at becomes, not itself, but another thing, which is bigger and much more important and yet remains the same thing."[2]

Most families are without a history older than the unrecorded memories of grandparents. Most lives are uninterpreted in relation to ancestry and descent. And, therefore, most people who become conscious of their indebtedness to the past do so through the appreciation of the public and common elements of inheritance: their language, their institutions, their monuments, their literature. But the mystique of *blood inheritance* is older and infinitely more compelling in its own mysterious way. It is as if such an heir comes by the sense of the continuity of life through necessity rather than by dint of application. Of course that is not always the case, as innumerable descendants of aristocrats demonstrate by their minimal appreciation of their personal heritage. However, V. Sackville-West was one of the few in whom the appreciation of her family history was as far as possible removed from a condition of being "taken for granted." She represents the opposite extreme. She was dominated, not to say obsessed, by her family history. She wrote *Knole and the Sackvilles* in 1922, edited the writings of one of her ancestors (*The Diary of Anne Clifford*) in 1923, and later published the biography of her grandmother and her mother in *Pepita*.

From Michael Stevens's book, we learn that the publication of *Knole and the Sackvilles* was the occasion for Virginia Woolf's becoming acquainted with V. Sackville-West.[3] It was Virginia Woolf who initiated their correspondence and, when she had been sent a copy of the book, wrote to the author: "There is nothing I enjoy more than family histories . . ." That may sound hyperbolic but there must have been a great deal of truth in it. Almost all of the reviews of non-fiction which Virginia Woolf published are of biographies and family histories. *The Common Reader, First Series*, begins with a lengthy essay on the Paston family letters, and one of the last articles she wrote is concerned with a book by Queen Marie of Rumania, enabling her to reflect on the character of a royal family.

---

2. Virginia Woolf, *Orlando* (London: The Hogarth Press, 1928; New York: New American Library, 1960), p. 187.

3. Michael Stevens, *V. Sackville-West* (London: Michael Joseph, 1973), p. 38.

Why should it have been for her that "There is nothing I enjoy more than family histories"? Ordinary biographies produce a distorted impression of the separateness, isolation or self-sufficiency of individuals, concentrating, as they do, on what appears to have been within the independent power of one person. They contribute to a misconception of individuality. They do not show (as a novelist can) how the influences of the past and the tensions toward the future, through the infinite ways of interrelating with others—experienced from the inside—enable a person to recognize the degree to which he is neither isolated nor self-sufficient, but is part of a whole greater than the self. Family histories are closer to poetic, narrative or dramatic works in which such relationships are demonstrated, for they make patterns visible. They trace influences; they show how Grandson Y was like Uncle X. Likenesses, then, reassure, because they demonstrate that much of what we are is the result of our being part of a chain, one more link in a chain of human life which we inherit and make the most (or the least) of that we can. The reason this reassures is that it makes us aware that we are not condemned to the fearful freedom of creating ourselves all by ourselves; nor are we shipwrecked, abandoned, isolated on a deserted island. We are no more totally responsible for what we make of our lives than we are totally victimized, as if our lives were biologically programmed or socially predetermined. An individual is free to do what he can, but only within the circumstances of what has formed him out of the past and how he responds—being influenced and exerting his influence—in the present. The most interesting family histories are those in which we are able to see, through a sequence of generations, how people make of their lives something "like" and something "different from" each other's out of very similar "material."

A world obsessed by "freedom," by the idea of "individuality" and the supreme ideal of "realizing the self," flounders for lack of models by which to estimate one's own worth, standards rejected out of misguided tolerance. If no invidious comparisons can be made, then no one stands to be ashamed of himself. The price paid for such freedom from standards is that one has no basis for pride; whereas the essence of Family Pride rests on respect for the character and accomplishments of ancestors, so that they constitute models of what subsequent generations are encouraged and expected to emulate. Most tribal religions begin with ancestor worship, with veneration and fear of the power of the spirits of the dead to influence the living. To the extent that one appreciates the past (either a personal or an impersonal past), one embodies it and thereby enhances one's own powers to cope, as an individual, "with the strength of hundreds." Thus, the sense in which one is a human being is much more valuable than the idea of only being "one's self." Or to put it another way, shared experience is more desirable than subjectively isolated experience, just as intercourse is more gratifying than masturbation: by reassuring, through socially confirming one's humanity, rather than satisfying merely in one's self-controlled solitude.

But an excess of Family Pride, without a counterbalancing development of individuality, is as dangerous to a personality as the lack of it is, and this is what emerges through the pages of Mr. Stevens's biography of V. Sackville-West. Brought up at Knole—that vast estate, characterized by its grandeur even more than by its luxury—for all practical purposes in isolation from nearly any other child, dominated by a mother with whose beauty, charm and willfulness she could not compete, her only escape was into the love of that great mansion and that illustrious ancestry.

To appreciate one's antecedents is a part of the answer to the question: "Who am I?" Her paternal descent consisted of four hundred years of noblemen actively engaged in the governance of the state, leaders of social life and appreciators of the arts. On her maternal side, she descended from the very same line plus the infusion of the most plebeian—possibly gypsy—Spanish blood, joined to the English aristocracy through her grandfather's long-lived but illegitimate affair with the dancer, Pepita, whose daughter became mistress of Knole; that ancient grandfather continued to live his austere and silent last years at Knole throughout her adolescence. The Great House was the embodiment of those antecedent forces and a symbol of their splendor.

She assimilated the history of Knole, and out of that strength sought to communicate to the outside world: she would make of herself a writer. One of her poems (unpublished in her lifetime, but included in Stevens's book) reads in part:

> God knows I gave you all my love, my agony,
> Scarcely a stone of you I had not kissed.

> Knole! Knole! I stretch my hands to you in prayer,
> You, great and solid; you, enduring, staid;
> You do not know what surges beat against your walls;
> Miss me a little, I who am your soul.

But Knole was not to become hers; she was not male and therefore could not inherit it. She, who had known paradise, then knew paradise lost. Her devotion to literature, to the writing of poems, histories, biographies, novels, sustained her for the rest of her life, for her love of writing offered her the same protection that her love of

Knole had done: it enabled her to overcome uncertainty in lived experience by exercising control over imagined experience.

Virginia Woolf experienced V. Sackville-West both as an aristocrat of ancient race and as an ambitious writer. V. Sackville-West wished to be a literary *artist*. It makes no difference how successful she was. What is important is that she represented both consciousness of her own personal and family history and consciousness of herself as a writer. And the differences between masculinity and femininity, in social life as well as subjectively experienced, which must have had a particular fascination for Virginia Woolf, were reflected in V. Sackville-West's life, especially in the reason why she was deprived of Knole. Moreover, there is no reason not to believe that, given the intimacy of their friendship in the late 1920s, Virginia Woolf learned at least as much about V. Sackville-West's private life as became public information in the 1970s—that both V. Sackville-West and her husband, Harold Nicolson, were bisexual and that Mrs. Nicolson had made adventurous experiments as a transvestite as well. The idea of changing roles by changing clothes must have been very much a part of the Bloomsbury sense of fun. Virginia Woolf herself was a participant in the prank played upon the British Navy, as a member of the group that dressed up as Ethiopians. It went with a sense of frivolity as well as a desire to shock.

For all that she believed herself to be a writer of fiction, Virginia Woolf was obsessed by the question of how to tell the story of someone's life. It is not the problem of marshaling factual information in chronological sequence. It is a question of selection and interpretation. To know "what happens" is of interest only in the light of knowing what it is worth, what it means, or what significance it has had, either for the subject of the biography himself or for others. The difference between "the story of a life" and whatever aspires to be non-interpretive or disinterested biography is that a story has an aesthetic or a moral consequence that is not to be expected from a conventional biography. The meaning of a life may never be assumed to be self-evident. The problem then is twofold: (1) What constitutes a life? that is, where are the limits to be drawn? and (2) what constitutes the truth? that is, wherein lies the significance?

With regard to "a life," I believe that the wisest definition ever devised is condensed into Ortega y Gasset's proposition: "I am myself plus my circumstance, and if I do not save it, I cannot save myself."

This enigmatic epigram returns one to the statement that an individual is free to do what he can, but only within the limits of the influences that have formed him. Ortega's remark forces one to recognize that the commonplace is more mysterious than it appears to be.

Etymologically, the word "influence" refers to an emanation from the stars; and historically, the poetry of the thought, moving from astrology to psychology, supposes a flowing from the stars of an ethereal fluid which acts upon the character and the destiny of a man—until it comes to be used for any kind of divine, moral or other secret power that flows from one thing or person into another. What remains is the belief in a power whose operation is unseen except in its effects. Even if one has not had the experience of trying to raise a child, one has only to meditate upon his own upbringing to recognize that the capacity for producing an effect that results in a genuine influence remains a profound mystery. The most blatant of all examples are the differences among siblings brought up as nearly as possible in the same way, by the same parents, under the same circumstances. This returns us to the point about how people make of their lives something "like" or "different from" each other's out of very similar material.

Where is the limit to be drawn? The answer is radically different depending upon whether the life is looked at from the outside or from the inside. To construct a biography of someone else is one way to "save" that life. The biographer may be in a position to know much "about" that life that the person who lived it did not know; thus, the circumference which delimits "myself and my circumstance" for a biographer may be very much narrower or very much broader than the location of the circumference experienced from the inside of the circle. "To save myself" is a function of the consciousness of each one of us, limited as it is by our powers of sympathy, intelligence and intuition. To the extent that one is appreciative of the influences that have formed the self, he assimilates them, accepts them to the point of recognizing a degree of identity between the self and the circumstance. It is in this sense that lives merge into each other's and it is impossible to draw a line so fine that it can delimit the point of separation. "From the inside," the sense of "myself" in contrast with "my circumstance" is felt most intensely in relation to rejection of influences, i.e., what one feels he is, *despite* the rest of the world. There is as much mystery about the relationship between one's public self and one's private self —with respect to the question of what one is—as about the function of influences with respect to the question of how one became what one is. But in that tension between the public and private is felt the keenest intensity of life as experienced subjectively. And although this is of the greatest difficulty for the biographer to recreate, it is where the writer of fiction may achieve mastery. Thus, one answer to the question of what constitutes the life to be taken as subject for a biography is that the limits should be drawn as close as possible, not to the limits of the public life, but to the larger circumference of the private life, with the same conscious subjectivity and intensity as the one has who lives it.

However, intensity is the enemy of certainty. One may achieve accuracy in understanding what was experienced subjectively only insofar as it involves no other person. But to the extent that lives merge one into another—that relationships rather than isolated entities illuminate, excite and fulfill a person—to the same degree certainty of knowledge declines. In all relationships, the question "What are the facts?", which appeals to a court of objectivity and aims at accuracy of evidence, is doomed to be disappointed. In this regard, it is not Ortega but the duc de la Rochefoucauld whose maxim comes to mind: "One is never as happy nor as unhappy as one imagines." I am myself *and* my circumstance to the extent that I appropriate my circumstance unto myself, as well as affirm myself independent of it; but much of what is most valuable to me in my circumstance consists of relationships with others that are always problematical. There can be no certainty, no last word regarding my knowledge of my own life, let alone the knowledge of the life of any other human being, for the social nature of human reality arises out of an interdependence of values which are indefinitely changeable, not out of facts which are stable in their arbitrarily truncated way.

Answers to both questions—"What is a life?", and what constitutes the truth and significance of that "story"—are found in functions of meanings determined by what one values. Neither is limited to what fits into any one conventional, abstract formula stressing objectivity.

In biography, the closest approximation to an abstract formula or convention in Western culture is the element assumed to be necessary for a newspaper obituary wherein one's public life, seen from the outside, is presented in the form of an outline under the tyranny of objective fact. That convention was discounted among the members of the Bloomsbury group, many of whom were particularly concerned with the problem of writing biography; their "debunking" attitude is nowhere more succinctly expressed than in Lytton Strachey's remarks in *Lancaster Gate:*

> The actual events of life are perhaps unimportant. One is born, grows up, falls in love, falls out of love, works, is happy, is unhappy, grows old, and dies—a tedious, a vulgar succession; but not there lies the significance of a personal history; it is the atmosphere that counts.[4]

But how is one to represent such "atmosphere"? Poetically. A bi-

---

4. Michael Holroyd, ed., *Lytton Strachey by Himself, A Self-Portrait* (New York: Holt, Rinehart & Winston, 1971), p. 17.

ography cannot be literal; it cannot be an actual recapturing in words of the historical sequence of self-enjoyment and the significance of a human life. It must be predominantly metaphorical. In *Orlando* Virginia Woolf was not in pursuit of biography in any conventional sense at all. What she was after was the *story* of a life—a goal of fiction. The imaginative grasp requires not only literal information but intuitive similes, analogies, metaphors that can take one from what is less well known to what is better known in order for comprehension to occur. Making such connections is the artistry that yields literary satisfaction.

In our secret lives, in ordinary conversation or in correspondence, we characterize other people's lives by such metaphorical treatments; we call a tedious but respectable person "a shopkeeper," or a con man "a bandit," or a superficial scene stealer "a nightclub entertainer," or a particularly obtuse mind in a gross body "the Neanderthal man." In *Eminent Victorians*, Lytton Strachey made use of such sobriquets. For example, early in the section on Florence Nightingale, we are told that Lord Panmure, a Scottish nobleman, then Secretary of State for War, was called "the Bison" by his friends. "The name fitted both his physical demeanor and his habit of mind. That large, low head seemed to have been created for butting rather than for anything else. There he stood, four-square and menacing, in the doorway of reform. . . . " Within a few pages, the metaphorical treatment enables Strachey to condense a library of debate and diplomatic maneuvering into a vignette:

> The Bison was no match for the Lady. It was in vain that he put down his head and planted his feet in the earth; he could not withstand her; the white hand forced him back. But the process was an extraordinarily gradual one. Dr. Andrew Smith and all his war office phalanx stood behind, blocking the way; the poor Bison groaned inwardly, and cast a wistful eye toward the happy pastures of the Free Church of Scotland; then slowly, with infinite reluctance, step by step, he retreated, disputing every inch of ground.[5]

Such metaphors and similes, which speak volumes, add sparkle to the enameled portraits of *Eminent Victorians*. But what Virginia Woolf does for a biography of V. Sackville-West is construct all of *Orlando* upon two extended metaphors, one regarding longevity and the other sexuality. Both are employed in order to demonstrate formative influences, to arrive at an understanding of the essence of the subject of the biography—poetically.

---

5. Lytton Strachey, *Eminent Victorians* (London: Chatto and Windus, 1918), p. 165.

There is a time-honored joke about the callow American tourist who visits one of the stately homes of England and, marveling at the acres of superb lawns, asks the resident guide—with the hope of obtaining immediate practical advice—how you get a lawn to look like that. "It's simple," the old man said. "You just clear the ground, level it, seed it, fertilize, and then mow it and water it for four hundred years."

Virginia Woolf's "aristocrat of ancient race" is characterized as a feudal lord. At the end of four hundred years of development, the feudal lord—who has become a lady—achieves identity as a literary artist. It is, of course, a joke; the quintessential Bloomsbury group joke, meant in perfect seriousness. Virginia Woolf undertakes to satirize everything: the nature of conventional biography—from the character of the acknowledgments to the nature of the index; society; the pomposity and the pretension of political leaders; literary aspirations and literary critics; doctors; the war between the sexes. But at the same time as she does this, with "joyous knowledge," she makes a literary argument for what she believes is true. If, in the course of one's development, one has assimilated the literary, political, cultural and social history of four hundred years, then it is *as if* one were four hundred years old.

If one has had sexual experiences which consist of the love of women and the love of men, then it is *as if* one were both a man and a woman. The idea of androgyny is a psychological equivalent to bisexuality; to the extent that one thinks and feels as a man, one is a man; and to the extent that one feels and thinks as a woman, one is a woman. Given the change in sex in *Orlando*, we read: "Orlando has become a woman—there is no denying it. But in every other respect, Orlando remained precisely as he had been. The change in sex, though it altered their future, did nothing whatever to alter their identity." And a little while later:

> The difference between the sexes is, happily, one of great profundity. Clothes are but a symbol of something hid deep beneath. . . . Different though the sexes are, they intermix. In every human being a vacillation from one sex to the other takes place, and often it is only the clothes that keep the male or female likeness, while underneath the sexes are very opposite to what it is above.[6]

Of course, there are differences of "great profundity" between men and women, but these are biologically determined and socially

------

6. *Orlando*, p. 123.

conditioned. This results in the necessity to "play different games" at different times or in different places. Why? In order to get what you want—to exercise your powers, which are the functions by which you establish your identity.

Orlando's changes through time and change in sex are qualified by social expectations, the mores of an epoch. Orlando as a male, young, handsome, talented, goes from jolly, occasional "rolls in the hay" with the common girls, to a willingness to marry as would be appropriate to his class and station, to the love affair with the exquisite foreign beauty, the Russian noblewoman who is not faithful to him; as the ambassador to Constantinople, whose achievements warrant his being made a duke, he marries a gypsy. The alteration, in such a passionate nature, is from propriety to individuality, and back again. Orlando as a woman of the eighteenth century, again young, handsome and talented, shares the cravings of the times for "Life and a Lover"— until she has no lack of lovers, male and female; but the nineteenth century converts the need into "Life and a Husband." In each period the possibility of identity is conditioned by social circumstances. Self-fulfillment is formed and shaped, pared away and burnished, between respectability and adventurousness. While the expectations differ for men and for women, identity for either is achieved only within those limits. One is primarily identified with the work one executes. And the possibility of being a writer is one of the few expectations of work which a woman could fulfill to greatness.

The most desirable exercise of feudal lordship is not merely to dominate but to justify the inherited power over others by the ability to win in the jousts oneself. And the analogous psychic power is subjective, the ability of the "Captain self" to command the obedience of enough of the rest of the innumerable selves—often antithetical and unsympathetic to each other—which go to make up "the self as a group," in order to achieve its purposes. The metaphoric expression for the purposes of a writer is "to find his own voice." The reference for the image is the experience of dialogue, of people talking with each other—some of which is sociable and non-competitive, but much of which is directed toward a goal that only one can win. To that one goes the Prize, be it the dukedom or the literary award. But there is no external prize as valuable as the internal command of what one prizes for oneself: to find one's own voice, to have self-mastery in the sense of being able to do the best one can, to be one's self as well as one's circumstance. The obverse of the image of the feudal lord who becomes a literary artist is the writer as a feudal lord: for which read Virginia Woolf's *auto*biographical intent in pursuing the story of the life of a contemporary author.

To this end, Virginia Woolf's *Orlando* convinces us. Seeing is believing. Her biography of V. Sackville-West is the *story* of the life of that particular person, who is also a representative of the artistocrat, as a member of an élite social class, and of the writer, as a member of an élite creative class. She is at once herself and her circumstance.

ERIC BENTLEY

From the Memoirs of Pontius Pilate:
Excerpts from a New Play

> "I am willing to be harangued by someone who knows as much
> as Mr. Bentley does about an impossible subject. . . . If he did
> not always sound like himself, he would be in the position of his
> hero, Bernard Shaw, who was accused in a public meeting of
> talking like two different people. To which Shaw truthfully re-
> plied: 'Why only two?' "
>
>

JACQUES BARZUN, reviewing Eric Bentley's "In Search
of Theatre," in *The Griffin,* Vol. 2, No. 5 (1953)

⧼ȝ

[*From the Memoirs of Pontius Pilate* is a monologue—Pilate, a retired
Roman official about sixty years of age, reads from his *Memoirs*—and
eight dialogues. Two parts of the monologue and the seventh and
eighth dialogues, in which Pilate appears as the thirty-year-old Governor of Judea, are printed here. In what precedes them the reader or
spectator has learned the following:

An insurrection against the Romans in Jerusalem, led by the militant Zealot, Barabbas, and Yeshu, whose constituency is the *am-haarets*
or Jewish "riff-raff," has failed. Barabbas has been taken prisoner,
along with his most conspicuous associate, Judas, who has already "betrayed" Yeshu to the Romans because he would not promise to fight on.
Pilate offers to let Yeshu return to Galilee and resume his earlier,
quietistic mission. At first Yeshu turns this offer down, but a visit from
former high priest Annas, who tries to convert Yeshu to his own vision
of Judaism—a vision of endurance and acceptance—reduces him to
apathy and despair. "Tell Pilate I will go to Galilee," he says, and is
brought before Pilate to sign and seal the arrangement.]

(The scene is Pilate's work room in the Antonia Fortress. Pilate, very
much the Roman soldier and efficient administrator, is seated at his

[249]

desk. His appearance suggests a Roman statue, his clean-shaven face
and short-cropped hair in marked contrast with the other heads in our
story, which are Jewish. Roman statues, however, are idealized and
suggest unalloyed dignity. Pilate is the man Tiberius chose to control
troublesome Judea: his harshness—even savagery—is not entirely hid-
den by his sophistication and poise. Yet, as the following Dialogue
opens, he is at his gentlest and most relaxed, and glances up almost
casually as Yeshu is ushered in.)

PILATE. "Tell Pilate I will go to Galilee." (To the Guards.) Leave us.
    (The guards leave the room.) (Silence.) Yes, I'm Pilate. Am I
    what you expected? Anyhow, I am what I am. (Silence.) Annas
    told me all. (Silence.) Not that he needed to. He himself, as he
    said, was covered by my spy at the door. So I know more than
    Annas told me. I know how little you sympathize with Annas. (Si-
    lence.) But, to be practical, you *will* go to Galilee? (Yeshu is im-
    passive before this question as before all the previous remarks.)
    No, this time, Yeshu, I have to have an answer. Will you go to
    Galilee?
YESHU (dully). I will go to Galilee.
PILATE. Returning to your former work? (Silence.) Answer please.
YESHU. Returning to my former work.
PILATE. Which was preaching and healing? (Silence.) Hm?
YESHU. Which was preaching and healing.
PILATE. Preaching peace. Goodwill. Harmlessness.
YESHU. Peace. Goodwill. Harmlessness.
PILATE. Which would represent a decisive break with the Zealots?
YESHU. A decisive break with the Zealots.
PILATE. Thank you. You can relax now. Sit down. I want to talk to you.
    (Yeshu might not be inclined to relax in a chair—is not used to
    chairs anyhow—but sinks down on one in sheer exhaustion.) It is
    strange to study someone so intently at a remove, to spy on them
    so long, and after all that meet them. Would we ever understand
    each other, we two? Let me hear the voice that has been reported
    to me so often by others. Say something.
YESHU. I have nothing to say.
PILATE. He has made a career out of speech-making and he is speech-
    less. He found a million words to rouse multitudes to fight Pilate:
    for Pilate himself he cannot find one word. (Silence.) If you will
    not harangue me, Jew, then satisfy my curiosity by answering a
    few natural questions. What, for instance, made you think your
    insurrection could succeed? (Silence.)

YESHU. Must I answer?

PILATE. Why not? (Silence.)

YESHU. We have a saying, If God is for us, who is against us?

PILATE. It didn't stand you in very good stead. We were against you and we won.

YESHU. God was not for us.

PILATE. Why put up with a God like that? We have many gods but would never tolerate a turncoat.

YESHU. I spoke of the One God.

PILATE. Brilliant idea. Like one Caesar. Who is, or can become, a god, and anyway is king of kings and lord of lords. Can your god be defeated by mere men?

YESHU. Never.

PILATE. It would take another god to defeat him. And since he has just been defeated, that proves there *is* another god. Self-evidently his name is Caesar.

YESHU. I did not wish to speak. Should not have spoken.

PILATE. You will not dispute the fact that Caesar exists. I will dispute the contention that Yahweh exists. And it does seem to me a distinct advantage, especially for a god, to exist, hm? (Silence.) Blessed are the peacemakers! Your line, but I'll fill in for you. Any actual peace is a peace that our god, Caesar, made by winning a war. Your nonexistent god offers—I must speak your lines again —a peace that passeth understanding. The merit of Caesar's peace is that everyone can understand it.

YESHU. "He makes a desert and calls it peace."

PILATE. A misplaced quotation indeed! Caesar irrigates the desert and it *is* peace. And plenty. And men smile for a change. Cities rise up and prosper where formerly there were only the tents of nomads and the huts of tribesmen. Such is the peace all men understand. (Silence.) Any comment?

YESHU. What can I say?

PILATE. At least say it.

YESHU (swallowing). Caesar kills Jews.

PILATE. No more than non-Jews. After the Spartacus revolt we crucified six thousand Italians. Caesar is absolutely without racial prejudice. Can Yahweh say as much? (Silence.) Yahweh cannot say as much. Romans kill Jews because Jews kill Romans, and you know it. You also know that the Romans will stop killing Jews just as soon as the Jews have stopped killing Romans.

YESHU (quickly). Rome was the aggressor. Rome broke the peace.

PILATE. Now you're talking. Thank you. Permit me simply to observe that you are mistaken. Provably. On matters of fact. While our peace, founded on war, is a fact, yours, founded on nothing, is mere legend. I have made it my business to study your country and its history. Every page stained with blood. Internecine strife and nothing else from time immemorial. Can you deny it? (Silence.) You cannot deny it. Primitive tribes forever at each other's throats exactly as in Italy, Germany, and distant Britain. And what ended this strife?

YESHU. Nothing. You continued it on an ever grander scale!

PILATE. Now you're arguing—and well. Yes, we make war on a somewhat grander scale, moving ever closer to a grander, and somewhat contrary goal: a peace that is enduring and, ultimately, universal. Pax Romana!

YESHU. Peace on earth—

PILATE. Peace on earth! The phrase is yours. The fact, however, is all ours. The Pax Romana is the only pax this earth has known, the only peace that is destined to spread over the *whole* earth. . . . Give or take a little of my rhetoric, can't you see a measure of truth in all this, Jew?

YESHU. "No ruler but God!"

PILATE. Zealot rhetoric! This is an odd moment for you to resort to Zealot rhetoric.

YESHU. Could *you* accept foreign rule?

PILATE. Continue.

YESHU. Where you see peace, my people see usurpation, theft, enslavement, and ask what business Romans have in Israel?

PILATE. Fair enough. Then let me ask what business your Moses had there and your Joshua and the rest? Didn't they move in uninvited like any Roman general, usurping authority, stealing the land, offering the inhabitants a choice of slavery or death?

YESHU. They were *not* uninvited.

PILATE. No?

YESHU. The Lord Himself invited them!

PILATE. Over the dead bodies of the native population, however. No ruler but Yahweh! And what kind of ruler does Yahweh make? By their fruits ye shall know them! Does that saying of yours apply to him?

YESHU. Above all to Him.

PILATE. He talks to you, doesn't he?

YESHU. He spoke to the patriarchs.

PILATE. He talks *too much*, your god. Talks a peace that he could never deliver. Never. For how would a tribal deity—and that is all Yahweh is, god of the Jews—deliver peace between tribes? For that you need an imperial deity: Caesar who imposes peace upon all the tribes. By their fruits ye shall know them. Eh? (Silence.) Your silence tells me *I* too talk too much, hm?

YESHU. You talk of peace. I think of—crucifixion.

PILATE. And what is crucifixion? Simply the Roman way with a rebel: placing him in plain view and saying to potential rebels, Pray think twice! Cruel? That is the point. But to be kind. Unlike your terrorists we Romans are not in love with violence.

YESHU. Six thousand crosses, and multiply that by—

PILATE. By many. What can justify that? What is worth such a price? I will answer that, and we shall see if you can answer my answer. Your Yahweh talks ideals but never impresses them on the actual world. Caesar, to the contrary, brings to the conquered this pearl beyond all price: civilization. You stare. The word means nothing to you? That is your loss. Your ignorance. What is civilization? If only you had seen these places, Britain, Gaul, yes, and Israel before the Romans came! If then you had witnessed the building of our cities, roads, bridges, the creation of cultural and commercial intercourse between nations—we have even set up a postal system —if you had witnessed, above all, the substitution of Roman law for the law of—I have to say it, the law of the jungle, you would think differently, even of crucifixion. Now civilization presupposes law and order; while law and order presuppose the Pax Romana. It follows that a threat to Rome is a threat to peace, to order, to law, to civilization. Rome is the one hope for this world, since this world's one alternative to Rome is barbarism. Or? (Silence.) You agree? (Silence.) You disagree so deeply you aren't talking? (Silence.) I ask you to talk and end up lecturing you on civilization. I apologize. By all means, let's return to the practicalities. (He is handling scrolls on his desk now.) Here are my spies' reports. I will not claim to have grasped all the subjective nuances and Semitic super-subtleties, but anyway. Tiberius has ordered me to release one of the two leaders of the revolt. To demonstrate Roman magnanimity. Barabbas being an intransigent Zealot, it is quite logical to release you. You accept this? (Pause. Then Yeshu nods.) And you will let us escort you back to Galilee?

YESHU (nods slowly, then raises his hand to his brow, as if dizzy). Can we end this interview?

PILATE. Just as soon as I have outlined the formalities. (Yeshu stirs uneasily at this word. Pilate notices this.) Our clemency to be valid, must be as rational as our cruelty. (Yeshu is now apprehensive.) No, Yeshu, we do not intend to push you beyond the position you have taken. We must, however, take reasonable advantage of that position.

YESHU (muttering). What?

PILATE. My lecture was not all that academic. Civilization means law, law entails procedure. The procedure we now propose, *im*pose, is recantation. You joined a conspiracy, Yeshu. You must now *re*nounce it, and *de*nounce any fellow conspirators who have not recanted.

YESHU. Barabbas. . . .

PILATE. Judas your betrayer and so on down to the rank and file: we have drawn up a list. . . . Your release will not only demonstrate our magnanimity. Better even than a crucifixion, it will serve to discourage potential rebels.

YESHU. What are you asking of me?

PILATE. A public recantation, thrice repeated. First you will read it before the common people in the Temple Courtyard; second before the captive rebels in the nearby jail; and third you will read it before the cross on which by then Barabbas will be hanging. That may not come easy but it will soon be over, and—what's the matter, Yeshu? (Lifting both hands to his head in an overpowering attack of vertigo, Yeshu has fallen unconscious to the floor.)

PILATE (reading from his Memoirs). I had him carried to his cell. "Bring him back when he comes to," I said. My doctor reported he could not return that day at all, he was in a coma. The same the second day. It was on the third day that he rose again from his bed, saying: Take me to Pilate. The final Dialogue, Number Eight, with apologies to brother Stephen, I entitle Resurrection.

PILATE. Well, Yeshu! We were worried about you. You're now ready to go through with the recantation?

YESHU. To go through with the discussion.

PILATE. Hm?

YESHU. I left without answering your question.

PILATE. But now the time for debate is over.

YESHU. Not however the time for answers. If I left a three-day pause it was not for dramatic effect. It was because I didn't know what to say.

PILATE. And after being three days unconscious?

YESHU. Only I wasn't. Rather, becoming conscious. I am now so conscious I think I was never conscious before.

PILATE. Conscious of what?

YESHU. The other day you spread out before me the panorama of what
    you call civilization. To hear you talk, Rome is all splendid insti-
    tutions and even more splendid principles. I am no historian, not
    even a traveler, but one need not study the archives, or journey
    to Italy, to learn the truth about Rome. Rome is the Abomination
    of Desolation! Its statecraft is murder, corruption and intrigue! Its
    god-emperors are slavering halfwits and rampaging maniacs!

PILATE. That is quite an answer.

YESHU. And you yourself with your talk of peace, law, order, etcetera,
    what is *your* record here in Israel? You have desecrated our tem-
    ples! You have persecuted our people!

PILATE. Have you become a Zealot again in these three days?

YESHU. I have become myself again—or for the first time.

PILATE. And that self is a Zealot?

YESHU. Is a Jew. A barbarian. If Rome is civilization, I *want* to be a
    barbarian. It is not in Rome that we Jews will find the answers.
    We shall reach into our own hearts, into our own minds, and find
    there—

PILATE. Old Annas said it: acceptance of oppression as your fate.

YESHU. God bless Annas! Wise and good about so many things, miss-
    ing out on the one thing.

PILATE. Namely?

YESHU. The Messiah.

PILATE. Him again! Tiberius told me when I left Rome, Bear in mind
    that the Jews, though very spiritual and all that, are completely
    crazy.

YESHU. You think I'm going mad?

PILATE. You must always have been mad. Wouldn't you call a village
    preacher mad if he claimed to be Julius Caesar? How about a vil-
    lage preacher who claimed to be God's undefeatable Messiah?

YESHU. I *was* mad.

PILATE. Your God forsook you, as you put it.

YESHU. As I wrongly put it. I was deluded. I don't blame Barabbas. I
    could have told him No. But I was so deluded I nearly did it again:
    invited Stephen to repeat the Barabbas experience on a grander
    scale, and on an invisible battlefield where my defeat could never
    be proved. It was bad enough to let someone else believe I am a
    god but when I started to entertain that possibility myself . . .
    you are right, Pilate, I have consorted with madness.

PILATE. But, in the person of old Annas, you consorted with sanity.

YESHU. In a way. The wrong way. Annas is sane the way the Roman

Empire is sane. For the oppressor it is sane to oppress; for the oppressed, it is sane to *be* oppressed.

PILATE. You choose *in*sanity? The insanity of Messiahship?

YESHU. No. No. I am not the Messiah. That *was* insane.

PILATE. Then the Messiah is someone else now? Barabbas? Judas?

YESHU. Not Barabbas either. Not Judas. Or a hundred other such. Not today. Not tomorrow. The Kingdom of God is *not* at hand!

PILATE. Ah! So you were wrong, all of you?

YESHU. Yochanan and Yeshu were wrong. Barabbas and Judas will continue to be wrong.

PILATE. And Annas was right.

YESHU. Annas was even wronger! He said never when he should just have said a long time. The Kingdom will be *a long time* coming. The blood spilt now in its name will be as a drop in the ocean beside the blood my people will shed before it comes. Before Messiah comes. But to say never is the sin against the holy spirit. "Where there is no vision, the people perish."

PILATE. Let me get this straight now. Your people, being visionaries, are going to await a Xerxes, an Alexander, a Julius Caesar?

YESHU. Must the Messiah be an individual? Might he not be Israel, God's suffering servant among nations? Might not every Israelite be an atom, a spark, of the Messiah? For me, at any rate, to say the Messiah will come is to say we Jews will *never* accept oppression as our fate. (Pilate starts to speak.) Yes, Annas lost that faith. And when the Insurrection failed, I lost it too, lost it because I could not be it, could not be the Messiah. Such was my arrogance. But wondrous are the ways of the Lord! Your arrogance has brought me to my senses. (Silence.) Have I answered your question?

PILATE. You have made my head swim. Where are we now? We were arranging a little deal, and you have taken me on a speculative journey like some Greek philosopher.

YESHU. Some Jewish philosopher.

PILATE. Where are we? Can we get this recantation over with now? A couple of hours will dispose of it.

YESHU. So you haven't understood.

PILATE. Civilization? The Messiah?

YESHU. Or even this little deal.

PILATE. I'm coming to fast. Yes, yes, Rabbi, this is your devious, sacerdotal way of telling me—the deal is unacceptable. You don't want to go to Galilee after all.

YESHU. You *have* understood.

PILATE. Have *you* understood your situation?

YESHU. It is all too clear. I have decided to die.

PILATE. *What?* What's the catch?

YESHU. Do you never look at people when you talk to them? (Pilate looks at him closely.)

PILATE (grunting). You're trying to show me the face of one who has "decided to die." To me, it looks pretty much like the face of someone desperately ill who suddenly decided to live.

YESHU. You do look at people. You've noticed I'm a new man. I was dead but am alive again.

PILATE. What?

YESHU. Died when the Insurrection failed. Came alive again only this morning.

PILATE. And coming alive again only this morning, decided to die this very evening?

YESHU. Very apt. Yes, that's right. Tiberius has ordered you to release one of us and to execute the other. You will execute me. You will release Barabbas.

PILATE. But you are no longer a Zealot!

YESHU. A war has two sides, not three. Choosing between the Zealots and you, I cannot but choose the Zealots.

PILATE. So now we have it. The whole story. I am to release Barabbas.

YESHU. You will have to. I am refusing to recant.

PILATE. I will have to. Hm. Well, Yeshu, my friend, we are moving now from your field, which is that of dreams, to mine which is action. Only Caesar tells Pilate what he *has* to do.

YESHU. Caesar says you have to release someone.

PILATE. Check. But not checkmate, brother Yeshu. Very well. I kill you. I release Barabbas. That will mean precisely nothing. He is far too important a rebel to be left at large. Confident of my Emperor's full approval, I would kill him too. Have him mysteriously disappear.

YESHU. You would do that? (Silence.) Of course you would do that.

PILATE. So where are we now? You wish to die for absolutely nothing?

YESHU. I will not denounce my brothers. I love them. Yes: including Judas. Nor will I insult the suffering body of Barabbas on his cross.

PILATE. Then you leave me no alternative.

YESHU. No alternative at all. (He prepares to leave the room.)

PILATE. One moment, though. A thought. Suppose we were to withdraw the demand for a recantation?

YESHU. All three recantations? All the denunciations?

PILATE. I have reached you now. Yes. All the recantations. All the denunciations. Hm? (Silence.) Rome is not known for flexibility perhaps, but we change course when we have to. I'll make it definite. We do withdraw our demand.

YESHU (with an intake of breath something like relief). Ah, then, so I need not—

PILATE. Need not go through all that after all. No. You may withdraw to Galilee and your old life *without* any obligation to us here in Jerusalem. (Silence.)

YESHU. I would really enjoy Galilee.

PILATE. Then you shall.

YESHU. And the deal is concluded. Except I am not interested in deals.

PILATE. Not . . . ? Look, Yeshu, think clear, think fast. We have just waived all our demands on you. We ask nothing. If you die now, it *will* be for absolutely nothing.

YESHU. You want me in Galilee for a reason: "better even than a crucifixion, it will serve to discourage potential rebels."

PILATE. And, since you are no longer a Zealot, what's wrong with that? Peace on earth, goodwill to men, a quiet harmless life, that was and will be your Galilean creed.

YESHU. The Zealots taught me this much: who acquiesces in your oppression is not harmless, he has betrayed my Kingdom to your Empire.

PILATE. You will die a Zealot?

YESHU. I shall die a Jew.

PILATE. To hang from a cross is to be accurst of God. That's what Jews believe. You yourself said it.

YESHU. I also said God had forsaken me, and He hadn't. Who accepts His curse for the good of Israel shall be blessed.

PILATE. Hm. Well, listen. You have everything figured. Except the actual, material cost: we have made the penalty a death—a dying— so hideous that no man, no man could willingly embrace it, least of all a man like yourself, far from the toughest, oozing timidity and panic a matter of hours ago. You have never thought what being crucified is like.

YESHU. It hurts.

PILATE (deliberately). Being suspended from the crossbeam of the so-called cross—it is actually just a T—imposes an unbearable strain on the heart. The waste which the heart cannot eliminate poisons the muscles, which go into convulsions. The victim is suffocated— to the point of the unendurable. Screams for someone to put him out of his agony. No one does. No one is allowed to. And death will not come for forty hours. Forty hours. During which the unendurable is endured.

YESHU. And this is what Barabbas and Judas are about to go through! Take me to them!

PILATE (at a loss momentarily). It's only *their* sufferings you feel? You bother me, Jew. We must get you on that cross fast. (He strides to the door to call the guards.)

YESHU. Oh, the pain! The pain of the Jews! (Pilate stops and looks at him.) At the same time, Pontius Pilate, this is the happiest day of my life.

PILATE (reading from his Memoirs). It was soon to be the happiest day in Stephen's life. Less than a week after Yeshu died on the cross Stephen announced he was still alive and popping up all over Palestine as a ghost, a "holy ghost." The legend that we nail men to crosses played a role here: for the ghost of Yeshu invited doubters to stick their fingers in the nailholes. Since which time, the friends of Stephen have become a cult, with Yeshu as their god. And the record has been touched up. The crucifixion is blamed on Caiaphas and the Jewish Establishment. We Romans had nothing to do with it. In this way Stephen's people seek to appease us. According to one legend, as I mentioned, Judas killed himself. Another has it that Barabbas was set free after all. What is truth? What is legend? I know the truth on one point. Yeshu was crucified alongside two other men, and these were not nameless bandits as the touched-up record would have it but the two leading Zealots—Barabbas and Judas. There is a story that, while on the cross, Yeshu said: "This night you will be with me in paradise." That too could be a legend, but, if he did say it, he said it to his seducer and his betrayer, respectively. Knowing Yeshu, I wouldn't put it past him. For when I tried to make him feel the pain of crucifixion he felt only *their* pain. "Love driveth out fear." Is that one of his sayings? It is something he demonstrated in action. It unsettled me. Yet what did *I* have to fear? Although from childhood on, Yeshu had been encouraged to believe he was so extraordinary, might well be the Messiah, he had in fact proved rather ordinary. Neither his teaching nor his poetry were original. Inept in politics, nonexistent as a soldier, outclassed by Barabbas as a leader, and now, it seems, by Stephen as an organizer, he was hardly what we Romans would consider a great man—only a victim of great delusions who in consequence let himself be pushed around by Barabbas, by Annas, even, up to a point, by the unspeakable Stephen.

And of course by me. Till that final meeting when he declared himself an ordinary Jew and thereupon proved extraordinary. I don't just mean he died gamely, though he did. All three of them did. Good dying is commoner than good living. I mean that when he told me he was a new man, he *was* a new man or, better, the ordinary man who must always have been there behind the extraordinary masks. But then it is really the wild masks of delusion and dream that are humanly ordinary, and authenticity that is extraordinary. I tried to undermine him, and couldn't touch him. No one should be *that* authentic. An ordinary Jew, powerless, about to die, a little man from a little people, who yet could scare the Roman Governor! His defeat *was* a victory, too. The news was soon around that Yeshu had died rather than cooperate, and this was a blow to the constituency not only of Caiaphas but of Annas. A boost to the constituency of Barabbas and Judas. Whatever his failures, Yeshu did help keep alive the spirit of resistance. Since his death, others have fanned the flame. And today we stand on the verge of a full-scale war between Rome and this incorrigible tribe. We shall win. We shall win if we have to take Jerusalem apart stone by stone. But let no one think I am changing the subject when I recall crying out to Yeshu that he was a madman yet feeling in the pit of my stomach that *I* had gone mad. Had always been mad in a mad world. The point I am trying to make is that such men are a threat to Empire. Study him, Romans, to know your enemy.

Thalia

THE HUMAN COMEDY

⬿

RICHARD FRANKO GOLDMAN

The Great-Great-Grandnephew of Rameau
(With profuse apologies)

"There can be a great deal of sound and but few notes."
JACQUES BARZUN, *Classic,*
Romantic and Modern

᷒

1975. A dismal August afternoon in New York, with the temperature in the nineties and the air a pale greenish brown. A seedy character, past middle age, is walking along 57th Street. He seems agitated and depressed, and brightens only slightly when he encounters an old friend who fancies himself a philosopher but is actually an interviewer for a television network. Let us call him Mr. Z. The seedy character is a great-great-grandnephew of Rameau who has, since settling in the United States, changed his name to Ramo.

Z. I say, you look as if you were ill.

R. And well I might.

Z. Is it anything in particular?

R. No . . . I have just come from a concert. . . .

Z. Oh, I see. Was it . . . ?

R. I could stand a drink . . . that is, if you'd really like to hear about it.

Z. By all means. (They repair to a bar.)

R. You and I have been around for a while. We can remember when there was something called "modern music." And of course you remember the days of The New Music Society. Well, what I have just attended was clearly a performance by The No Music Society. A gala, in fact. By a Mongolian who studied in Darmstadt and Wuppertal.

Z. Inner or Outer Mongolian?

R.   Oh, I rather think Hypo-Mongolian. More *à la mode*, not that it matters. The concert lasted well over four hours. The composer during that time ripped apart three violas, bent a trombone into the shape of a pretzel, blew a police whistle every seven minutes and thirteen seconds, painted a huge poster saying "I love Italo Montemezzi," tied up several of his assistants with piano wire, eviscerated a harpsichord while the old Russian national anthem was performed twenty-three times by a quartet of counter-tenors, rolled a bass drum filled with marbles around the stage, sprayed the audience with a fire extinguisher, then excused himself saying he had to go to the men's room, and telephoned forty minutes later to say that the concert was over, but would someone flush the toilet please.[1]

Z.   Did anyone?

R.   No. I think it was generally felt that this would be anticlimactic. Also, it would destroy the evidence that history requires. Besides . . .

Z.   Mightn't that be construed as criticism? Or an unwillingness to become involved?

R.   My dear friend, *everything* is criticism. Nietzsche pointed that out years ago. I forgot to mention that the afternoon's composition was called "Etude for Bass Ocarina and Armadillo." A fine title, I think. And titles are ever so important. When you give a name to nothing, it immediately becomes something.

Z.   You may have a point there, but I will have to think about it. You are right—it's a fine title. Much better than "Paradigm XXIV" or "Rhomboidal Structures," which are rather the more usual thing these days. I wish I had attended the concert with you. It seems to have upset you. Couldn't you think of it as simply amusing foolishness?

R.   Well, there is an element of deadly fun, I suppose. But there is so much more of anger and hatred and contempt. What the composer and his accomplices are trying to tell us is that everything hurts so much that it must be destroyed by symbolic gesture, and eventually by absolute action. I find it frightening, which it is intended to be.

Z.   Surely you are attaching too much importance to an event

---

1. Anyone who thinks that this account is distorted or exaggerated should see the Calvin Tomkins Profile of Nam June Paik in *The New Yorker*, May 5, 1975, especially pp. 47–48.

like this. Granted that there are more of them all the time, it seems to me that there is nothing very serious to protest.

R. You misunderstand me. I am not protesting against the absurd. I am trying to understand it. In a way, I am testing my own capacity for survival. It's a long downhill road and one has to wonder from what peak it started and what depths it may reach. I do admit that I am disturbed. Chaos is frightening, and chaos is the essence of these concerts or events. I wonder if the intention is not a kind of preventive chaos . . . that is, if you act it all out, it becomes a therapy or a propitiation of what awaits you around the corner. Further, you annihilate the past, which threatens you, by actually destroying some of its tools—pianos and cellos, for example—and its materials (bits of Chopin or Tchaikovsky or anyone else) and you proclaim that all is useless . . .

Z. You make it seem like a fantasy of destruction.

R. Isn't that what it really is? It's a way of saying that the past is meaningless and therefore dead, the present is intolerable and the future holds no hope. It's a rather shallow and immature stance, even if one concedes that there is some truth in all the assumptions. It's also a way of saying that we have had enough, which is also partly true. We have exhumed everything from history, studied it and created a micro-pedantry that is death-dealing. The total weight of this past is not stimulating; it is paralyzing. And it is hard to blame anyone for wanting to escape from it. Surely there are more courageous attitudes, but we are not always brave. The desire to abolish or annihilate—which has been dealt with by an eminent philosopher-historian of my acquaintance[2]—may not be brave or even reasonable, but surely it is not too hard to understand.

Z. Have another drink and relax. You are reading far too much into an afternoon's antics. It seems to me that you are reaching for meanings that don't exist.

R. I think not. Let me pursue it a bit. Stravinsky, in his own subtle, terribly intelligent, marvelously skillful way, was in a sense also an abolitionist. He was, like my uncle, a man of genius, a composer of genius, but he was also a *parodist* of genius. He took the history of music from Machaut to Webern and rewrote it. And in doing so, incidentally,

---

2. Jacques Barzun, *Classic, Romantic and Modern* (Boston: Little, Brown, 1961), pp. 140 ff.

taught us more about style than a thousand dissertations or analyses. But also, in a manner peculiar to his genius, he *abolished* Machaut. Or at least we might assume that that was his intention.

Z.   Now you're really losing me. Your reasoning seems a bit dense. Why abolish Machaut?

R.   Well, Machaut had been dead for hundreds of years. Suddenly, in our century, he is brought back to life, studied, performed and admired. Then Stravinsky puts him away again, has the last word about Machaut, certainly in the *Mass,* and eliminates the need for having Machaut around at all. He accomplishes a magnificent reconstruction or evocation of place and time and style. Of course I suppose that we could call this "creative" abolition. . . .

Z.   Please watch your language. I've heard of "creative" movies, "creative" skyscrapers and a few others. But "creative" abolition . . . ? Anyhow, I detect another contradiction. If the musicologists, the exhumers, whom you seem to mistrust, hadn't resurrected Machaut, Stravinsky might never have discovered him or recreated him.

R.   He would still have had Tchaikovsky, Pergolesi, and quite a few others within fairly easy reach.

Z.   I see that you are in a bad humor. Perhaps you need an antidote. Would you care to go with me to the all-Schoenberg program this evening?

R.   (Shudders) Thank you, no. Listening to Schoenberg makes me restless. Schoenberg was a theoretical man. Sometimes I wonder if he would not have been happier writing waltzes. His music is not happy, but neither is it tragic. It is solemn, extremely self-conscious, and always begs you to notice how important it is. These are some of the cardinal sins of so much of the music of our time.

Z.   But Schoenberg is a giant! A master! One of the greatest . . . an influence . . . a teacher!

R.   Yes, the father of us all. No doubt. He is historical, of course . . . perhaps more historical than musical. A complete art requires gifts he did not have—a sense of comedy, for example.

Z.   You are being difficult indeed. You condemn solemnity, frivolity and everything in between.

R.   We haven't even mentioned anything in between. No, I'll try to explain. An art dependent on theorizing or on verbal justification, or at the lowest, on program notes, is a deficient art. Look at Schoenberg's many defensive and quarrelsome dicta. His comments on his first American work, the *Suite in G,* for example. But even putting such arrogance aside, you remember his saying that great works could still be written in C major? Well, his own music doesn't prove this at all. The *G Major Suite,* the *Theme and Variations,* are really dreadful bores. It was Prokofiev and Stravinsky and a few others who proved that one could still write in C major.

Z. You're making too much out of a few little examples.

R. Well, I'll give you the *Ode to Napoleon* too. You know, I'm beginning to think that I must have enjoyed this afternoon's nonsense.

Z. You are incorrigible and perverse. You condemn only yourself. There is a point beyond which frivolity and irresponsibility shouldn't go.

R. I am only thinking to myself that we are condemned to experience our own time completely. And that means everything. This afternoon was certainly less boring than, say, a concert by members of the American Society of University Composers, or a concert of electronic music. At least one isn't quite sure what's going to happen, except that one knows it will be outrageous, whereas in concerts of electronic music one knows, alas, all too well what's going to happen, or more likely not happen. Has anyone ever heard any joyous electronic music?

Z. Why joyous? We don't live in a joyous world, do we?

R. No. But it does seem to me that art should provide something to live on, perhaps even a momentary joy, an excitement, a quickened sense of life. Excuse me if I sound like Pater. I was thinking of so much of Haydn and Mozart, who were both joyous and tragic.

Z. If your own theorizing is correct, why haven't they been abolished too?

R. Because we still have our museums. It's very simple. We have concerts of what is known as standard repertoire. And we have recordings. And then, too, Haydn and Mozart are somewhat bigger targets than Machaut. What's more, the abolitionists are merely asserting intent or disposition. They tell us how they feel about the past, but they haven't yet been as successful as they might wish to be.

Z. Exactly my point. You are exaggerating the significance of a small cluster of cultural hoodlums. They exist in painting and literature as well as in music. But they really don't matter, do they?

R.   They matter. Of course they do. Maybe they are even necessary.

Z.   Why do you say that? It seems to me that's a *volte-face*.

R.   They force us to reconsider our notions, that's why.

Z.   You may reconsider to such an extent that you will end up exactly where you started.

R.   There's always that danger. To come back to solemnity and frivolity: both distress me, and we are heavily afflicted by both. Our so-called serious art is often merely solemn and humorless, and that is why chopping up pianos is such an attractive gesture for some people. But Satie attacked solemnity a long time ago, and he wrote some charming music while doing it. People confuse solemnity and seriousness. Haydn was a serious composer, but one smiles with pleasure and joy while listening to his symphonies. At least if one can hear. Why did the nineteenth century start taking length and size for seriousness and importance?

Z.   Nothing satisfies you. Does all the music of the last fifty years seem to you a waste?

R.   Not at all. I am unhappy with most of the music that is based on theorizing. And there is so much of it. I recall my teacher, whose most vigorous expression of disapproval was to say that something was *gesucht*. There is a difference between artifice and contrivance . . .

Z.   I take it you agree with your teacher about contriving effects, or reaching out for them. In that case, I suppose that you must be sympathetic to music that employs chance or improvisation?

R.   No. That sort of thing is precisely contrivance, and irresponsible contrivance at that. It's the abdication of the ear, and is exactly the opposite of artifice. Good composers are artificers, not contrivers.

Z.   Name six of each.

R.   We'll never agree, and I'm really not looking for an argument. Stravinsky's music, though, for all the paradoxes of his style, is full of the most exquisite and ingenious artifice from first to last. Stravinsky also had almost perfect taste and a sense of comedy. They must go together of course. You can't have one without the other. And there is real pas-

sion in Stravinsky too. As there is in Bartók, for that matter, or . . .

Z.   You are, after all, beginning to pick up my challenge, and
I am beginning to see your bias. You don't like formulas
or machines.

R.   True. And it puts me out of step. We live in the midst of
formulas and machines. They are what make the world go
round, are they not?

Z.   I daresay it's easier that way. But it doesn't matter. You're
right, of course—for a change. We live by them, whether we
like it or not. But, by the way, aren't the symphonies of Haydn
also a matter of formula?

R.   Superficially, I suppose you could say so. They generally have
four movements, a conventionalized scheme of tonality and
key relationships, a well-defined field of harmonic gravitation,
and so on. But there is infinite variety in them, extraordinary
invention, high comedy, great artifice, passion, wit . . . they
contain everything. Great art must work within conventions,
but that is not the same as formula or theory. The well-made
machine is not enough, and that is what the uninteresting
composer so often gives us.

Z.   I expect you have Hindemith in mind, among others.

R.   You can draw your own conclusions. He was a theorizer, of
course. And a bad influence, especially in America. All very
successful teachers tend to be bad influences. They produce
little copies of themselves which are seldom very interesting.

Z.   Especially in America! Why do you say that?

R.   Because I think we give encouragement too easily. There is
something appalling about the sheer number of students
"majoring" in composition. I've just come across an interesting book, by the way. It's called *Teach Yourself to Compose
Music*, and it is designed, the publisher claims, for "promising amateurs who haven't had the benefit of technical training. . . . " Well, I think it would make an ideal Christmas
present for ever so many people I know. You too can be a
composer. And that's the way it is today.

Z.   I'm afraid you're right. The quantity of stuff written is a problem. And a great lot of it is performed because no one is sure
that it oughtn't to be.

R.   Amen.

Z.   But isn't there at least some good or interesting music being written today? And must we not be patient about sorting the good and the bad?

R. To both questions, yes. There is still genius among us. Of course there is. And some talent, some originality, some life . . . But you've got to get along to your concert. Have we time for another?

Z. I'm afraid not. I'm glad I extorted some hope from you. Stay away from concerts for a few weeks and you'll probably be all right.

R. Sound advice. There are lots of cantatas still to be written, and I'm sure that there are words enough for all of them.

Z. Please don't even contemplate writing a cantata. You should first learn to sing.

R. True. I am only a poor onlooker—I am not "creative." Anyone, therefore, can impute my opinions to my frustrations. I have nothing except my ephemeral observations and my reputation as a good companion over drinks. But I am one of the last who enjoys conversation, as opposed, let's say, to monologue or cross-examination. Let the word fall where it may. Who knows if it will be fertilized?

JAMES HARVEY YOUNG

Euclid + Lincoln = Kent

"... a man of today thinks he sees the truth of science demonstrated in every gadget he uses."
JACQUES BARZUN, *Science: The Glorious Entertainment*

When late in the New Deal the Congress expanded the authority of the
Food and Drug Administration to include control over specious medical
devices, the first case to reach trial in court concerned a gadget manu-
factured in Peoria. Much of quackery has a shabby, down-at-the-heels,
end-of-the-line vaudevillian quality about it, and this characterization
applies to the case of the Electreat Mechanical Heart.

Not that the Electreat's inventor and promoter did not possess
more grandiose pretensions. During the years when Congress wrestled
with the bill that became the Food, Drug and Cosmetic Act of 1938,
Charles Willie Kent strove to become "the Aristotle of modern times."[1]
In his *Grammar of Nature or Key to the Master's Mind*, Kent pierced
through to an insight that reduced the complexity of the cosmos to a
simplicity of crystal clarity: $A + B = C$. On this fundamental theme,
he played numerous variations. Father + Mother = Son, Daughter;
hence, Adam + Eve = Cain, Abel. Wood + Workshop = Chair; hence,
Substance + Handiwork = Finished Product.

This "universal formula" pushed on toward the abstract and the
arcane: Noun + Verb = Idea; Substance + Motion = Creation; Impulse + Prejudice = Intelligence; Curiosity + Elimination = Education. Kent found the pattern wherever he probed and eagerly replicated
its variant forms. He admired Euclid for his logic—although Euclidian
logic rested on the noun and Kentian upon the verb—and esteemed
Lincoln for his "Elliptical Momentum," a devious verbal adroitness by
which the prairie statesman had been able to confuse his opponents.

---

1. C. W. Kent, *Grammar of Nature* (Peoria: C. W. Kent, 1934). The 64-page
abridged edition is used here.

Kent acknowledged but improved upon both these heroes, and proudly formulated the fact in his favorite way: Euclid + Lincoln = Kent.

Kent's conceptual breakthrough allowed him to solve some of the riddles of the ages, like that puzzling problem of priority often debated on Illinois farms. "With clear thinking," Kent asserted, "it is plain that the hen can lay an egg to make another hen, but she cannot lay an egg, nor can any other hen lay an egg to make herself, therefore she must be prior, subject and before the egg which is her predicate."

Such a universal scheme as Kent's inevitably encompassed human health, which proved to be the sum of Nourishment + Freedom of Movement. By nourishment Kent seemed to mean food and medicines, articles of substance, the province of regular physicians. By freedom of movement he meant a sort of external and internal limberness—and implied that chiropractors helped sustain it—without which the body's nervous system went awry, producing disease. This structure of nervous controls consisted of two parts, the central nervous system, headed by the brain, which, like a proprietor, made the key decisions; and the sympathetic nervous system, headed by the solar plexus, which, like a secretary, performed detail work at the proprietor's direction. Long ago the brain had handed over digestion to the solar plexus, which kept on working while the brain slept to restore the body's vital energy. A sleepless brain exhausted the supply of vital energy, stole reserve strength from the solar plexus, ruined digestion, induced constipation and provoked nervous prostration. "Keep on thinking," Kent warned, "and you soon get apoplexy or paralysis." Brain and solar plexus must function in harmony. "When the bowels lose their energy to eliminate, the mind will cease to elucidate."

Whereas Kent elaborated on these principles at considerable length, he did not explain in the pages of the *Grammar of Nature* how mankind might extricate itself from such a plight. In the equation, Sickness + B = Health, he did not reveal the unknown B. He seemed reluctant to sully philosophy with commerce.

Perhaps Kent merely felt no need to restate in his emulation of Aristotle what he had already enunciated in an earlier Aesculapian role. For Kent knew full well the unknown B, because he had invented it and had devoted a decade and a half to its vigorous promotion.

While still a young man, just before the end of the nineteenth century, Willie Kent was to assert, he had suffered a throat injury that so impaired his left vocal cord he could barely speak above a whisper.[2] Inspired to treat his affliction with an electrical device called the S.O.S. Pulser, he received "wonderful restorative benefits." His

---

2. Kent to Senator Scott Lucas, June 18, 1940, Electreat Mechanical Heart

own cure so impressed him that Kent, in time, became a Pulser sales-
man. By reading books on the use of electricity in the healing art and
by tinkering, he built a better mousetrap than the one he sold. In
1918 he began to manufacture the Electreat; in 1921 he received from
the Patent Office a trademark for this name, declaring his device an
electric massage machine. In 1929 Kent expanded this trademark to
include the words "Mechanical Heart," and in 1931 secured a patent
for his "Electric Massage Machine Vibrator." While describing the device in minute detail, patent 1,812,960 referred neither to its trade-
marked name nor to the Electreat's therapeutic merits, for which Kent
had long been beating a booming drum.[3]

The Electreat's healing prowess received the most glowing elaboration in a thick pamphlet always enclosed with the machine and also
circulated separately.[4] Frequently revised, *Electreat Relieves Pain* had
little to say about the proprietor. Kent referred to himself only as a
graduate of the American Institute of Phrenology. He later acknowledged that he had received some help in drafting his brochure. L. V.
Bates, M.D., Kent said, had been his collaborator. "I employed him for
the special purpose of his long experience as a student of Abrams'
electronics."[5]

In the words of an inveterate foe of quackery, writing in the
1930s, Albert Abrams "easily ranked as the dean of twentieth century
charlatans."[6] A renegade physician, Abrams had devised a whole series
of bewildering machines, operating, he claimed, on "electronic reactions." Whether in the very room with a person who was sick or thousands of miles away, the machines not only could diagnose the suf-
ferer's ailment but could produce a ready cure. The judicious might
grieve, like the noted physicist Robert Millikan, who termed Abrams's
machines "the kind of device a ten-year-old boy would build to fool an
eight-year-old," yet before Abrams died in 1924 he had fooled enough
adults, who thought cures over great distances no stranger than the
new wonder of radio, to accumulate $2 million which he bequeathed to
an association dedicated to perpetuating his principles.[7]

---

case, Interstate Sample No. 16222-E, Food and Drug Administration Records,
Record Group 88, Washington National Records Center, Suitland, Md.

3. Photostats of the two trademark registrations (144,424 and 259,609)
and of the patent grant are included in the I.S. no. 16222-E file.

4. Copies in *ibid.* and in Electreat file, Department of Investigation, American
Medical Association, Chicago, Ill.

5. Summary of seizure trial prepared by FDA, I.S. no. 16222-E file.

6. Arthur J. Cramp, *Nostrums and Quackery and Pseudo-Medicine* (Chicago:
American Medical Association, 1936), p. 112.

7. See J. H. Young, *The Medical Messiahs* (Princeton, N.J.: Princeton Univ.
Press, 1967), pp. 137–142.

That Willie Kent hoped his promotion might become infused with the magic of electronic reactions says much about the nature of his enterprise. Abrams's bevy of boxes with their jumbled wiring differed considerably from Kent's Electreat Mechanical Heart. Kent's patented device was not a heart, was not mechanical, and opinion certainly differed as to whether it could be deemed either treat or treatment.

A Food and Drug official thought the Electreat "resembled some bastard offspring of a rolling pin and a flashlight."[8] The flashlight-like case contained a primary coil, consisting of a few turns of insulated wire wound around a soft iron core, powered by two batteries.[9] A button switch activated the circuit. A current interrupter attached to the apparatus continuously broke and remade this primary circuit at a rate of about 180 times each second. The interrupted flow of direct current created an intermittent magnetic field around the primary coil. This field passed through a secondary coil with which the gadget was equipped. The secondary coil, consisting of many turns of very fine wire, could be moved up and down around the fixed primary coil by pushing the switch along a small groove. The strength of the flow of electrical charges through the secondary coil depended on its position in relation to the primary coil. Interrupted, alternating current flowed from the secondary coil to the "rolling pin," a metal roller attached to one end of the device.

A person who activated the Electreat Mechanical Heart by pressing the switch felt a jolt of electricity through the hand with which he held the case and another jolt at the site where the roller touched his body. The intensity of the shock increased as the switch was pushed along the groove. Both the tube and the roller head contained small sockets into which wires could be inserted to convey the current to "extension applicators." These applicators, packaged with the Electreat kit, consisted of sponges which, when wet, made better contact and increased the impact, and of "internal electrodes," slender metal rods for inserting in the body's orifices.

While ingenious in its compactness, Kent's gadget offered the world nothing electrically new. Michael Faraday, the distinguished English scientist, had first described the principle it embodied in 1831 and thereafter had been honored by having the faradic current bear his name. For a time physicians made a vogue of Faraday's "medical

---

8. K. W. Brimmer, "Faith, Hope and Cure-Alls," *Journal of the Missouri State Medical Association*, 39 (1942), pp. 335–338. Dr. Brimmer was responsible for assembling the expert witnesses for both court trials described below.

9. The description and evaluation of the Electreat is based on testimony in Summary of seizure trial, I.S. no. 16222-E file.

battery," impressed with its angry buzzing, the painful sensations it caused in patients, the jerking of the tetanic muscle contractions it produced. But before long reputable medicine came to recognize that faradic current possessed no therapeutic merit and gave it up, leaving its tingling, binding effect to pseudo-medicine and penny arcades. "The rag-bag of folk-medicine," Edward Eggleston once noted, "is filled with the cast-off clothes of science."[10]

Kent's exploitation of faradic current combined a number of appeals. The cover of *Electreat Relieves Pain* smacked of patriotism, displaying the Statue of Liberty, her customary torch replaced by a new beacon to the world, the Electreat Mechanical Heart. Concepts Kent would later develop more elaborately appeared in this brochure in a primitive form: the joint sovereignty of brain and solar plexus, the former termed the body's "positive pole," the latter its "negative"; the hazard of too constant cerebration; the dread danger of constipation.

As to just what body system went wrong to cause disease, Kent seemed not quite sure. In some passages the nerve networks got priority, encountering difficulty in their normal tasks of rushing protectones from the brain or speeding irritones to it. Elsewhere Kent focused upon the muscles, which might fail at either end of a contraction-relaxation spectrum: if they relaxed and did not contract, a person failed to develop strength and vitality; if they contracted and did not relax, he soon exhausted his strength and vitality. Again, Kent seemed to blame the blood, which stagnated and thus thwarted Mother Nature's plan of using it "to cleanse those tissues which compose our inner bodies."

Whatever the theory of disease, Kent explained how the Electreat functioned to remedy the trouble. The device added protectones and subtracted irritones, short-circuited pain, contracted and relaxed muscles as needed (the machine, indeed, was "a short cut to exercise"), and forced an increased cleansing circulation of blood to any desired part of the body. "Applying Electreat to a muscle," Kent wrote, "causing rhythmic contractions of the arteries and veins is like priming a pump. That is why we call it the Mechanical Heart." With the Electreat, "we can say to the ear, stomach, bowels, breast, etc., Perform thy function, and behold! they perform."

For each of these—and most other—segments of the anatomy, Kent's pamphlet told users how to hook up the machine in order to treat each ailment. To make things simple, the author resorted to

---

10. E. Eggleston, *The Transit of Civilization from England to America in the Seventeenth Century* (New York: Appleton, 1901), p. 60.

chart, illustration and primer prose. The list of treatable circumstances ran on and on, not excluding dandruff, weak eyes, goiter, chest pains, small bust, large prostate and sweaty feet. For piles and "female weakness," the internal electrode was recommended. Nor did Kent rely solely on his own catalogue of complaints. The pamphlet cited numerous testimonials, genuine in the sense that they were truly written by Electreat users, which added to the diseases which the device could conquer, e.g., appendicitis, milk leg and infantile paralysis.

The device control provisions of the 1938 law became effective on New Year's Day of 1940, and Food and Drug inspectors began immediately to survey their new field of regulatory responsibility. In a Kansas City health-food store, an inspector ran across an Electreat Mechanical Heart which was for sale. Certainly its striking name caught his attention. Included in the carton was a copy of *Electreat Relieves Pain*. The claims in the booklet impressed the inspector as being of such extravagant dimensions that he acquired six devices with their accompanying labeling, permitting the government to fire one of the legal weapons provided by Food and Drug law: the Electreat was seized as misbranded.[11] Under the law, Kent had the right to contest the seizure in court and defend his labeling against the misbranding charge. He chose to do so. After the usual delays, the case came to trial in Kansas City on January 27, 1941, before a federal district judge.

Because this was the first device case to come to court, Food and Drug Administration officials spared no pains to make a persuasive presentation. Deciding to rely exclusively on expert testimony, they assembled an all-star cast, a judicious mixture of national authorities and local specialists. In his opening remarks, an assistant district attorney let the judge know that Kent's device was no backyard operation relying on neighborhood sales. Electreat's distribution had spanned the nation. Through the years Kent had sold nearly a quarter of a million of the gadgets at $7 each to retail dealers, who resold them to common citizens for $15. Earning an average of $100,000 a year, Kent had become a millionaire.[12]

The millionaire's invention, testified Frank E. Hoecker, a University of Kansas City physicist who had helped invent electrical instruments for studying heart currents, proved to be only old-fashioned faradic current in a new disguise. Bringing a galvonometer and an

---

11. I.S. no. 16222-E file contains the documents in the case.
12. This discussion of the trial is based on Summary of seizure trial and on clippings from the *Kansas City Journal*, *Kansas City Star* and *Kansas City Times* in *ibid.*

oscillograph to the witness stand, Dr. Hoecker proceeded to demonstrate this point. Faradic current, he said, unlike galvanic current, had no positive and negative poles, so all of Kent's pamphlet references to polarity were ridiculously wrong.

A University of Kansas City biologist, Lester Eisenbrandt, struck at the heart of one of Kent's principal claims, namely, that the Electreat wrought cures by stimulating blood circulation. Kent's machine did just the opposite, slowing blood flow to a standstill. When applied to a normal motor nerve, Dr. Eisenbrandt said, faradic current caused muscles supplied by that nerve to go into a sustained tetanic contraction, which lasted until either the current ceased or the muscles became exhausted. He had reached his conclusions in part from experiments with frogs.

The differences between proper and improper uses of electricity in medicine were explained by Frank H. Krusen, head of the Department of Physical Therapy at the Mayo Clinic. Neither electrochemical nor thermal effects, which physicians often used electricity to achieve, could be secured by low-frequency faradic current because of the pain produced. The Electreat, used indiscriminately, Dr. Krusen testified, was not only worthless for treating all human ailments but in some cases dangerous.

Several Kansas City physicians of various specialties documented the danger, pointing to conditions listed in Kent's pamphlet for which use of the Electreat might pose a particular threat. Among them were glaucoma, apoplectic stroke and Parkinson's Disease.

Star of stars and final witness for the government was Anton J. Carlson, Professor Emeritus of Physiology at the University of Chicago. It took the judge forty minutes just to list "Ajax" Carlson's qualifications. A month after the trial, *Time* featured Carlson's rugged face upon its cover, pointing to his extensive pioneering research in hunger, digestion and nutrition, and calling the Swedish immigrant "the most colorful figure among U.S. scientists."[13] He was no stranger to the witness stand in Food and Drug cases, having for more than two decades testified about such disparate products as saccharin, maple syrup, pesticide residues, abortifacient pastes and bust developers.[14] During the Electreat trial, Food and Drug officials honored Dr. Carl-

---

13. *Time* magazine, vol. 37 (February 10, 1941), cover and pp. 44–48.
14. J. H. Young, "Historical Aspects of Food Cultism and Nutrition Quackery," *Symposia of the Swedish Nutrition Foundation VIII*, Uppsala, 1970, p. 9; J. H. Young, "Saccharin: A Bitter Regulatory Controversy," in Frank B. Evans and Harold T. Pinkett, eds., *Research in the Administration of Public Policy* (Washington, D.C.: Howard Univ. Press, 1975), pp. 39–49.

son's long record of aid to them by tendering him a dinner on his sixty-sixth birthday.

On the witness stand, Dr. Carlson called the Electreat a "blooming fake" and Kent's pamphlet a promiscuous mixture of 5 to 10 percent truth with 90 to 95 percent artistic falsification. Pointing to one of the anatomical charts, Carlson testified: "This chart is [only] accurate in that on one end of the body there is a head and on the other end a rump." Confronting the issue of conflicting schools of medical opinion, which the defense attorney had brought up in earlier cross-examination, Carlson denied that the case under trial involved that question. Rather, it concerned "a difference in mental attitudes between the scientific mind prepared to seek new proofs and accept scientific truths contrasted with those unthinking 'peculiar people' who blindly adhere possibly in faith to weird unproven scientific tenets of their various so-called schools."[15]

In defense of the weird Electreat, two witnesses took the stand, a physician who had known Kent for half a century and Kent himself. Kent's medical friend squirmed through a rigorous cross-examination and failed to give unequivocal support to many claims made in Kent's pamphlet. The doctor insisted, however, that he had used the Electreat with success in treating goiter, "muscular neuritis" and some cases of otitis media.

Kent's appearance came at his own insistence. Just prior to his testimony, a private colloquy between Kent and his lawyer happened to be overheard by Food and Drug officials. "My God!" the attorney exclaimed. "If you get on the stand they will crucify you." Kent went ahead.

As witness, Willie Kent did not come across as the confident and convoluted philosopher of the *Grammar of Nature*. He had taken a physics course in high school, he testified, from which he had graduated in 1893. He had attended the American Institute of Phrenology in New York, enrolled briefly in an evening course on motors and magnetism at Bradley Polytechnic Institute, and through the years had read a host of books. Besides the Electreat Mechanical Heart, he said, he had invented the "electrical kiss." A defense objection blocked Kent from defining this marvel.

Kent did not answer precisely questions put to him about electricity.

"What is a battery, Mr. Kent?"

"There are 100,000 batteries, no two of them alike."

---

15. This citation from the Summary of seizure trial may not reproduce Carlson's exact words.

"What is a plus charge?"

"As applied to electricity an advancement forward from the starting point. Negative is subtraction."

"What is an electrical transformer?"

"I am not a walking dictionary. It is an unanswerable question."

Had Kent used the Electreat to treat himself?

"Yes, sir! For menopause."[16]

Judge John C. Collet wasted no time in reaching a verdict against the seized device. The conclusion was "irresistible," he ruled, that claims made for the Electreat in Kent's pamphlet were "as falsely misleading as might well be possible by the use of the English language."[17] The judge paid tribute to the persuasiveness of government witnesses in his written decision, singling out "Ajax" Carlson for praise. "His testimony and the illustrations he gave supporting his conclusions were in all respects as fully convincing of the accuracy of his judgments as was his test for the determination of which of two fluids was a sugar solution." In a footnote the judge explained this reference by citing the article about Carlson that had appeared in *Time*. Confronted by two beakers of liquid, one containing urine, the other sugar, Carlson had stuck his finger into one of the containers, tasted it and said: "Ya, dot's sugar."

So, under the law, the Electreat Mechanical Heart was condemned. In due course a federal marshal destroyed the device.

Within a year Willie Kent had stopped manufacturing the Electreat, not, however, because he had lost the case in court. In a nation now at war, Kent could not get the raw materials he needed.[18] When shortages eased in 1946, he resumed production and distribution. Kent displayed a degree of caution. He excised "Mechanical Heart" from the name of his device. And he removed from his pamphlet his own therapeutic promises, although continuing to print testimonials.

When the FDA seized one of his postwar devices, Kent expressed a type of surprise Food and Drug officials had grown accustomed to observing. He wished, he said, to "continue to operate an honorable business."[19] He had discarded the pamphlet that had lost him the trial. He certainly did not know that quoting genuine testimonials

---

16. These questions and answers occurred at various points in Kent's testimony.

17. *United States* v. *6 Devices*, "Electreat Mechanical Heart," 38 F. Supp. 236 (W.D., Mo., 1941). The decision is cited in FDA Drug Notice of Judgment 376.

18. Kent's activities between the two trials are described in various documents contained in Electreat case, Interstate Sample no. 49–77OH, FDA Records, RG 88, WNRC, Suitland.

19. Kent to George P. Larrick, June 5, 1947, in *ibid.*

could bring him new difficulty, and now employed both an advertising firm and a special medical consultant to help him bring his labeling within the law's bounds.

Food and Drug officials believed it impossible for Kent to sell the Electreat in interstate commerce "for any recognized therapeutic use."[20] Moreover, they deemed him "calculating" and "unregenerate" because he had seemed to learn nothing but a little caginess from his defeat in court. So they went to court again, this time not seizing Kent's gadget, but launching a criminal prosecution against Kent himself.[21]

When the case came to trial in Peoria during September 1950, the government's case greatly resembled its presentation in Kansas City of nearly a decade before.[22] Indeed, three of the central witnesses, Drs. Hoecker, Krusen and Carlson, repeated their earlier testimony. Peoria physicians testified to the Electreat's inefficacy and hazards.

The defense case differed greatly. Kent, now a man of seventy-six, did not brave the witness stand again. The government had been prepared to show that some events in his earlier autobiographical accounts could hardly have been true, because Kent had spent seven years in prison, convicted of manslaughter for shooting his brother.[23]

Testifying for the defense, a Bradley Professor of Electrical Engineering denied that the Electreat produced faradic current and suggested that its heat output might do some therapeutic good. Preparing for possible rebuttal testimony, the FDA had experiments run at the Department of Agriculture's Northern Regional Research Laboratories in Peoria. In the year of the Kansas City trial these laboratories, by their contributions to the mass production of penicillin, including the discovery of a new and more potent strain from the mold on a rotting cantaloupe, had begun to make a more worthy place for

---

20. Larrick to Kent, June 26, 1947, in *ibid*.

21. St. Louis Station Summary and Recommendations, August 1, 1947, in *ibid*. A successful seizure action bars the device from interstate commerce, but does not bring the promoter into personal jeopardy, as does criminal prosecution. Misbranding is the basis for both types of action.

22. The discussion of this trial is based on a summary prepared by various FDA officials, which is included with "Termination of Prosecution Action in U.S.A. *v*. Charles Willie Kent," January 29, 1951; on a series of letters written during the course of the trial from Van Smart to John L. Harvey in Washington; and on clippings from the *Peoria Journal* and the *Peoria Star*, all in I.S. no. 49-77OH file.

23. Certified copy, July 21, 1950, by Clerk of the Circuit Court of Macoupin County, Illinois, of verdict in 1901 case, *The People* v. *Willie Kent*, and report on records of Illinois State Prison, Menard, cited in William C. Hill to Chief, St. Louis District, FDA, August 8, 1950, in I.S. no. 49-77OH file.

Peoria in the history of health than Kent's Electreat provided.[24] Now, a decade later, the laboratories had discovered errors in the Bradley professor's research.

Kent's main defense before the jury in Peoria rested on testimonials. A box of 2,800 letters was admitted into evidence, and more than a dozen live witnesses—men and women who were elderly, poorly dressed and scantily educated—paraded to the stand.[25] Loyal to Kent and his device, these humble people spoke of recurrent aches and pains in head and stomach, back and limbs, and of how self-treatment with the Electreat banished each attack. Sometimes a more serious ailment, usually self-diagnosed, like hemorrhoids, cropped up in the testimony.

A woman from Texas with a correspondence-school degree in Swedish massage sold Electreats, used them in her practice and employed them in self-treatment of her swollen feet. A Peoria chiropractor also plied the Electreat on both her patients and herself. She described how the device had helped her move an accumulation of bad blood at the base of her brain on a zigzagging path up across the top of her skull and on down to her nose, where it was released, thus eliminating a host of ominous symptoms. On cross-examination, unable to define the most elementary medical terms, she presented the same pathetic spectacle that Kent himself had exhibited on the witness stand in Kansas City.

The chiropractor was one of 4,756 drugless practitioners, according to Kent's secretary, who had bought the Electreat, and 90 M.D.s were also included among the purchasers of the 229,273 instruments that Kent had sold. But most of these devices had been bought for self-treatment by the ordinary men and women of America who had applied a buzzing, shocking placebo that relieved minor emotional ills possessing physiological overtones, or who had recuperated in the course of nature from simple transitory ailments while giving Kent's gadget credit. Many unknown users, who did not appear to testify in Peoria, must have done serious damage to themselves when applying the Electreat's vibrations, in accordance with Kent's directions, to afflictions like appendicitis, hemorrhoids and boils.

Less impressed with Kent's dedicated disciples than with the gov-

---

24. See Lennard Bickel, *Rise Up to Life, A Biography of Howard Walter Florey Who Gave Penicillin to the World* (London: Angus & Robertson, 1972), pp. 142–149, 183–187.

25. This characterization was made by an inspector who contributed to the Summary of the trial included with Termination of Prosecution Action, in I.S. no. 49-77OH file.

ernment's expert witnesses, the jury, after deliberating for three hours, found the defendant guilty. Taking Kent's age into account, the judge did not impose a prison sentence as he might have done under the 1938 law. He levied on the millionaire a $1,000 fine, the maximum possible for the offense.[26]

In at least one sentence of his *Grammar of Nature*, Charles Willie Kent had unwittingly pointed to a failing in both his customers and himself. "Accepting sophisms for truisms," he had written, "constitute [sic] the intellectual mistakes of mankind." Many promoters of pseudo-medical wares and many common citizens continue similarly to err.

---

26. FDA Drug Notice of Judgment 3357.

Terpsichore

THE PERFORMING ARTS

ح§

HUGH MACDONALD

"Un pays où tous sont musiciens..."

> "Race, moreover, makes the critic shirk his proper task. He should tell us what he finds, refer us to Rabelais's wit, style, vocabulary, and opinions, to Berlioz's imagination, orchestral skill, and melodic genius, describing these in human and, if need be, technical, terms of art, instead of talking about either's Latin soul or German race."
>
> JACQUES BARZUN, *Race: A Study in Superstition*,
> revised edition, 1965.

&

"Un pays où tous sont musiciens . . . la race, qu'on dit la plus musicienne du monde. . . ." The words are French, the nation is Germany, and the voice is Romain Rolland, very early in *Jean-Christophe*, setting the scene for his exhaustive fictional exploration of what was for him the most burning problem of the time. Rolland's wide cultural interests encountered the problem of national identity at many levels political, ethnic, social and artistic—but nowhere did it engage his personal attention so pressingly as in music, the art he loved and studied more than any other. His problem was a simple one, and yet he seems to have been alone in seeking its very roots. Were the Germans, or were they not, more musical than the French? What was it that made German music German and French music French? The calmness of Rolland's attempt to disentangle truth from prejudice was the more remarkable for coming at a time when nonsense and bigotry were delivered in absurd abundance on both sides of the Rhine, and when the military arms race had a less publicised parallel in music criticism. By 1914, "la victoire musicale de la France d'aujourd'hui sur l'Allemagne d'aujourd'hui"[1] was a goal at which French musicians gazed

---

1. G. J.-Aubry, *La musique française d'aujourd'hui* (Paris: Perrin, 1916), p. 16.

with confidence and pride. Rolland's own view of it was more detached: music could be good or bad, French or German, but it was meaningless to speak of it as victorious.

Musical nationalism is too often glibly referred to as a phenomenon that touched the fringes of Europe—Russia, Bohemia, Scandinavia and Spain—as a late fruit of Romanticism. For Russia, at least, the issue was a crucial one for a whole generation. Yet the two countries that most truly reflected the swell of nationalist feeling in their music were Germany and France. German Romantic music had a powerful national element, especially in Weber, but in France the very opposite was at first the case. Nothing was so striking in the Paris of the 1830s as its cosmopolitanism. The musical scene was an international parade of extraordinary richness; the glittering list of foreign names is headed by Chopin and Liszt, and includes Hiller, Kalkbrenner, Cherubini, Moscheles, Hallé, Habeneck, Fétis, Schlesinger and many others less celebrated. Italian music belonged, in Paris, to Rossini, and the spirit of cosmopolitanism was embodied in the most successful of them all, Meyerbeer, whose capacity for turning any element, from whatever source, to good effect was legendary. Beulé, in an obituary address to the Académie des Beaux-Arts in 1865, spoke of Meyerbeer's eclecticism as the leading characteristic of the age.[2]

What bitter resentment, one might suppose, this state of affairs must have provoked in the hearts of the French themselves! But no. Berlioz never once grumbled that he was the single Frenchman to shine in the constellation. Félicien David, the perfect Saint-Simonian, cultivated the exotic and the foreign as his own. The passion for foreign literature—Shakespeare, Goethe, Byron, Scott, Cooper, Hoffmann —that ignited the French Romantics was born neither of snobbery nor of a desire to belittle French genius; it was a passion for passion, a spontaneous admiration for greatness that paid no heed whatever to frontiers of nation or race. On that famous September evening in 1827 at the Odéon theatre Berlioz and his fellow-Romantics encountered Shakespeare in a language few of them understood (Jean-Christophe, aping Berlioz, discovered *Hamlet* at one further remove—in French).

While Schumann studiously cultivated the notion of Germanness (he is perhaps the most to be thanked—or blamed—for the idea that the Germans are the most musical nation in Europe), one foreigner in Paris felt bitterly foreign. To the *Revue et gazette musicale* in 1840 Wagner contributed an article, "De la musique allemande," whose national self-awareness must have seemed shockingly parochial and discriminatory to Parisians. The French must have taken offence to see

2. *Revue et gazette musicale*, XXXII (1865), p. 349.

the Italians described as singers, the French themselves as virtuosi, and the Germans as—musicians. In 1841, "Un musicien étranger à Paris" developed the theme. Wagner's humiliations in Paris are well known (Jean-Christophe's first experiences in Paris were identical to Wagner's) and are clearly enough seen as a source of his anti-Jewish and anti-French outbursts of later years. His antagonism was the most dangerous crack in the structure of international fraternity in Paris and his later insistence, in *Oper und Drama*, that music-dramas can be fittingly expressed only in the German language was a cause of French resentment and a provocation of a long campaign to rehabilitate France's national greatness. The Second Empire's belief in a renewal of national glory, the humiliation of 1870, Wagner's disastrously tactless *Eine Kapitulation* of 1873, and the passing of the openness and enthusiasm that characterised French Romanticism, all these heralded new attitudes, new contortions and new prejudices.

More and more the French came to see the Germans as cultural as well as military invaders. Barbarians from the Nordic mists who were at the same time unhealthily decadent—this was an extreme view; while the Germans saw nothing but the frivolity of Paris in a headlong decadence of its own. Of course the Germans were not so wide of the mark. The French themselves, surveying the state of their music in 1871, concluded that all was not well. Tastes and standards had sunk abysmally low; Meyerbeer and Offenbach still held sway; Berlioz's lessons had fallen on deaf ears; Wagner, with the failure of *Tann häuser* in 1861 to fan his resentment, was mocking them from Triebschen. Could it be that Wagner was right in suggesting that the Jews, Meyerbeer and Offenbach, were not so much leading French music as usurping it? In admitting that he was right, the builders of French national music betrayed their ambivalent regard for Wagner: he was both the natural enemy of French music and at the same time the propounder of ideas of national resurgence that were eagerly grasped, an age-old dilemma for nationalist thinkers in political as well as cultural affairs.

The history of French response to Wagner is well chronicled,[3] and his role in the development of French nationalism is not to be underestimated. Yet national consciousness was already evident in this sphere in the 1860s. Gustave Bertrand, in 1863, in an article in *Le ménestrel* entitled "Des nationalités en musique," believed that national identity must be preserved and national traits emphasised. This would

---

3. See for example G. Servières, *Richard Wagner jugé en France* (Paris: Librairie illustrée, 1887); "Wagner en France," special number of *La revue musicale* (1923); and Elliott Zuckerman, *The First Hundred Years of Wagner's Tristan* (New York: Columbia Univ. Press, 1964).

in itself produce a new cosmopolitanism, a kind of league of patriotisms. Four years later Edouard Fétis, the lexicographer's son, spoke of the need to combat internationalism as being "le préjugé de notre temps."[4]

The war brought these nascent ideas into sharp relief. The most tangible expression of the new movement was Saint-Saëns's and Bussine's Société Nationale de Musique, with its motto "Ars gallica," launched in November 1871, and its exclusive devotion not only to French music but to "healthy" music, as opposed to the Wagnerian infection. No foreign music was heard in its programmes until 1886, and its achievement in bringing forward younger French composers was very positive. An abundance of composers of at least second rank —Bizet, Lalo, Duparc, Dukas, Lekeu, Chausson, Bruneau and of course Saint-Saëns himself and César Franck—constitutes a school only rarely equalled, in numbers and productivity, at other times in history. The remarkable thing is that one of the society's aims, the encouragement of instrumental and chamber music, so long neglected in France, had the effect of Germanising style. Where were Lalo or Fauré to turn for chamber music models if not to Beethoven, Mendelssohn and Schumann? Fauré has even been called the French Schumann. In the 1870s, a spirit of classicism permitted this leaning on German models while the Wagnerian influence was easily resisted. In the following decade, as Saint-Saëns began to lose interest in the society's doings, a new guiding spirit came forward in the person of César Franck. Historical and foreign music was now heard, and even Wagner on one occasion (a piano transcription of the *Venusberg* music). The anti-Wagnerian animus had receded, in fact it had failed, and literary Wagnerism, in the mid-1880s, swept all before it. Franck, and more especially his pupils, indulged in a style so rich in red corpuscles and of such gravity that one might be forgiven for thinking that it was German. Lekeu, Chausson, Augusta Holmès and d'Indy were none of them scared of the Bayreuth blight.

If d'Indy seems to represent the whole-hearted acceptance of Wagnerian music he was also close to nationalist movements, such as the Action française, that worked for the creation of a truly representative French culture, and he was a violent anti-Dreyfusard.[5] D'Indy found himself in more than one cleft stick. His passionate Catholic and

---

4. E. Fétis, "De l'affaiblissement des types et des caractères en musique," *Revue et gazette musicale*, XXXIV (1867), pp. 33–37. The ideas of Bertrand, Fétis and others are more fully examined in Ursula Eckart-Bäcker, *Frankreichs Musik zwischen Romantik und Moderne* (Regensburg: Bosse, 1965), pp. 148–154.

5. See Charles B. Paul, "Rameau, d'Indy and French Nationalism," *Musical Quarterly*, LVIII (1972), pp. 46–56.

royalist principles turned the Schola Cantorum, which he founded with Bordes and Guilmant in 1894, into a school of severely dogmatic mien, upholding the finest musical heritage of the Catholic Church—especially Gregorian chant, Josquin, Palestrina, Lassus and Victoria—and pursuing the saintly example of Franck. Protestantism, along with Romanticism and republicanism, was proscribed. D'Indy was happy to accept Wagner's excuse that the Jews (i.e., Meyerbeer) had wrecked the 1861 *Tannhäuser,* and in his *Cours de composition musicale* is reproduced a twelfth-century illustration of Satan vomiting two Jews, with the comment: "Art symbolique et expressif, s'il en fut!" Yet he admired Bach and had to find an excuse for the Lutheran element: "S'il est grand, ce n'est pas *en raison de,* mais *malgré* l'esprit dogmatique et desséchant de la Réforme."[6] Rolland cites the even more acrobatic argument of Edgar Tinel in the *Tribune de Saint-Gervais* of 1902: "Bach, cet artiste si profondément chrétien, *protestant par erreur,* sans doute, puisque en son immortel *Credo,* il confessa sa foi en l'église une, sainte, catholique et apostolique . . ."[7]

Gradually anti-German feeling subsumed anti-Protestant feeling, though discrediting Bach was never easy. By the 1890s Wagnerism was again on the defensive, and d'Indy's position became equivocal. The purest French ideals were invoked once more, and this time it was Debussy who led the revolt against Wagnermania. It was now convenient that Franck was after all a Belgian (d'Indy persisted in describing Franck's Wallonia as "ce pays si français"),[8] just as, a century earlier, it had been helpful that Rousseau was Genevan. Lekeu could equally be dismissed as Belgian and Augusta Holmès was Irish. Chausson, according to Debussy, had been tainted by the Flemish influence of Franck, and while Franck himself was parcelled off to Belgium to discredit him, Beethoven was passed to the Low Countries for the opposite purpose. Ancestry revealed him not to be German, but Flemish, to the relief of his many French admirers. Raymond Bouyer, in *Le secret de Beethoven* (1905), never mentioned the word "German," but treated the composer as if he were born, lived and worked in Flanders. Furthermore the argument could be extended to the point of saying that because Beethoven was a Fleming, his music must be regarded as the "purest form of the French genius."[9]

Rolland was not ashamed to admire Beethoven as a German,

6. Cited by Romain Rolland in his *Musiciens d'aujourd'hui* (2nd ed., Paris: Hachette, 1908), p. 103.

7. *Ibid.*

8. Vincent d'Indy, *César Franck* (Paris: Alcan, 1906), p. 1.

9. Cited by Leo Schrade in his *Beethoven in France; The Growth of an Idea* (New Haven, Conn.: Yale Univ. Press, 1942), p. 212.

indeed, his admiration is as clear in *Jean-Christophe* as it is in his *La vie de Beethoven*, with its clarion-call to moral regeneration, to strength, purity and excellence—all ideals shared by Péguy, in whose *Cahiers de la quinzaine* it first appeared in 1903. Rolland borrowed the warmongers' own language when he named the enemy none of them had noticed:

> C'est le devoir de l'historien de signaler les dangers de l'heure présente, et de rappeler à des artistes français, trop facilement convaincus d'avoir gagné la victoire,—dès la première victoire,—que l'avenir n'est rien moins qu'assuré, et qu'il ne faut jamais désarmer contre l'ennemi commun, plus dangereux dans une démocratie qu'ailleurs:— la médiocrité.[10]

But enemies continued to be marked off for their ancestral sins, while new, purified strains were put in their place. Against Bach's towering stature at the head of German music the French pitted their ablest champion, Rameau. Rameau's music appeared constantly in the Schola Cantorum's concerts and luxuriously edited scores issued from such leading figures as Saint-Saëns, Dukas and d'Indy himself. In 1900 Bruneau described Adam de la Halle as the founder of "une musique essentiellement nationale," with Rameau as the next landmark: "C'est la tradition française, faite des qualités inhérentes à notre race: la mesure, la clarté, l'esprit, le coeur, la franchise et l'audace."[11] Debussy took up the call of Rameau's spirit and the heritage of French classicism (French Romanticism was not so favoured): "Couperin, Rameau, voilà de vrais français! . . . La musique française, c'est la clarté, l'élégance, la déclamation simple et naturelle."[12] Thus it was chauvinism, not reason, that spurred Debussy to challenge the clearness and supremely simple natural declamation of Gluck. Rameau, it seems, has yet to recover from his unworthy treatment for many years as a mere flagpole.

A good working compromise was that reached by, among others, G. Jean-Aubry in his *La musique française d'aujourd'hui*, written during the war, when even Beethoven's music was no longer to be heard in Paris (Marliave and his friends played the quartets at the front to boost their spirits, but only in private). For Jean-Aubry it was folly to eradicate the great German music of the past, since belittling Bach,

---

10. Rolland, *Musiciens d'aujourd'hui*, p. 277.
11. Alfred Bruneau, *La musique française; rapport sur la musique en France du XIIIème au XXème siècle* (Paris: E. Fasquelle, 1901), p. 9.
12. Claude Debussy, *Monsieur Croche et autres écrits*, ed. François Lesure (Paris: Gallimard, 1971), p. 272.

Beethoven and Wagner was clearly a superhuman task.[13] Jean-Aubry was delighted to find contemporary German music unworthy of its heritage and therefore easily dismissed. Strauss has only "l'apparence de génie"; he and Mahler simply build up the orchestra to become "le rival de Krupp." The failure of Strauss's *Die Josephslegende* in Paris in 1914 seemed to prove beyond question that all modern German music was worthless: "La musique européenne n'aurait pas reculé d'un pas si on en supprimait la production straussiste ou mahlérienne; il est aisé de sentir ce qui manquerait à notre vocabulaire musical si nous n'avions eu ni Rimsky, ni Albeniz, ni Debussy." Rolland, on the other hand, swimming once more against the tide, was convinced that Strauss was the leading musical personality in Europe, an opinion from which no party line would dislodge him.

At a crucial moment in the debate, 1902, when national issues were beginning to glow with heat, Debussy gave *Pelléas et Mélisande* to the world, asserting his identity as a Frenchman and proclaiming the necessity of freeing himself from the pervasive evils of Wagner. Here was exactly what the builders of French national culture sought above all else: a palpable masterpiece. No one dreamed of denying that it was anything but purely and wholly French; no one wanted to notice that the libretto, to which the music is so inalienably grafted, was Belgian, and to this day the work is regarded as the purest example of Frenchness. The assumption is universally repeated. Martin Cooper, whose understanding of the French character is profound, is himself voicing that assumption when he says: "Heaven knows, it was not necessary for Debussy to insist on his Frenchness."[14] But insist he did, with "musicien français" discreetly but purposefully appended to his signature in the last works.

This is scarcely the place to establish the true contours of French and German national character, in music or in anything else; but it may be valuable to draw attention to the confusion that existed then and still exists today, between being national and acting national, between giving to a tradition and drawing upon it. No composer between 1870 and 1914 could be unaware of his own frontiers, and for French composers at least it was often sufficient to write like other French composers and to reproduce the currently approved marks of

---

13. Jacques Barzun draws attention to the fact that Mozart was never discussed in this context, perhaps because his name *sounds* French. (*Race: A Study in Superstition* [rev. ed., New York: Harper & Row, 1965], p. 142.) Perhaps, too, he could have been claimed, albeit on flimsy grounds, by the Austrians.

14. In *French Music from the Death of Berlioz to the Death of Fauré* (London: Oxford Univ. Press, 1951), p. 177.

Frenchness. Their hearers, and often they themselves, were deceived into thinking that such a procedure was the expression of instinctive, tribal roots with a claim to superiority over other nations, and the deception fed upon itself.

Pelléas et Mélisande can be seen to have won a propaganda battle and to have been awarded the palm of Frenchness. Yet it is a deeply original work and has little in common with much French music of its own day. Its success and standing have dislocated an earlier notion of French music and bequeathed to the world the idea that French music is, typically, effeminate and willowy (in contrast to the heavy vigour we call Teutonic). But there are two serious fallacies: first, apart from Debussy and some imitators and two composers of the previous generation (Fauré and Massenet), French music is red-blooded and muscular everywhere we look. Heaviness was easily condemned as Wagnerian or as merely foreign: if Franck was Belgian, Schmitt Lorrainian and Lalo half-Spanish, Magnard, on the other hand, was a Parisian and a patriot, and his music is as strong as a boar. Roussel has a hardness of outline that seems remote from the half-lights of the Impressionists. And *Carmen!* How could such a work spring from France if it were really true that French music is frail, suggestive, delicate and naïve?

Second, *Pelléas et Mélisande* itself is not the water-colour many have taken it to be. The myth of *Pelléas* was exploded recently when Pierre Boulez recorded it with no French singers in the cast. To this opera, he pointed out, many misunderstandings had become attached, not least being its national distinctness:

> Une certaine "tradition" particulariste a recouvert le tout d'un vernis d'élégance, auquel se joint inévitablement la fameuse clarté française. Or, ni l'élégance, ni la clarté n'ont de rôle à jouer dans le sens conventionnel qu'on attribue à ces termes. L'atmosphère est sombre, incroyablement pesante. . . . Il me paraît démoralisant que cette soi-disant tradition de l'exsangue puisse passer pour le comble de "l'esprit français" en musique![15]

Boulez is concerned as much to universalise *Pelléas* as to de-Frenchify it, but his impatience with the notion of bloodlessness is timely. The half-lights and human frailties are theatrical sleight-of-hand; *Pelléas* is indeed ponderous and sombre, with passages of great force.[16]

---

15. *Miroirs pour Pelléas et Mélisande*, record sleeve, CBS 77324.
16. It is time, too, to question the notion that *Pelléas* is untranslatable; is not the free unemphatic prosody perfectly suited to translation?

Romain Rolland's intentions were worthy, but like every critic of his day became ensnared in the problem of national identity, even though he strove to engage what seemed to him profounder issues. However often he stated that a man's work is more important than his origins, he was nonetheless obsessed with national differences and studied them with the closeness of a jeweller. Rolland spoke of Berlioz, for example, as being wholly French: "S'il est naturel que l'Allemagne, plus musicienne que la France, se soit rendu compte, avant la France, de la grandeur et de l'originalité musicale de Berlioz, il est douteux qu'elle arrive à sentir parfaitement une âme aussi française." And later on: "C'est la première fois peut-être qu'un grand musicien fran- çais ose penser en français!"[17] How would Rolland have convinced Cornelius, who saw Berlioz as "wie von gotischen Blut erfüllt, von germanischer Milch genährt"?[18] Cornelius concluded that for Berlioz, "So ist Deutschland seine geistige Heimat, nach welcher er immer sehnsüchtig strebt, und in welcher ihm einzig das rechte Verständnis werden kann."

Hans von Bülow likewise argued that Berlioz's spirit was German through and through.[19] On the other hand, Rolland regarded Saint- Saëns as distinctively German in temperament—which cannot have pleased him—even if French in "la parfaite clarté." Later on in *Musiciens d'aujourd'hui* we read:" La clarté! c'est la marque de l'intelli- gence de M. d'Indy. Pas d'esprit plus français."[20] With *clarté* so re- peatedly put forward as the hallmark of France, it is hard to believe that a movement such as Impressionism with its deliberate unclear- ness could spring from the same land. Logic is similarly invoked in many instances, although if that were truly a characteristic of French music we would have to acknowledge Brahms as more French than Fauré.

Rolland was only being cautious when he declared that the French genius was many-sided and that in music Debussy represents only one aspect of it.

> Il y a un tout autre côté de ce génie, qui n'est nullement représenté ici: c'est l'action héroïque, l'ivresse de la raison, le rire, la passion de la lumière, la France de Rabelais, de Molière, de Diderot, et, en musique, dirons-nous—(faute de mieux)—la France de Berlioz et de

---

17. Rolland, *Musiciens d'aujourd'hui*, pp. 4 and 50.
18. P. Cornelius, *Ausgewählte Schriften und Briefe* (Berlin: B. Hahnefeld, 1938), p. 307.
19. H. G. von Bülow, *Ausgewählte Schriften, 1850–1892*, ed. Marie von Bülow (2 vols. in one, Leipzig: Breitkopf & Härtel, 1911), p. 91.
20. Rolland, *Musiciens d'aujourd'hui*, p. 107.

Bizet. Pour dire la vérité, c'est celle que je préfère. Mais Dieu me garde de renier l'autre! C'est l'équilibre de ces deux Frances qui fait le génie français.[21]

"Faute de mieux"! So that other side is *not* properly represented by Berlioz and Bizet, and indeed to burden them with the traits of Rabelais, Molière and Diderot is unfair, not to say downright false. Rolland, without knowing it, has defined French musical character not as something he can measure from literature, but more simply as the sum of its parts; these composers are French because they are French, not because they conform to a parochial construct of what a French composer ought to be. Rolland might perhaps have added that Debussy's art represents not the central zone of national character but a rarer region where few composers join him.

The critics' war was every bit as futile as the real war. Where was the victory of French music in 1918? For Cocteau and his friends the great issues of 1900 were to be laughed off the stage; importance and unimportance exchanged roles, and Stravinsky swept in a new cosmopolitanism, unthinkable before the war. The most musical nation in the world (as a concept) had simply ceased to exist.

---

21. *Ibid.,* p. 206.

WILLIAM A. OWENS

From Isaac Watts to "Heaven's Radio"

"There is moreover a directness, almost a crudity, about great art that many cannot stand. It brings life too close to the observer, who feels alternately scorched and chilled. Art may be beauty, but it is not easy beauty. It lacks the smooth contours that conventional moods and words insure. For example, in the original version of 'Rock of Ages' occurs the line:

> When mine eye-strings break in death

But it was later revised to read:

> When mine eyelids close in death

which being weaker and less upsetting may be sung without thinking about it.

"The study of the arts in their great manifestations is thus a gradual and deliberate accustoming of the feelings to strong sensations and precise ideas. It is a breaking down of self-will for the sake of finding out what life and its objects may really be like. And this means that most esthetic matters turn out to be moral ones in the end. Great art offers a choice—that of preferring strength to weakness, truth to softness, life to lotus-eating."

JACQUES BARZUN, *Teacher in America*

Out of the slave holds they came, survivors of the Middle Passage, a few weeks or months away from the Slave Coast, the Ivory Coast, the Gold Coast, the Congo, subdued, worn in body and spirit by the struggle against the iron collar and the shackles that bound their feet. Some were victims of tribal warfare; some had been captured by black traders on lonely roads. All had been passed from black captor to white factor in exchange for gold, rum, bright-colored cloth.

By the time the captives went down to the slave decks, much of their family and tribal identity had been lost. In their buying and selling, slave merchants cared not what family or tribe had been violated. In fact, they took some care to mix people from different tribes, upland, coastal. They thus lessened the danger of mutiny. In the slave factory, waiting for the sails of the slaver to appear, the captives shouted and cried in their own confusion of languages but with little communication. Only by signs could they share their common experience—the capture, the sale, the march to the sea. On the slave deck, chained to ring bolts, they might listen in vain for the sound of a familiar word.

Out of the slave holds they came at last, those who had survived sickness, eluded death, and on to slave marts in Boston, New York, Philadelphia, Baltimore, Charleston, New Orleans, where the slaver sold them as house servants or field hands. Sale on the slave block, by accident or intention, marked another separation from kin or tribe. House servants went singly or in small groups. Buyers for large plantations, except for a few on the Carolina coast, made certain that no more than a handful came from the same tribe. English was forced upon them, and African languages disappeared through disuse. Except for a few words, as if the process had been carefully calculated, the slave lost the language that might have bound him to his past. After a generation or so a slave did not know whether he was Dahoman, Yoruba, Congolese, or a tribal mixture. All he knew was that he was African and that his skin was black.

As quickly, he lost the beliefs and rituals that could have preserved for him some sense of identity, some tie from one generation to the next. His tribal language was unwritten; so was his tribal history, tribal law. Back in Africa slaves had, at the age of puberty, listened to old men and women recite their history and instruct them in belief and ritual. Only after they had demonstrated sufficient knowledge could they go through the rituals that admitted them to manhood, womanhood. The old were the keepers of both tradition and ritual. But buyers of slaves knew there was no market for the old and the old were left behind. Abruptly the tribal chain was broken and there was no way to restore it, no way even for those who had gone through the rites of puberty in Africa to pass on their knowledge. Tribal training, tribal ritual faded in one generation.

During the transition slaves lived in a state of non-history, non-law, other than that provided by their owners. It was not, however, entirely a state of non-memory. Certain cultural remnants could not be so easily erased. They remembered the rhythm of the drumbeat, the sound of the ritualistic chant. They retained a distinctive timbre of voice. They learned English but were not trained in it. In the isolation of field or cabin they sounded words as they thought they had heard them, in voices that carried African overtones. Some of the slaves were taught by their masters to read and write. For the majority, however, English was a sub-language, ungrammatical, unsyntactical, dialectal. It was also the only language they had. Whatever they shaped in song or poetry or story had to be shaped in it.

Likewise the tribal beliefs and rituals were largely submerged in the Christian. It was the practice of more conscientious slave traders to have a priest baptize and give Christian names to captives before they left the West Coast of Africa. Neither conversion nor exorcism was required and witch doctors and workers of magic were baptized indiscriminately with the rest. In certain parts of the Caribbean and in predominantly Catholic countries in South America voodoo survived and flourished, initially because tribal dispersion had not been so effectively practiced, later because voodooism was tolerated and partially absorbed into Catholic belief and ritual. In the Protestant South, African religions were soon forgotten as the slaves were exposed to Protestant teachings and rituals. In the isolation of field and cabin, however, strains of voodooism survived in scattered areas, the magic of voodoo sometimes merged with the miracle of Christianity. Many a plantation, whether the master was aware or not, had its resident conjure man.

In North America, especially in the South, there was a gradual melding of folk custom, folk lore into what is now called Afro-American. In its simplest statement it is the hybridization of African tribal culture with Anglo-Saxon culture, in a process similar to the coming together of European tribes centuries earlier to form the Anglo-Saxon. A more incongruous melding can hardly be imagined, the components coming as they did on the one hand from the cold climate, the austere peoples of Northern Europe, on the other from the hot climate, the less restrained peoples of the West Coast of Africa. They were as different, whites insisted, as black from white, yet they were alike—human, creative, capable of absorbing one from the other, capable of synthesizing, consciously or unconsciously. The result is clearly a new culture, largely folk in development, chiefly oral in retention and transmission, dominant in a few geographical areas, nigh predominant in areas of creativity.

The Anglo-Saxon folk culture came almost full-blown to America, carried in the minds of pioneers who traveled in groups, settled in communities, clung together in the presence of hardship, shared and passed on whatever they remembered from the past. Many of them unable to read or write, they could hand down only what had been handed down to them. The culture they handed down, an accumulation of centuries of folk history and folk experience, was rich and varied. The richness and variety were no better displayed than in the music: English, Scottish and Irish ballads and songs; fiddle and dance tunes; and the spiritual songs compatible with the beliefs of religious dissenters. In contrast, the Africans, stripped of language and culture, could make no comparable contribution; but as time has proved they had much to give in the sense of poetry, rhythm, harmony, and other less definable attributes. Fortunately, no racial barrier ever erected has been able to keep a folk tune or folk wisdom from crossing over. This crossing over, this melding together, has enhanced the strengths of both, and the richness.

Of all the art forms in this new culture, the Negro spiritual demonstrates most clearly the process of synthesis. It did not come about, as some have claimed, as a kind of spontaneous overflowing. Nor is it a special derivative from either the African or the Anglo-Saxon. In the combining of the two it has a pattern of growth that can be defined and analyzed in both the poetry and the music. Ideas expressed—religious overtones, secular undertones—have their counterparts in the developing liberalism of the frontier and the struggle for equality in dissenting congregations. Though slave owners all along the Atlantic seaboard tried with varying enthusiasm to bring Christianity to the slaves and the slaves to church, successes were more marked in the South, where slavery had proved profitable, where Negroes soon numbered almost as many as whites, in some areas more. The beginnings of the Negro spiritual were in the South.

In Virginia, from early days the Anglican Church permitted slaves to attend Sunday services, and to sit in slave balconies or on benches on the sides or at the back. Generally unable to read or write, they could not follow the liturgy in *The Book of Common Prayer* except as they memorized parts like the Kyrie Eleison and the General Confession.

The sung Kyrie gave them a melody and a simple structure, both easily imitated. Less easy were the prayers chanted by the priest, or the English plainsong sung in unison by priest and people. Unlike any tribal chant that might have echoed in their minds, the plainsong was a severe, disciplined form, restrained in emotion, restraining in rhythm. Yet it left a residue in mind that could be taken to cotton field or kitchen, to become the plaint of some lonesome singer—to be taken from or added to in words or tune or rhythm as the singer pleased, the changes inspired from Africa remembered, from new religious experience, from the emotional needs and artistic sense of the singer.

Quite likely the Negro spiritual had some of its origin in the Anglican liturgy. Anglican plainsong was probably precursor to the wordless chant—the "moanin' low"—of black field hands who toward sundown raised their voices in sounds low and gentle and full of lament. The blossoming, however, came later, toward the end of the eighteenth century, and farther west on the frontier, where the migration of white owners and black slaves stretched beyond the hold of the Anglican Church and merged with the migration of white dissenters—Baptist, Presbyterian, Methodist—who had peopled the Valley of Virginia and were pushing on beyond the Alleghenies into Kentucky. These dissenters had rejected formal liturgy, as they had rejected the display of the cross or any other symbol that reminded them of the established Church. For worship, led by a preacher, often ordained from among them, they used the Bible, prayers made up on the instant, and songs— white spirituals, some sung from song books, a greater number from memory. Having rejected the General Confession, they replaced it with a testimonial time in which sinners cried out their sins, and the faithful testified how Jesus had taken their feet out of the miry clay of sin and set them on the road to glory, hallelujah.

By the end of the eighteenth century, in the farther reaches of the frontier, Negro slaves were welcomed as members in white churches, especially the Baptist, and to a lesser extent the Methodist. Equally with the whites they were called "Brother" George and "Sister" Betsy. They went down into the baptismal waters with the whites, sometimes with their own masters, ate the bread and drank the wine with them, and joined with them in praying, singing and testifying. This was at the beginning of a great revival movement, the movement that gave rise to camp meetings.

Some of the songs they sang came directly from the great English hymn makers: the Wesleys, Isaac Watts, William Cowper, John Newton. Some from the same makers were so changed in oral transmission that they were in effect new songs. Some were of frontier origin with neither words nor music in written form. Many were a jumble of words from one source, tunes from another, often with sacred words set to secular tunes, tunes taken from dance hall songs to traditional ballads.

Of the hymn composers, Isaac Watts was probably the best known on the Western frontier. His years, 1674–1748, spanned the time of vast migrations of German Mennonites, English and Welsh Quakers, Scots and Scots-Irish Presbyterians, and other dissenters into Pennsylvania and then Virginia. A dissenting minister himself, he wrote hundreds of hymns, many of which appeared in his *Psalms of David in the Language of the New Testament* in 1719, and many of which became a regular part of worship in dissenting churches. Frontiersmen faced with hardship and danger took comfort from such words as:

> O God, our help in ages past,
> Our hope for years to come,
> Our shelter from the stormy blast,
> And our eternal home!

or,

> When I survey the wondrous cross,
> On which the Prince of glory died,
> My richest gain I count but loss,
> And pour contempt on all my pride.

These songs were in simple metrical form, simple melody, simple words, and easy to sing by illiterate slave or almost as illiterate white overseer, or master, or preacher himself. They were steeped in religious emotion, the doctrine they proclaimed simple and direct enough to be understood by the least educated.

In log cabin meetings, where there were no song books, or where the people could not read, the preacher sometimes turned the responsive psalm reading of the Anglican liturgy into what came to be called "lining out." He would "h'ist" a tune and then recite the first line. The people would sing that line and wait for him to give the next. In this lining out, beyond the control of printed word or music, the people developed a freer use of rhythm and stanza form.

The worship in the white churches became also the worship of the black members. Still in the eighteenth century white preachers reported on how effectively black slaves sang white hymns, and how their voices seemed peculiarly suited to hymn singing. They were probably describing a timbre of voice. They did not mention rhythm or the effect of the drumbeat, but the drumbeat had not been lost to memory.

Drumless in an Anglo-Saxon world, Africans whittled down two rib bones and holding them between fingers "knocked the bones" in a variable rhythm, good for dancing. Or they whittled wooden clubs and beat out their rhythms on barrel heads, again for dancing. But these belonged not to spiritual songs but to "sinful songs," and religious whites proscribed them as rather childish remnants of a savage past.

Negroes were admitted to church membership at a time when there was a great surge in religious fervor and evangelism. In church or camp meeting revival songs were sung and at times shouted through by both whites and blacks. The words of these songs were usually simple, the stanza form uncomplicated—often a line repeated three times and then a final line that suggests or clinches a thought. A popular form was the chain song, with its repetition of all except certain key words. The whites used this form in a perennial favorite:

> Where, oh, where are the Hebrew children?
> Where, oh, where are the Hebrew children?
> Where, oh, where are the Hebrew children?
> Safe over in the Promised Land.

As the singers repeated the stanzas with such substitutions as "the Twelve Apostles" and "Paul and Silas," their emotions rose higher and higher. When they sang "Where, oh, where is my sainted mother?" there was general weeping and the opening of mind and spirit to the words, the power of the revivalist. At the height of their emotion, the revivalist himself might lead them to the altar and back in a slow religious dance, a kind of lockstep of the faithful.

These white spirituals, steeped in the Calvinist tradition, often drew their messages from the fear of death and the hope of heaven. Images from the Old Testament were, also in the manner of Isaac Watts, reshaped in the Christian terms of the New Testament, with the imprint of Jesus ever present. To them in their songs Jesus might be Lord or King; he was also the Saviour who could save and heal the "sin-sick soul."

Slaves, when they were converted to Christianity, took the beliefs and the forms of worship of their masters. Called to preach, they exhorted in the words and manner of white preachers. In worship they prayed the prayers, sang the songs the whites taught them. Stirred to "make a new song unto the Lord," they followed forms and tunes already set for them. Parallels were broken chiefly as a result of dialect or of faulty memory. For example, instead of "Where, oh, where are the Hebrew children?" they sang:

> Wonder where is good ole Daniel,
> Wonder where is good ole Daniel,
> Wonder where is good ole Daniel,
> Safe over in de Promise' Lan'.

From 1619 on, whites and blacks in America had consciously or unconsciously been progressing toward a common language, a common folk tradition, a common religious experience. This is not to say that racial and cultural amalgamation was complete, or that it would ever be, or that complete amalgamation would be desirable. It might prove stultifying, especially in areas of creativity. These common grounds do, however, provide the essentials for examination of the Negro spiritual as religious and artistic experience.

Had common church membership continued, the course of American music might have been different—less segregationist on one hand, less bitter on the other, and less distinctive. But common church membership virtually disappeared during the rising arguments over the institution of slavery and the nature of the Negro. (As late as 1819 the constitution of the state of Missouri defined a Negro slave as "not being Christian," yet during the same years Negro Christians had become so numerous that they could establish and maintain their own churches and preachers.) The racial equality of the earlier frontier was diminished. With improvement in general education for whites, white churches became more fixed in their forms of worship. There was a proliferation of hymn books in which the words of white spirituals were set to conventional musical forms. Congregations sang from these books and the freedom of frontier singing was lost to the authority of the printed page. A new song from whatever source had to be reduced to conventional forms before it could appear in a book. Negro variations of white spirituals were not easily adapted and were for this, if for no other reason, omitted. From then on for a century or so, whites could listen sentimentally to Negroes singing spirituals but not join in the singing.

Negroes in their churches had no such restrictions. They could listen to the preacher in the height of emotion turn his sermon into a kind of chant, or they could follow a leader as he turned a white spiritual into a hand-clapping, foot-tapping, jig-dancing jump-up. For more than half a century—through a period of intense creativity— their spirituals were entirely oral, the words and music unfettered by the white man's forms. Solitary singers made up songs as they worked. Songs came about in meetings. A brother or a sister, after a prayer or a testimony that stirred the emotions, would pick up a phrase like "He'p me, Lawd" and sing it out to an old tune or one made up at the moment. Others would repeat it, and they were singing in unison or in harmony: "He'p me, he'p me, he'p me, Lawd." Or lines that expressed a particularly poignant thought like

> If religion was a thing that money could buy,
> The rich would live and the po' would die

would be dragged into one song after another.

In the isolation of small black churches, Negroes were free to turn back in time to dimly remembered sounds from Africa. Then they began their own synthesis of the sounds of Africa and the sounds and images of religious America. As they improvised more freely, they moved farther and farther from their gleanings from the whites. For the common meter they substituted syncopation, with the beat of the drum echoed in stomping feet. Instead of using scales, in the white man's way, singers, at times seeming independent of each other, let their voices slide up and down in search of some satisfying tone, of a chord that would bring them all together at the end.

Half a century or so later, Negro spirituals began following white spirituals into print, frequently as "collected and arranged" for solo or for choral groups. Parallels between white model and black spiritual are often obvious. As often, blurrings of words and tunes through faulty memory, or through the Negro's penchant for improvisation through substituting his own words and tonal effects, obscure the parallels. Arrangers of Negro spirituals for print have encountered well-nigh insuperable difficulties when they tried to show in conventional notation sounds and rhythmic patterns that sprang from African rather than European sources and inspiration.

These difficulties can be illustrated by two versions of "Amazing Grace," a favorite of whites and blacks alike. The words were by John Newton, an English clergyman who with the poet William Cowper wrote the hymns published in *Olney Hymns* in 1779. The words, set to a popular secular tune, appeared as follows:

> Amazing grace! how sweet the sound,
> That saved a wretch like me!
> I once was lost, but now am found,
> Was blind but now I see.

In the two centuries since they were published the words have been faithfully reprinted in countless song books. During the same time garbled versions of the text have been widely sung in the South and a few have appeared in print with tunes also garbled.

At present the tune most widely sung in both white and black churches in the South is listed simply as a Southern melody. As it appears in white hymnals the tune is simple, unadorned. As it is sung by Negro quartets a method of quartet singing in black churches is illustrated. The leader sings the verses, the others, as a black singer explained, "offer comment." It is this "offering comment" in both words and harmony that transforms the song into a Negro spiritual:

> Ama—It was de Lawd—zing grace—It was de Lawd—
>   how sweet—It was de Lawd—the sound—It was de Lawd—
> That-a saved—It was de Lawd—a wretch—It was de Lawd—like-a me;
> I once—It was de Lawd—was lost—It was de Lawd—
>   but now—It was de Lawd—I'm found—It was de Lawd—
> Was blind—It was de Lawd—but now—It was de Lawd—
>   I see—It was de Lawd.

Rarely if ever would a black singer in a black church know that before his conversion to Christianity John Newton was a slave trader and served as master of ships taking holds full of slaves across the Middle Passage. Readers of his diary may suspect that he was distilling his days on the West Coast of Africa and the guilt he felt for them when he wrote another line in the song:

> Thro' many dangers, toils and snares,
> I have already come . . .

Though separation between white and black churches, even within the same denomination, became firmly established and there was little communication one to another, parallels in white and black spirituals persisted, chiefly because they both drew from Bible stories and life experience. But differences are to be found in methods and meanings.

White singers had traditionally sung of the burdens of life, of the fear of death, the hope for glory. Negro singers sang of the same burdens and added one of their own: the burden of slavery. The Negro was using his own meanings and his own sense of poetry and music when he sang:

> Sometimes I'm up, sometimes I'm down,
> I'm gonna lay down this heavy load;
> Sometimes I'm almost to the ground,
> I'm gonna lay down this heavy load.
>
> I know my robe's gonna fit me well;
> I tried it on at the gates o' hell . . .

When he sang of the condition of servitude his statements were likely to be phrased in the subtlety of irony. No white, whether he caught true meanings or not, could fault a Negro for singing straight from the Old Testament:

> Go down, Moses, 'way down in Egypt land,
> Tell old Pharoah, let my people go.

Irony they used and parody—parody without subtlety, broad, sometimes angry, often less than poetic, penetrating in its report on the Negro condition:

> Oh, it jes' keeps on a-leakin' in this ole buildin',
> It jes' keeps a-leakin' in this ole buildin',
> It jes' keeps on a-leakin' in this ole buildin',
> I believe I'll have to move,
> I'll find a better home, home, home . . .

By the time the Negro was able to make such a spiritual he had moved a long way away from the European heritage, a long way toward the African.

In the nineteenth century both white and black singers expressed spiritual feelings in the metaphor of technology, the white open, above board, the blacks in a kind of gospel double talk. There was, for instance, a frontier belief that the gun speaks the gospel. Slaves on the run knew the kind of gospel a "paterroller's" gun could speak. They knew what they were saying when they sang:

> Oh, Lawd, how de devil run
> When he seen dat gospel gun.

Whites saw the railroad as a kind of passage to heaven; the blacks saw it as an underground passage to the freedom of Canada. Whites sang a tune with predictable intervals, words with pedestrian imagery:

> Life is like a mountain railroad with an engineer that's brave.
> We must make the run successful from the cradle to the grave.
> Watch the curves, the fills, the tunnels, never falter, never quail,
> Keep your hand upon the throttle and your eye upon the rail.

Compared with the trip north by underground railroad the trip to heaven on this mountain railway seems relatively easy. Double meanings in "The Gospel Train" and "I'll Meet You at the Station" suggest real urgency, real danger:

> The gospel train's a-coming,
> I hear it jes' at hand;
> I hear the wheels a-rumbling,
> And a-rolling through the land.
> Git on board, little children,
> Git on board, little children,
> Git on board, little children,
> There's room for many a more.

In chain form the second song moves from "blind" to "dumb" to "lame," all human conditions that can be overcome whether the train is headed up north or straight up:

> I may be blind and I cannot see
> But I'll meet you at the station
> When the train comes along.
> Brother, when the train comes along,
> Brother, when the train comes along,
> I'll meet you at the station
> When the train comes along.

This metaphor of multiple meaning is fully apparent in the lines of a song whimsically called "Swinging on the Golden Gates":

> Sister Lou, Brother Joe, Aunt Maria
> Done caught that train and gone.

A few years after the slaves were freed, the telephone became a part of American life. No longer with a need for communicating in double meanings, Negro singers responded with spirituals like "I Rung Up Jesus on the Heavenly Telephone." At the same time whites were singing "Hello, Central, Give Me Heaven."

Though the radio did not come into general use in the South until after the Depression, it did inspire a spiritual that had spread in several versions by the beginning of the Second World War. A singer who claimed to have made it up sang the words as follows:

> There's a wonderful invention,
> It is called the radio;
> You can hear it almost every place you go,
> But the static in the air
> Makes it sometimes hard to hear,
> But it is not so with heaven's radio.
>
> Heaven's radio is on the other shore
> Where my precious Savior listens in;
> There's no static in the air
> And it never needs repair,
> 'Cause my precious Savior listens in.

Unlike earlier songs, this has neither words nor images that would mark it as unmistakably black or white. The music, set for piano accompaniment, has none of the wanderings in scale or meter. At least one version showed up as a kind of dance tune in a honkytonk. But so did other spirituals of earlier origin.

The movement of the spiritual to the secular song was as easily accomplished as had been the earlier movement of the secular to the spiritual. The remnant of African voodoo had attached itself to Christianity early. Conjure men, conjure women, making no distinction between magic and miracle, used Christian prayers and spirituals to evoke powers nebulous in form, dark in suggestion, equally strong for healing the sick or casting a spell over the enemy. Satan was powerful, Jesus more powerful. Singers put their warnings in words:

> Satan's a liar and a conjure too;
> If you don't look out he'll conjure you.

Jesus casting out devils was also a kind of conjure man, but "Jesus was a preacher too." When they sang

> Satan's like a snake in the grass,
> Always in some Christian's path

it was Jesus who could out-conjure.

Elements of what became blues, jazz, "soul," had existed in the spiritual since the first one became less white, more African in form and style. In church, people in religious ecstasy danced to spirituals like "When the Saints Go Marching In." In dim dance halls, with a bluesy piano in the background, men and women—singly, not in couples—twisted and turned and beat the rhythm to the same song:

> Oh, when the moon—oh, when the moon—
> Is red with blood—is red with blood—
> Oh, when the moon is red with blood—
> Oh, Lawd, I wants to be among that number
> When the moon is red with blood.

A blood red moon is from the world of voodoo.

Such were the minglings of spiritual and secular, minglings that formed the basis for new creativity in American music—creativity distinctly Afro-American whether achieved by either black or white.

In the twentieth century, larger black churches increasingly used white hymn books, and the spiritual was regarded by many a part of the past they were trying to erase; but in smaller churches it never lost its place in worship or its power to inspire religious rapture:

A Sunday service was in progress at the Old North New Hope Baptist Church at Franklin, Texas. There had been preaching and praying, testifying and singing. Women in white robes had "labored" with the few who had come to the "mo'nuh's bench." The preacher talked of the fullness of spirit like a dove descending. Women spoke of the power of Jesus: "He be's better'n liniment fuh achin' bones." "He gives me stren'th fuh hoein'." Still they had not reached the "upper plain" of feeling.

Then a quartet of young men and women, all in white, moved slowly from among the people and stood before the table that was the altar. The preacher stood to one side with his head bowed. Sounds of praying and "laboring" and humming subsided and gave way to silence deep as the void before creation. Then a young woman began in a voice strong and firm and prayerful:

> Precious Lawd, take my hand,
> Lead me on, let me stand.
> I am so tired, I am weak, I am worn—

"Sho' nuff!" The woman's voice sounded not as interruption but as affirmation.

> Through the storm, through the night,
> Lead yo' child to the light.
> Take my hand, precious Lawd,
> Lead me on.

Before she came to a pause there was an overtone of "Amen" and "Praise the Lawd" and an undertone of harmony from the other three singers.

Then she began the words again, the rhythm more accented, more syncopated, supported by the sound of clapping hands and tapping feet, and the three in harmony repeating over and over: "Leadin' me, leadin' me, leadin' me," in what might have been a kind of drone but was turned into a kind of orchestration. With her face lifted, her eyes closed, the leader took up another stanza:

> When my death draws near in the night so still,
> When my work on earth is done,
> At the river I'll take my stand,
> Help me over to the Promised Land,
> Take my hand, Precious Lawd,
> Lead me on.

Her voice drifted lower, the other three louder. Together they rose above the drone of the congregation, the hands clapping, the feet stomping. The preacher moved neither hand nor foot but his body began weaving to the rhythm. Then a woman in white stood up and began a slow dance toward the altar. Almost as if on cue another woman and a man started up along the aisles. Feeling caught on. People stood and danced in place. Others in unlinked chains worked their way to the altar and back again, singing, clapping, dancing, weeping, praising, the spiritual at the heart of the common experience, individual feelings guiding the body, the lips. Then there was a waning of sound and rhythm. The mountain peak reached, there had to be a return to the valley. Back in their own places, with heads bowed low, hands and feet still, the faithful prayed themselves back to silence. When all was still the preacher lifted his hand in voiceless dismissal.

It was all there—poetry, music, dance—three muses come together in a deeply religious moment, each esthetically satisfying, each drawn from the Anglo-Saxon tradition, the riches of Europe and remembrances of what has been called "darkest Africa."

b) Spiritual

The transcription is only a rough approximation of the music, partly because the subtleties of rhythm and pitch are not easily expressed with standard Western staff notation, and partly because the quality of the original recording and the equipment used for transcription do not permit further refinement. The original pitch is one half-step lower (Db). Bar lines indicate the pattern of stress:

> A | máz   in' | gráce
> | It wás de Láwd |

There are four singers, a female soloist and a chorus consisting of two women and one man. The chorus provides the familiar chordal underlay of tonal music (tonic, dominant, subdominant) to the melody.

(Transcription and notes by Jessie Ann Owens)

a) Traditional

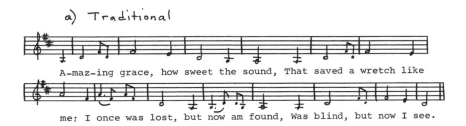

A–maz–ing grace, how sweet the sound, That saved a wretch like me; I once was lost, but now am found, Was blind, but now I see.

Urania

SCIENCE AND PSEUDOSCIENCE

DONALD A. COWAN

Science, History and the Evidence
of Things Not Seen

> "The activities of science are properly a game, because in it con-
> vention and chance divide the interest; phenomena are as may
> be, but the rules restrict their handling, no favors asked or
> given."
>
> JACQUES BARZUN, *Science: The Glorious Entertainment*

A few years back, a physicist in Rumania began an article with a
statement which illuminated, quite unintentionally, the entire discipline of physics. "One of the most remarkable facts in the field of weak
interaction physics," he wrote, "is the non-observation of bosonic
leptons."[1] The note was in *Physical Review Letters*, a little journal that
reports the latest scientific discoveries to an expectant, highly specialized audience almost on an emergency basis. To most people, no doubt,
a fact of non-observation would seem to be the stuff of which satire,
not science, is made. And, as it happened, the note appeared at the
same time that one of our most prominent cartoonists was depicting
a somewhat Aristophanic sequence: the people of his mythical kingdom were lining up for days to not-see the country's greatest treasure,
the "bashful blobolink," whose appearances were so brief as to be invisible, though no one doubted his existence. Satire, of course, has
many edges, and may at any moment slice through inadvertently to a
basic truth. It could indeed be true, as the cartoonist may or may not
have intended to imply, that a country's greatest treasure is something
that its people can not-see. It is, after all, the grace of office, not a
naked man, that resides inside the Emperor's clothes. And though the
modern physicist is frequently reproached for admitting to his ken
only entities whose existence can be demonstrated, he is not insensi-

---

1. Richard Wiener, "Bosonic Leptons," *Physical Review Letters*, 19 (March
1967), p. 376.

tive to the importance of the non-observation of the bosonic lepton.

A lepton is a light elementary particle which responds to the "weak force" (one of the four fundamental forces—the others being the gravitational, the electromagnetic and the "strong"). Muons, electrons and neutrinos are leptons which have been "observed"; but they are not bosons—they are fermions, that is, they obey the Fermi-Dirac statistics of the exclusion principle, according to which no more than one can occupy any given set of quantum numbers. Bosons obey Bose-Einstein statistics not limited by the exclusion principle. A photon is bosonic, but is not a lepton. The Rumanian physicist quoted earlier was saying that theory allows for the existence of a particle responding to the weak force which does not obey the exclusion principle, but that so far none has been observed.

The explanation does not greatly diminish the urge to satire. Before indulging it, however, we should remind ourselves that non-observation has a long and honored career among scientists. The most memorable of the events of non-observation was the "failure" of the Michelson-Morley experiment in 1887 to measure the drift of the earth through the ether. Actually, what was not observed was any change in the apparent velocity of light caused by the addition of the earth's motion to that of light in the ether. H. A. Lorentz suggested (1892) that the velocity actually did change but that the length of all measuring devices contracted in the direction of motion just sufficiently to obscure the change. Einstein took a simpler but more daring approach (1905) by *postulating* a uniform velocity of light for all observers, regardless of their states of motion.[2] The consequence of this egalitarian postulate was the special theory of relativity, according to which the length of a moving body does, indeed, contract in the direction of motion and time dilates as well; but the velocity of light stays the same. The fact that change was not observed was, to Einstein, evidence that change did not occur.

The null result of a crucial experiment is, of course, an important event, although its importance, indeed its cruciality, does not become fixed until some simplifying postulate changes the world view. History, in a sense, ordains the experiment—in truth, captures it as material for its own discipline. For a time the experiment exists in science as part of the logical structure leading to the postulate; but soon the positive results of the new manner of thought take over the task of authenticating its reality, and the experiment itself, no longer needed, falls away from the coherent and active body of knowledge

---

2. The account may be found in many places, including Ronald W. Clark, *Einstein, His Life and Times* (New York: World, 1971), pp. 77 ff.

that is science. The "special history" of science preserves the story of the experiment as a memorable anecdote for use in the psychology of innovation, or for whatever other purpose it might serve in the pursuit of other disciplines in the *speculum mentis.* But its original utility in the sciences is gone. For unlike most other disciplines, science is residual, not accretional, and this characteristic gives it a kind of primitive innocence.

The nomenclature of physics commemorates its saints—an Ampère of current, a Volt of potential difference, a Faraday of capacitance, a Coulomb of charge, Newton's laws, Maxwell's equations, Planck's constant—the litany is extensive. Such piety bespeaks a concern for the past and a desire for its conservation. But these marks of deference are more memorials than *memoria,* monuments to the past rather than its preservation. The reason for this anti-historical bent lies in the nature of scientific discovery: discoveries of science are generally not contained in an artifact. No critical return to an original text is likely to reveal a further truth, nor will it deepen the understanding of a principle, as it does, say, for a poem or a painting. Certainly a scientific model exists once the discovery is made; but it exists in a communal imagination, not in a single work of art. It is discovered, not revealed—even in ambiguity. The model, not the incident of its discovery, is open to exploration. Only the residue of discovery remains.

Fame of neither sort awaits the leptonic writing cited at the beginning of this paper. The non-observation of the bosonic lepton as reported in the scientific journal is not the outcome of a crucial experiment; it is, rather, an observation on the part of a theorist of a lack of expected findings in experimental data. The theorist goes on to comment that evidence such as he seeks may actually be present in experiments already performed, unnoticed by investigators. Such an oversight would not be unique in the annals of physics; the great physicist Enrico Fermi did not discover fission because he did not imagine it, though the evidence was before him. Awareness of the facts alone did not constitute "observation" of the phenomenon. What it is that sets the imagination going in a certain direction is not easily ascertained, but one of its progenitors is surely a *theme*—an activated postulate, a possible idea—in its local culture, local in the sense of a current community of like-minded scholars.

Gerald Holton speaks of the effect of thematic commitment on explanation, noting the way in which pertinent themes are subject to a prevailing style.[3] As an example, he points to the recurring reversals

---

3. Gerald Holton, "The Humanistic Basis of Scientific Work," *Change* 7: 6 (1975), p. 24.

in the causal relation of chaos and order. Kinetic theory (1860) explains pressure as the elastic bumping of molecules moving in random fashion against a surface—order out of chaos; but Einstein's account (1905) of the Brownian movement explains the seeming randomness of molecular motion as the result of a great number of quite predictable collisions—chaos out of order. The Uncertainty Principle (1927) again reverses the roles. Similarly, Holton points to the frequent reversals of commitment to a view of reality as either continuous or discrete, particles or waves being alternately in style. He has identified fifty such themes in the physical sciences and supposes that the total number is not much greater. In thus mapping out his field of explanation, Holton illustrates a physicist's preference in style for a theme of normal coordinates—if he is in the continuous mode—or a set of quantum numbers—if he is in the discrete. Even with so modest a set as fifty binary choices, Holton would have available some million billion variations, which one would suppose to be adequate.

Whether the style at any one time limits or frees the imagination is a matter of speculation. No age can anticipate a future epoch except the one it is busy preparing. Such ideas as atomicity and continuity may alternate in style from age to age, but even so, Democritus' atom, despite the verbal similarity, was not the progenitor of the current model. The concept had to arise out of contemporaneous material. The atom worked its way up from Dalton through chemistry, found a sort of confirmation in Maxwell's kinetic theory of gases, gained components through Thompson's electron and Rutherford's nucleus, was structuralized by Bohr's model, became sophisticated with wave mechanics, then spallated into elementary particles—all in about 150 years. An earlier age, one can speculate, could not have conceived of such a development, would not have accepted what we now take for experimental evidence as actual observation. The chain of evidence has indeed been indirect, sometimes remote. Even the most direct and irrefutable evidence seems somewhat nebulous: the track in a cloud chamber, for instance, which an observer or a camera sees as the reflection of light from droplets of moisture formed on ions remaining along a path supposedly followed by the electron or other charged particle. That evidence is fairly "hard," as data go. Uncharged particles leave no such track. The observation of uncharged particles, therefore, is of a more removed order: it is filling in unseen bits of data in agreement with conservation principles—the substance of things hoped for, the evidence of things not seen. The faith of a medieval scientist would not likely have been up to an act such as not-seeing elementary particles, any more than a modern investigator can not-see angels. The themes are different.

Angels have fled the imagination of men who find no utility in their presences. We can no longer turn a stone "and start a wing." There was a time, however, when an elaborate angelology gave rise to heated debate of theoretical questions.

The well-established nine choirs with their three hierarchies are in fact the product of angelologists, though the names of the choirs occur in Scripture and the arrangement is partly exegetical. Both Dante and Thomas Aquinas follow Dionysius, the Pseudo-Areopagite, in placing in the highest category the Seraphim, the Cherubim and the Thrones; in the second the Dominations, the Virtues and the Powers; and in the third the Principalities, the Archangels and the Angels— with man a little lower. Angelologists did not seem to carry out serious investigations of distinguishing characteristics of the various choirs; for example, the debate continues even now whether St. Michael the Archangel was not, in fact, a Seraph.

Do angels observe an exclusion principle? The number that can occupy the head of a pin[4] might lead one to think that angels, like photons, are bosons, observing no exclusion principle—as one might suspect from their identification with light. Of course, these particular angels might be only one class of angels—those of the host of angels which are indistinguishable from one another.

The tenet of angelic indistinguishability is not supported by authority: in the 1950 Encyclical *Humani Generis,* Pius XII chides theologians who cast doubt on the personhood of angels. Only three angels, however, are officially allowed names: Michael, Gabriel and Raphael. Other names which occur in apocryphal works and rabbinical literature—and were used by Milton—were rejected by Pope Zachary in 745 and again by a synod at Aix-la-Chapelle in 789.[5] Lacking names, the angels also lack individual characteristics that would cause an exchange of assignments among them to be noticed. It is in this sense that they are taken here to be indistinguishable.

Thomas reasoned that each angel was of a different species— that angels are as different from one another as cats are from dogs (Question 50, article 4). The Schoolmen accepted Thomas's authority on this matter. The argument was not persuasive to the Scotists, however, who continued to believe that all angels are of one species, nor

---

4. Modern Scholastics deny that such a question was a subject of medieval disputation. See James Collins, *The Thomistic Philosophy of the Angels* (Washington, D.C.: Catholic Univ. Press, 1947), p. x. However, see Thomas Aquinas, *Summa Theologica IX,* trans. Kenelm Foster (New York: Blackfriars, 1968), Question 52, art. 3, p. 53. Subsequent references to Thomas are from this volume.

5. See Pascal Parente, *The Angels* (St. Meinrad, Indiana: Grail Publications, 1958), p. 75.

to the followers of Suarez, who held several species to exist. Judging from the depiction of angels in works of art, one would suppose the popular belief favored the Scotist position.

Guardian angels are, likely enough, indistinguishable in a technical sense, but since they do have exclusive assignments in our parallel system they would have to be fermions. The special assignments of these angels, with a Scriptural basis in Daniel and a usefulness in lullabies, was generally accepted up to the Renaissance but came under question by some of the later angelologists, depending, as Holton might put it, on what theme each was following—the Protestant camp rather disliking the possibility of intervention between man and maker.[6] Milton's angels, one might recall, stayed in Heaven except for the two messengers to the Garden, Raphael and Michael.

The corporeality of angels, like that of neutrinos, was another matter not easily settled. The probability that they had mass seemed to overlap zero. In the end, the weight of the evidence, as for neutrinos, favored no mass.[7] In such a circumstance arose the question of how angels could be seen, as they were from time to time; it was suggested by Aquinas that the angels themselves could not be seen, but that they caused a condensation of clouds which reflected light in a shape that would have meaning for the observer (Question 51, article 2). Usually angels were not seen but were known by their effect on observable things.

Angels had their anti-particles in the fallen angels. A good conservation principle operating at the time of the separation of the good and the bad would have set up as many minuses as pluses, which would have made for sounder drama—the outcome of the battle in Heaven would have seemed to be in more doubt—but the opportunity was, apparently, overlooked; prevailing opinion held for about a third as many bad angels as good ones.[8] Neither does there seem to be any record of the two coming together to annihilate each other in a burst of glory as anti-particles should, although, with some shifting of suppositions, the concept might have had appeal.

It is difficult to be objective about the myth in which one lives. B. M. G. Reardon has commented:

> Myth appears as an organic function of the culture within which it
> occurs. . . . In the beginning myth is a mode of existence, an inte-

---

6. See Robert H. West, *Milton and the Angels* (Athens, Ga.: Univ. of Georgia Press, 1955), pp. 18–19. West credits Swedenborg with initiating the identification of angels as "separated souls."

7. Aquinas, *op. cit.*, p. 31n.

8. Parente, *op. cit.*, p. 51.

gration of thought, feeling, and action. It may acquire expression in words, but only as these are pointers to a concrete reality. For a myth is lived—and projected ritually—before ever it begins to be clearly thought about . . . [being] in its primary state . . . not so much the object of thought as its condition.[9]

The myth of fact so engulfs the present that reality itself often becomes obscured. Extensive and fanciful constructions are frequently put forth in speculative disciplines under the guise of fact and in the trappings of science. Jacques Barzun has warned the historian against this danger, particularly in the use of pseudo-facts imported from other disciplines.[10] José Ortega y Gasset, writing forty years before, says quite flatly, "By themselves, facts do not give us reality."[11]

These two sages have both concerned themselves with the relation of history to science and seemingly have reached quite opposite evaluations. Barzun concludes that science and history are totally other; "the substance of history, we know, is not amenable to measurement in the scientific sense. . . ." He identifies science with method: "in science the elements are clear, abstract, and unchangeable. . . . Because of this clarity and fixity, it is easy to use these concepts correctly once their strange artificiality has been firmly grasped; it is then but the application of a method." The elements of history, on the other hand, he indicates, elude definition and consequently no historical method can exist. "Obviously, the two modes of thought do not mix well; there are no natural transitions from the one to the other, the movement of the mind in each goes counter to the other" (p. 92).

Ortega, on the contrary, views physics as the norm of modern knowledge for all disciplines—history in particular. This opinion, diametrically opposed to Barzun's, arises from a difference of understanding about science and about history. Ortega sees science as sister to poetry because of its imaginative character:

> In order to discover reality we must for a moment lay aside the facts that surge about us, and remain alone with our minds. Then we construct an imaginary reality, a pure invention of our own; then, following in solitude the guidance of our own imagining, we find what aspect, what visible shapes, in short, what facts will produce that imaginary reality.

---

9. "Philosophy and Myth," *Theology*, LXV (April 1962), p. 135.
10. See Jacques Barzun, *Clio and the Doctors* (Chicago: Univ. of Chicago Press, 1974). Subsequent references to Barzun are from this volume.
11. José Ortega y Gasset, *Man and Crisis*, trans. Mildred Adams (New York: Norton, 1962), p. 13. Subsequent references to Ortega are from this volume.

It is then, Ortega says, that we compare the observed facts with our imagined ones, and if they "mate happily," we have discovered reality (p. 13).

This process of discovery, as described by Ortega, has been recounted frequently by scientists.[12] Often, when the imagination has given the correct shape to the concept, a snap of recognition occurs so that the scientist is quite certain what the data will tell him long before he sees them. There is a rightness about the concept, just as there is about a true line of poetry, which gives to its discoverer a certainty and a deep satisfaction. The role of facts prior to this act of the imagination is ambiguous; the facts indicate the problem, as Ortega noted, and set the imagination in motion, but the facts then retire from the scene; discovery is by no means a process of induction by method from facts.

Now this kind of science, which Ortega is describing, is the science of discovery and, as Thomas Kuhn points out, is quite different from normal science.[13] In his consideration of ordinary and extraordinary science, Kuhn first establishes a modern schoolman's outlook: "If science is the constellation of facts, theories, and methods collected in current texts, then scientists are the men who, successfully or not, have striven to contribute one or another element to that particular constellation" (p. 6). This picture of science supposes an "ever-growing stockpile" of scientific technique and knowledge which results from scientific development. What Kuhn calls normal science is somewhat more imaginative than this textbook science, but it partakes of the same methodical character. Discovery, on the other hand, violates the methods of its time; it is deeply intuitive, highly non-systematic. Because of the residual nature of science, the results of discovery—the revolutions in science, Kuhn calls them—sink finally into ordinary science and become part of method. It is this afterview of discovery sunk into normal science that Barzun is describing when he states, " . . . genius in science consists in adding to the stock of . . . defined entities and showing their place and meaning within the whole system of science and number" (p. 91). At any one time, this ordinary science appears to the outside observer complete and efficient. These characteristics tempt other disciplines to model themselves upon ordinary science, mistaking efficiency for genius. Barzun rejects the method of

---

12. See, for instance, Henri Poincaré, *Science and Method*, trans. Francis Maitland (New York: Dover, n.d.), p. 52.
13. See Thomas S. Kuhn, *The Structure of Scientific Revolutions* (Chicago: Univ. of Chicago Press, 1973).

this science for his model of the discipline of history. It is, of course, a different science from the one Ortega accepts as his model.

Ortega sees in physics a habit of the intuitive mind grasping phenomena and building an imaginary construction, then checking for conformity with reality at every observable point. It is this model of physics as a paradigm for other disciplines which he urges on historians. Other than in its identification with physics, Barzun has much the same model; associating history with intuitive thought, he declares that "genius in the realm of intuition consists in discovering pattern and significance in the uncontrollable confusion of life and embodying the discovery in intelligible form" (p. 92). The two views differ, certainly. Barzun does not suggest for the historian the *play* of the imagination which Ortega recognizes in the physicist. Indeed, this play might lead to the very danger of unwarranted assumptions and preposterous conclusions in the works of history against which Barzun inveighs. But the views are similar enough to be within the range of reconciliation.

Ortega is careful to point out that it is only in the habit of construction that he urges physics upon history; "The other characteristics of physics are not such as to be desirable for history" (p. 20). He views history as mission-oriented. "The primary and most elemental task of history is hermeneutic, which is to say interpretive," Ortega remarks (p. 17), and points out that interpretation occurs in the very selection of facts to be arranged. Barzun maintains that interpretation is optional, and some histories can do without it. His criteria for history—narrative, chronology, concreteness, memorability—would not seem to be in conflict with Ortega's views except on the third point, for here the hermeneutical mission and his theory of generations bring Ortega close to abstractions. "The investigation of human lives is not possible," he claims, "if the wide variety in these animals does not hide an identical basic structure" (p. 18). To put it in other terms, for Ortega persons in the same generation evince a common aspect which allows them to be viewed as indistinguishable particles. Barzun is not so much on the side of the angels as of the Greek gods; for him, every event, every person must maintain his individual character. It is up to other disciplines to abstract what they will from the careful delineation of history.

Barzun and Ortega agree that history must be grasped intuitively, that patterns must be perceived if one is to make sense of history. For Ortega, the pattern is imagined, put together theoretically, then checked against observation. Barzun seeks in the midst of events a pattern that meets his criteria for genuine history. The two methods may result in equivalent patterns—indeed, are likely to do so, since history accounts for events which have actually happened rather than predicting events which may or may not happen. But only if the patterns are *inevitably* equivalent, as are those of Schrödinger's equations and Heisenberg's matrices for quantum mechanics, can one say that the choice of approaches is at the disposal of the historian—a matter of style. The possibilities for variance, however, are manifestly evident. Therefore a decision of legitimacy regarding the two approaches is, in a sense, crucial.

The utility of unseen presences is one of the points on which the two approaches are likely to differ. All ages have invisible agencies which they accept on non-empirical evidence. Angels are as much historical entities as are elementary particles, and the historian has the duty to treat both in a manner free of cynical enlightenment. But the employment of non-observable elements by the historian himself is suspect in the discipline of history. Admittedly, Ortega is as quick as Barzun to reject psychological interpretations of history, yet his hermeneutical method calls for the completion of imagined patterns by some means—invention if necessary, in the manner of physics.

Perhaps there are instances when the historian may legitimately use the second level of observation—the completion of a pattern by a process of imagined data. But to use physics as a paradigm for history would require further abstraction: the observation of unseen presences not only at the second level but at a third as well. The familiarly observable leptons seem to be truly elementary, but the far more numerous hadrons—the generally heavier particles, including protons and neutrons, which obey the strong nuclear force and many of which are observable only on the second level—exhibit structure and therefore are themselves apparently made up of components. These components have only recently been christened "quarks," three of which seem to be necessary, each with a set of quantum numbers which, when assigned, account for the composition of all hadrons. However, in late 1974, two unexpected unseen hadrons were "observed," their existence requiring a fourth quark with a different set of quantum numbers, which, in the self-mocking patois of physicists at play, is said to have the property of *Charm*.[14] As investigations proceed, it is not impossible that the levels could multiply and the quantum numbers in-

---

14. See Sidney D. Drell, "Electron-positron Annihilation and the New Particles," *Scientific American*, 232 (June 1975), p. 50; and William D. Metz, "The New Particle Mystery: Solid Clues Now Lead to Charm," *Science*, 189 (August 8, 1975), p. 443.

crease until the possible variations outnumber the varieties on Holton's themes—indeed, justify the hypothesis of St. Thomas that each angel is a separate species.

Such constructions, in all their elaborateness, represent the appropriate operation of physics, whereas they do not seem to be legitimate for history. As intuitive and poetic as physics may be, it is not the right model for the discipline of history. The constructions of science are those which build a residual discipline. And history is, *par excellence*, accretional.

BANESH HOFFMANN

Magic, Science and Evaluation

> ". . . Bring me to the test,
> And I the matter will re-word . . ."
> *Hamlet,* Act III, scene iv.

~§

> Black is the color of my true love's hair.

So runs the opening verse of the ballad, and there is magic in it.

How do we know? There can be no rational answer. Somehow we just know. We sense the magic instinctively. And if, for some reason, we feel a need to be further persuaded, we can perform the simple maneuver of rearranging the words. Not so as to convert them into a meaningless jumble. That would be far too drastic to be persuasive. It is enough merely to place them in their natural prose order, like this:

> The color of my true love's hair is black.

At once we have an admirably straightforward declaratory sentence. But where now is the magic? Magically, it has vanished. A rapturous outburst has been turned into a dreary catalogue item—and this by a logical change of word order that we might well have expected to bring a significant improvement.

If all merit were as easy to recognize as the magic above, life would be simpler for those whose business it is to evaluate. Of the various types of evaluators, the professional critics have, for the most part, long recognized that their calling cannot be reduced to objectivity. True, they are sometimes unanimous—as we would expect them to be, for example, in sensing the magic and lack thereof above. In such special cases we might feel that the critics had transcended subjectivity and, by their unanimity, established the objective presence and absence of magic. Even so, they, and we too, are likely to feel overawed by the elusiveness of the crannies through which the magic comes and goes. And those who would reduce criticism to a set of rules must feel shaken, because even when the presence of magic is plain to all, its essence still lies mysteriously beyond the grasp of reason.

No universal prescription can be given for its creation. Schubert often snatched beauty from the air, setting it down without premeditation on whatever scrap of paper or table linen lay conveniently to hand. When shown Beethoven's work books he was horrified at the drudgery they revealed. For Beethoven would struggle painfully with a banal theme, somehow convinced that there was beauty to be found in it. Nudging it bit by bit, he would remold it a dozen times and more, its triteness apparently little diminished, until after a final, seemingly minor adjustment it blazed forth as a thing of beauty. Schubert and Beethoven, each in his own way, made magic; and who shall say that the one followed a better path than the other?

Just as there is no universal prescription for creating magic, so too is there none for detecting it. To recognize its presence we depend on an inconstant inner sense that, in most of us, is easily turned awry by novelty, prevailing opinion, our own ever-changing moods, and other obtruding influences too numerous to mention.

The field of evaluation is clearly a quagmire. Because of this, when an ego-aching critic pontificates we make allowances for the pressures under which he works and we readily realize that his utterance, no matter how learned, expresses a subjective, personal view. For even the most doctrinaire of critics does not go so far as to claim to have reduced the art of evaluation to an impersonal formula yielding precise numerical ratings that are scientific and objective.

There are other professional evaluators, however, who do make this sort of claim, and a look at their procedures can provide a valuable antidote to the temptation to succumb to the seemingly scientific aura with which they surround their work. Here is a case in point. It has to do with the evaluation of essays written by students. The evaluation of students' essays by teachers is notoriously unreliable. That different teachers have different standards hardly comes as a surprise —after all, so do different critics. But the problem goes deeper than that. For example, if a teacher evaluates an essay and a few days later evaluates it again, he can find himself giving it startlingly different grades.

Faced with this situation we would be inclined to bow to the inevitable while doing what little we could to increase the uniformity of grading standards. But psychometrists, those professional evaluators who seek to reduce evaluation to a science, have had other ideas: If grading essays causes problems, then stop giving essays on tests; or, alternatively, as was proposed a decade ago, give essays but dispense with the human graders and replace them by a computer. Who could fail to be impressed by the innocent simplicity of these solutions?

Can human essay graders really be replaced by a computer—satisfactorily? Here is the evidence adduced by the two researchers who devised the computer program. They pitted their computer against four experienced human graders, displayed statistical correlations of the five sets of grades, and showed that it was quite impossible to tell from the statistics which set of grades had come from the computer. This is an impressive result, and if we are susceptible to the blandishments of statistics we may well feel that it makes a convincing scientific case for the proposition that experienced essay graders can indeed be satisfactorily replaced by a computer—so far as grading essays is concerned.

Yet there are aspects of the computer grading of essays that should give us pause. For example, the computer gives essay grades on a scale from 0 to 5. This seems reasonable enough. But the evaluations are given to two decimal places, and this means that the computer actually yields essay grades representing some five hundred different gradations of merit. Given the subjectivity and unreliability of evaluation by human beings, are we mistaken if we regard such a degree of refinement as unrealistic?

There is more to tell. The computer is quite incapable of detecting magic, or even sense. The researchers therefore made an elaborate statistical study of several essays and the grades assigned to them by qualified human graders. From this they came up with a list of those essay attributes that correlated best with the grades while conforming to the limited capabilities of the computer. These attributes may surprise us, although they should not. The computer bases its essay grades solely on some thirty carefully weighted statistical criteria such as—I am not making this up—the length of the essay, the number of commas, the average word length and the standard deviation (a technical statistical measure of variability) of the lengths of its words.

The danger is clear. Imagine an essay pervaded by magic comparable to that of the verse of the ballad. Rearrange its words just enough to destroy its magic, making it comparable to the verse's prosaic counterpart. Also, prepare a third version by jumbling the words just enough to convert them into nonsense. Feed all three into the computer and they will receive identical essay grades.

The computer grading of essays ignores essentials. Yet, given the limitations of computers, the psychometrists who conceived the idea were able to create an extraordinarily successful computer program. This is clear from the striking correlation statistics that they obtained, which allowed them to claim in a statistically persuasive way that the computer was on a par with well-qualified human graders. As far as those statistics were concerned, this was true. And the moral is clear: even impressive statistics can be gravely misleading.

An analogy will underline the moral. Suppose I claim to have a pill that, if taken by someone not suffering from cancer, will ensure him immunity from cancer for the rest of his life. And suppose that by impeccable scientific procedures I compile statistics to show that the pill performs precisely as claimed in more than 99.965 percent of the cases. In view of such statistics, the conclusion will perhaps seem inescapable that the pill has great merit. Nevertheless, the statistics will be gravely misleading if the secret of the pill is that it contains a fast-acting lethal dose of cyanide.

So far as I know, the computer grading of essays has not caught on. Given the manifest limitations of such an approach to evaluation, we may regard this as only to be expected. But to do so would betray naïveté concerning what can go on in the field of education. For the idea of replacing human graders by a computer was proposed in all seriousness by responsible people—one of the two was actually a former Professor of English—and it created quite a flurry of interest. There were psychometrists who looked on it with favor, and organizations sufficiently impressed to give it financial support.

For the most part, the evaluation of ability in English composition remains, as it long has been, in the hands not of qualified essay graders but of psychometrists who favor the use of so-called objective instruments such as multiple-choice tests, which can deal only with peripheral aspects of the art of writing—and none too well even with those.

A major drawback of multiple-choice tests, whether intended as measures of ability in English composition or not, is that they are concerned only with choices, and not with the all-important reasons for those choices. It happens all too often that students pick wanted answers for incorrect reasons, and unwanted ones for reasons that are impeccable.

A related fact is that different students read different things into the same wording, and this too is ignored, even though variety of response to a given stimulus is well known. Detectives and trial lawyers, for example, have to struggle to extract an element of truth from the conflicting testimony of honest eyewitnesses. And, as every author of a widely reviewed book knows, each reviewer seems to have read a different version of it.

Again, in a major article on the legal aspects of the misuse of tests of personnel in industry, two distinguished professors of law, George Cooper of Columbia University and Richard B. Sobel of the University of Michigan, took exception[1] to specific items on a widely used test. Here is one of these items:

> 19. REFLECT   REFLEX—Do these words have
>   1   similar meanings   2   contradictory
>   3   mean neither same nor opposite?

It is a matter of elementary politeness—or is it?—to assume that the publisher of the test believes the items in it to be satisfactory. The publisher's presumptive satisfaction gives us one possible opinion —a wholly favorable one—of item 19. Here is a second opinion. It comes from Cooper and Sobel:

> The vocabulary questions call for an appreciation of subtle differences in word meanings and parts of speech. Question 19 is particularly obscure, but fairly indicates something of the level of difficulty of the examination. "Reflect," a verb ("to bend or throw back" says Webster) and "reflex," as an adjective ("turned, bent or reflected back" says Webster) have similar meanings in one sense. But in the sense that it is inaccurate to equate meanings of different parts of speech, they mean "neither same nor opposite."[2]

Their point is well taken, and we may think they have left nothing further to be said. Let us venture a third opinion even so. As professors of law, Cooper and Sobel use words with precision. We see them doing so in their criticism. Yet, like eyewitnesses, book reviewers and indeed all of us, they have been unconsciously selective in what they saw. The test item is in fact atrociously worded. For example, note the misfit of choice 3 and the stem. Here is what they ask when joined together: ". . . Do these words have mean neither same nor opposite?"

What of choice 2? Here is how it reads when joined to the stem: ". . . Do these words have contradictory"—without even a question mark.

Perhaps the test taker is expected to make allowances for the test maker's sloppy workmanship and guess from the question as a

---

1. "Seniority and Testing under Fair Employment Laws: A General Approach to Objective Criteria of Hiring and Promotion," *Harvard Law Review*, Vol. 82, No. 8 (June 1969), pp. 1598–1679. See pp. 1642–3.

2. *Ibid.*

whole the intended meaning of each of its parts. This is a distressing principle. There is enough ambiguity in multiple-choice tests without our expecting test takers to ignore the plain meaning of words. In the present case, the principle calls for drastic rewording. For example, in the case of choice 3 we cannot simply make a good fit by omitting the "have" from the stem like this: "REFLECT REFLEX—Do these words mean neither same nor opposite?" For, *if we accept this wording for what it actually says*, might we not find ourselves accepting choice 3 on the presumably unintended ground that neither REFLECT nor REFLEX means SAME or OPPOSITE? Alternatively, we might find ourselves rejecting choice 3 on the presumably equally unintended ground that neither REFLECT nor REFLEX means something neutral that is implied by the phrase "neither same nor opposite."

We have now discussed three views of item 19. They surely do not exhaust the issue. Yet no account is taken of all the different possible views when the response to the question—the mere choice of an answer—is graded. The narrow scope of the multiple-choice format is deliberate. By ignoring essentials and concentrating solely on what can be graded by machine, psychometrists neatly sidestep the problems that arise when human beings grade less coercive examinations. With their machine-graded tests, the psychometrists achieve what they call objectivity—the elimination of dispute and uncertainty in the assignment of scores. This does not mean that the assignment of scores is sensible or truly fair. It is fair only in the trivial and misleading sense that all people choosing a particular answer, no matter how profound or stupid their reasons, will receive identical scores for the question. And one is hard put to find a worthwhile sense in which the sacrifice of so much for the sake of this meager sort of objectivity can be regarded as sensible.

The attainment of this objectivity is a major element in the psychometrists' claim to be evaluating scientifically; and against this posture of precision, the critics of arts and letters must seem like wild, undisciplined romantics. The psychometrists extract from their machine-graded tests voluminous statistics on both individual questions and tests as a whole. These statistics are insensitive to the penalizing of thoughtful students and totally blind to the squelching of creativity and other baleful effects of machine-graded tests on education in general. Yet the psychometrists rely heavily on the statistics to guide them in the construction of further questions and further tests—so heavily that they seem to be not the masters but the slaves of their statistics.

These statistics can cast an almost irresistible spell. Many educational leaders succumb to them with little sign of struggle. But would we be wise to let the statistics dominate us as they dominate the psychometrists and their friends? Surely experience has taught us that numbers, often purely because they are numbers, can possess a hypnotic magic.

We have already prepared a counter to this magic of what is numerical. Recall the statistics adduced in favor of the computer grading of essays, and their hypothetical counterpart in favor of the anti-cancer pill. Did we not feel that, despite their patina of science, the statistics were seriously misleading? Why, then, should we rush to accept as cogent the statistics adduced in favor of multiple-choice tests?

There is magic, of course, in even a patina of science. But using the tools and techniques of science does not necessarily make one a scientist. Let us hold back from declaring psychometrists non-scientists. If we so declare them because their statistics ignore intangibles that they cannot reduce to numbers, we show a misunderstanding of the nature of science. For scientists achieve spectacular successes by similarly ignoring whatever transcends the limitations of their procedures. Because of these limitations, science gives only a one-sided insight into what is. Much of science is plodding, but that is not its nature. Nor is science a precise, cold-blooded exercise in logic. On the contrary, in its essence, and at its most profound, it is one of the creative arts, practiced with awe and passion by people seeking in the universe a special poetic magic. And finding it too—but finding it, strangely enough, by ignoring particulars.

The ancient Greeks, for example, spoke of the perfection of the heavens, which they thought of as made up of an unearthly quintessence or ether exquisitely appropriate to its perfection. They thought the stars lay fixed on a crystal sphere that rotated majestically once a day about the imperfect earth. But they were illogical—or let us say, rather, that they closed their minds to what they could not help seeing. For to the eye, the stars seem to have been strewn haphazardly on the celestial sphere, marring its spherical perfection—though apparently not marring in the eyes of the ancients the pervasive perfection they ascribed to the heavens.

We have learned much since the days of the Greeks. Scientists have found general laws of cosmic scope and staggering beauty. But before these laws can be applied, they must be supplemented by special data that describe the particular situation; and often these data lack beauty. For example, there is a magic simplicity in Newton's law of gravitation, which says that every particle of matter attracts every other particle of matter *throughout the universe* with a force that is specified by a simple, universal rule. But if we want to apply it to the solar system, we must supplement this magic by a catalogue of such things as the masses and present positions and motions of the various planets. And although there is ample cause for wonder in the existence of these planets—as there is in the very existence of the universe—the catalogue notably lacks the beauty of the universal law.

This situation is typical. The world as viewed by the present-day scientist has a sort of schizophrenia: singularly beautiful general laws tied to special data that bespeak a seeming wantonness in what is particular. In a sense we face the same sort of problem as that confronting the Greeks: If the ultimate laws of nature have inner beauty and symmetry, how does it happen that the stars are not evenly distributed in space—that the universe seems untidy?

As for the general laws, do not think that because they are scientific they are "true" or final. Scientific theories come and go. Einstein repeatedly spoke of them as "free creations of the human mind." Of course, one expects a good theory to agree with experiment; but agreement is easily achieved if the theory has enough adjustable parameters, and when agreement is achieved at the expense of elegance and an inner economy of means, it usually carries little weight.

What about conflict with experiment, then? That, too, is by no means as important as one might expect. For example, when a new theory is in the process of superseding an old, there is often an initial period when the old can account for experimental effects that the new cannot. Besides, no theory accounts for everything.

What about internal consistency? Again, it is less important than we might think. Bohr's epoch-making theory of the atom was a manifestly self-contradictory jumble of new ideas and old.

What, then, is science? As we have seen, the usual pat answers do not hold up well. Indeed, great science seems more like an exercise in aesthetics than in what we usually think of as science. In evaluating a scientific theory the scientist has to balance facts against intangibles, numerical experimental confirmation against aesthetic feel. As the famous physicist Paul Dirac put it: "A theory with mathematical beauty is more likely to be correct than an ugly one that fits some experimental data."[3] His own celebrated relativistic equations for the electron are among the most beautiful in all physics. In judging a theory, Einstein would ask himself whether, if he were God, he

---

3. P. A. M. Dirac, "Can Equations of Motion Be Used in High-Energy Physics?" *Physics Today*, Vol. 23, No. 4 (April 1970), pp. 29–32.

would have made the universe in that way. And he rejected many theories that seemed to him unworthy of God. But he also had standards that were less exacting: on coming upon Louis de Broglie's revolutionary idea that particles of matter (for example, electrons) are accompanied by guiding waves, Einstein immediately sensed its profound importance and urged physicists to take it seriously even though, as he said, it looked crazy. And Niels Bohr, discussing an idea put forward by an outstanding scientist, gently expressed his disfavor by saying he thought the idea crazy but wondered whether it was sufficiently crazy to be true.

What, then, of our question "What is science?" The best definitions of science are those that beg the question. The standard multistep specification of "the scientific method" conforms little to what scientists actually do. Even this statement begs the question. For, what is a scientist? And if the work done by a particular "scientist" is easily faulted, shall we for the purposes of our definition still count him as a scientist—albeit a bad one? Or should we cast him forth with the brand of a charlatan?

Let us not become entangled further in this maze of semantics. Let us not ask whether psychometrists are scientists. The crucial question is not one of nomenclature. Rather, it is the extent to which their actions and conclusions are worthy of approval. And this, like all worthwhile questions of evaluation, involves taste and a respect for intangibles. It cannot be answered by the methods of the psychometrists.

CODA

We can give a particularly strong impression of being "scientific" if we are willing to go beyond where even the psychometrists have ventured. Here, for example, is a modest proposal that emerged swiftly one sunny day in the course of a pleasant stroll with a colleague, Richard Emery, who must bear half of the responsibility. It relates to the method of programmed learning, in which, as is well known, the topic to be studied is broken into minuscule bits. Test questions are given after the presentation of each morsel and the student is immediately rewarded when he responds in the wanted way. His reward is of a somewhat sophisticated sort: the knowledge that his response was the wanted one, and the consequent permission to go on to study the next morsel of subject matter.

The initial laboratory experiments on which the idea of programmed learning is based were not done on free human beings but on captive, non-human creatures; and the rewards, far from being sophisticated, were definitely down to earth: morsels of food.

It occurred to Emery and me that in programmed learning one would achieve a more seemly semblance of science by staying close to the laboratory situation. We proposed, therefore, that the students be kept locked in cages, and that they be rewarded for wanted responses by being given morsels of food. It then dawned on us that there was an unexpected advantage in staying thus close to the laboratory situation: the problem of assigning course grades was automatically solved. One simply weighed each student before and after.

What could be more objective What more scientific? As I said, it was a pleasant stroll that sunny day. The only qualms I have about telling of our project arise from the fear that a foundation may take it seriously.

Jacques Barzun
at Columbia

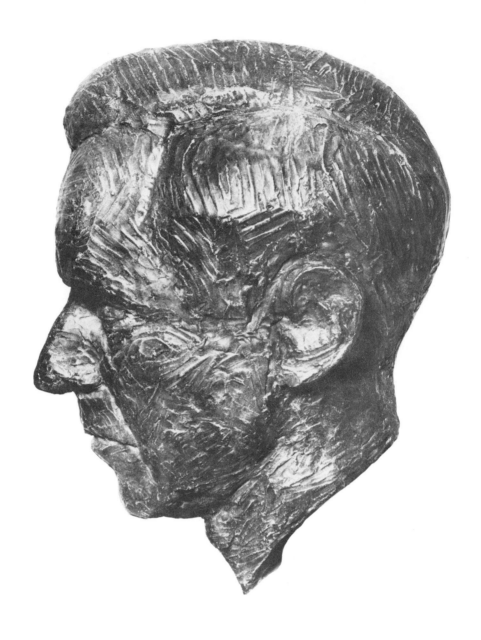

JACQUES BARZUN, 1958

Bronze sculpture by Vera Kuffner Eberstadt

KENNETH B. CLARK

The Impact of a Personality

> ". . . we may say that educational nonsense consists in proposing or promoting something else than the prime object of the school, which is the removal of ignorance.
>
> "These are the signs of a turning point in civilization. The high Renaissance ideas on which we have lived for 500 years have lost their power, and we drift. We shall do so until the collective mind is emptied of dogmas and slogans and turns once again to the actualities of teaching and the plain limits of schooling. Then, some of the principles found in the perennial philosophy of the old reformers will regain their place of honor, after being restated by some crusading genius and being hailed as great new discoveries."
>
> JACQUES BARZUN, "Where the Educational Nonsense Comes From," *Papers on Educational Reform*, Volume II, pp 1–13.

The name Jacques Barzun first came to my attention in the late 1930s when I was a graduate student in psychology at Columbia University. For me, Jacques Barzun was part of that mosaic of Columbia names which included Lionel Trilling, Selig Hecht, Franz Boas, Ruth Benedict and Otto Kleinberg among a few others—names that stood for scholarship, and the highest standards of academic excellence, and had about them an aura of severity. Oddly enough, the name Nicholas Murray Butler was not a part of this vague pattern which dominated my image of intellectual Columbia: I saw that name as merely a symbol of perennial and remote university power. Jacques Barzun, on the other hand, was part of that to me foreboding shadow of standards which any aspiring Columbia graduate student had to reckon with because, according to my fantasy, it would somehow determine one's success or failure in obtaining a Ph.D. in Psychology, or any other subject, at Columbia University.

When confronted with this peculiar phenomenon of a name which projects qualities and characteristics of its own, one tends to respond in rather complex and ambivalent ways. Among the ingredients of this pattern of response is a fear, barely conscious, of ever meeting the person behind the name lest the name and its intrinsic qualities be in any way spoiled by the actuality of the person. This is particularly true when the qualities of the name are dominated by positives. At times this anxiety can be so intense as to lead to a reluctance even to read the articles and the books published under the formidable name. Conversely, the name sometimes has such a powerful gravitational force that you are pulled toward the writings. You find yourself seeking them out, reading them and evaluating them to see whether they confirm or refute your *a priori* assumptions about the author. Sometimes the reading results in a more or less drastic reevaluation of the image suggested by the name alone.

At this point, relating the name to the writings generally ceases because there is rarely the opportunity to get to know the author as a person with whom one can actually interact. For the most part one continues to read the articles of the name, agrees with them or argues with them, or writes notes about them, either in the margin or on fragments of paper. If one is strongly moved by a particular book or article one might be stimulated to write an article in support or in refutation. But even this degree of interaction with the name and his written works remains impersonal, although it can be intensely intellectual.

The final step in the process of responding to a name is in actually meeting the person. For me, this step invariably is associated with some degree of awkwardness, particularly when the name and the writings of the person are admired and respected. When I actually meet a writer whom I respect, I am anxious that I not betray an adolescent form of hero-worship. For some set of complex reasons, I feel the need to try to communicate to the person the extent of my admiration and respect without fawning and with a minimum of words. This was my predicament when I first met Jacques Barzun.

I am not clear about the actual situation in which I had the opportunity to associate the name and the writings with the person, Jacques Barzun. It might have been at a seminar or symposium sponsored by the Council on Basic Education or one of the activities of Phi Beta Kappa or, more probably, my first meeting as a member of the editorial board of *The American Scholar*. I am only sure that it was not in the context of Columbia University. While I was a student at Columbia and in my early post-student associations there, Jacques

Barzun remained only a name and a compelling writer with whom I more often than not agreed. My uncertain memory as to where I met him is made even more confusing by the possibility that I met Jacques Barzun at the same time that I first met Hiram Hayden. Hiram was another name I had admired and respected, and Jacques and Hiram reinforced each other quite positively in my mind. Thus I did not meet Jacques Barzun, the person, pure, and what follows is influenced by the vagueness and uncertainty of the circumstances.

Jacques Barzun, the person, fitted all too perfectly with Jacques Barzun, the name and the writer. He looked like his name. He personified prestige, authority and self-confidence. The severity of his standards and his unapologetic insistence upon excellence in academic pursuits dominated all aspects of his person. As I got to know him better, these qualities occasionally seemed associated with a quiet, unstated form of self-assurance. I am fascinated by the fact that the positive aura and admiration which I associated with his name and his writings were strongly influencing my evaluation of and response to the person. Probably because of this I felt that it was important for me to try to be as objective as possible in my understanding of my admiration for Jacques Barzun, the person. In some unclear way this seemed essential for my understanding of important aspects of myself, and my association with Jacques Barzun became an ongoing introspective exercise for me.

Without question, I shared his values concerning the importance of solid standards and high quality basic education in elementary, secondary, collegiate and graduate education. I shared his opinion concerning the importance of a rational, intellectual approach to human problems as providing the substance for humanity and civilization. I respected his regard for the English language and I identified totally with his intolerance of intellectual laziness. But these areas of like-mindedness were certainly not enough to account for the depth of my admiration for Jacques Barzun. As our association developed and continued, it was plain that it was based not on an increasing and expressed closeness of personal friendship, but rather, from my viewpoint, on a complex admiration of the total quality of intellectual courage and academic excellence which he personified. But even this did not seem to be enough.

It was not until I received in the mail a short book on race with a very simple and short note from the author, Jacques Barzun, that I realized what there was about him that held my attention. I had not known, although I should have, that he had written on this important and complex human and American problem. The book was simple and direct, and discussed the problem of race and racial prejudice in terms of the need to free human beings from the shackles of ignorance and superstition.

Although in candor, which he would respect, I could not state that Jacques Barzun's book on race is one of the classics which have been written on this problem, what his book did for me was to help me understand a number of other things about Jacques Barzun, the person. Here was a man who was so concerned with the positive potentials of human beings that he had no patience with the variety of excuses which interfered with the stimulation and development of these potentials. I now understand why my personal relations with Jacques Barzun never seemed flawed by the fact that he was white and I was not. He always seemed to respond to the nature and the quality of the ideas of others rather than to superficial irrelevances.

I understood that Jacques Barzun, the person, with whom I interacted on the Council on Basic Education and in Phi Beta Kappa and on the editorial board of *The American Scholar*, reminded me of some of my best teachers in elementary and high school and in college and graduate school. These teachers had held me to exactly the same standards they held for others. Like them, Jacques Barzun was in no way condescending. If one believes that an individual with high standards of excellence who respects solid creativity and thought is an elitist, then Jacques Barzun and some of my best teachers are elitists. From my perspective, they are democratic elitists. They did not contaminate their elitism with the idiocy that intelligence, creativity and sensitivity are in any way determined by the color of one's skin or one's economic status. They related to their fellow human beings on the basis of the fact that excellence can come in the package of a white or black skin; that whites and blacks can be mediocre and —the ultimate test of liberation from the subtle forms of American racial condescension—that there can be white and black idiots.

Excellence, sensitivity and creativity are rare commodities which should not only be respected but must be identified, encouraged and conserved without apology. My admiration of Jacques Barzun was based upon the fact that he had passed my most severe test of a truly liberated, civilized human being. The more I came to know him, to interact with him, to listen to him and, occasionally, to argue with him, the more I became aware of the fact that my fantasy in the late 1930s and early 1940s about the name Jacques Barzun and the realities of the person were compatible.

Characteristically, in his note explaining the gift of his book on race, Jacques stated that it was not necessary for me to respond. I did not respond in writing but resorted to a studied casual expression of thanks the next time I saw him. He replied with appropriate casualness. This brief interchange somehow characterized the quality of my relationship with Jacques Barzun, the person.

This essay is my written expression of appreciation for Jacques Barzun, the defender of standards of excellence, the person who believes in the power of trained and disciplined intelligence as a foundation for social justice and for a genuinely civilized society.

COURTNEY C. BROWN

The Scholar as Administrator

> "Give five thousand talented people diversified responsibilities under a minimum of hierarchy, yet with intersecting orbits, and their duties and their talents alike will produce daily innovation and impatience, rash promises and unruly acts, resistance to system and forgetfulness of forms. (p. 13) . . . Good administrators are frequently accused of wanting to keep everything tidy. The charge is correct, and so are the administrators. That is what they are there for—to contain natural chaos." (p. 98)
> JACQUES BARZUN, *The American University**

It was in the middle of the third decade of this century that Jacques Barzun began his long career at Columbia University. Like other educational institutions of the time, the Columbia of 1923 that he came to as an undergraduate was a relatively quiet and unworldly place. It had prospered in its intellectual and physical development, but the material rewards of a career on its faculty were modest—the compensations for Columbia professors were of a different sort altogether. And one's colleagues were kindly souls, committed to teaching and scholarly effort. In this atmosphere, which minimized pretension and exalted integrity, the recent graduate of Columbia College—soon to become the brilliant young lecturer—must have felt in 1927 that he had arrived on the heights of Parnassus, if not Olympus.

During the succeeding half-century, much happened on the Morningside campus, some of which shaped Barzun's career, but much of which was shaped by him. Some of the events at Columbia that Barzun became involved with could hardly be rendered in prose from Parnas-

---

*Unless otherwise noted, the quotations in this essay are from Jacques Barzun's own account of his career at Columbia, *The American University: How It Runs, Where It Is Going* (New York, Harper & Row, 1968).

sus, inspired by one of the Muses. Indeed, a part of the story seems more to have been composed under the influence of Pluto in the environs of Hades. Yet even a brief account of the ideas he contributed, the decisions he made, and the actions he took at Columbia reveal Barzun to have been a uniquely constructive, loyal, and persistent influence on Alma Mater. Despite his constitutional preference for teaching and scholarship on the agreeable heights of Parnassus, he was willing to spend extended periods as a hardworking and effective administrative officer of the university, sometimes on Olympus and sometimes in Hades.

Barzun had been a member of the faculty as a lecturer and instructor for a decade when I first had the opportunity to know him in 1937. He had just been named an assistant professor—teaching careers developed more slowly in those days. Although we were about the same age, he seemed a giant to this newly appointed instructor. Indeed, the corridors of Hamilton Hall were filled at that time with bright young men, many of whom were destined for great success both within and without the university: men such as Harry Schwartz, Walt Rostow, Henry Graff, Louis Hacker, and others. But none were more luminous then or in subsequent years than Jacques Barzun. At that time we knew nothing of his administrative talents, but we were already convinced that he communed regularly with all the Muses, so wide and so lively were his cultural and intellectual concerns.

Most scholars enter the portals of academic administration through their interest in curriculum, and such was the case with Barzun. In 1944 Provost Frank D. Fackenthal, observing Barzun's effectiveness as acting chairman of the Columbia College Committee on Instruction, appointed him a special representative of the university administration for curriculum study. Nor did the prize of a professorship in 1945 protect him from further administrative assignments; the following year he was named the secretary of the Committee on Plans for Columbia College, which produced under his guidance and authorship (with H. R. Steeves) *A College Program in Action.* The Columbia University Press published this volume and then induced Barzun to become a member of its publications committee and to edit several works, including the *Records of Civilization Series, The Bicentennial Editions and Studies* (12 volumes), and the *Bicentennial History of the Faculty of Political Science.*

Following these activities, what could have been more appropriate than Barzun's designation in 1951 as Secretary of the Faculty of Political Science and in 1952 as Chairman of the university committee for the Columbia University Bicentennial Celebration? The pace of his life was further accelerated by two off-campus activities: he was consultant on cultural history to *Life* magazine and a member of the Ford Foundation's Graduate Meetings Concerning the Ph.D. The pattern of his future and, indeed, the future of university life on Morningside Heights was beginning to become apparent.

For most members of academic faculties, a life of perceptive scholarship terminates with the acceptance of an important administrative assignment. It is an unusual man or woman who can simultaneously be both scholar and administrator with distinction. As evidenced by his record of publications and by the observations of those who have contributed to this book, there was no sign of a diminution in Barzun's scholarly contributions after he was induced, in 1955, to plunge deeply into administrative life and serve as the Dean of Columbia's Graduate Faculties. Nor was the frequently observed phenomenon of a good teacher making a poor administrator repeated. Barzun's was a remarkable record of success in all he undertook.

The year 1955 was a propitious one in which to start an administrative assignment. Columbia had just emerged from the celebration of its bicentennial. Professor Arthur McMahan had been named the chairman of a small committee to study the future of the university and to recommend in specific terms what should be done to shape its development. Among the proposals, which were accepted after the committee reported in 1957, was the creation of a new post, Dean of the Faculties and Provost of the University, to oversee the university's entire academic program. Barzun was the logical—one might say the inevitable—recipient, in 1958, of the post. His task was to balance academic programs within the framework of the report's conception of the university's goals, guiding the faculties of the undergraduate schools, the professional graduate schools, and the graduate faculties of the arts and sciences. All of his enormous intellectual resources were called into play as he worked with the sixteen deans of the various schools of the university, the directors of the many institutes and centers, and the approximately forty department chairmen—each of whom had a fully developed capacity for representing with determination and vigor the interests of his or her particular constituency.

Barzun's work in this role was diverse and unending. His travels to represent the university at alumni functions throughout the nation were frequent and exhausting. Numerous students and their organizations felt no restraint about appropriating his time. To clarify and codify student and faculty rules and procedures he compiled the *Graduate Student Guide* and the *Faculty Handbook of Columbia University*. It must have required extraordinary self-discipline and patience for a mind attracted by intellectual matters to concentrate on the mundane details of academic procedure. His additional appointment as special assistant on the arts to the president of Columbia, however, could not fail to have been a source of considerable delight and a welcome relief from the chores of day-to-day administration.

Despite the fact that, for him, teaching was a demanding and exhausting activity, Barzun continued to teach throughout the long period of heavy administrative responsibilities. In 1960, he was named Seth Low Professor of History at Columbia, and in 1961 he received an appointment as Extraordinary Fellow at Churchill College, Cambridge University. Both appointments were concurrent with his administrative duties at Columbia.

Sophistry is not unknown on academic campuses, and Barzun has ever been a skillful foe of the fraudulent. His disdain for the disingenuous was no doubt affirmed and refined in his long association with Lionel Trilling. Both recognized, to use Trilling's phrase, the "necessity of conscious self-definition and self-criticism, of the need to make private judgments of reality."[1] A champion of research as the enriching source of new knowledge, Barzun nevertheless sees most doctoral dissertations for what they are: "exercises in fact-gathering rather than contributions to knowledge."[2] He deplores the fact that an interest in good teaching has become secondary to research and publication in the development of a professional academic career. His personal commitment to research and publication has always been strong, as is evidenced by the proliferation of his widely read books, but teaching, he believes, is equally central to the scholar's work.

In the 1950s and 1960s, students became aware that teaching was no longer the main concern of the university or of its faculty. Barzun charitably attributed this more to cultural change than to any lassitude on the part of the faculties. "Students come last, not by selfish choice, not on any theory, but simply because everything else is a group activity. . . . In other words, the flight from teaching is a fact but, apart from the singular laziness or escapism of a few, it is a cultural fact. To put it in still another way, the new university is the product of a new society and the flight is the by-product."[3] The new university is staffed by faculty members "in transit" who are fluid both in their physical movements and in their academic affiliations, professors whose loyalties are more to their disciplines and others in their field than to any one institution of higher learning. The availability of large

---

1. Lionel Trilling, "Emma and the Legend of Jane Austen" in *Beyond Culture* (New York: Viking Press, 1965).
2. P. 93.
3. P. 54.

research grants from government agencies, foundations, and corpora-
tions, which serve as an alternative employer for university faculty
members, has also diverted them from their traditional role of teaching.

"Teaching . . . is extremely hard work; it is the original and literal
brain-drain, being the continual readjustment of one's thought to another's, not to placate or even to persuade, but to strengthen and enlarge and make more complex."[4] Not for Barzun the prevalent notion
that the teacher and the taught are "both students, exploring together,
each learning from the other."[5] The task of the teacher is to help the
student achieve control of his own mental powers so that they become
flexible and strong. ". . . [N]obody can 'broaden somebody else's horizons'; the somebody else himself doesn't broaden them—*they broaden*,
perhaps after the learner has learned something which can be taught
and which fits itself into his whole previous mental organization."[6]

An educated mind is one that has acquired the ability to think
comprehensively about complex matters and to talk and write co-
herently about them. Barzun was convinced that most students have
an inner power to fashion their own values, built out of their observation of details but not enslaved to precision, and the courage to depart,
not on principle but with judgment, from conventional opinion. To
him, "education in the strict sense, [is] the cultivation and tempering
of the mind. . . ."[7] There can, then, be no higher calling than teaching.

How Columbia induced Jacques Barzun to surrender so large a
part of his time and energies to its administrative chores, to leave the
agreeable delights of Parnassus for the frequently rough journeys between Olympus and Hades, will always be a mystery. For the administrator's "occupational disease is the bends, or caisson disease, which
comes from violent changes of pressure."[8] The explanation in his own
words provides a measure of the man: ". . . the reasons that moved a
thereupto blameless member of the institution . . . to give up for a
time his chosen work and submit to a sentence of hard labor—the long
hours and grueling conditions of the executive life, coupled as it is
with overt pity and envious disdain of one's colleagues. The decisive
reasons in my case were my long attachment to the university."[9]

A mere recitation of Barzun's assignments and achievements fails

---

4. P. 242.
5. P. 90.
6. P. 223.
7. P. 220.
8. P. 167.
9. P. 8.

to reveal the painful adjustments and frustrations that accompanied the emergence of present-day Columbia University. When he took his first administrative assignment, in the mid-1940s, the university had a long tradition of centralized control. President Nicholas Murray Butler and a few of his immediate associates had made all of the significant institutional decisions and had kept the place nourished. An interregnum of perhaps two decades followed the time of Butler's lessening capabilities and the issuance of the McMahan report. During this period, Dwight D. Eisenhower was president for a while, but unfortunately spent too brief a time on Morningside Heights to achieve meaningful change. Thus the university was ready for—indeed, in need of—substantial restructuring to prepare for anticipated growth when Barzun became Dean of the Graduate Faculties in 1955.

The magnitude of the change that occurred is measured in one way by noting the increase in Columbia's annual budget from $20 million in 1953–54 to the $200 million planned for 1976. The quality of the change is evident in the growth of the peripatetic habits of the professoriate and the opportunities it has acquired for work off the campus; in student insistence on participation in university governance; in the inflation of the grading scales; and in the proliferation and diversification of activities on the campus. "The suspicion grows that diversity, generally deemed a sign of corporate strength, has for *this* institution become a means of escaping responsibilities, a means which all alike employ—students, faculties, and administration."[10]

It was realized at the outset that growth would require a redistribution of decision-making throughout the university, but few anticipated the rapidity and extent of the expansion. It was necessary to review almost continuously the structural shape as well as the physical dimensions of the university concurrently with the conduct of its daily life. Barzun's was one of the talents that helped to hold things together and to give at least partial denial to Robert Hutchins' notion that "The multiversity does not appear to be a viable institution. There is nothing to hold it together, and something that is not held together is likely to fall apart."[11]

The administration of educational institutions is divisible into two kinds of activities: institutional administration and academic administration. At Columbia, institutional administration—the housekeeping and financing of the university—was for the most part handled by others besides Barzun, although as a member of the ad-

---

10. P. 242.
11. P. 240.

visory group that met regularly with President Kirk, he was exposed to many purely business matters. It was the administration of the university's academic program that occupied his full attention: procedures for the appointment of faculty members and decisions about programs, tenure arrangements and promotions, fellowships, research activities, faculty salaries and budget procedures, committee assignments, sabbaticals and visitations; in other words, all of the variety of activities involved in the intellectual life of a great university.

Academic administration can be, and frequently is, great fun, but in a period of rapidly changing circumstances and values it can also be baffling; " . . . the essence of university administration defies analysis; it is a branch of the black art."[12] The resources available— space, equipment, time and money—are never adequate to satisfy all of the legitimate claimants. Moreover, faculties quite properly exercise the major influence on the structure of the academic program, a program that must nevertheless be accommodated to the finances that are available. Effective academic administration relies on the art of persuasion—not on authoritative control; there is, after all, in many faculty members a desire for administrative authority, accompanied by a great readiness to shed responsibility when it is acquired. The intangibles of personality and the equivalent of patronage must be supplemented by the marshaling and presentation of facts if a reasonably balanced program is to be achieved. Barzun lived with these subtle pressures over many years and was still able to retain the objectivity of the scholar.

Fortunately, Barzun was spared the punishment experienced by all Columbia administrators during the student occupations and "bust" in 1968. He had received the university's highest academic honor in 1967 with his appointment as a university professor, at which time he surrendered his administrative responsibilities. He retained his ample office in Low Library, however, and it may have been more than coincidence that this was the only space that remained available to the central administration during the occupation of that building by students, professional radicals, and other assorted adventurers from the sidewalks of New York City.

Academe is indeed a wonderful and complex world, and its rewards as well as its penalties are uniquely its own. No one knows this so well as Jacques Barzun, whose career at Columbia spanned fifty-two years, first as a student, then as a teacher and scholar, and finally as an academic administrator who surrendered neither his

---

12. P. 114.

scholarship nor his teaching. Many have shared in the construction of the great university on Morningside Heights in the more than two centuries of Columbia's existence, but none with more distinction than Barzun. The university community has been the grateful beneficiary of his sense of commitment, so rare on the contemporary academic campus. Columbia could never have been so stimulating and agreeable a place without him.

Bibliography

VIRGINIA XANTHOS FAGGI

Bibliography: The Writings of Jacques Barzun

"A man who writes, as Hardy said, stands up to be shot at, but Hardy was wrong to resent the shooting."
JACQUES BARZUN, "Calamophobia, or Hints Towards a Writer's Discipline," in *A Writer's Book*, ed. by Helen Hull (1950).

I.   Books

II.   Books Edited

III. Translations

IV.   Chapters Contributed to Books by Others

V.   Introductions

VI.   Selected Articles and Reviews

       1.   On Education

       2.   On History and Biography

       3.   In Cultural Criticism

I. BOOKS

The French Race. New York: Columbia University Press, 1932. Reissued in limited ed., New York: Kennikat Press, 1966.

Race, A Study in Modern Superstition. New York: Harcourt, Brace, 1937. Rev. ed., *A Study in Superstition.* New York: Harper & Row, 1965.

Of Human Freedom. Boston: Atlantic-Little, Brown, 1939. Rev. ed., New York: Lippincott, 1964.

Darwin, Marx, Wagner: Critique of a Heritage. Boston: Atlantic-Little, Brown, 1941. Rev. ed., New York: Anchor Books, 1958.

Romanticism and the Modern Ego. Boston: Atlantic-Little, Brown, 1943.

Introduction to Naval History (with Paul Beik, George Crothers, E. O. Golob). Philadelphia & New York: Lippincott, 1944.

Teacher in America. Boston: Atlantic-Little, Brown, 1945. English ed., entitled *We Who Teach,* London: Gollancz, 1946. 2nd ed., with new Preface, New York: Anchor Books, 1954, 1959. Reissue of original ed., Boston: Atlantic-Little, Brown, 1971.

A College Program in Action: A Review of Working Principles at Columbia College, by the Committee on Plans; H. R. Steeves, Chairman; Jacques Barzun, Secretary. New York: Columbia University Press, 1946.

Berlioz and the Romantic Century, 2 vols. Boston: Atlantic-Little, Brown, 1950. Rev. and abridged ed., *Berlioz and His Century* (1 vol.). New York: Meridian Books, 1956. 3rd and rev. ed. of 2 vols. New York: Columbia University Press, 1969.

God's Country and Mine. Boston: Atlantic-Little, Brown, 1954. English ed., London: Gollancz, 1955. New York: Vintage Books, 1959.

The Energies of Art. New York: Harper and Bros., 1956. Rev. ed., New York: Vintage Books, 1962. Reprint of original ed., Westport, Conn: Greenwood Press, 1975.

Music in American Life. New York: Doubleday, 1956. Bloomington, Ind.: Indiana University Press, Midland Books, 1962.

The Modern Researcher (with Henry Graff). New York: Harcourt, Brace, 1957. (Harbinger Book, 1962). Rev. ed., Harcourt, Brace, and World, 1970.

The House of Intellect. New York: Harper and Bros., 1959. English ed., London: Secker & Warburg, 1959. (Harper Torchbooks, 1961). Reissue. Chicago: University of Chicago Press, Midway Books, 1975.

Lincoln, The Literary Genius. Evanston, Ill.: The Schori Private Press, 1960. (Reprint of article, "Lincoln, The Literary Genius," *Saturday Evening*

Post, February 14, 1959; also included in *Jacques Barzun On Writing, Editing and Publishing*, see Section IV.)

Classic, Romantic and Modern. Boston: Atlantic-Little, Brown, 1961. New York: Anchor Books, 1961. (Revision of *Romanticism and the Modern Ego*). Re-issue, Chicago: University of Chicago Press, 1975.

Science: The Glorious Entertainment. New York: Harper & Row, 1964. English ed., London: Secker & Warburg, 1964.

The American University. New York: Harper & Row, 1968. English ed., London: Oxford University Press, 1969. (Harper Colophon Books, 1970).

A Catalogue of Crime (with Wendell Hertig Taylor). New York: Harper & Row, 1971. 2nd imp., corrected, 1974.

Clio and the Doctors: Psycho-History, Quanto-History and History. Chicago: University of Chicago Press, 1974.

The Use and Abuse of Art. Princeton, N.J.: Princeton University Press, Bollingen Series XXV, 22, 1974. (Princeton Paperback, 1975). (A publication of the Mellon Lectures of 1973 as delivered; the author did not see the book through the press.)

Simple & Direct: A Rhetoric for Writers. New York: Harper & Row, 1975.

II. BOOKS EDITED

Samplings and Chronicles (a short history of the Philolexian Society History, with literary selections, from 1912 to 1927, with a Foreword by John Erskine). New York: Columbia College, 1927.

The Later Ego, by James Agate. Edited with an Introduction and Notes. New York: Crown Publishers, 1951.

Pleasures of Music. Edited and translated, with an Introduction. New York: Viking Press, 1951. English ed., London: Michael Joseph, 1952. Viking Compass Editions, 1960.

The Selected Letters of Lord Byron. Edited with an Introduction and Notes. New York: Farrar, Straus and Young, 1953. Grosset and Dunlap, 1957.

A History of the Faculty of Philosophy of Columbia University (in the Bicentennial History of Columbia University Series). New York: Columbia University Press, 1957.

The Selected Writings of John Jay Chapman. Edited with an Introduction. New York: Farrar, Straus & Cudahy, 1957. Anchor Books, 1959. Funk & Wagnalls, Minerva Press editions, 1968.

The Delights of Detection. Edited with an Introduction. New York: Criterion Books, 1961.

Modern American Usage, by Wilson Follett. Completed and edited with Carlos Baker, Frederick Dupee, Dudley Fitts, James D. Hart, Phyllis McGinley, and Lionel Trilling. New York: Hill and Wang, 1966. Warner Paperback Library, 1974.

Burke and Hare: The Resurrection Men. Edited with an Introduction and Notes. Metuchen, N.J.: Scarecrow Press, 1974.

III. TRANSLATIONS

Becque, *La Parisienne*, in *From the Modern Repertoire, Series One,* edited
by Eric Bentley. Denver, Col.: University of Denver Press, 1949. In
The Modern Theatre, Vol. 1, edited by Eric Bentley. New York:
Doubleday Anchor Books, 1955.

Diderot, *Rameau's Nephew,* in *Great French Short Novels,* edited by F. W.
Dupee. New York: Dial Press, 1952. Revised version (with other dia-
logues translated by Ralph Bowen), *Diderot: Rameau's Nephew and
Other Works.* New York: Doubleday Anchor Books, 1956. Reprinted in
Rameau's Nephew and Other Works. Indianapolis, Ind.: Bobbs-Merrill
Library of Liberal Arts, 1964.

"Four Portraits," by Colette. *The Griffin,* Vol. 1, No. 4, 1952.

Mirbeau, *The Epidemic,* in *From the Modern Repertoire, Series Two,* edited
by Eric Bentley. Denver, Col.: University of Denver Press, 1952.

"Berlioz's Romeo and Juliet." Notes and Translation for RCA recording
of performance by Boston Symphony Orchestra, 1953. Reprintings:
New York Philharmonic concert notes, January 29, 1961; Cleveland
Orchestra Program for March 1 and 3, 1962; Stanford University
Music Department program notes for May 1964; NBC Symphony
Orchestra recording on RCA Victor, 1965; San Francisco Symphony
Orchestra program notes for May 1972; Toronto Symphony Orchestra
program notes for October 31 and November 1, 1972; Boston Sym-
phony Orchestra program note for January 19 and 20, 1968; October
1975.

New Letters of Berlioz, 1830–1868. Translated with Introduction (bilingual
ed.). New York: Columbia University Press, 1954. 2nd ed., Westport,
Conn.: Greenwood Press, 1974.

Berlioz, Eleven Unpublished Letters 1830–1864. Private printing of eleven
additional letters, translated, annotated, and introduced by Jacques
Barzun. The Berlioz Society, Exeter, New Hampshire, December 1954.
(Issued also by *The Berlioz Society Bulletin,* London, December 1954.)

Flaubert, *Dictionary of Accepted Ideas.* New York: New Directions, 1954.
2nd ed., London: Max Reinhardt, 1954. 3rd ed., New York: New
Directions, 1968.

Berlioz: "Lelio: A Lyric Monodrama," in *City College Music Department
Program Notes.* New York, May 1955.

Musset, *Fantasio,* in *The Modern Theatre,* Vol. 2, edited by Eric Bentley.
New York: Doubleday Anchor Books, 1955.

Berlioz, *Evenings with the Orchestra.* Translated with an Introduction. New
York: Knopf, 1956. 2nd ed., Chicago: University of Chicago Press,
1973.

Musset, *A Door Should Be Either Open or Shut,* in *From the Modern
Repertoire, Series Three,* edited by Eric Bentley. Bloomington, Ind.:
Indiana University Press, 1956.

"The World's Second Detective" (abridged version of letter from Beaumarchais to the London *Morning Chronicle* in 1776), in *Ellery Queen's Mystery Magazine,* November 1956. Reprinted in *The Delights of Detection.* New York: Criterion Books, 1961.

Courteline, *A Rule Is a Rule* (four playlets: "The Torn Transfer," "The Registered Letter," "Article 330," and "The Scales of Justice"). Translated with Introductory Notes. *The Tulane Drama Review,* October 1958. "Article 330" republished in *The Plays of Georges Courteline,* edited by Albert Bermel. London: Heinemann, 1960. Reprinted by Theatre Arts Books, New York, 1961.

Beaumarchais, *Figaro's Marriage* (with Robert Lowell's translation of Racine's *Phaedra*). New York: Farrar, Straus and Cudahy, 1961. In paperback *The Classic Theatre,* Vol. IV, edited by Eric Bentley. New York: Doubleday Anchor Books, 1961.

IV. CHAPTERS CONTRIBUTED TO BOOKS BY OTHERS

"The Period and Character of the Renaissance," "The Meaning of Romantic," "A Rationale of Modern Culture," "The Plastic Arts: Nineteenth Century and Modern," and "Music in the Nineteenth and Twentieth Centuries," in *An Introduction to Contemporary Civilization in the West,* Vol. II. 9th ed., Vols. I and II, with Columbia College Associates. New York: Columbia University Press, 1933–34. 10th ed., Vol. I, 1935; Vol. II, 1936.

"Education in France: Its Theory, Practice and Worth" (with R. Valeur), in *Redirecting Education,* Vol. II, edited by R. G. Tugwell and L. H. Keyserling, New York: Columbia University Press, 1935. (Fuller version in *Columbia University Quarterly,* December 1932.)

"Race-Prejudice," in *America Now,* edited by Harold E. Stearns. New York: Charles Scribner's Sons, 1938.

Conversations in *The New Invitation to Learning,* edited by Mark Van Doren. New York: Random House, 1942. (Discussions of books with various panelists over CBS program "Invitation to Learning" 1940–42.)

"The Romantic Period," in *Contemporary Civilization Manual and Source Book,* Part 2, Section 8. New York: Columbia University Press, 1942. (Expanded into article "Romanticism," in *Collier's Encyclopedia,* 1956.)

"History, Popular and Unpopular," in *The Interpretation of History,* by Joseph P. Strayer. Princeton, N. J.: Princeton University Press, 1943.

"The Idea of a Career," in *A Man's Reach: Some Choices Facing Youth Today,* edited by Thomas H. Johnson. New York: Putnam's Sons, 1947.

"Calamophobia or, Hints Toward a Writer's Discipline," in *The Writer's Book,* edited by Helen Hull. New York: Harper and Bros., 1950. (Included in *Jacques Barzun on Writing, Editing and Publishing,* see below.)

"Cultural Nationalism and the Makings of Fame," in *Nationalism and Internationalism: Essays in Honor of Carlton J. H. Hayes,* edited by Edward M. Earle. New York: Columbia University Press, 1950.

"The Artist Against Society," in *The New Partisan Reader,* edited by William Phillips and Philip Rahv. New York: Harcourt, Brace, 1953.

"Cultural History: A Synthesis," in *The Varieties of History,* edited by Fritz Stern. New York: Meridian Books, 1956.

Several notes on American classics, in *American Panorama,* edited by Eric Larrabee. New York: New York University Press, 1957.

"The Oddest Profession in the World," in *Expanding Resources for College Teaching,* edited by G. Dobbins (Report of The Conference on College Teaching, January 20, 1956). Washington, D.C.: American Council on Education, 1957.

"The Scholar-Critic," in *Contemporary Literary Scholarship,* edited by Lewis Leary. New York: Appleton-Century-Crofts, 1958. (Revised from a statement for the *Report of National Commission on the Humanities,* edited by Howard Mumford Jones, April 1956.)

"The Tyranny of Idealism in Education," in *Education in the Nation's Service.* New York: Frederick Praeger, in cooperation with the Woodrow Wilson Foundation, 1960.

"From the Nineteenth Century to the Twentieth," in *Chapters in Western Civilization,* Vol. II, edited by Bernard Wishy. New York: Columbia University Press, 1962.

"Why Diderot?", in *Varieties of Literary Experience,* edited by Stanley Burnshaw. New York: New York University Press, 1962.

"Verses on the Death of Dr. Swift, D.S.P.D.," in *Master Poems of the English Language,* edited by Oscar Williams. New York: Trident Press, 1966.

"Fewer Facts: More Theory," in *Washington Colloquium on Science and Society, Second Series,* edited by Morton Leeds. Georgetown University, Mono Book Corp., 1967.

"Ideas Just in Time," in *Naturalism and Historical Understanding: Essays on the Philosophy of John Herman Randall, Jr.,* edited by John P. Anton. Albany, N.Y.: State University of New York Press, 1967.

"As We Were," in *University on the Heights,* edited by Wesley First. New York: Doubleday, 1969.

"The Quality of Life," in *Man and Life: A Sesquicentennial Symposium.:* Printed by University of Cincinnati, 1969–70.

"Detection and the Literary Art," in *The Mystery Writer's Art,* edited by Francis M. Nevins, Jr., Bowling Green, Ohio: Bowling Green University Popular Press, 1970. (Revised version of the Introduction to *The Delights of Detection.*)

Jacques Barzun on Writing, Editing and Publishing. A collection of previously published essays, edited with a Foreword by Morris Philipson. Chicago: University of Chicago Press, 1971.

"The Decline of University Independence," in *Education: Threatened Standards,* edited by Rhodes Boyson, M.P. London: Churchill Press Ltd., 1972.

"Society and Politics," "Science and Theology," "Romanticism and After," "From Liberalism to Democracy," and "The State of Culture Today," in *The Columbia History of the World,* edited by John Garraty and Peter Gay. New York: Harper & Row, 1972.

V. INTRODUCTIONS

Introduction to *Mademoiselle de Maupin,* by Théophile Gautier. New York: Limited Editions Club, 1944.

"Swift, Gulliver, and Mortal Men." Introduction to Jonathan Swift's *Gulliver's Travels.* New York: Crown Publishers, 1947.

"Bagehot, or the Critic as Statesman." Introduction to *Physics and Politics,* by Walter Bagehot. New York: Knopf, 1948.

General Editor's Preface to the *Columbia University Bicentennial Editions and Studies.* New York: Columbia University Press, 1954.

Introduction and Notes to Goethe's *Faust: A Tragedy, Part One,* translated by Alice Raphael. New York: Holt, Rinehart & Winston, 1955.

Introduction to *The Edge of Perfect: The Tragedy of Abelard and Heloïse,* by Nicolas Monjo. New York: Grove Press, 1956.

Foreword to *The Academic Marketplace,* by Theodore Caplow and Reece J. McGee. New York: Basic Books, 1958.

Foreword to *The Varieties of Religious Experience,* by William James. New York: Mentor Books (New American Library), 1958.

Preface to *Watch Your Language,* by Theodore Bernstein. New York: Channel Press, 1958.

"Remarks," in *Approaches to the Oriental Classics,* edited by Wm. Theodore deBary. New York: Columbia University Press, 1959.

Foreword to *Foresight and Understanding,* by Stephen Toulmin. Bloomington, Ind.: Indiana University Press, 1961.

Preface to *Tomorrow's Illiterates: The State of Reading Instruction Today,* edited by Charles C. Walcutt. Boston: Atlantic-Little, Brown, 1961.

Introduction to *Africa for Beginners,* by Melvin J. Lasky. New York: Lippincott, 1962.

"Columbia and the Parker School." Foreword to *International Contracts: Choice of Law and Language,* edited by Willis L. Reese. Published for the Parker School of Foreign and Comparative Law of Columbia University by Oceana Publications, Inc., 1962.

"The Poet in Zola." Introduction to Emile Zola's *Germinal,* translated by Willard R. Trask. New York: Bantam Books, 1962.

Afterword to Stendhal's *The Charterhouse of Parma,* translated by C. K. Scott Moncrieff. New York: New American Library, 1962.

Foreword to *The Tyranny of Testing,* by Banesh Hoffmann. New York: Crowell-Collier, 1962.

"The Permanence of Oscar Wilde." Introduction to Oscar Wilde's *De Profundis.* New York: Vintage Books, 1964.

"Restif de la Bretonne." Introduction to Restif's *Les Nuits de Paris,* translated by Linda Asher and Ellen Fertig. New York: Random House, 1964.

Preface to *The Clash and Attraction of Two Cultures,* by Angel del Rio, translated by James G. Shearer. Baton Rouge, La.: Louisiana State University Press, 1965.

"What Man Has Built." Introduction to *Great Ages of Man: A History of the World's Cultures.* New York: Time-Life, Inc., 1965.

Introduction to *The Guilt of the Templars,* by G. Legman. New York: Basic Books, 1966.

"Bagehot as Historian." Introduction to *The Historical Essays of Walter Bagehot.* Collected Works, Vol. 3, edited by Norman St. John-Stevas. London: *The Economist,* 1968. (Cambridge: Harvard University Press, 1970).

Introduction to *The Columbia University Forum Anthology,* edited by Peter Spackman and Lee Ambrose. New York: Atheneum, 1968.

"Remarks," in *Illusions,* by André Maurois. New York: Columbia University Press, 1968.

"Albert Jay Nock." Preface to *Cogitations from Albert Jay Nock.* Irvington, N.Y.: The Nockian Society, 1970.

Foreword to *The Parsons College Bubble: A Tale of Higher Education in America,* by James D. Koerner. New York: Basic Books, 1970.

Introduction to *The New Music: The Sense Behind the Sound,* by Joan Peyser. New York: Delacorte Press, 1971.

"A Request for the Loan of Your Ears." Preface to *The Liberation of Sound: An Introduction to Electronic Music,* by Herbert Russcol. Englewood Cliffs, N.J.: Prentice-Hall, 1972. (Expanded version of a speech delivered by Jacques Barzun at May 9 and 10, 1961, concerts of the Columbia-Princeton Electronic Music Center at McMillin Theatre, Columbia University.)

"The Young Raymond Chandler." Foreword to *Chandler Before Marlowe,* edited by Matthew J. Bruccoli. Columbia, S.C.: University of South Carolina Press, 1973.

VI. SELECTED ARTICLES AND REVIEWS

1. *On Education*

"Textbooks and Tediousness," *The Columbia Varsity,* October 1926.

"Irrelevant Maturity," *The Columbia Varsity,* December 1926.

Review of *Essays on Research in the Social Sciences,* by Swann, Beard, Llewellyn, Schlesinger, Ogburn, and others. *New York Herald Tribune Books,* September 27, 1931.

"Teaching the Humanities," *Columbia University Quarterly,* September 1938.

"The Humanities—Proper Study of Mankind," *English Journal,* October 1938.

"Read, Do Not Run"; review of *How to Read a Book,* by Mortimer J. Adler. *Saturday Review,* March 9, 1940.

"Maritain and the Pragmatists"; review of *Education at the Crossroads,* by Jacques Maritain. *New York Times Book Review,* November 14, 1943.

"Report of the Proceedings of the Conference of University Administrators on General and Liberal Education" (with others), University of Oklahoma, March 1944.

"Whom Shall We Teach?", *New Leader,* February 24, 1945.

"Harvard Takes Stock"; review of Harvard University's *General Education in a Free Society. Atlantic,* October 1945.

Review of *Literary Study and the Scholarly Profession,* by Hardin Craig. *American Historical Review,* January 1946.

"The Scholar Looks at the Library," *College and Research Libraries,* April 1946.

"The Higher Learning in America," *Horizon,* London, October 1947.

"The Scholar Is an Institution," *Journal of Higher Education,* November 1947.

"Education," *The Lawrentian,* Lawrenceville, N.J., Spring 1948.

"The Backwardness of Present-Day Science Teaching," *Proceedings of American Conference of Academic Deans,* January 1949.

"The Educated Man," *Life,* October 16, 1950.

"A Loyalty Oath for Scholars," *American Scholar,* Summer 1951 (signed "Hippocrates, Jr.").

Review of *Chambers' Encyclopedia,* Oxford University Press; and *The Columbia Encyclopedia,* 2nd ed., Columbia University Press. *New York Herald Tribune Book Review,* September 2, 1951.

"The Great Books"; review of *Great Books of the Western World. Atlantic,* December 1952.

"English as She's Not Taught," *Atlantic,* December 1953. (Included in *Jacques Barzun on Writing, Editing and Publishing,* see Section IV.)

"The Battle Over Brains in Democratic Education," *University of Toronto Quarterly,* January 1954.

"The Indispensable Amateur: Music in the Liberal Arts College," *Juilliard Review,* January 1954.

"The Care and Feeding of the Mind," *Phillips Exeter Bulletin, Supplement,* April 1955. (Recording in Spoken Arts, No. 713, Distinguished Teachers' Series, Westminster Records, 1956.)

"The Graduate School Today and Tomorrow" (with others), Report of the Committee of Fifteen. Fund for the Advancement of Education, New York, December 1955.

"Report of the Dean of the Graduate Faculties, 1955–56," Columbia University, 1956.

"Teachers, Parents, and Money," *Harper's,* February 1956 (Anonymous).

"Report of the Educational Policies Committee of the Association of Graduate Schools" (with others), *Journal of Proceedings and Addresses,* October 1956.

"Report of the Dean of the Graduate Faculties, 1956–57," Columbia University, 1957.

"Doctors and Masters—Good and Bad" (with others), *Journal of Proceedings and Addresses of the Association of Graduate Schools,* October 1957. (Report of the Committee on Policies in Graduate Education, *New York Times,* November 13, 1957.)

"Report of the Dean of the Graduate Faculties, 1957–58," Columbia University, 1958.

"Science vs. the Humanities," *Saturday Evening Post,* May 3, 1958.

"The Discovery and Encouragement of Humanists" (with others), Report of the American Council of Learned Societies Conference, May 16–17, 1958.

"Research and Creativity," *Report of the Seventh Conference of the Association of Princeton Graduate Alumni,* December 27–28, 1958.

"The Place and the Price of Excellence," *Vogue,* February 1, 1959. (Originally a convocation address at the Lawrenceville School, printed for private circulation October 1958.)

"Publish or Perish. Scholarship and Security: An Uneasy Alliance," *The Times Literary Supplement,* November 6, 1959 (Anonymous).

"The Conduct of Oral Examinations" and "Scholarship and the Ansley Awards," Columbia University, 1960.

"Centering the Arts," *Columbia University Forum,* Winter 1960.

"The Conditions of Success," *Vogue,* March 1, 1960.

"How Much Science in Our Mental Diet?", printed for private circulation by Industrial Indemnity Co., San Francisco, May 1960.

"Our Universities: Unguided Missiles," *Think,* November 1960.

"The American College in Double Jeopardy," *Proceedings of the American Philosophical Society,* Vol. 104, No. 6, December 15, 1960.

The Education of Historians in the United States (with members of the Committee on Graduate Education of the American Historical Association). The Carnegie Series in American Education, New York: McGraw-Hill, 1962.

"Notes on the Making of a World Encyclopedia," *American Behavioral Scientist,* September 1962; and "Further Notes on Encyclopedias: The Organization of Knowledge," June 20, 1962. (Memoranda to the Board of Editors, *Encyclopaedia Britannica.*)

"What Is a University?", *College and University Journal,* Vol. I, No. 4, Fall 1962.

"College to University—and After," *The American Scholar,* Spring 1964.

"Fighting for Your Education," *Milton Academy Bulletin,* December 1964.

"Computers for the Humanities?", Yale University, 1965. (Record of Conference on Man and the Machine, January 22–23, 1965.)

"Conflicts Between the Federal Research Programs and the Nation's Goals for Higher Education" (with others), U.S. Government Printing Office,

Washington, D.C., June 1965. (Response to inquiry by Subcommittee on Government Operations.)

"College Administration and Crime," Middle States Association of Collegiate Registrars and Officers of Admission, December 1965.

"Science as a Social Institution," *Proceedings of the Academy of Political Science,* April 1966.

"Art and Science—How Soon the Fatal Dose?", *Chancellor's Occasional Papers,* University of California, Berkeley, May 1966.

"The University as the Beloved Republic," Center for the Study of Democratic Institutions, Los Angeles, Fall 1966.

"The Sciences and the Humanities in the Schools After a Decade of Reform: Present and Future Needs" (with Glenn Seaborg), Council for Basic Education, April 1967.

"The Intellectual Life and the School System," Aspen Institute on Education and the Human Potential, Aspen, Colorado, August 15, 1967.

"Career Thinking . . . Advice to Advisors," *Journal of College Placement,* October–November 1967.

Review of *Catholic Education Faces Its Future,* by Neil G. McCluskey, S.J. *America,* April 5, 1969.

Statement to the Special Subcommittee on Education of the Committee on Education and Labor, House of Representatives, 91st Congress, May 9, 1969. Printed in volume containing the hearings held before the Subcommittee, *Campus Unrest,* pp. 765–781.

"Tomorrow's University—Back to the Middle Ages?", *Saturday Review,* November 15, 1969.

"Testing, Grades, Standards," *Papers on Educational Reform,* Vol. I. La Salle, Ill.: Open Court Publishing Co., 1970.

"The Conflict of Action and Liberty: The Humanities in the Melting Pot," *The Humanist,* September–October 1970.

"The Centrality of Reading," *Michigan Quarterly Review,* Winter 1970. Reprinted in *The Written Word,* by Sheridan Baker, Jacques Barzun, and I. A. Richards. Rowley, Mass.: Newbury House Publishers, 1971.

"Where the Educational Nonsense Comes From," *Papers on Educational Reform,* Vol. II. La Salle, Ill.: Open Court Publishing Co., 1971. (Published with some changes, under title "The Sources and Symptoms of Educational Nonsense," in *Conference,* Vol. 9, No. 1, February 1972, Journal of the Headmasters' Conference, Norwich, England.)

Review of *The Catholic University: A Modern Appraisal,* edited by Neil G. McCluskey, S.J. *Thought Quarterly Review,* Spring 1971.

"Open Admissions: The Pros and Cons" (with others), Council for Basic Education, Washington, D.C., 1972.

"Career Education—An American View," *Public Schools Appointments Bureau News Bulletin,* 144 (London), Autumn 1972.

Review of *Social Sciences as Sorcery,* by Stanislav Andreski. *New Leader,* December 11, 1972.

"The Education of Candidates for Medical School," *Bulletin of the New York Academy of Medicine*, April 1973.

"The Recasting of Liberal Education," *Columbia College Today*, Summer 1973.

"Humanities, Pieties, Practicalities, Universities," *Columbia University Seminar Reports* and *Columbia University Spectator*, November 14, 1973.

"The Use of Tradition in Educational Disputes," *Encounter*, November 1973. Reprinted in *Papers on Educational Reform*, Vol. IV. La Salle, Ill.: Open Court Publishing Co., 1974.

"To Give an Education," *Black Paper 1975*, edited by C. B. Cox and Rhodes Boyson, M.P. London: J. M. Dent, 1975.

2. *On History and Biography*

Review of *Europe Since 1914*, by F. Lee Benns. *The Historical Outlook*, March 1930.

Review of *Figures of the Revolution*, by Louis Madelin. *The Historical Outlook*, May 1930.

Review of *The Romance of Madame du Châtelet and Voltaire*, by André Maurel. *New York Herald Tribune Books*, August 16, 1931.

Review of *English Biography in the Eighteenth Century*, by Mark Longaker. *New York Herald Tribune Books*, October 4, 1931.

Review of *Englishmen at Rest and Play*, edited by Reginald Lennard. *New York Herald Tribune Books*, December 13, 1931.

Review of *The Jacobins*, by C. Crane Brinton. *The Historical Outlook*, January 1932.

Review of *Studies in Modern History*, by G. P. Gooch. *New York Herald Tribune Books*, March 27, 1932.

Review of *Does History Repeat Itself?*, by R. F. McWilliams. *The Historical Outlook*, February 1933.

Review of *The Pendulum of Progress*, by Sir George Young. *The Historical Outlook*, February 1933.

Review of *Dialogues Curieux, et Mémoires de l'Amérique Septentrionale*, by Baron de Lahontan, edited by Gilbert Chinard. *Historical Outlook*, October 1933.

"Stendhal prophète," *Chimère* (Columbia University), April 1937.

Review of *The Romantic Age*, by R. B. Mowat. *American Historical Review*, October 1938.

"Truth in Biography: Berlioz," *The University Review* (Kansas City), Summer 1939. Reprinted with minor revisions in *Biography as an Art*, edited by James Clifford. London: Oxford University Press, 1962.

"The Uses of History"; review of *Historian and Scientist*, by Gaetano Salvemini. *Saturday Review*, December 23, 1939.

"Truth in Biography: Leonardo and Freud," *The University Review* (Kansas City), June 1940.

Review of *Enchanted Wanderer: The Life of C. M. von Weber,* by Lucy and Richard Poate Stebbins. *The Nation,* August 3, 1940.

Review of *Nietzsche,* by Crane Brinton. *Saturday Review,* March 22, 1941.

"The Cry for Order," *Saturday Review,* April 12, 1941.

Review of *History as the Story of Liberty,* by Benedetto Croce. *Saturday Review,* May 17, 1941.

"Romantic Historiography as a Political Force in France," *Journal of the History of Ideas,* June 1941.

"Using the Past"; review of *The Ground We Stand On,* by John Dos Passos. *The Nation,* September 13, 1941.

"Our Tradition and Its Critics"; review of *From Luther to Hitler,* by William M. McGovern, and *What Nietzsche Means,* by George Allen Morgan. *Saturday Review,* September 27, 1941.

"Max Eastman and History," *New Leader,* February 14, 1942.

"Recent European Historians"; review of *Some Historians of Modern Europe,* edited by Bernadotte E. Schmitt. *The Nation,* April 4, 1942.

"The Bridge of Clio"; review of *A History of Historical Writing,* by James Westfall Thompson. *The New Republic,* December 7, 1942.

"Men and History"; review of *The Hero in History,* by Sidney Hook. *The Nation,* September 18, 1943.

Review of *Two Currents in the Thought Stream of Europe,* by Elmer G. Suhr. *American Historical Review,* October 1943.

"Tiger in the Night"; review of *Clemenceau,* by Geoffrey Bruun. *The New Republic,* December 6, 1943.

"The Muse Resents the Soapbox"; review of *Man the Measure,* by Erich Kahler. *Saturday Review,* May 13, 1944.

Review of *From Despotism to Revolution: 1763–1789,* by Leo Gershoy. *New York Herald Tribune Book Review,* August 13, 1944.

"History as a Liberal Art," *Journal of the History of Ideas,* January 1945.

Review of *The Philosophy of American History,* by Morris Zucker. *Saturday Review,* March 31, 1945.

Review of *Prophets and Peoples,* by Hans Kohn. *Political Science Quarterly,* September 1946.

Review of *The Pilgrimage of Western Man,* by Stringfellow Barr. *New York Herald Tribune Book Review,* July 24, 1949.

Review of *G.B.S.: A Postscript,* by Hesketh Pearson. *Saturday Review,* December 23, 1950.

"Why Not the Third Cheer?", *The Griffin,* Vol. 1, No. 1, 1951.

Review of *Goethe and the Modern Age,* by Arnold Bergstraesser, and *Goethe the Thinker,* by Karl Victor. *New York Herald Tribune Book Review,* January 14, 1951.

"Last Years of a Great Doer"; review of *G.B.S.,* by Hesketh Pearson. *Shaw Society Bulletin,* New York, February 1951.

"Gide's Finest Work"; review of *The Journals of André Gide,* Vol. IV, translated by Justin O'Brien. *New Leader,* May 14, 1951.

"Time Out of Mind," *The Griffin*, Vol. 1, No. 7, 1952.

Review of *Bernard Shaw*, by A. C. Ward, and *Bernard Shaw: A Chronicle*, by E. F. Rattray. *Saturday Review*, March 29, 1952.

"Dr. Freud of Vienna," *The Griffin*, Vol. 2, No. 11, December 1953.

"Some Principles of Musical Biography," *Perspective*, No. 2, Winter 1953.

Review of *Studies in Intellectual History*, by George Boas, *et al. American Historical Review*, July 1954.

" 'The Blest Group of Us,' " *The Griffin*, Vol. 5, No. 6, June 1956.

"Erich Kleiber: The Passing of a Free Spirit," *High Fidelity*, August 1956.

"Himself When Older," *The Griffin*, Vol. 5, No. 12, November 1956.

"Intellect and the Hungarian Revolution," *The Griffin*, Vol. 6, No. 7, August 1957.

"On First Looking Into Our Own Chapman," *The Griffin*, Vol. 6, No. 8, September 1957.

"Lawrence in Life and Letters," *The Griffin*, Vol. 7, No. 2, February 1958.

Review of *The Nature of Biography*, by John A. Garraty. *Mississippi Valley Historical Review*, March 1958.

"The Sense of History," *The Griffin*, Vol. 7, No. 5, May 1958.

"Two Letters" (exchange between Enid Starkie and Jacques Barzun), *The Griffin*, Vol. 7, No. 6, June 1958.

"Life Into Words," *The Mid-Century*, No. 3, September 1959.

"The Siege at Peking," *The Mid-Century*, No. 4, October 1959.

"Out of Many, One," *The Mid-Century*, No. 6, November 1959.

Review of *A History of Western Morals*, by Crane Brinton. *Science*, December 18, 1959.

"On the Death of an American Artist" (Anne Goodwin Winslow), *The Mid-Century*, No. 8, January 1960.

Review of *The Education of Nations: A Comparison in Historical Perspective*, by R. Ulich. *Science*, April 28, 1961.

"Trial Now or by Posterity," *The Mid-Century*, No. 25, May 1961.

"The Cutting of an Agate," *The Mid-Century*, No. 30, September 1961.

Review of *The Artist and Social Reform: France and Belgium, 1885–1898*, by E. W. Herbert. *American Historical Review*, April 1962.

"Berlioz"; article in *Colliers' Encyclopedia*, Vol. 4. New York: Crowell-Collier, 1962.

"Unknown? Misknown? Worth Knowing?", *The Mid-Century*, No. 40, June 1962.

"Exploring the Space of Time," *The Mid-Century*, No. 42, Midsummer 1962.

"The Spectre of Decadence," *The Mid-Century*, No. 43, August 1962.

"Berlioz"; article in *New Catholic Encyclopedia*, Vol 2. New York: McGraw-Hill, 1967.

"Berlioz"; article in *Dictionnaire de la Musique*, edited by Marc Honegger. Paris: Bordas, 1970.

Review of *Dictionary of Scientific Biography*, Vols. 1 and 2, edited by Charles C. Gillispie. *Science*, November 6, 1970.

"Eugène Delacroix"; biographical entry in *Atlantic Brief Lives: A Biographical Companion to the Arts*, edited by Louis Kronenberger. Boston: Atlantic-Little, Brown, 1971.

"Hector Berlioz"; biographical entry in *Atlantic Brief Lives: A Biographical Companion to the Arts*, edited by Louis Kronenberger. Boston: Atlantic-Little, Brown, 1971.

"William James"; article in *The Encyclopedia of Education*. New York: Crowell-Collier and Macmillan, 1971.

"A Warm Cold Fish"; review of *Prosper Mérimée*, by A. W. Raitt. *The Nation*, April 26, 1971.

Review of *Sources of Cultural Estrangement*, by Deric Regin. *Canadian Journal of History*, September 1971.

"Confounding the Happy Few"; review of *Life of Rossini*, by Stendhal; new and revised edition, translated by Richard Coe. *The Nation*, January 24, 1972.

"History: The Muse and Her Doctors," *American Historical Review*, February 1972.

"Thomas Beddoes or, Medicine and Social Conscience," *Journal of the American Medical Association*, April 3, 1972.

"Hector Berlioz"; article in *Encyclopaedia Britannica*, 15th edition, Vol. I. Chicago: Encyclopaedia Britannica, Inc., 1974.

"The Point and Pleasure of Reading History," in *Encyclopaedia Britannica*, 15th edition, Vol. I. Chicago: Encyclopaedia Britannica, Inc., 1974.

"Biography and Criticism—A Misalliance Disputed," *Critical Inquiry*, March 1975.

3. *In Cultural Criticism*

"The Wise Youth at the Theatre," *The Columbian*, Columbia University, 1927.

Review of *HIM*, by E. E. Cummings. *Columbia Spectator*, April 26, 1928.

"A Logical View of Aesthetics"; review of *A Study in Aesthetics*, by Louis Arnaud Reid. *New York Herald Tribune Books*, November 1, 1931.

"Havelock Ellis: Impressionist M.D."; review of *From Rousseau to Proust, A Study of Modern French Literature*, by Havelock Ellis. *The Columbia Review*, Columbia University, December 1935.

"Blast"; review of *Blast at Ballet*, by Lincoln Kirstein. *The Nation*, December 17, 1938.

"A Music Critic to the Rescue"; review of *Music on Records*, by B. H. Haggin. *The Nation*, December 31, 1938.

Review of *Les Idées traditionalistes en France de Rivarol à Charles Maurras*, by Alphonse V. Roche; and *France Faces the Future*, by Ralph Fox. *Political Science Quarterly*, March, 1939.

"Why Dictators Prefer Blonds"; review of *Race Against Man*, by Herbert J. Seligmann. *Saturday Review*, April 8, 1939.

"Scientific Humanism," *The Nation*, April 29, 1939.

"Tower with Windows"; review of *Personal Record, 1928–1939*, by Julian Green. *Saturday Review*, November 11, 1939.

Review of *The Races of Europe*, by Carleton S. Coon. *Social Education*, March 1940.

"To the Rescue of Romanticism," *The American Scholar*, Spring 1940.

"A Religion of Science"; review of *Dangerous Thoughts*, by Lancelot Hogben. *The Nation*, April 13, 1940.

"Hamlet's Politics," *Saturday Review*, April 15, 1940.

Review of *Race: A History of Modern Ethnic Theories*, by Louis L. Snyder. *Political Science Quarterly*, June 1940.

"Truth and Poetry in Thomas Hardy," *The Southern Review*, Summer 1940.

"The American as Critic"; review of *The Arts and the Art of Criticism*, by Theodore M. Greene. *Saturday Review*, December 7, 1940.

"Mr. Tate's 'Radical Dualism' "; review of *Reason in Madness*, by Allen Tate. *Saturday Review*, May 31, 1941.

Review of *France: 1815 to the Present*, by John B. Wolf. *Social Education*, December, 1941.

Review of *Metapolitics: From the Romantics to Hitler*, by Peter Viereck. *Journal of the History of Ideas*, January 1942.

"Aesthetic Theology"; review of *The Mind of the Maker*, by Dorothy L. Sayers. *The Nation*, February 21, 1942.

" 'The Republic' in Basic"; review of *The Republic of Plato: A New Version Founded on Basic English*, and *How to Read a Page*, both by I. A. Richards. *The Nation*, April 25, 1942.

"Evolution, Religion and Materialistic Science," in *Contemporary Civilization Manual and Source Book*, Part II, Section IV. New York: Columbia University Press, 1943.

"William James"; review of *In Commemoration of William James*, by Arnold Metzger. *The Nation*, February 6, 1943.

"How to Suffocate the English Language," *Saturday Review*, February 13, 1943.

"William James as Artist," *The New Republic*, February 15, 1943.

"Strawinsky as Critic"; review of *Poétique musicale sous forme de six leçons*, by Igor Strawinsky. *The Nation*, March 27, 1943.

"Invitation to Learning." CBS radio discussion by Harry D. Gideonse, Joseph D. McGoldrick, and Jacques Barzun, of *Progress and Poverty*, by Henry George. *Land and Freedom*, April–May 1943.

"What Is a Romantic Life?", *Saturday Review*, September 11, 1943.

"A Second Language," *Saturday Review*, October 2, 1943.

"What Is Faith?"; review of *The Primacy of Faith*, by Richard Kroner. *The Nation*, March 18, 1944.

"Architects of Babel"; review of *Say What You Mean*, by John B. Opdycke, and *The Loom of Language*, by Frederick Bodmer. *Saturday Review*, July 1, 1944.

"Poetry and Portmanteaus"; review of *A Skeleton Key to Finnegans Wake*, by Joseph Campbell and H. M. Robinson. *Saturday Review*, October 14, 1944.

"Who's Who in Shaw's 'What's What'"; review of *Everybody's Political What's What*, by George Bernard Shaw. *The Nation*, October 28, 1944.

Review of *Germany: A Winter's Tale: 1844*, by Heinrich Heine, translated by Herman Salinger. *New York Times Book Review*, January 14, 1945.

Review of *Democracy in America*, by Alexis de Tocqueville, edited by Phillips Bradley. *New York Herald Tribune Book Review*, April 15, 1945.

"Machiavelli Dead and Gone," *The American Scholar*, Spring 1945.

Review of *American Romantic Painting*, by Edgar P. Richardson. *Magazine of Art*, May 1945.

"Quote 'em Is Taboo," *Saturday Review*, September 22, 1945. (Included in *Jacques Barzun on Writing, Editing and Publishing*, see Section IV.)

"Some Notes on Créteil and French Poetry," *New Directions* 9, New York, 1946.

"Mencken's America Speaking," *Atlantic*, January 1946.

Review of *Values for Survival*, by Lewis Mumford; *Western World*, by Royce Brier; and *On the Nature of Value: The Philosophy of Samuel Alexander*, by Milton R. Konvitz. *Saturday Review*, April 27, 1946.

"Myths for Materialists," *Chimera*, Spring 1946.

"The Counterfeiters," *Atlantic*, May 1946.

"Of Making Books," in *The American Scholar*, Summer 1946. (Included in *Jacques Barzun on Writing, Editing and Publishing*, see Section IV.)

"Our Non-Fiction Novelists," *Atlantic*, July 1946.

Review of *The Wayward Bus*, by John Steinbeck. *Harper's*, April 1947.

"Moralists for Your Muddles"; review of *Essays on Morals* by Philip Wylie, and other books. *Harper's*, May 1947.

"Consumer's Goods: Science and Letters"; review of *On Understanding Science*, by James Conant, and other books. *Harper's*, July 1947.

"Workers in Monumental Brass"; review of *The Age of Anxiety*, by W. H. Auden, and other books. *Harper's*, September 1947.

"Lincoln, Liberals, Lillibullero"; review of *The Age of Reason*, by Jean-Paul Sartre; *The Cult of Power*, by Rex Warner; *Lincoln, the Liberal Statesman*, by J. G. Randall; and other books. *Harper's*, November 1947.

"French Music," in *Encyclopaedia Americana*. New York: Americana Corp., 1948. (Revision of article by C. Koechlin and E. Pendleton.)

"Four in America and What They Found There"; review of *America in Perspective*, edited by Henry Steele Commager; *The American Experience*, by H. B. Parkes; and other books. *Harper's*, February 1948.

"American Sensuality," *The Nation*, March 27, 1948.

"On the Art of Saying 'Quite Mad'"; review of *Wit and Wisdom of Whitehead*, by A. H. Johnson; Whitehead's *Essays in Science and Philosophy*; and other books. *Harper's*, March 1948.

"Light Literature and the Poet Historian"; review of *Civilization on Trial,* by Arnold J. Toynbee, and other books. *Harper's,* July 1948.

"Thomas Mann as Critic," *The Nation,* July 3, 1948.

"Interpreters of the Modern Temper"; review of *The Heart of the Matter,* by Graham Greene; *The Loved One,* by Evelyn Waugh; and other books. *Harper's,* September 1948.

"Our Economic Future: The Lady or the Tiger?"; review of *Individualism and Economic Order,* by F. A. Hayek, and other books. *Harper's,* November 1948.

"Advice from the Lovelorn"; review of *The Plague,* by Albert Camus; *Intruder in the Dust,* by William Faulkner; and other books. *Harper's,* December 1948.

"Critics: Connolly to Koestler"; review of *Literary History of the United States,* and other books. *Harper's,* March 1949.

Review of *Degas Letters,* by Marcel Guérin, translated by Marguerite Kay. *Magazine of Art,* April 1949.

"Past Masters and New Blood: Elizabeth Bowen, Arthur Bryant"; review of *The Heat of the Day,* by Elizabeth Bowen; *The Valley of St. Ives,* by Arthur Bryant; and other books. *Harper's,* April 1949.

"With Goethe in Colorado," *The Nation,* May 28, 1949.

"A Poet on Culture—And Who Reads What"; review of *Notes Towards the Definition of Culture,* by T. S. Eliot, and other books. *Harper's,* July 1949.

"The Mind of the Young Berlioz," *Musical Quarterly,* October 1949.

Review of *The Complete Plays of Henry James,* edited with an Introduction and Notes by Leon Edel. *New York Herald Tribune Books,* October 20, 1949.

"Romanticism: Definition of a Period," *Magazine of Art,* November 1949.

"More on Sound Repetitions," *Word Study,* April 1950.

"Berlioz and the Bard," *Saturday Review,* April 29, 1950.

"Berlioz's Second Symphony and Its 'Orgy,'" *WABF Program Magazine,* May 1950.

"Auden on Romanticism"; review of *The Enchafèd Flood,* by W. H. Auden. *Yale Review,* Summer 1950.

"A Symposium: Government in Art," *Magazine of Art,* November 1950.

"Victor Hugo: Bard on Olympus," *Saturday Review,* November 4, 1950.

"Purpose in Paint"; text of brochure for Cleve Gray's *Youth and Age* Exhibition, October 30–November 18, 1950.

"Scenes from 'The Infant Christ' "; program notes for performances by Cincinnati Symphony Orchestra, December 21, 22, 1950.

"A Burst of Berlioz," *Saturday Review,* December 30, 1950.

"The Retort Circumstantial," *The American Scholar,* Summer 1951.

Review of *The Musical Experience,* by Roger Sessions. *Saturday Review,* July 28, 1951.

"Two Fausts"; review of recordings "Liszt: A Faust Symphony" and "Berlioz: La Damnation de Faust." *Saturday Review,* July 28, 1951.

Review of *Shaw's Plays in Review*, by Desmond MacCarthy. *Saturday Review*, October 13, 1951.

"The Undesirability of a National Theatre," *Forestage* (The Questors' Theatre Magazine, London), November 1951.

Notes for recording of Bernard Shaw's *Don Juan in Hell*. Columbia Masterworks, 1952.

"Lorenzo the Magniloquent," *The Griffin*, Vol. 1, No. 4, 1952.

"Berenson and the Boot," *The Griffin*, Vol. 1, No. 10, 1952.

Review of *A Bibliography of the Musical and Literary Works of Hector Berlioz*, by Cecil Hopkinson. *Musical Quarterly*, January 1952.

"Artist Against Society: Some Articles of War," *Partisan Review*, January–February 1952. (Reprinted in *The New Partisan Reader*, New York, 1953, see Section IV.)

"America's Romance with Practicality," *Harper's*, February 1952.

"The Greater Garble," *Saturday Review*, April 12, 1952.

Article in "Our Country and Our Culture: A Symposium II," *Partisan Review*, July–August 1952.

Review of *Words and Ways of American English*, by Thomas Pyles. *New York Herald Tribune Book Review*, August 3, 1952.

Review of *Bernard Shaw and Mrs. Patrick Campbell: Their Correspondence*, edited by Alan Dent. *The New Republic*, November 3, 1952.

"Trial by Translation"; review of *The Chief Plays of Corneille*, translated by Lacy Lockert. *The New Republic*, December 8, 1952.

"Music into Words," Library of Congress Elson Lecture reprint, Washington, D.C., 1953. Reprinted in *The Score*, December 1954; and in *Lectures on the History and Art of Music*. New York: De Capo Press, 1968.

"The Inexhaustible Bernard Shaw," *The Griffin*, Vol. 2, No. 2, 1953.

"The Three Faces of the Drama," *The Griffin*, Vol. 2, No. 5, 1953.

Review of *Notes Without Music: An Autobiography*, by Darius Milhaud. *Notes*, June 1953.

Review of *Lexicon of Musical Invective*, by Nicolas Slonimsky. *Notes*, September 1953.

Program notes for performance of Berlioz's *Harold in Italy*, Philharmonic Symphony, New York, October 11, 1953.

"The Secretary's Turban and the Story Behind It," *The Griffin*, Vol. 2, No. 10, November 1953.

"Food for the N.R.F.," *Partisan Review*, November–December 1953. (Included in *Jacques Barzun on Writing, Editing and Publishing*, see Section IV.)

"The Indispensable Amateur," *Juilliard Review*, January 1954.

Review of *The Letters of Franz Liszt to Marie zu Sayn-Wittgenstein*, translated and edited by Howard E. Hugo. *Musical Quarterly*, January 1954.

"Rereading Santayana," *The Griffin*, Vol. 3, No. 2, February 1954.

Review of *The Manner Is Ordinary*, by John LaFarge, S.J. *New York Times Book Review*, February 14, 1954.

"America's Passion for Culture," *Harper's*, March 1954.

Review of *The Relaxed Sell*, by Thomas Whiteside. *New York Herald Tribune Book Review*, May 9, 1954.

Review of *Individualism Reconsidered*, by David Riesman. *New York Times Book Review*, June 13, 1954.

"As Uncomfortable as a Modern Self," *The Griffin*, Vol. 3, No. 7, July 1954.

"Modern Life Begins at *Forte*," *The Griffin*, Vol. 3, No. 9, September 1954.

"When Manet was Anathema"; review of *Manet and His Critics*, by George Hamilton. *Art News*, September 1954.

"O'Casey at Your Bedside," *The Griffin*, Vol. 3, No. 10, October 1954.

Program notes for performance of Berlioz, *The Damnation of Faust*, Carnegie Hall, December 14, 1954.

"French Literature Today"; review of *Présences contemporaines*, by Pierre Brodin. *New Leader*, January 31, 1955.

"The American and His Gadgets," *The Griffin*, Vol. 4, No. 3, March 1955.

"Each Age Picks Its Literary Greats," *New York Times Book Review*, March 6, 1955.

Notes for the recording of Berlioz, *Symphonie fantastique*, by Angel Records, Spring 1955.

"Shaw and Rousseau: No Paradox," *Shaw Society Bulletin* (New York), May 1955.

"Why Talk About Art?", *The Griffin*, Vol. 4, No. 5, May 1955.

Review of *La Mélodie française de Berlioz à Duparc*, by Frits Noske. *Notes*, June 1955.

"Not Gobbledygook—But Plain Words"; review of *Plain Words*, by Sir Ernest Gowers. *New York Times Magazine*, August 21, 1955.

"Japan—Roads to Interpretation," *The Griffin*, Vol. 4, No. 10, October 1955.

"Sophocles: Oedipus"; review of recording of music by Harry Partch. *American Record Guide*, January 1956.

"Proust's Way," *The Griffin*, Vol. 5, No. 4, April 1956.

"The Rain in Spain, Etc.," *The Griffin*, Vol. 5, No. 8, July 1956.

"The New Man in the Arts," *The American Scholar*, Autumn 1956.

"The Wondrous Kind," *The Griffin*, Vol. 5, No. 14, December 1956.

"Two French Poets," *The Griffin*, Vol. 6, No. 2, March 1957.

"The Anatomy of Book Publishing," in *New Leader*, May 13, 1957. (Included in *Jacques Barzun On Writing, Editing and Publishing*, see Section IV.)

"Fowler's Generation," *The American Scholar*, Summer 1957.

"The Anti-Modern Essays of Aldous Huxley"; review of *Adonis and the Alphabet*, by Aldous Huxley. *The London Magazine*, August 1957.

Review of *Parisian Sketches*, edited by Leon Edel and Ilse Dusoir Lind. *New York Herald Tribune Book Review*, October 20, 1957.

"The Man-Mountain," *The Griffin*, Vol. 6, No. 10, November 1957.

"A Chance to Tinker to Evans"; review of a *Dictionary of American-English Usage*, by Bergen Evans. *The American Scholar*, Winter 1957–58.

"The Requiem of Berlioz"; notes for the recording by Westminster Records, 1958.

Review of *The Honor of Being a Man: The World of André Malraux,* by Edward Gannon, S. J. *America,* March 15, 1958.

"The Literary Mind," *The Griffin,* Vol. 7, No. 4, April 1958.

"The Truth at Any Cost," *The Griffin,* Vol. 7, No. 8, Summer 1958.

"The Artistry of Discontent," *The Griffin,* Vol. 7, No. 12, Christmas 1958.

"The Esthetic Society," *The Griffin,* Vol. 8, No. 1, January 1959.

"The Saddest Pack—Translators"; review of *On Translation,* edited by Reuben A. Brower. *New Leader,* May 11, 1959.

"The Artist as Scapegoat," *The Mid-Century,* No. 1, July 1959.

"The Ages of Man," *The Mid-Century,* No. 2, August 1959.

"A Further Word on Cars," *The Mid-Century,* No. 3, September 1959.

"The Poet as Man in a Box," *The Mid-Century,* No. 5, Fall 1959.

"The Tradition of the New," *The Mid-Century,* No. 7, December 1959.

"Trains and the Mind of Man," *Holiday,* February 1960.

"TV in the World of Letters," in *The American Scholar,* Spring 1960. (Included in *Jacques Barzun On Writing, Editing and Publishing,* see Section IV.)

"Tragedy à la Shakespeare," *The Mid-Century,* No. 11, April 1960.

"Not All Are O.O.O.," *The Mid-Century,* No. 12, May 1960.

"The Charge of the Light Brigade," *The Mid-Century,* No. 15, August 1960.

"The Comedy of Comedies," *The Mid-Century,* No. 17, Fall 1960.

"Found: A Novel with a Hero," *The Mid-Century,* No. 19, November 1960.

Remarks at a panel discussion on "Liszt, Wagner, and the Relations Between Music and Literature in the 19th Century," at a meeting of the International Musicological Society. *Report of the Eighth Congress,* New York, 1961.

"The Narrator in Command," *The Mid-Century,* No. 21, January 1961.

"The Playwright as Critic—of Music," *The Mid-Century,* No. 26, June 1961.

"When Thought Is Air-Borne," *The Mid-Century,* No. 27, Summer 1961.

"The Practical Life Described and Directed," *The Mid-Century,* No. 29, August 1961.

"Ultima Thule," *The Mid-Century,* No. 29, August 1961.

"Modern Architecture: The Road to Abstraction," *Columbia University Forum,* Vol. IV, No. 4, Fall 1961.

"High Jinks and Pathos," *The Mid-Century,* No. 32, November 1961.

"Ten Rillington Place," *The Mid-Century,* No. 32, November 1961.

"The Grand Pretense," *The Mid-Century,* No. 35, January 1962.

"Modern Mores and the Law," *The Mid-Century,* No. 36, February 1962.

"The Artist in Public Life," *The Mid-Century,* No. 37, March 1962.

"In Favor of Capital Punishment," *The American Scholar,* Spring 1962.

"Speaking of Means and Ends"; review of *The Concept of Method,* by Justus Buchler, and *Case Method in Human Relations,* by Paul and Faith Pigors. *The American Scholar,* Summer 1962.

Review of *On Knowing: Essays for the Left Hand,* by Jerome Bruner. *Science,* January 25, 1963.

"What Is a Dictionary?"; review of *Webster's Third New International Dictionary. The American Scholar,* Spring 1963.

"Shaw Against the Alphabet," *The Independent Shavian* (New York), April 1963.

"Money and the Man," *Church History,* June 1963. (Slightly revised and reprinted as "A diller, a dollar, a very expensive scholar," *Horizon,* September 1963.)

Review of *Criminal Law, Problems for Decision in the Promulgation, Invocation, and Administration of a Law of Crimes,* by Donnelly, Goldstein and Schwartz. *Yale Law Journal,* November 1963.

"Aldous Huxley on the Two Cultures"; review of *Literature and Science,* by Aldous Huxley. *Science,* January 3, 1964.

"Infidelity in the Sixties," *The Cambridge Review* (England), Vol. 85, No. 2079, June 6, 1964.

"Why Are We Here? The Scientific Style of Life," *Report on Science and Contemporary Social Problems.* Oak Ridge Institute, Tennessee, September 1964.

"Berlioz and Cellini"; program notes for performance of Berlioz, *Benvenuto Cellini* at Philharmonic Hall. Concert Opera Association, March 22, 1965.

"Meditations on the Literature of Spying," *The American Scholar,* Spring 1965.

"The Man in the American Mask," *Foreign Affairs,* April 1965.

"What We Expect of Criticism—Old or New"; précis of remarks given at 52nd Biennial Convention of the American Federation of Arts in Boston, April 1965; published by the Federation in "The Critic and the Visual Arts."

"Art—By Act of Congress," *The Public Interest,* No. 1, Fall 1965.

"Modern Man in Search of Himself," *St. Louis Post Dispatch,* September 26, 1965.

"About Rex Stout," in *A Birthday Tribute to Rex Stout.* New York: Viking Press, December 1, 1965.

"A Fantasy on Fencing," *Columbia College Fencing Program,* 1965–66.

"Venus at Large—Sexuality and the Limits of Literature," *Encounter,* March 1966.

"To Praise Varèse," *Columbia University Forum,* Spring 1966.

"Why Opera?" *Opera News,* January 28, 1967.

"Liberalism and the Religion of Art—De Mortuis," *Midway* (University of Chicago Press), Autumn 1967 (Anonymous).

Presentation of the Emerson-Thoreau Award to Joseph Wood Krutch, on May 10, 1967, at the American Academy of Arts and Sciences. *Bulletin of the American Academy of Arts and Sciences,* October 1967.

"The Price and Preparation of Genius"; review of *William James,* by Gay Wilson Allen. *Science,* October 27, 1967.

"Museum Piece, 1967," *Museum News,* April 1968.

"Berlioz, Our Contemporary"; summary of Colloquium at the French Institute in London, held in recognition of the 100th anniversary of Berlioz's death, on October 23, 1969. *The Berlioz Society Bulletin* (London), No. 65, October 1969.

"The Professional Is a Marked Man," *Cornell University Medical College Booklet,* October 1969.

"This Business of Conformity," *Peabody Notes,* November 1969.

"The New Librarian to the Rescue," *Library Journal,* November 1, 1969.

"The Book, the Bibliographer, and the Absence of Mind," *The American Scholar,* Winter 1969. (Included in *Jacques Barzun On Writing, Editing and Publishing,* see Section IV.)

"Berlioz a Hundred Years After," *Musical Quarterly,* January 1970.

"A Note on the Inadequacy of Poe as a Proofreader and of His Editors as French Scholars," *Romantic Review,* February 1970. (Included in *Jacques Barzun On Writing, Editing and Publishing,* see Section IV.)

"Loyalty and Dissent: Catholic Radicals Today"; review of *Divine Disobedience: Profiles in Catholic Radicalism,* by Francine du Plessix Gray. *America,* June 27, 1970.

"Publicity, Advertising, and Applied Arts," in *The Encyclopedia of Education.* New York: Crowell-Collier and Macmillan, 1971.

"Soliman the Mag," *Quarterly of the Encyclopaedia Britannica Society,* Vol. I, No. 1, 1971.

"A Critical Vocabulary for Crime Fiction," *The Armchair Detective,* January 1971.

"So Long as Doctors Have to Think," *Bulletin of the New York Academy of Medicine,* March 1971.

"The Novel Turned Tale," *Mosaic* (University of Manitoba Press), Spring 1971.

"Doctors Afield: Doctors Criminal and Criminous," *New England Journal of Medicine,* April 1, 1971.

"A Summary of the Seminar on Central Influences on American Life" (November 22–24, 1971), sponsored by the Council for Biology in Human Affairs. The Salk Institute, December 1971.

"The Arts To-Day: Consolation or Confrontation?", *Journal of the Royal Society of Arts,* March 1972.

Review of *Theatre of War,* by Eric Bentley. *The Independent Shavian* (New York), Winter 1972–73.

"The Mystery in Rameau's Nephew"; review of *Diderot the Satirist,* by Donal O'Gorman. *Diderot Studies XVII,* edited by Otis Fellows and Diana Guiragossian. Geneva: Librairie Droz S.A., 1973.

"Sidelights on Further Conversations About the Contemporary Scene." An addendum to the Seminar on "Central Influences on American Life" (September 21–23, 1972), sponsored by the Council for Biology in Human Affairs. The Salk Institute, January 1973.

"In Favor of Particular Clichés," *Translation* 73, Vol. 1, No. 1, Winter 1973 (Columbia University).

"A Few Words on a Few Words," *Columbia Forum*, Summer 1974.

Review of *Henry James and Pragmatistic Thought*, by Richard A. Hocks. *American Literature*, May 1975.

"The Bibliophile of the Future: His Complaints About the Twentieth Century." Bromsen Lecture in Humanistic Bibliography. Boston Public Library reprint, Boston, 1976.

"Administering and the Law," *American Bar Association Journal*, May 1976.

"Remembering Lionel Trilling," *Encounter*, September 1976.

Biographies of Contributors

MORTIMER J. ADLER   Chairman of the Board of Editors of the *Encyclopaedia Britannica* and Director of Editorial Planning for the 15th edition. Director of the Institute for Philosophical Research.

> "Jacques Barzun was a student of mine at Columbia in 1925–27, both in a psychology course and in General Honors. Subsequently he became a personal and intellectual friend for over fifty years and a colleague in many enterprises, including the Aspen Institute for Humanistic Studies and work on the *Encyclopaedia Britannica*."

ERIC BENTLEY'S   association with Jacques Barzun dates from 1944. Indeed, Jacques Barzun tried to attach Bentley to the Columbia History Department at that time. This did not work out, but in the fifties Bentley went to Columbia to replace Joseph Wood Krutch and occupy the Brander Matthews chair in drama. When, later, Barzun was Dean of the Faculties, Bentley served as an acting dean of the School of Arts along with him. . . . Eric Bentley's book *Bernard Shaw* (1947) is dedicated to Jacques Barzun and Lionel Trilling. . . . Bentley tells us he likes to think of his several chronicle plays as what he did *instead of* becoming a Columbia historian.

COURTNEY C. BROWN   Dean Emeritus and Paul Garrett Professor Emeritus of Public Policy and Business Responsibility, Columbia University Graduate School of Business. Educated at Dartmouth and Columbia, Dr. Brown was Dean of Columbia's Business School for fifteen years, from 1954 to 1969. For over a year during his deanship, he assumed the additional post of Vice-President in charge of Business Affairs. From 1943 to 1945 he served the Department of State as chief of the Division of War Supply and Resources and in 1946 served as Vice-Chairman of President Truman's Famine Emergency Committee. Chairman of the Governor's Commission on Minimum Wage in New York State in 1965, Dr. Brown recently served as a member of President Nixon's Commission on International Trade and Investment Policy. He was the Director of Arden House for two decades. He is now Chairman of the American Assembly and trustee of the Academy of Political Science, the Council for Financial Aid to Education, and the International Executive Service Corps.

DAVID CAIRNS   A freelance writer, critic, and gramophone record producer who resides in London, Cairns has been a friend of Jacques Barzun's since the early 1960s. He is the translator of *The Memoirs of Hector Berlioz* (1969) and the author of *Responses: Musical Essays and Reviews* (1973). As the classical program coordinator of Philips Records between 1969 and 1972, he participated in the planning and production of the Philips Berlioz Cycle. He is currently at work on a biography of Berlioz.

THEODORE CAPLOW   Commonwealth Professor of Sociology at the University of Virginia and author of *The Sociology of Work* (1954), *Principles of Organization* (1964), *Two Against One: Coalitions in Triads* (1968), and *Toward Social Hope* (1975).

"I was a student of Jacques Barzun's at Columbia College in 1937 and have remained in touch with him ever since. Over the years, we have kept up a running conversation, in which one thread has been Jacques's devastating critique of empirical sociology and my defense of it. His position in this debate was initially strong, but has been undermined by his passionate interest in sociological topics and his own talents as a sociological observer."

KENNETH B. CLARK   received his A.B. and M.S. degrees from Howard University and his Ph.D. from Columbia in 1940. A specialist in child, social and clinical psychology, he has been Professor of Psychology at the City College of New York since 1960, and was appointed Distinguished University Professor in 1970. He has served as research director at the Northside Center for Child Development since 1946 and as a consultant to the N.A.A.C.P. since 1950. The author of *Prejudice and Your Child* (1955), *Dark Ghetto* (1965) and *A Relevant War Against Poverty* (1968), he has served with Jacques Barzun on the Council for Basic Education and on the editorial board of *The American Scholar*.

DONALD A. COWAN   President of the University of Dallas, Cowan was host to Professor Jacques Barzun during his stay as the first Eugene McDermott Professor at that institution. Professor Barzun taught a course in the origins of Modernism, including its major changes in science as well as in philosophy and the arts.

Professor Cowan, a physicist, has published in nuclear spectroscopy, the desalination of water, the history of science, and education.

C. BRIAN COX   Professor of English Literature at the University of Manchester, England, and co-editor with A. E. Dyson of *Critical Quarterly*. Cox and Dyson edited the famous Black Papers on education in 1969–70. *Black Paper Two* included extensive quotation from Jacques Barzun's *The House of Intellect*. This pamphlet aroused huge controversy in Britain, and led to the first meeting among Cox, Dyson, and Barzun.

VERA KUFFNER EBERSTADT   A graduate of Vassar College, Vera Eberstadt was a participant in the Barzun-Trilling graduate history seminar at Columbia and, for several years, Barzun's secretary. As a sculptor, she studied with William Zorach at the Art Students League in New York City and with Jean Arp in Meudon, near Paris. Her sculptures have been exhibited in group shows and are represented in numerous private collections.

"When I became a sculptor instead of an historian, Jacques remained my loyal supporter and friend and was an excellent model."

NELL EURICH   Special Adviser to the International Council for Educational Development, Nell Eurich has been a family and social friend of Jacques Barzun's for many years. She has served as Vice-President for Academic Affairs, Manhattanville College; Dean of Faculty, Vassar College; acting president of two colleges, teacher of English Literature at New York University, trustee of several institutions, and consultant to various agencies. Her publications include *Science in Utopia* (1967) and various articles and monographs.

VIRGINIA XANTHOS FAGGI   Assistant to the Executive Vice-President for Academic Affairs at Columbia University.

"I began to work as Jacques Barzun's secretary in 1954 and became his administrative assistant when he was appointed Dean of the Graduate Faculties in 1955, Provost in 1958 and, from 1967–1975, while he held the position of University Professor and Special Advisor on the Arts to the President. I was involved in the preparation of the university's *Graduate Student Guide, Faculty Handbook*, and *Administrative Guide*, and have prepared the indexes for all of Barzun's books published since 1956. It was an incomparable experience to work with Jacques, and I shall treasure the many memories of all those twenty-two wonderful years."

PETER GAY   Durfee Professor of History, Yale University, and author of *Voltaire's Politics* (1959), *Weimar Culture* (1968), *The Enlightenment, An Interpretation* (2 vols., 1966, 1969), *Style in History* (1974), and *Art and Act* (1976). Peter Gay was Barzun's junior colleague in the Columbia History Department from his transfer there in 1956 until his departure from Columbia in 1969; since 1970 they have been colleagues on the editorial board of *The American Scholar*.

RICHARD FRANKO GOLDMAN   is President of the Peabody Institute of the City of Baltimore. His acquaintance with Jacques Barzun goes back to 1927 when they were both undergraduates at Columbia College. He has been active as composer, conductor, author, educator, and consultant, and has taught or lectured at colleges and universities throughout the United States. He has been a frequent contributor to *The American Scholar, Musical Quarterly*, and other scholarly and non-scholarly periodicals.

HENRY F. GRAFF   Professor of History, Columbia University. He has written and lectured extensively on the presidency. He is the author of *The Tuesday Cabinet*, a study of Lyndon Johnson's Vietnam policies.

"Jacques Barzun and I had our first extended conversation in 1947. It took place late one Saturday afternoon, to my best recollection, on the seventh floor of Hamilton Hall where he and I had neighboring offices. He was a professor of history and I an instructor, yet somehow he did not make me feel my juniority. Our friendship has been gradually sealed through almost thirty years of mutual participatoin in the pleasures and vicissitudes of the department and university. We were permanently bonded by our collaboration in teaching History 201 ("Nature and Types of History and Historiography") between 1953 and 1957, and in writing *The Modern Researcher,* a book that grew out of that course. Always we have enjoyed a shared confidence that on too many matters the world is more intractable and unreasoning than it ought to be because it is more misguided and more misinformed than he and I seem to be."

CLEVE GRAY   "Jacques came to see my first exhibit in New York City in 1947. He may have read that I had studied in Paris with Jacques Villon and André Lhote; Cubist painting was an important part of his childhood environment and continued to be of great interest to him. In 1956 he dedicated to me, as a representative of artistic continuity, his book, *The Energies of Art.*

"During the years he served as editor or advisor of many publications, I would occasionally receive a request to write about an aspect of contemporary painting. My first piece for him was on Albert Gleizes (*Magazine of Art,* 1950); there followed one on Villon (*Perspectives USA,* 1953); an essay on abstract art (*The American Scholar,* 1959); and so on.

"Jacques owns several of my paintings and prints; and in 1950 he wrote a fine introduction to my fourth exhibit at the Jacques Seligmann Galleries. When a few years later I was asked to paint his portrait, I was delighted. I did a second, more abstract version, less gentle, perhaps, than the first.

"Fortunately, my wife, Francine du Plessix Gray, is always as eager as I am to talk with Jacques. We never see him frequently enough."

SHIRLEY HAZZARD   is a novelist and short story writer, having previously worked for ten years on the staff of the United Nations. Her novels and collections of fiction include *Cliffs of Fall, The Evening of the Holiday, People in Glass Houses,* and *The Bay of Noon.* She has contributed many short stories to *The New Yorker* and is the author of *Defeat of an Ideal: A Study of the Self-Destruction of the United Nations* (1973).

"I came to know Jacques Barzun twelve years ago, through my marriage to Francis Steegmuller who had been Barzun's classmate at Columbia College. I had become a reader of Barzun a decade earlier, with the publication of *Berlioz and the Romantic Century.* I first met him in a New York theatre in an interval of a French performance of *Phèdre,* inaugurating a friendship that has given me intense pleasures of conversation and new knowledge, and an envy for those taught by this immensely learned man."

CAROLYN G. HEILBRUN   Carolyn G. Heilbrun is a Professor of English at

Columbia University and a writer. She has known Jacques Barzun since 1953 when she was his student. Since she became his colleague, they have exchanged theories on detective fiction, certain nineteenth-century English writers, biography, and the ideal seminar and lecture course. His discovery, just prior to the publication of *A Catalogue of Crime*, that she was Amanda Cross, inspired him to offer her plots, none of which she felt she was talented enough to use. Her recent publication, *Towards a Recognition of Androgyny*, while counter to most Barzun inclinations, received his support, as its author had always enjoyed his encouragement. More in his line were Heilbrun's *The Garnett Family* and her essay on Sayers, in admiration of whom she and Barzun are united. She has written, as Amanda Cross, four detective novels; a fifth will be published soon. In April 1976 she was awarded a Rockefeller Foundation Humanities Fellowship to study the subject of her essay in this volume. She has also been appointed a Fellow of the Radcliffe Institute and will spend the academic year 1976–77 there working on problems of female identity and the female imagination.

BANESH HOFFMANN Banesh Hoffmann, theoretical physicist, investitured Baker Street Irregular, long-time critic of multiple-choice tests, and author of a variety of articles and books, is Professor of Mathematics at Queens College of CUNY. He collaborated with Einstein, and recently wrote with Einstein's secretary, Helen Dukas, the prize-winning biography *Albert Einstein, Creator and Rebel*. His book *The Tyranny of Testing* and related articles owe much to Jacques Barzun's crucial encouragement during two decades.

WILLIAM R. KEYLOR is Associate Professor of History at Boston University, specializing in modern French history and European diplomatic history. He received his B.A. from Stanford University in 1966 and his M.A. and Ph.D. from Columbia University in 1966 and 1971, respectively. He was a member of Jacques Barzun's graduate seminar and was one of his last Ph.D. students at Columbia. He is the author of *Academy and Community: The Foundation of the French Historical Profession* (1975) and *Jacques Bainville and the Renaissance of Royalist History in Twentieth-Century France* (forthcoming), both of which were begun under Barzun's supervision. He is currently engaged in a study of Franco-American relations since the First World War on a Guggenheim fellowship. His interest in Charles Péguy as a critic of academic history was stimulated by a conversation with Jacques Barzun amid the student demonstrations at Columbia in May 1968, during which teacher and student discussed the nature of historical instruction and research in the university.

HUGH MACDONALD is a Lecturer in Music at the University of Oxford. He is general editor of the New Berlioz Edition, a monumental enterprise that was made possible by the new climate of Berlioz studies initiated by Jacques Barzun's *Berlioz and the Romantic Century*, and he has published numerous articles and studies on Berlioz.

STEVEN MARCUS   is Professor of English at Columbia University, where he has been a student and colleague of Jacques Barzun's. Author of *Dickens: From Pickwick to Dombey, The Other Victorians, Engels, Manchester and the Working Class*, and *Representations*, he also serves as associate editor of *Partisan Review*.

WILLIAM A. OWENS   is Professor Emeritus and Dean Emeritus, Columbia University. He received his B.A. and M.A. from Southern Methodist University, his Ph.D. from the University of Iowa. Before coming to Columbia in 1947 he taught in several schools and colleges. He was born at Pin Hook, Texas.

Professor Owens has traveled the back roads of the American Southwest in search of folk songs, especially English ballads and Negro spirituals. From this research he published *Texas Folk Songs* and a novel on black and white education, *Walking on Borrowed Land*. *This Stubborn Soil* is a narrative of his Texas boyhood. His latest book, *A Fair and Happy Land*, traces two hundred years of American frontier experience.

ROSEMARY PARK   Professor of Higher Education and Vice-Chancellor for Educational Planning at the University of California, Los Angeles, since 1975 retired. As President of Barnard College (1962–67), she had esteemed the works of Jacques Barzun, the critic, long before confronting Jacques Barzun, the Provost of Columbia University, where his style in administration proved to colleagues and students alike that intellectual grasp and operational skill can be happily and enviably combined.

MORRIS PHILIPSON   Director, the University of Chicago Press, was a student and became a friend of Jacques Barzun's. He has taught philosophy and cultural history at the Juilliard School, Hunter College, and the University of Chicago, and is the author of *Bourgeois Anonymous* and *Outline of a Jungian Aesthetics*, and the editor of *Aldous Huxley on Art and Artists, Leonardo Da Vinci, Aesthetics Today*, and *Jacques Barzun on Writing, Editing and Publishing*. His latest book is a novel, *The Wallpaper Fox*.

JOHN SIMON   taught literature at several colleges and universities and writes diverse types of criticism for a number of publications such as *The New Leader* and *The Hudson Review*. His books include *Acid Test, Private Screenings, Movies into Film, Ingmar Bergman Directs, Uneasy Stages*, and *Singularities*.

He knew Jacques Barzun when he served as associate editor of The Mid-Century Book Society and its magazine, *The Mid-Century*, under Barzun, Trilling, and Auden. He "learned a lot from the experience."

C. P. SNOW   was born in Leicester, England, and went to Christ College,

Cambridge, where he held a fellowship in physics and later became tutor. His career as a novelist began in 1934 with *The Search*. His "Strangers and Brothers" series, begun in 1940, ended recently with the publication of *Last Things*. His other novels are *The Malcontents* and, most recently, *In Their Wisdom*.

With the outbreak of the Second World War, C. P. Snow entered public affairs as advisor to the Ministry of Labour and Civil Service Commissioner. He was knighted in 1957 and was created a life peer in 1964. Also in 1964, he joined Harold Wilson's government as Parliamentary Secretary to the Ministry of Technology. He resigned from that post in 1966 to devote his full time to writing. C. P. Snow is married to the novelist Pamela Hansford Johnson. He writes:

"I have known Jacques Barzun for many years, first through literary acquaintances and then later as a close personal friend. For a long time, whenever my wife and I came to New York, we almost always dined in the Barzuns' apartment on the first night we arrived, usually with the Trillings also."

ALAN B. SPITZER is Professor of History at the University of Iowa. He received his Ph.D. from Columbia University in 1955; his field is modern French political and social history. His publications include *The Revolutionary Theories of Louis-Auguste Blanqui* (1957) and *Old Hatreds and Young Hopes: The French Carbonari Against the Bourbon Restoration* (1971).

FRITZ STERN "In 1944, as an undergraduate in Columbia College, I became a student of Jacques Barzun's; at the time I was a pre-medical student, and his example inspired my decision to set out on a different course. I belong to the fortunate few who took not only Jacques Barzun's course in cultural history and his seminar on Rousseau, but also the Colloquium on Great Books and the Ph.D. seminar which in those years he taught together with Lionel Trilling. It was under Mr. Barzun's guidance that I wrote my dissertation. My student days were the beginning of an association that has grown ever since through two decades as colleagues at Columbia and friends everywhere.

"In my first books, *The Varieties of History* (ed., 1956) and *The Politics of Cultural Despair: A Study in the Rise of the Germanic Ideology* (1961), I benefited from what in the latter I called Jacques Barzun's 'incomparable combination of advice, encouragement, and relentless expectation.' He was also a superb critic of many of the essays in *The Failure of Illiberalism: Essays on the Political Culture of Modern Germany* (1972)."

LIONEL TRILLING (1905–1975) was a member of the Department of English and Comparative Literature at Columbia University from 1932 to 1975, holding the George Edward Woodberry Chair from 1965 until he was made University Professor in 1970. He was George Eastman Visiting

Professor at Oxford and Charles Eliot Norton Visiting Professor of Poetry at Harvard and was awarded honorary degrees by Harvard, Yale, Brandeis, Northwestern and other universities. He received the first annual Thomas Jefferson Award in the Humanities in 1972. A member of the American Academy of Arts and Sciences and of the National Institute of Arts and Letters, he was the author of *Matthew Arnold* (1939), *E. M. Forster* (1943), *The Middle of the Journey* (1947), *The Liberal Imagination* (1950), *The Opposing Self* (1955), *A Gathering of Fugitives* (1956), *Beyond Culture* (1965), *The Experience of Literature* (1967), *Sincerity and Authenticity* (1972), and *Mind in the Modern World* (1973).

DORA B. WEINER   A graduate of Smith College, now Associate Professor of History at Manhattanville College, Dora Weiner was Barzun's assistant, Ph.D. candidate, and junior colleague. She has taught at Columbia University, Barnard, and Sarah Lawrence Colleges; is the author of *Raspail: Scientist and Reformer* (1968); and is preparing *The Politics of Health in Revolutionary and Napoleonic France.*

"Among my treasured experiences is participation in the Barzun-Trilling Colloquium and the continuing privilege of Jacques' tough and creative critique of my English and French prose. How difficult it is to be 'simple and direct'!"

JAMES HARVEY YOUNG   Professor of History, Emory University. Harvey Young began his friendship with Jacques Barzun during two post-doctoral years at Columbia University, one to learn about Columbia's Contemporary Civilization and Humanities programs by participating in them, the other to study intellectual history with Barzun and to do research. Young has traced the course of health quackery through American history in *The Toadstool Millionaires* and *The Medical Messiahs,* and has written on other aspects of the history of food and drug regulation.